The Reconstructed Chronology of the Divided Kingdom

The Reconstructed Chronology of the Divided Kingdom

M. Christine Tetley

Winona Lake, Indiana
Eisenbrauns
2005

© Copyright 2005 by Eisenbrauns.
All rights reserved.
Printed in the United States of America.

Library of Congress Cataloging-in-Publication Data

Tetley, M. Christine, 1944–
    The reconstructed chronology of the Divided Kingdom /
      M. Christine Tetley.
          p. cm.
    Includes bibliographical references and index.
    ISBN 1-57506-072-8 (hardback : alk. paper)
    1. Bible. O.T. Kings—Chronology. 2. Jews—History—953–
586 B.C.—Chronology. I. Title.
BS1335.55.T48   2004
222′.5095—dc22

                                              2004017731

The paper used in this publication meets the minimum requirements of the American National Standard for Information Sciences—Permanence of Paper for Printed Library Materials, ANSI Z39.48-1984. ♾™

To Barry

with love and gratitude for his unfailing support

Contents

List of Tables xi
Acknowledgments xiii
Abbreviations xiv

1. Introduction 1
    1.1. Significance of Divided Kingdom Chronology 1
    1.2. Establishing Divided Kingdom Chronology 2
        1.2.1. Relative Chronology 2
        1.2.2. Absolute Chronology 3
    1.3. Conventional Approaches to Divided Kingdom Chronology 4
        1.3.1. Biblical Sources 4
        1.3.2. Dating Systems 5
        1.3.3. Assyrian Eponym Canon 7
        1.3.4. Tiglath-pileser III and Menahem 7
    1.4. Alternative Approach to Divided Kingdom Chronology 8
    1.5. New Proposal for Divided Kingdom Chronology 10
    1.6. Names of Kings 12

2. Transmission History 14
    2.1. Early Compilation of the Books of Kings 14
    2.2. Transmission History of the Old Testament Text 15
        2.2.1. Hebrew Text and Qumran Manuscripts 15
        2.2.2. Old Greek and *Kaige* 19
        2.2.3. Lucianic Manuscripts 21
        2.2.4. Aquila, Symmachus, and Theodotion 24
        2.2.5. Origen's Hexapla 24
        2.2.6. Insights from Recensional Development 26
    2.3. Thiele's Approach to the Text of Kings 27

3. Chronological Data 30
    3.1. Regnal Years in the Divided Kingdom 30
        3.1.1. Regnal Years in the Early Divided Kingdom 30
        3.1.2. Regnal Years in the Late Divided Kingdom 32
        3.1.3. Total Regnal Years in the Divided Kingdom 32
        3.1.4. Thiele's Discussion of Regnal Years 33
    3.2 Divided Kingdom Chronological Data 34
    3.2.1. Accession Synchronisms in the Divided Kingdom 34
    3.2.2. Accession Synchronisms in the Early Divided Kingdom 34

   3.2.3. Accession Synchronisms in the Late Divided Kingdom . .   44
   3.2.4. Thiele's Approach to Accession Synchronisms   48

4. **Chronological Data in Manuscript c_2**   54
  4.1. Regnal Years in the Divided Kingdom according to c_2   54
  4.2. Accession Synchronisms in the Divided Kingdom
    according to c_2   56
  4.3. Conclusions concerning c_2 Data   60
  4.4. Scholarly Discussion of c_2   60
   4.4.1. Thiele and Shenkel   60
   4.4.2. Galil   61
   4.4.3. Significance of c_2   63

5. **Regnal Formulas**   64
  5.1. Patterns of Opening and Closing Formulas   64
   5.1.1. Opening Formulas   65
   5.1.2. Closing Formulas   66
  5.2. Distribution of Opening Formulas   69
  5.3. Supplementary Notices   72
   5.3.1. Rehoboam   72
   5.3.2. Asa   73
   5.3.3. Nadab and Elah   73
   5.3.4. Baasha   73
   5.3.5. Omri   75
   5.3.6. Jehoshaphat   75
   5.3.7. Ahaziah-I   76
   5.3.8. Joash-J   78
   5.3.9. Joash-I   78
   5.3.10. Amaziah   79
   5.3.11. Jeroboam II   79
   5.3.12. Zechariah   79
   5.3.13. Menahem   79
   5.3.14. Hoshea   79
   5.3.15. Jotham   79
   5.3.16. Conclusion   79
  5.4. Sequence of Reigns in the Books of Kings   79
  5.5. Translation of מלך   86
  5.6. Thiele's Analysis of Regnal Formulas' Patterns   87

6. **Reconstructing Chronology**   91
  6.1. Establishing Relative Chronology   91
   6.1.1. Methodology for Reconstructing Chronology   91
   6.1.2. Methodology for Identifying Original Numbers   93
  6.2. Establishing Absolute Chronology   95
   6.2.1. Establishing a Starting Date for the Divided Kingdom . .   95
   6.2.2. Reliability of the Assyrian Eponym Canon   97

6.3. Thiele's Methodology 104
    6.3.1. Using MT Data in Preference to the Greek 104
    6.3.2. Using Postdating and Antedating 104
    6.3.3. Using Tishri Years for Judah, Nisan Years for Israel 105
    6.3.4. Using Coregencies 106
    6.3.5. Using the AEC to Establish a Starting Date 117
6.4. Taking up Thiele's Challenge 118

7. Relative Chronology of the Early Divided Kingdom 119

7.1. Explanation of Table 7.1 119
7.2. Explanation of Early Divided Kingdom Chronology 119
    7.2.1. Rehoboam (Judah); Jeroboam I (Israel) 119
    7.2.2. Abijam and Asa (Judah); Nadab and Baasha (Israel) 120
    7.2.3. Asa (Judah); Baasha, Elah, Zimri, Omri (Israel) 123
    7.2.4. Asa and Jehoshaphat (Judah); Omri and Ahab (Israel) .. 125
    7.2.5. Jehoshaphat (Judah); Ahab, Ahaziah-I,
        and Joram (Israel) 127
    7.2.6. Jehoram and Ahaziah-J (Judah); Joram (Israel) 128
    7.2.7. Identity of *Iaúa* 129
7.3. Textual Solutions for Early Divided Kingdom Chronology 130
    7.3.1. Abijam's Reign Changed from 6 Years to 3 Years 130
    7.3.2. Baasha's Reign Changed from 17 Years to 24 Years 131
    7.3.3. Ahaziah-I's Accession Changed from
        Jehoshaphat's 24th Year to 17th Year 132
    7.3.4. Summary of Textual Solutions 132
    7.3.5. Two Additional Matters regarding Numbers 132
    7.3.6. Suggested Explanation for Changes in Numbers 133
7.4. Assessment of the Early Divided Kingdom Chronology
    by Thiele and Other Scholars 136
    7.4.1. Abijam and Asa 138
    7.4.2. The Omride Period to the End of the
        Early Divided Kingdom 138

8. Relative Chronology of the Late Divided Kingdom 145

8.1. Explanation of Table 8.1 145
8.2. Explanation of Late Divided Kingdom Chronology 145
    8.2.1. Athaliah and Joash-J (Judah); Jehu and
        Jehoahaz (Israel) 145
    8.2.2. Joash-J, Amaziah, Azariah (Judah); Jehoahaz, Joash-I,
        Jeroboam II (Israel) 145
    8.2.3. Azariah (Judah); Jeroboam II, Zechariah, Shallum,
        Menahem, and Pekahiah (Israel) 148
    8.2.4. Jotham, Ahaz, and Hezekiah (Judah);
        Pekah and Hoshea (Israel) 151
    8.2.5. Summary of Late Divided Kingdom Chronology 152
8.3. Establishing a Starting Date: The Fall of Samaria 153

   8.3.1. The Earliest Established Date 153
   8.3.2. Sennacherib's Campaign to Jerusalem 153
   8.3.3. Tiglath-pileser III and Hoshea's Accession 155
   8.3.4. Who Was King of Assyria When Samaria Fell? 157
   8.3.5. Date of Samaria's Fall 162

9. **Absolute Chronology of the Divided Kingdom** 165
 9.1. The Priority of the Hebrew Record 165
 9.2. Explanation of the Julian-Year Tables 166
 9.3. Synchronization of Hebrew, Assyrian, Tyrian,
   and Egyptian Chronologies 166
   9.3.1. Shalmaneser III of Assyria; Ahab and *Iaúa*
     "Son of Omri" 166
   9.3.2. Adad-nirari III of Assyria and Joash-I 169
   9.3.3. Hebrew Chronology and the Kings of Tyre 170
   9.3.4. Adad-nirari III of Assyria and a Discontinuity in the
     Eponyms of His Reign 173
   9.3.5. Pul of Assyria and Menahem 176
   9.3.6. Shishak of Egypt and Rehoboam 178
 9.4. A New Julian Chronology for the Divided Kingdom 180
   9.4.1. Explanation of Table 9.9 180
   9.4.2. Significant Dates in Ancient Near Eastern History 183
 9.5. Resolution to the Problems of Divided Kingdom Chronology .. 185

Indexes 187
 Index of Authors 187
 Index of Scripture 189
 Index of Royal Names 193

List of Tables

1.1.	Divided Kingdom Rulers according to Kingdom	12
1.2	Divided Kingdom Rulers in Alphabetic Order	13
2.1	Textual History of the Old Testament according to F. M. Cross	17
2.2	Text-Types in Samuel–Kings in Codex Vaticanus	19
2.3	Lucianic Manuscripts	23
2.4	Origen's Hexapla	25
3.1	Regnal Years in the Early Divided Kingdom	31
3.2	Regnal Years in the Late Divided Kingdom	31
3.3	Regnal Years in the Divided Kingdom	32
3.4	Early Divided Kingdom Chronological Data	35
3.5	Late Divided Kingdom Chronological Data	38
3.6	Divided Kingdom Timeline	40
3.7	Thiele's Chart 3 ($MNHK^3$ 82)	49
3.8	Thiele's Chart 11 ($MNHK^3$ 106)	51
3.9	Thiele's Chart 12 ($MNHK^3$ 106)	52
3.10	Thiele's Chart 13 ($MNHK^3$ 109)	52
4.1	Regnal Years in the Early Divided Kingdom according to c_2	55
4.2	Regnal Years in the Late Divided Kingdom according to c_2	55
4.3	Regnal Years in the Divided Kingdom according to c_2	56
4.4	Divided Kingdom Timeline according to c_2	58
5.1	Opening Formulas	65
5.2	Closing Formula: Pattern A (Kings of Judah and Israel Succeeded by a Son)	66
5.3	Closing Formula: Pattern B1 (Assassinated Kings of Israel Not Succeeded by a Son)	68
5.4	Closing Formula: Pattern B2 (Assassinated Kings of Israel Not Succeeded by a Son)	68
5.5	Distribution of Opening Regnal Formulas	70
5.6	Baasha's Closing and Elah's Opening Formulas (1 Kgs 16:6–8 MT/OG/L)	74
5.7	Hypothetical Original of 1 Kgs 16:6–8 according to the Typical Format	75
5.8	Ahaziah-I's Closing Formula (2 Kgs 1:17–18 MT/KR/L)	77
5.9	Translation of מלך by βασιλεύει (= HP) and ἐβασίλευσεν (= A)	88
6.1	Assyrian Eponym Canon for Shalmaneser IV and Ashur-dan III	96
6.2	Eponyms during Adad-nirari III's Reign according to the Assyrian Eponym Canon	98
6.3	Reconstruction of Eponyms during Adad-nirari III's Reign	99
6.4	Nonsynchronization of Adad-nirari III's 5th Year with the Regnal Years of Joash-I	100
6.5	Thiele's Chart 6 ($MNHK^3$ 85)	109
6.6	Thiele's Chart 8 ($MNHK^3$ 97)	110

6.7	Thiele's Chart 9 (*MNHK*[3] 101)	111
6.8	Thiele's Diagram 12 (*MNHK*[3] 98)	111
6.9	Thiele's Diagram 16 (*MNHK*[3] 118)	112
6.10	Thiele's Diagram 18 (*MNHK*[3] 130)	114
6.11	Thiele's Diagram 17 (*MNHK*[3] 121)	115
7.1	Early Divided Kingdom Chronology	120
7.2	Egyptian Hieratic Symbols in the Samaria Ostraca	135
7.3	Hebrew Alphabets (source: M. Lidzbarski in *Gesenius' Hebrew Grammar*)	137
8.1	Late Divided Kingdom Chronology Reconstructed from MT/KR, L, and c_2 Data	146
8.2	Calendar Years 196–229 according to MT/KR	148
8.3	Calendar Years 196–229 according to L	149
8.4	Calendar Years 196–229 according to c_2	150
8.5	The Assyrian Eponym Canon during the Fall of Samaria	158
8.6	Years 746–717 Synchronized with Assyrian and Hebrew Chronology	161
9.1	Correlation of Reigns of Joram and Shalmaneser III	167
9.2	Correlating Adad-nirari III with Joash-I on Current AEC Reckoning of Shamshi-Adad V's Reign	168
9.3	Revised Correlation of Adad-nirari III and Joash-I	169
9.4	Tyrian Data and Reconstructed Late Divided Kingdom Chronology	172
9.5	Assyrian Eponym Canon 810–781	174
9.6	Revised Correlation of Adad-nirari III's Later Reign with Hebrew Chronology	175
9.7	Menahem and Tiglath-pileser III	177
9.8	Egypt's 22nd Dynasty according to Kitchen	179
9.9	Reconstructed Divided Kingdom Chronology for Julian Years 981–718	180
9.10	Reigns for the Divided Kingdom	182
9.11	Significant Dates in Ancient Near Eastern History	184

Acknowledgments

The present work is a revision of my doctoral thesis of the same name approved by the Australian College of Theology in 2000. I wish to acknowledge the special help of my supervisors, Dr. Geoffrey Jenkins of the University of Melbourne, Australia, and Rev Dr Keith Carley of The College of St John the Evangelist, Auckland, New Zealand.

Over the past three decades, my exploration of ancient Near Eastern chronology, and the Divided Kingdom in particular, has been an absorbing labour of love in pursuit of the truth. Without the commitment of my husband, Barry, my research and writing could not have continued through our 16 years of mission ministry in the Philippines, 12 years in theological education in Auckland, and now alongside the ministry leadership of a busy urban parish. I am indebted also to our children, Bruce, Paul and Carolyn for their consideration and practical help.

Many friends and colleagues have supported me materially by accessing information, through sustained encouragement, or contributing in other ways, including staff of the Bible College of New Zealand and the Australian Institute of Archaeology. I am profoundly grateful to Eisenbrauns for bringing this work into the public arena.

M. CHRISTINE TETLEY
July 2004

Abbreviations

General

AEC	Assyrian Eponym Canon
boc_2e_2	Lucianic minuscule manuscripts
DK	divided kingdom
EDK	early divided kingdom
KR	*kaige* recension
L	Lucian, Lucianic
LDK	late divided kingdom
LXX	Septuagint
MT	Masoretic Text
OG	Old Greek

Bibliographic

ABC	A. K. Grayson, *Assyrian and Babylonian Chronicles* (Texts from Cuneiform Sources 5; Locust Valley, N.Y.: Augustin, 1975)
ANET	J. B. Pritchard (ed.), *Ancient Near Eastern Texts Relating to the Old Testament* (3rd ed.; Princeton: Princeton University Press, 1969)
ARAB	D. D. Luckenbill, *Ancient Records of Assyria and Babylonia* (2 vols.; repr. New York: Greenwood, 1968 [orig. Chicago: University of Chicago Press, 1926–27])
BASOR	*Bulletin of the American Schools of Oriental Research*
CKIJ	Gershon Galil, *The Chronology of the Kings of Israel and Judah* (Studies in the History and Culture of the Ancient Near East 9; Leiden: Brill, 1996)
CRD	James Donald Shenkel, *Chronology and Recensional Development in the Greek Text of Kings* (Harvard Semitic Monographs 1; Cambridge: Harvard University Press, 1968)
HAIJ	J. Maxwell Miller and John H. Hayes, *A History of Ancient Israel and Judah* (Philadelphia: Westminster/London: SCM, 1986)
JBL	*Journal of Biblical Literature*
MNHK[1]	Edwin R. Thiele, *The Mysterious Numbers of the Hebrew Kings: A Reconstruction of the Chronology of the Kingdoms of Israel and Judah* (1st ed.; Chicago: University of Chicago, Press, 1951)
MNHK[2]	Edwin R. Thiele, *The Mysterious Numbers of the Hebrew Kings: A Reconstruction of the Chronology of the Kingdoms of Israel and Judah* (2nd ed.; Grand Rapids: Eerdmans/Exeter: Paternoster, 1965)
MNHK[3]	Edwin R. Thiele, *The Mysterious Numbers of the Hebrew Kings* (3rd ed.; Grand Rapids: Zondervan, 1983)
QHBT	Frank Moore Cross Jr. and Shemaryahu Talmon (eds.), *Qumran and the History of the Biblical Text* (Cambridge: Harvard University Press, 1975)
VT	*Vetus Testamentum*

1

Introduction

T. R. Hobbs writes, "No problem associated with 2 Kings, and indeed the OT in its entirety, is more complicated than that of chronology, that is, the placing of events recorded in the OT in their proper sequence and assigning them their proper moment in the broader history of the ANE."[1] These chronological problems have intrigued scholars for centuries, and to the present day they remain the subject of ongoing debate. Recent publications witness to the continuing quest for a resolution to the chronology of the Hebrew kings.

The present uncertainty concerning the dates for the DK and its individual kings inspires my interest in the chronology of this period. I will attempt to reconstruct the chronology in the Books of Kings and to date the DK kings in the context of the ancient Near East using the Julian calendar.

1.1. Significance of Divided Kingdom Chronology

The Books of 1–2 Samuel and 1–2 Kings purport to record the history of the Hebrew monarchy during its three recognized divisions: the united kingdom under three kings, Saul, David, and Solomon, lasting approximately 120 years; the divided kingdom, comprising the nations of Israel and Judah each with their own monarch and lasting to the fall of Samaria; and the remaining single kingdom of Judah, lasting for over 130 years to the fall of Jerusalem.

The chronological data contained in the Books of 1–2 Kings, composed of a coordinated system of regnal years and accession synchronisms, offer a unique opportunity to propose a time frame for Hebrew monarchical history.[2] These data, supplemented from other sources, promote the expectation that a reconstruction of the Hebrew kings' chronology is possible. Yet it has proven intractably difficult.

An accurately dated chronology for the monarchy is important for understanding contemporary history and also for dating the preceding periods of the Hebrew and other nations in the ancient Near East. But the paucity of corroborating evidence for the existence of Israel prior to the monarchy and even for the united kingdom has given rise to debate concerning the historicity described in the biblical record. A convincing chronological reconstruction of the DK, synchronized with extrabiblical kings and events, would contribute to this debate and provide base dates for reckoning periods particularly relevant to the reconstruction of the chronologies of Egypt and Assyria. In addition, the establishment of the beginning date of the DK would provide the end date for the united kingdom, suggest a date for the monarchy's inception, and supply

---

1. T. R. Hobbs, *2 Kings* (Word Biblical Commentary 13; Waco: Word, 1985), xxxix.
2. Chronological data for Judah are also found in 2 Chronicles, with a few statements in other biblical books.

more precise dates for the end of Iron Age I and the onset of Iron Age II, associated with the commencement of the monarchy. In other words, an accurately dated DK would provide a springboard for dating archeological levels with more confidence.

1.2. Establishing Divided Kingdom Chronology

The determination of the Hebrew kings' reigns depends on establishing both relative and absolute chronology. Relative chronology relates the reigns of the kings of Israel and Judah to each other by their regnal years and accession synchronisms. Absolute chronology places the kings' reigns within the broader perspective of the ancient Near East and dates them to a recognized calendar.

1.2.1. Relative Chronology

The data for constructing relative chronology for the reigns of the Hebrew kings are contained in synchronistic formulas in which the accession of a king, whether of Israel or Judah, is synchronized with a regnal year of the contemporary king of the neighboring kingdom and followed by the number of years the king reigned. A typical formula states, "In xth year of King A of Judah, King B of Israel began to reign and he reigned y years." The formula implies that a king's reign occurs between his own accession synchronism and the accession synchronism of his successor. At the conclusion of the narrative of a king's reign another formula states his death and names his successor. The two interwoven chronologies of Israel and Judah provide a framework in which each king's reign is secured to both his predecessor and successor and is further secured by being synchronized with contemporaries of the other kingdom. This arrangement seems designed to establish and preserve an accurate record of the kings' reigns. Even so, reconstructing chronology from the data is problematic.

This basic chronology is provided by Hebrew and Greek biblical manuscripts. The earliest extant Hebrew manuscripts of the Books of Kings preserve the Masoretic text-type (as represented in Codex Leningrad B19^A, dating to 1008/1009 C.E.). These MT data are most commonly used to reconstruct the DK chronology. Codex Vaticanus (a Greek manuscript dating to the 4th century C.E.) contains two text-types approximating the pre-Masoretic division of 1–2 Kings. The text-type of 1 Kings is dated to about the 2nd century B.C.E., and 2 Kings to the 1st century B.C.E. Later Greek cursive manuscripts (minuscules known collectively as boc$_2$e$_2$) date from the 10th to 14th centuries C.E. and exhibit a text-type known as Lucianic, thought to date from the 3rd century C.E. and believed to be based on an earlier text dating back to the 2nd century B.C.E. This L text is extant throughout 1–2 Kings and plays a significant role in textual analysis.

The important feature about these early texts is that they exhibit two variant arrangements of the chronological data. One arrangement is found in 1 Kings in Codex Vaticanus ending with Ahab's reign and in the L manuscripts (except c$_2$) to the end of the EDK (i.e., the deaths of Ahaziah-J and Joram by Jehu). The second arrangement of chronological data is found in the MT for all of 1–2 Kings and in Codex Vaticanus from 1 Kings 22 to the end of 2 Kings. From the beginning of the LDK (commencing with Athaliah in Judah and Jehu in Israel) the Hebrew and Greek texts (except c$_2$) exhibit the same chronological data apart from a variant for the reign of Pekahiah.

The two systems are not completely independent. Some EDK data are identical in both Hebrew and Greek texts and other data are different for the same kings, creating variants. But in neither the Hebrew nor the Greek texts are the data internally consistent. The inconsistency caused by regnal years and synchronisms in Israel and Judah not corresponding to the kings' allocated years makes reconstructing chronology from the data in either the Greek or Hebrew texts very difficult. A proposal to reconstruct relative chronology must explain the presence of variant chronological EDK data in Greek and Hebrew texts and resolve the problems of inconsistency throughout the DK.

1.2.2. Absolute Chronology

The second criterion used in reconstructing chronology is the establishment of absolute chronology in which the kings' reigns are dated to a recognized calendar. The Julian calendar is used by Western scholars to date the events of the ancient Near East.[3] The Hebrew kings derive their absolute dates from synchronization with Assyrian kings named in the Assyrian Eponym Canon, to which Julian years have been assigned. Any attempt to establish absolute chronology must, however, consider the reliability of the AEC.

The AEC is a list of Assyrian officials, each one giving his name (eponym, Akkadian *limmu*) to a year of a king's reign, with the most important officials heading the list. The king held the office of eponym in his 1st or 2nd regnal year, but commencing with Shalmaneser V (727–722) the king's eponym was allocated to a later year of his reign. Some lists comprise only the eponyms, while others add the title of the official and a few words indicating an important event in that year (frequently a military campaign against another country). The AEC is reconstructed from fragmentary tablets, each containing parts of the list, that overlap to give an apparently continuous list of names.

A solar eclipse recorded in the AEC during the month Siwan in the 9th eponym of Assyrian king Ashur-dan III is dated by astronomers to 15/16 June 763 B.C.E. and provides a reliable fixed point for synchronizing the AEC with the Julian calendar. Beginning with Nabu-nasir in 747 B.C.E. it is possible to correlate Assyrian kings listed in the AEC with the Canon of Ptolemy, a list of Babylonian kings.[4] This known correlation between Assyria and Babylonia confirms the accuracy of the AEC from 763 onward. Various king lists (generically related to the AEC) allow scholars to calculate the total years that each king reigned, and on this basis eponyms have been dated between 910 B.C.E. and 612 B.C.E.[5]

To establish absolute chronology, a synchronism has to be established between a Hebrew king and an Assyrian king. The earliest known synchronism, for example, comes from the records of Shalmaneser III of Assyria, which mention two kings of Israel: *Aḫabbu* (Ahab) in a campaign record from Shalmaneser's 6th regnal year and *Iaúa* (Jehu) in a campaign in Shalmaneser's 18th year. According to 1 Kgs 22:52 MT, Ahaziah-I reigned for 2 years after his father Ahab's death, followed by his brother Joram's 12-year reign (2 Kgs 3:1) before Jehu usurped the throne. The 14 years required in the biblical record between the death of Ahab and the accession of Jehu seem to conflict with the 12 years given in the AEC between Shalmaneser's 6th and 18th years. Thus, before the Hebrew kings can be dated to the Julian calendar, problems of synchronizing Israel's and Judah's kings with the AEC must be resolved.

---

3. The Julian calendar was introduced in 45 B.C.E. and slightly modified in 1582, when it was replaced by the Gregorian calendar. Both calendars have 365-day years, with a leap day every 4th year. See Ptolemy, *The Almagest* (trans. R. C. Taliaferro; Great Books of the Western World 16; Chicago: Benton, 1952), 467; J. Finegan, *Handbook of Biblical Chronology* (Princeton: Princeton University Press, 1964), 76–77; C. A. Ronan, "Calendar" in *Encyclopaedia Britannica* (Chicago: Benton, 1968), 4:615–19.

4. Ptolemy, "Almagest," 466; L. Depuydt, "'More Valuable than All Gold': Ptolemy's Royal Canon and Babylonian Chronology," *Journal of Cuneiform Studies* 47 (1995): 97–117.

5. A. Millard, *The Eponyms of the Assyrian Empire 910–612 B.C.* (State Archives of Assyria Studies 2; Helsinki: Neo-Assyrian Text Corpus Project, 1994), 6–7, 13; see also J. Gray, *1 and 2 Kings* (Old Testament Library; London: SCM, 1970), 58–59.

1.3. Conventional Approaches to Divided Kingdom Chronology

Establishing both relative and absolute chronology for the DK kings involves basic problems like those just illustrated. How then do scholars attempt to reconcile the conflicting data (both internal and external criteria) and reconstruct DK chronology? The majority of chronologies produced in the last half century or so have at least four features in common:

1. The chronological data of the Hebrew text are preferred to the Greek data.
2. More than one dating system is proposed to reconcile disparate numbers.
3. Dates assigned to the AEC are relied upon to date the Hebrew kings.
4. Menahem of Israel is understood to be a contemporary of Tiglath-pileser III, the latter identified as King Pul of Assyria, to whom Menahem paid tribute (2 Kgs 15:19).

These common features gave rise to what I call the conventional approach to biblical chronology, which does, of course, exhibit some variation of methodology, particularly with regard to the treatment of biblical sources and data and to dating systems. The leading proponent of the conventional approach during the last half of the 20th century was Edwin R. Thiele, whose best known work, *The Mysterious Numbers of the Hebrew Kings*, was published in three editions. While Thiele has been critiqued by scholars,[6] he still had followers as late as the mid-1990s.[7] In order to contrast my chronology with the conventional approach, in the following chapters I will analyze and assess Thiele's chronology.[8] In the meantime, it is important to review some of the more significant aspects of the conventional methodology and the problems raised by its main tenets.

1.3.1. Biblical Sources

Scholars differ on how the MT data should be regarded. Thiele, for example, writes:

> The many seeming contradictions in the chronological data of the Hebrew kings have long been regarded as evidence of certain error. Before, however, a final verdict can be pronounced against those data, it must be ascertained whether the data themselves are at fault, or whether our misapprehensions are based on our own failure to understand the basic chronological practices followed by the ancient Hebrew recorders.[9]

Thiele goes on to describe what he thought the practices were and claims that

> when these principles are applied to the chronological data of the MT, and when the coregencies and overlapping reigns . . . are taken into consideration, the seeming discrepancies in the regnal

---

6. E.g., "Thiele is forced to project innumerable coregencies, to reconstruct a complex interchange of calendars, and to fall back on unique patterns of calculation. . . . He has found few followers of his system apart from those who are committed apologetically to a doctrine of scripture's absolute harmony"; B. S. Childs, *Introduction to the Old Testament as Scripture* (Philadelphia: Fortress, 1979), 296. Cf. W. F. Albright, "Prolegomenon," in C. F. Burney, *The Books of Judges with Introduction and Notes and Notes on the Hebrew Text of the Books of Kings* (repr. New York: Ktav, 1970), 36; G. H. Jones, *1 and 2 Kings* (New Century Bible Commentary; Grand Rapids: Eerdmans, 1984), 19; Hobbs, *2 Kings*, xliii–xliv.

7. E.g., "The chronology most widely accepted today is one based on the meticulous study by Thiele"; D. J. Wiseman, *1 and 2 Kings* (Tyndale Old Testament Commentaries; Leicester: Inter-Varsity, 1993), 27. Cf. K. A. Strand's endorsement in "Thiele's Biblical Chronology as a Corrective for Extrabiblical Dates," *Andrews University Seminary Studies* 34 (1996): 295–317.

8. Space does not permit further critique of other proposals, some of which can be accessed readily in W. F. Albright, "The Chronology of the Divided Monarchy of Israel," *BASOR* 100 (1945): 16–17; Childs, *Introduction to the Old Testament as Scripture*, 295–97; J. Hughes, *Secrets of the Times: Myth and History in Biblical Chronology* (Journal for the Study of the Old Testament Supplement 66; Sheffield: JSOT Press, 1990), 99–122; L. McFall, "Has the Chronology of the Hebrew Kings Been Finally Settled?" *Themelios* 17/1 (1991): 6–7; Galil, *CKIJ* 1–11.

9. E. R. Thiele, "Coregencies and Overlapping Reigns among the Hebrew Kings," *JBL* 93 (1974): 177.

data of Kings will disappear, and there will be a pattern of years for the Hebrew rulers which will agree with the years of contemporary nations at every point where an exact contact can be made.[10]

Most scholars, however, allow for some textual errors or deliberate alteration to the MT numbers over centuries of transmission,[11] and they compose chronology using variations of dating systems incorporating some textual changes and/or coregencies.[12] The conventional approach, by uncritically preferring data of the Hebrew text over that of the Greek text, displays a flawed method of textual analysis and leaves a considerable amount of chronological data inadequately considered. Very little textual analysis attempts to resolve the origin of alternative data for the various kings in the Hebrew and Greek texts. Instead, the MT data alone are subjected to analysis.

1.3.2. Dating Systems

The conventional approach employs various dating systems and methodologies to reconcile conflicting numbers in the MT:

1. Antedating (also called nonaccession-year reckoning) counts a king's accession year as his first year, and his second regnal year begins after the next New Year's Day (*MNHK*³ 43–44, 48–50, 54–60, 231). Thiele interprets Jeroboam I's 22-year reign (1 Kgs 14:20) as his "official years" according to Israel's antedating system but reckons these as 21 "actual years" (*MNHK*³ 81).
2. Postdating (also called accession-year reckoning) counts a king's reign from the New Year's Day after his accession. In any particular year, antedating credits a king with one year more than postdating (*MNHK*³ 43–44, 47–50, 54–60, 231).
3. Switching between postdating and antedating is used at times to reconcile conflicting MT data (*MNHK*³ 47, 56–60, 215–16).
4. Variant calendars are used to reconcile the MT data. Some scholars propose that Israel's calendar began in Nisan (spring) and Judah's calendar began in Tishri (autumn). Israel's year began 6 months ahead of Judah's.[13]
5. Each nation used its own calendar to record the reigns of its own kings and even the kings in the other kingdom. Thus, Israel used antedating for Israel and Judah, even

---

10. Ibid., 178.
11. Discussed by Hughes, *Secrets of the Times*, 107–14.
12. Scholars who have produced chronology using these variations include Albright, "Chronology of the Divided Monarchy," 16–22; C. Schedl, "Textkritische Bemerkungen zu den Synchronismen der Könige von Israel und Juda," *VT* 12 (1962): 88–119; V. Pavlovský and E. Vogt, "Die Jahre der Könige von Juda und Israel," *Biblica* 45 (1964): 321–47; K. T. Andersen, "Die Chronologie der Könige von Israel und Juda," *Studia Theologica* 23 (1969): 69–114, revised in "Noch Einmal: Die Chronologie der Könige von Israel und Juda," *Scandinavian Journal of the Old Testament* 3 (1989): 1–45; H. Tadmor, "The Chronology of the First Temple Period," in *The World History of the Jewish People*, 1st series: *Ancient Times: The Age of the Monarchies: Political History*, vol. 4/1 (ed. A. Malamat; Jerusalem: Massada, 1979), 44–60, 318–20; M. Cogan and H. Tadmor, *II Kings: A New Translation with Introduction and Commentary* (Anchor Bible 11; Garden City, N.Y.: Doubleday, 1988), 341; J. H. Hayes and P. K. Hooker, *A New Chronology for the Kings of Israel and Judah and Its Implications for Biblical History and Literature* (Atlanta: John Knox, 1988); W. H. Barnes, *Studies in the Chronology of the Divided Monarchy of Israel* (Harvard Semitic Monographs 48; Atlanta: Scholars Press, 1991), esp. 1–27, 137–58; Galil, *CKIJ*; M. Cogan, *1 Kings: A New Translation with Introduction and Commentary* (Anchor Bible 10; New York: Doubleday, 2000), 100–103, 508.
13. Thiele, *MNHK*³ 44–54; McFall, "Has the Chronology," 7; idem, "A Translation Guide to the Chronological Data in Kings and Chronicles," *Bibliotheca Sacra* 148 (1991): 6–9; Galil, *CKIJ* 9–10. Other scholars propose an autumn calendar in both Israel and Judah during the DK (see Jones, *1 and 2 Kings*, 15–17); Hayes and Hooker (*New Chronology*, 13) assume a 1-month difference in the winter months, with Judah's year beginning in Tishri and Israel's in Marheshvan.

though Judah itself used postdating (*MNHK*³ 49–50, 55 [diagram 7], and 82 [chart 3, reproduced as my table 3.7]).

6. Coregency—defined by Thiele as "a period of rulership when a son sits on the throne with his father" (*MNHK*³ 231)—is used especially by Thiele, Gray, and McFall to reconcile the MT data.[14] Other scholars typically see coregencies as either without biblical warrant or based on circular argumentation.[15]

7. Finally, seemingly arbitrary changes in numbers are used to make sense of the MT data.

Scholars usually do not use a single one of these systems, but some combination of them. McFall, for example, uses four systems (antedating, postdating, Nisan and Tishri calendars, and coregencies) to reconcile the MT data about Israel and Judah.[16] And, although McFall does not allow changes to MT numbers, he changes instead the natural meaning of the regnal formulas by overwriting them with his own dating assumptions. He does not apply his system to the Greek data.

On the other hand, for the Greek texts, Thiele hypothesizes an inconsequent accession-year dating system in which "the year when a ruler is set forth as having begun his reign is actually the year after his reign began" (*MNHK*³ 93; cf. *MNHK*¹ 172–76, 185–87). Finding that this system does not work, Thiele concludes (*MNHK*³ 210) that "in no instance is a Greek variation an improvement over the Hebrew. The fallacies of the Greek innovations may be proved by the wide divergence of the patterns of reigns they call for from the years of contemporary chronology."

A different explanation for conflicting data is given by Jeremy Hughes, who rejects coregencies and asserts that chronological discrepancies are neither textual corruptions nor miscalculations.[17] Instead, he proposes that the chronology was altered from an original historical chronology to a schematic pre-priestly (Deuteronomistic) chronology and subsequently to a priestly schematic chronology before a final revision using noninclusive antedating. Seeming discrepancies, therefore, are alterations made to fit the kings' reigns into a scheme of 430 years from the foundation of Solomon's temple to its destruction, with some figures representing conflations of schemes between MT and LXX.[18] This system seems to be no less drastic than those to which Hughes objects.[19]

---

14. E.g., Thiele, *MNHK*³ 61–65 and passim; idem, "The Question of Coregencies among the Hebrew Kings," in *A Stubborn Faith: Papers on the Old Testament and Related Subjects Presented to Honor William Andrew Irwin* (ed. E. C. Hobbs; Dallas: Southern Methodist University Press, 1956), 39–52; idem, "Coregencies and Overlapping Reigns," 174–200; Gray, *1 and 2 Kings*, 65–75; Jones, *1 and 2 Kings*, 17–19; McFall, "Has the Chronology," 8–10; idem, "Did Thiele Overlook Hezekiah's Coregency?" *Bibliotheca Sacra* 143 (1989): 393–404; idem, "Translation Guide," 3–45; idem, "Some Missing Coregencies in Thiele's Chronology," *Andrews University Seminary Studies* 30 (1992): 35–58.

15. See J. M. Miller, "Another Look at the Chronology of the Early Divided Monarchy," *JBL* 86 (1967): 276–88, esp. 278; Shenkel, *CRD* 75 (see Barnes's comments in support of Thiele against Shenkel in *Chronology of the Divided Monarchy*, 26–27 n. 65); Jones, *1 and 2 Kings*, 18–19; Hayes and Hooker, *New Chronology*, 11, 12; Hughes, *Secrets of the Times*, 98–107, esp. 100.

16. McFall, "Translation Guide," 3–45.

17. Hughes, *Secrets of the Times*, 114.

18. Ibid., 94, 96, 98, 121–54.

19. See Galil's criticism of Hughes's methodology in *CKIJ* 6–7. Hughes's interest in "mythical" or schematic chronology (*Secrets of the Times*, v) was aroused by James Barr, who has himself written articles that propose a legendary chronology: "Why the World Was Created in 4004 B.C.: Archbishop Ussher and Biblical Chronology," *Bulletin of the John Rylands Library* 67 (1985): 575–608; *Biblical Chronology: Legend or Science?* (Ethel M. Wood Lecture 1987; London: University of London, 1987); and "Luther and Biblical Chronology," *Bulletin of the John Rylands Library* 72 (1989): 51–67.

The problem with these complex dating systems is that they are at variance with the regnal formulas, which are written in clear, stylized statements. Each formula states that a king began to reign *in* the given year of the king of the other kingdom, not that the reigns were calculated from different points according to different dating systems or that the reigns of father and son sometimes overlapped. In conventional chronology, these dating systems, especially coregency, are posited whenever a conflict in numbers is observed in the text—not on the basis of their direct attestation in Israel or Judah.[20] These systems are not supported by the text itself and are dubious assumptions to make about a text that intends to display chronological detail and synchronicity.

1.3.3. Assyrian Eponym Canon

Conventional chronologists assume that the AEC is reliable *before* as well as after the solar eclipse of 763 B.C.E. Hughes, for example, writes:

> The primary source of external evidence relating to Israelite and Judean chronology are the historical records of Assyria and Babylonia. We are therefore fortunate in having an accurate chronological framework for Assyrian and Babylonian history during the first millennium BC. This framework, which is based upon Mesopotamian chronographic texts (kinglists, eponym lists, and chronicles), is securely related to Julian chronology through the Ptolemaic Canon, a kinglist compiled by Alexandrian astronomers for use in astronomical calculations.[21]

In spite of this confident assertion, Hughes goes on to footnote uncertainty whether the eponym Balatu should be included in the eponyms for the reign of Adad-nirari III.[22] This confused area of eponyms comes *before* 763 B.C.E.

Kitchen and Mitchell's confident statement also illustrates the conventional approach: "From comparison of the Assyrian *limmu* or eponym lists, king-lists and historical texts, the date 853 BC can be fixed for the battle of Qarqar, the death of Ahab and accession of Ahaziah in Israel; and likewise Jehu's accession at Joram's death in 841 B.C."[23] It is assumed that dates before 763 B.C.E. can be relied upon, yet with no corroborating evidence 853 or 841 are used to establish the beginning of the DK in the 930s or 920s B.C.E.[24] Methodology that accepts the reliability of the AEC before 763 B.C.E. without first testing its veracity, especially when there are significant problems involved in reconciling the Hebrew regnal years with the years assigned to the AEC, is suspect.

1.3.4. Tiglath-pileser III and Menahem

Conventional chronologists assume that Menahem, who paid tribute to King Pul of Assyria (2 Kgs 15:19), was contemporary with Tiglath-pileser III because Tiglath-pileser was also known

---

20. Some scholars point to David's appointment of Solomon as his heir before he died (1 Kgs 1:1–48) and Jotham's rulership over the land after his father became leprous (2 Kgs 15:5) as evidence for coregencies, while others reject these examples; see discussion in Hughes, *Secrets of the Times*, 103–5.

21. Ibid., 182.

22. Ibid., 182 n. 53.

23. K. A. Kitchen and T. C. Mitchell, "Chronology of the Old Testament," in *Illustrated Bible Dictionary* (ed. N. Hillyer; London: Inter-Varsity, 1980), 1:276.

24. The beginning of the DK is variously calculated (some of these dates are taken from J. H. Hayes and J. M. Miller, *Israelite and Judaean History* [London: SCM, 1977], 682–83):

937	Hughes	931/930	Thiele, McFall, Galil	926	Begrich-Jepsen
932	Barnes	928	Cogan and Tadmor	925	Miller
932/931	Andersen	927/926	Hayes and Hooker	922	Albright

as Pul.²⁵ Tiglath-pileser's identity with Pul is confirmed by comparing the Babylonian Chronicle and Babylonian King List A (cf. 1 Chr 5:26). Menahem has been identified on tribute lists apparently from the time of Tiglath-pileser III.

The AEC and the Canon of Ptolemy confirm Tiglath-pileser III's reign as 745–727. But viewing Menahem as Tiglath-pileser's contemporary conflicts with 2 Kgs 15:29 and 16:1–18, in which Tiglath-pileser is contemporary with Pekah in Israel and Ahaz in Judah — but not with Menahem. For his entire reign Menahem was contemporary with Azariah (15:17–23). To locate Menahem in Tiglath-pileser's reign, scholars either posit Menahem and Pekah as rival rulers in Israel²⁶ or reduce Pekah's reign from 20 years to much less.²⁷ Methodology that makes Menahem and Tiglath-pileser III contemporaries should be viewed with considerable caution.

1.4. Alternative Approach to Divided Kingdom Chronology

An alternative approach to resolving the chronological problems of the Books of Kings was broached in 1964 by J. Maxwell Miller.²⁸ In the period following Omri's accession, Miller finds two different patterns of synchronisms, one dominating the MT and the other L, but both texts contained elements of both patterns. Miller concludes: "The Lucianic pattern of synchronisms is probably the best starting point for reconstructing the chronology of the Omride period."²⁹ In 1967 Miller argued for the acceptance of "the Lucianic pattern in preference to that of the masoretic tradition."³⁰ He suggests an EDK chronology that altered reign lengths to accommodate synchronisms without providing support from a text-critical analysis.

In contrast to Miller, working from a text-critical perspective James D. Shenkel analyzed EDK chronological data in his Harvard thesis, subsequently revised and published in 1968 as *Chronology and Recensional Development in the Greek Text of Kings*. Concerning the value of the Greek data, Shenkel proposed: "Any treatment of the chronological problems in the Books of Kings would be inadequate unless it were based upon an understanding of the Greek text as an independent body of traditions deserving of study in its own right, and not merely as a source for occasionally interesting variants to readings found in the Masoretic text" (*CRD* 5). Shenkel hopes that "better understanding of the recensional development of the Greek text will provide a new perspective for conducting research into the chronology of the Books of Kings" (*CRD* 4). But Shenkel himself does not attempt to construct chronology. Shenkel's work has been viewed favorably:

---

25. E.g., Thiele, *MNHK*³ 125, 139–41; Tadmor, "Chronology of the First Temple Period," 54; Barnes, *Chronology of the Divided Monarchy*, 157; Hughes, *Secrets of the Times*, 198–201; Galil, *CKIJ* 62–65.

26. Thiele, *MNHK*³ 63, 120–21 (diagram 17), 124, 129; McFall, "Translation Guide," 29–31.

27. Schedl ("Textkritische Bemerkungen," 91, 96) and Pavlovský and Vogt ("Jahre der Könige," 325, 337–38) give Pekah 10 years; J. Reade suggests that Pekahiah and Pekah were the same person and that Pekah's 20 years are illusory ("Mesopotamian Guidelines for Biblical Chronology," *Syro-Mesopotamian Studies* 4 [1981]: 5–6); Miller and Hayes give Pekahiah 2 years and Pekah 4 years (*HAIJ* 229); Barnes gives 8 years to Menahem and 5 to Pekah (*Chronology of the Divided Monarchy*, 153–54, 157); Andersen gives Pekah 4 years ("Noch Einmal: Die Chronologie," 8, 11–12); Hughes gives Pekah 4 years, claiming the 20 years to be schematic (*Secrets of the Times*, 205); and Galil gives Pekah a 5-year reign as sole monarch (*CKIJ* 65, 82; cf. 129 n. 10).

28. J. M. Miller, *The Omride Dynasty in the Light of Recent Literary and Archaeological Research* (Ph.D. diss.; Emory University, 1964), cited in "Another Look," 279–80 n. 21. Miller identifies the king of Israel referred to in 1 Kgs 22:1–40 as Jehoahaz, not Ahab. His arguments are summarized in "The Elisha Cycle and the Accounts of the Omride Wars," *JBL* 85 (1966): 441–54.

29. Miller, "Elisha Cycle," 454; see similar comments concerning the chronology of the Omride period in idem, "Another Look," 284–86; idem, *The Old Testament and the Historian* (London: SPCK, 1976), 37–38; idem, *HAIJ* 264–65.

30. Miller, "Another Look," 285.

The fresh perspective on the problem which has been opened up by the brilliant dissertation of J. D. Shenkel must be seriously considered by all future research. Shenkel, who has built on the textual work of F. M. Cross, was able to demonstrate that the variant chronological data of the Old Greek textual recension of Reigns represents an ancient and integral chronological tradition, and is not simply to be dismissed as a late, secondary reinterpretation of the Masoretic text. Moreover, Shenkel has dealt a severe blow to such reconstructions as those of Begrich and Thiele which have depended solely on the MT for recovering the original tradition. In addition, he has shown the textual basis for some of the tension in the present MT and has seriously damaged Thiele's explanations of co-regencies. However, Shenkel's own attempt to describe the historical process by which the various chronologies were related makes use of several projections of how biblical books were redacted which are far from obvious.[31]

Shenkel . . . has argued that extremely valuable chronological data are obtained from the Greek translations. Instead of taking the chronological data of the Greek as evidence of arbitrary tampering by a late translator, Shenkel, by investigating such data against the background of the development of the Greek and Hebrew texts, finds in them a variant tradition which may indeed be more ancient than the one preserved in the Hebrew.[32]

Despite Miller's and Shenkel's publications, scholars who have proposed chronologies since 1968 have taken only incidental interest in the chronological data of the Greek text and have continued to work mainly with the MT.[33] Galil, for example, constructs his chronology based on the MT data and only in the last chapter does he consider the variants of the Greek text (*CKIJ* 127–44).

The main criticism of Shenkel's work comes from his handling of the chronological issues, not his work on recensional development. For example, he identifies Ahaziah-J or Jehoram as the king of Judah who went with Joram on the Moabite campaign of 2 Kings 3, identifications indicated by the Greek regnal data. Shenkel explains (*CRD* 92–108, 111) that the naming of Jehoshaphat in the MT was done by a pious redactor who wanted to make good King Jehoshaphat the contemporary of Elisha the prophet and that the MT data had been changed backward to the reign of Omri to effect this. The weakness of this hypothesis seems to have undermined acceptance of the Greek variants as valuable witnesses to an early chronology.[34] Nevertheless, Shenkel's work on chronology has been taken seriously by a number of scholars, and as the recensional development of the Greek texts becomes more widely recognized the credibility of the Greek chronological data is gaining further support.[35]

---

31. Childs, *Introduction to the Old Testament as Scripture*, 296–97.

32. Jones, *1 and 2 Kings*, 5–6.

33. Thiele's response is discussed in §2.3. Note Barnes's comments about Shenkel's work in *Chronology of the Divided Monarchy*, 23–27.

34. Criticism of Shenkel comes from: D. W. Gooding, review of *CRD* in *Journal of Theological Studies* 21 (1970): 118–31; S. J. De Vries, "Chronology, OT," in *Interpreter's Dictionary of the Bible: Supplementary Volume* (ed. K. Crim; Nashville: Abingdon, 1976), 163; idem, *1 Kings* (Word Biblical Commentary 12; Waco: Word, 1985), 181–82; idem, "The Three Comparisons in 1 Kings XXII 4B and Its Parallel and 2 Kings III 7B," *VT* 39 (1989): 305–6; P. J. Williams, "Some Remarks Preliminary to a Biblical Chronology," *Creation Ex Nihilo Technical Journal* 12 (1998): 100; A. R. Green, "Regnal Formulas in the Hebrew and Greek Texts of the Books of Kings," *Journal of Near Eastern Studies* 42 (1983): 167–80; A. R. Millard, "Texts and Archaeology: Weighing the Evidence—the Case for King Solomon," *Palestine Exploration Quarterly* 123 (1991): 19–20.

35. See, e.g., Albright, "Prolegomenon," 27–28, 33–36; R. W. Klein, *Textual Criticism of the Old Testament: The Septuagint after Qumran* (Philadelphia: Fortress, 1974), 36–40; Julio Trebolle [Barrera], "Redaction, Recension, and Midrash in the Books of Kings," *Bulletin of the International Organization for Septuagint and Cognate Studies* 15 (1982): 12–35; Jones, *1 and 2 Kings*, 19–21; Hobbs, *2 Kings*, xliv–xlv; R. B. Dillard and T. Longman, *An Introduction to the Old Testament* (Leicester: Apollos, 1995), 156.

1.5. New Proposal for Divided Kingdom Chronology

Each of the methods discussed above proves to be problematic. Conventional approaches reconstruct chronology by analyzing only the MT data and by manipulating these data in various unconventional ways. Miller's reconstruction of the chronology gives more credence to the Greek data (especially the L data), but lacks supporting text-critical analysis. And Shenkel subjects the data to text-critical analysis based on his theory of recensional development in the Greek texts, but does not test his conclusions by reconstructing chronology. A new approach to reconstructing DK chronology is thus called for. The following features will be given fuller treatment in later chapters:

1. It is necessary to resolve conflicting data in the Hebrew and Greek texts. While scholars recognize two apparently alternative chronological patterns in the Greek and Hebrew, with some of the same data appearing in both patterns, the actual relationship between the Hebrew data and the Greek data has yet to be established. If the Greek was originally translated from a Hebrew text and was not an independent rendition of Hebrew history, why do we find variant and conflicting data alongside identical or similar data in the respective texts? I will analyze the data to find the factors that produced the textual variants and the two divergent patterns. Understanding the process or factors that produced divergency ought to provide a pathway back to the data first preserved in earlier Hebrew texts. It is not a matter of first trying to make consistent chronology from the Hebrew data or, failing that, from the Greek data. Rather it is a matter of seeing how each datum is placed in the overall picture of the whole transmission process. When each datum is seen in its appropriate place, indicators pointing to the earliest text (perhaps represented in late manuscripts) should emerge. The chronological data—that is, reign lengths and accession synchronisms—must be analyzed and evaluated within their context to elucidate their part in the transmission process and the chronological data they contain. I will seek to determine and isolate original data from secondary based on a text-critical analysis of the regnal formulas.
2. Chronology must be based on a dating system (or systems). As distinct from conventional chronologists who propose antedating, postdating, coregencies, etc., I will seek to establish a dating system consistent with the textual terminology of the regnal formulas, which assert that a king began to reign *in* the given regnal year of the contemporary king of the other kingdom and that the king acceded to the throne upon the death of his predecessor.
3. Using supposed synchronisms between the Assyrian kings and Hebrew kings with dates derived from the AEC as a baseline, most chronologies assign dates to the Hebrew kings at the same time as they construct relative chronology. I will instead first construct relative chronology from the dual chronologies of Israel and Judah before attempting to establish absolute chronology.
4. When relative chronology has been established, I will then correlate it to the Julian calendar to provide absolute chronology. This may necessitate reconciling the Hebrew and Assyrian chronologies.

From these foundational concepts I hope to propose a credible chronology for the DK. On the basis of conclusions arrived at by gathering and examining the evidence (chapters 2–5), I will propose a methodology (chapter 6) and reconstruct the chronology (chapters 7–9).

Chapter 2 reviews the transmission history of the Greek and Hebrew texts of the Books of Kings in order to gain an understanding of their origin and characteristics before reconstructing their chronology. The Greek texts—especially the L family—give valuable witness to the earliest chronology. My examination of these texts and their transmission history is contrasted with Thiele's approach, which depends on the Hebrew text to supply the chronological data and on various dating systems to make these data harmonize.

Chapter 3 surveys the chronological data in the Hebrew and Greek texts. The DK synchronisms and reign lengths found in MT, OG, L, and Josephus's *Antiquities* are tabulated and analyzed, and discrepancies noted. Thiele's analysis of the same data receives comment and is followed by a discussion of the problems attached to reconciling the data in the Greek and Hebrew texts.

Chapter 4 surveys the chronological data found in c_2, an L manuscript with its own unique variants. c_2 used a year-for-year approach to compile its coherent record, which fills in some gaps in the LDK in the texts analyzed in chapter 3.

Chapter 5 analyzes patterns of opening and closing regnal formulas, the word order of accession synchronisms, the position of supplementary material, the sequence of kings' reigns, and the translation of the Hebrew verb מלך. The resulting patterns and discrepancies help distinguish primary from secondary text.

Chapter 6 proposes a methodology for reconstructing relative chronology and absolute chronology on the basis of information analyzed in chapters 2–5. The method for constructing relative chronology relies on my understanding of several matters: the dating system used to record the kings' reigns, how final years were reckoned, how to account for variant numbers in the texts, how to distinguish original numbers from secondary, how numbers were written in early Hebrew manuscripts, and how to reckon regnal years by calendar years. The method for constructing absolute chronology must establish a starting date, which I do by investigating the reliability of the AEC. Since my analysis suggests that the AEC is reliable only after 763 B.C.E., we must, therefore, gain our starting date subsequent to this date and work backward to date the kings.

Chapter 7 reconstructs EDK relative chronology by employing the methodology outlined in the previous chapter. Text-critical analysis of the chronological data identifies primary and secondary text, indicates where variants entered the text(s) and caused a new system of chronology to emerge, and recognizes that both Hebrew and Greek retain some of the earliest data, showing their common origin. Relative chronology is reconstructed from the primary data, with explanations given for the appearance of the secondary.

Chapter 8 continues the discussion of relative chronology into the LDK. The data for this section exhibit little variation between text-types but the totals for Israel and Judah differ. Explanations for this anomaly and for reconciling the data are proposed. I also discuss a starting date for absolute chronology and provide a Julian date for the fall of Samaria using biblical and Assyrian records.

Chapter 9 proposes absolute chronology for the entire DK by relating Hebrew chronology to the AEC. Some synchronisms between the Assyrian and Hebrew kings are irreconcilable unless the years currently attributed to the AEC for Shamshi-Adad V and Adad-nirari III are revised (which has implications for Egyptian chronology). The end product of my investigation—the reconstruction of DK chronology—is presented in a continuous table for the entire period.

Table 1.1. Divided Kingdom Rulers according to Kingdom

	Judah	Israel	
	Rehoboam	Jeroboam I	
	Abijam	Nadab	
	Asa	Baasha	
	Jehoshaphat	Elah	
	Jehoram	Zimri	
EDK	Ahaziah-J	Omri	
LDK	Athaliah	Ahab	
	Joash-J	Ahaziah-I	
	Amaziah	Joram	EDK
	Azariah	Jehu	LDK
	Jotham	Jehoahaz	
	Ahaz	Joash-I	
	Hezekiah	Jeroboam II	
		Zechariah	
		Shallum	
		Menahem	
		Pekahiah	
		Pekah	
		Hoshea	

1.6. Names of Kings

The DK rulers of Judah and Israel are not consistently named in the various texts, nor are their names consistently spelled. In addition, some names are used for rulers of both kingdoms, and interchangeable names are occasionally used for the same king. To reduce confusion in an already complex discussion, I use standard names for the DK kings, adjusted by the following naming conventions:

1. The first and thirteenth rulers of Israel are both named Jeroboam; I refer to these kings as Jeroboam I and Jeroboam II.
2. The sons of Ahaziah of Judah and Jehoahaz of Israel are both named Joash (which is frequently interchanged with Jehoash); I refer to these kings as Joash-J and Joash-I.
3. The sons of Jehoram of Judah and of Ahab of Israel are both named Ahaziah; I refer to these kings as Ahaziah-J and Ahaziah-I.
4. The sons of Jehoshaphat of Judah and of Ahab of Israel are interchangeably named Jehoram and Joram; I refer to the Judahite king as Jehoram and to the Israelite king as Joram.
5. Abijam of Judah is also called Abijah (2 Chronicles 13); I refer to this king as Abijam.

Table 1.2. Divided Kingdom Rulers in Alphabetic Order

King	Kingdom	King	Kingdom
Abijam	Judah	Jehu	Israel
Ahab	Israel	Jeroboam I	Israel
Ahaz	Judah	Jeroboam II	Israel
Ahaziah-I	Israel	Joash-I	Israel
Ahaziah-J	Judah	Joash-J	Judah
Amaziah	Judah	Joram	Israel
Asa	Judah	Jotham	Judah
Athaliah	Judah	Menahem	Israel
Azariah	Judah	Nadab	Israel
Baasha	Israel	Omri	Israel
Elah	Israel	Pekah	Israel
Hezekiah	Judah	Pekahiah	Israel
Hoshea	Israel	Rehoboam	Judah
Jehoahaz	Israel	Shallum	Israel
Jehoram	Judah	Zechariah	Israel
Jehoshaphat	Judah	Zimri	Israel

6. Jehoahaz of Israel is also called Joahaz (2 Kgs 14:1); I refer to this king as Jehoahaz.
7. Azariah of Judah is also called Uzziah (2 Chronicles 26); I refer to this king as Azariah.

Table 1.1 presents the names used in this book for the DK kings and queen. Table 1.2 presents the DK rulers in alphabetic order so that readers can be easily reminded which kingdom any one king ruled.

2

Transmission History

Shenkel regards the Greek text of Kings as "one of the primary sources for any adequate reconstruction of a chronology" (*CRD* 4). His understanding of the recensional development of the Greek texts in parallel to that of the Hebrew text provides a new perspective that helps resolve the chronological problems of 1–2 Kings. Review of the transmission history of the Hebrew and Greek texts of the Books of 1–2 Kings may elicit information that will help reconstruct DK chronology.

2.1. Early Compilation of the Books of Kings

Statements in the Books of Kings refer to earlier sources that could be consulted for additional information about the kings' reigns: "The Book of the Acts of Solomon" (1 Kgs 11:41), "The Book of the Chronicles of the Kings of Judah" (15:23), and "The Book of the Chronicles of the Kings of Israel" (15:31). These chronicles—spanning several centuries and presumably recorded separately in Israel and Judah[1]—are mentioned in stylized regnal formulas at the end of most kings' narratives, implying that the narratives and/or the details of the regnal formulas were derived from the same or similar sources.[2] Regnal formulas, the kings' narratives, and other material (e.g., prophetic narratives concerning Elijah and Elisha) were subsequently compiled into one account to form what we now recognize as 1–2 Kings. But how and when the Books of Kings attained their present literary form is still a matter of debate.[3]

---

1. See S. R. Bin-Nun, "Formulas from Royal Records of Israel and of Judah," *VT* 18 (1968): 414–32; critiqued by R. D. Nelson, *The Double Redaction of the Deuteronomistic History* (Journal for the Study of the Old Testament Supplement 18; Sheffield: JSOT Press, 1981), 30–31; A. F. Campbell, *Of Prophets and Kings: A Late Ninth-Century Document (1 Samuel 1–2 Kings 10)* (Catholic Biblical Quarterly Monograph Series 17; Washington, D.C.: Catholic Biblical Association of America, 1986), 140 n. 1; and W. H. Barnes, *Studies in the Chronology of the Divided Monarchy of Israel* (Harvard Semitic Monographs 48; Atlanta: Scholars Press, 1991), 138–42.

2. M. Haran views these chronicles as official records of an annalistic nature rather than "narrative and literary material of the sort we find displayed in the canonical Books of Kings"; "The Books of the Chronicles 'of the Kings of Judah' and 'of the Kings of Israel': What Sort of Books Were They?" *VT* 49 (1999): 158.

3. The redaction history of the Books of Kings is an area of specialist study in itself. See M. Noth, *The Deuteronomistic History* (Journal for the Study of the Old Testament Supplement 15; Sheffield: JSOT Press, 1981), translated from *Überlieferungsgeschichtliche Studien* (2nd ed.; Tübingen: Max Niemeyer, 1957); F. M. Cross, *Canaanite Myth and Hebrew Epic: Essays in the History of the Religion of Israel* (Cambridge: Harvard University Press, 1973), 274–89; Nelson, *Double Redaction of the Deuteronomistic History*; G. H. Jones, *1 and 2 Kings* (New Century Bible Commentary; Grand Rapids: Eerdmans, 1984), 28–48; S. J. De Vries, *1 Kings* (Word Biblical Commentary 12; Waco: Word, 1985), xxxviii–lxix; M. A. O'Brien, *The Deuteronomistic History Hypothesis: A Reassessment* (Orbis Biblicus et Orientalis 92; Göttingen: Vandenhoeck

Translating and copying this final compilation over subsequent centuries gave opportunity not only for editorial activity, but also increased the chance of corruptions or variants entering the text. Emanuel Tov points out that our earliest extant texts are the products of a transmission process during which the original text suffered textual alterations:

> Most of the texts—ancient and modern—which have been transmitted from one generation to the next have been *corrupted* in one way or another. For modern compositions the process of textual transmission from the writing of the autograph until its final printing is relatively short, so that the possibilities of its corruption are limited. In ancient texts, however, such as the Hebrew Bible, these corruptions (the technical term for various forms of "mistakes") are found more frequently because of the difficult physical conditions of the copying and the length of the process of transmission.[4]

Julio Trebolle Barrera concurs:

> It is absolutely indispensable to know the history of transmission of the biblical text throughout more than two thousand years for further work in criticism and restoration of the "original" biblical text. It is necessary to know the wealth of variants which the manuscripts in Hebrew, Greek and other versions have transmitted to us, including rabbinic and patristic quotations. It is also necessary to determine which of these variants are guaranteed to go back to the oldest stages of textual transmission and which are the work of later revisions or the result of some type of textual corruption.[5]

Since the study of chronology deals with variant numbers in Greek and Hebrew texts, I will thus follow Shenkel's and Trebolle Barrera's recommendations to elucidate the transmission history of the biblical text, in this case the Books of Kings, before seeking a methodology to reconstruct the chronology.

2.2. Transmission History of the Old Testament Text

2.2.1. Hebrew Text and Qumran Manuscripts

The earliest known Old Testament Hebrew manuscripts—dated between the 3rd century B.C.E. and 70 C.E.[6]—were found in the Judean Desert between 1947 and 1956. The MT was not found at Qumran, even though its presumed forerunner, a proto-MT, is present.[7] After 70 C.E.,

---

& Ruprecht, 1989); B. Halpern and D. S. Vanderhooft, "The Editions of Kings in the 7th–6th Centuries B.C.E.," *Hebrew Union College Annual* 62 (1991): 179–244; S. L. McKenzie, *The Trouble with Kings: The Composition of the Book of Kings in the Deuteronomistic History* (Vetus Testamentum Supplement 42; Leiden: Brill, 1991); idem, "The Books of Kings in the Deuteronomistic History," in *The History of Israel's Traditions: The Heritage of Martin Noth* (ed. S. L. McKenzie and M. P. Graham; Journal for the Study of the Old Testament Supplement 182; Sheffield: Sheffield Academic Press, 1994), 281–307; A. G. Auld, *Kings without Privilege: David and Moses in the Story of the Bible's Kings* (Edinburgh: Clark, 1994); A. Lemaire, "Toward a Redactional History of the Books of Kings," in *Reconsidering Israel and Judah: Recent Studies on the Deuteronomistic History* (ed. G. N. Knoppers and J. G. McConville; Sources for Biblical and Theological Study 8; Winona Lake, Ind.: Eisenbrauns, 2000), 446–61.

4. E. Tov, *Textual Criticism of the Hebrew Bible* (2nd ed.; Minneapolis: Fortress, 2001), 8.

5. J. Trebolle Barrera, *The Jewish Bible and the Christian Bible: An Introduction to the History of the Bible* (trans. W. G. E. Watson; Leiden: Brill/Grand Rapids: Eerdmans, 1998), 267.

6. F. M. Cross, "A New Qumran Biblical Fragment Related to the Original Hebrew Underlying the Septuagint," *BASOR* 132 (1953): 16–17; M. Greenberg, "The Stabilization of the Text of the Hebrew Bible, Reviewed in the Light of the Biblical Materials from the Judean Desert," *Journal of the American Oriental Society* 76 (1965): 163; S. H. Horn, "The Old Testament Text in Antiquity," *Ministry* (Nov. 1987): 5.

7. F. M. Cross, "The Contribution of the Qumrân Discoveries to the Study of the Biblical Text," *Israel Exploration Journal* 16 (1966): 95 = *QHBT* 292; idem, "The Evolution of a Theory of Local Texts," in *QHBT* 314.

Hebrew texts of a provenance other than the proto-MT began to diminish in number, whether by accident or design, and their exemplars were lost to history—apart from those deposited at Qumran or kept by an isolated community such as the Samaritans[8]—leading to the widespread adoption of the MT by about the 8th century.[9]

Frank Cross identifies three Hebrew text-types in the Pentateuch and Former Prophets (Joshua, Judges, Samuel, Kings), which he traces to three stages in the recensional development of the LXX, and suggests a local-text theory of provenance, elaborating an earlier suggestion by W. F. Albright.[10] Even though Cross's hypothesis has not been accepted by all scholars (some propose even greater textual diversity),[11] his theory (table 2.1) is useful as a basis for discussion. According to Cross, the Qumran Hebrew texts developed from a 5th-century B.C.E. Palestinian archetype, and from this text developed at least three different branches or text-types, identified according to their assumed provenance: Egypt, Palestine, and Babylon.[12]

2.2.1.1. Egyptian Text

Cross finds "evidence that the Septuagint of Samuel and Kings was translated from an Egyptian Hebrew text that separated from the Old Palestinian textual tradition no later than the fourth century B.C. This text differed sharply from the *textus receptus*, and while more closely allied to Palestinian texts from Qumrân, nevertheless is distinct from them."[13] Elsewhere he comments: "The Egyptian and Palestinian families are closely related. Early exemplars of the Palestinian text in the Former Prophets, and Pentateuchal texts which reflect an early stage of the Palestinian tradition, so nearly merge with the Egyptian, that we are warranted in describing the Egyptian text-type as a branch of the Old Palestinian family."[14]

Objecting to Cross's theory that this Egyptian text was utilized by the LXX translators, Tov points out that "the reconstructed Hebrew *Vorlage* of 𝔊 does not reflect any proven Egyptian characteristics; rather, it is more likely that 𝔊 was translated from Palestinian texts, as claimed by the Epistle of Aristeas."[15] Whatever its origin, the first Greek translation is not extant but is be-

---

8. Cross, "Contribution of the Qumrân Discoveries," 95 = *QHBT* 292; cf. S. Talmon, "The Old Testament Text," in *The Cambridge History of the Bible*, vol. 1: *From the Beginnings to Jerome* (ed. P. R. Ackroyd and C. F. Evans; Cambridge: Cambridge University Press, 1970), 170–71, 187 = *QHBT* 12–13, 29; Tov, *Textual Criticism of the Hebrew Bible*, 34–35, 194–95, 316.

9. Tov, *Textual Criticism of the Hebrew Bible*, 33, 35.

10. F. M. Cross, "The History of the Biblical Text in the Light of Discoveries in the Judaean Desert," *Harvard Theological Review* 57 (1964): 297–99 = *QHBT* 193–95; idem, "Contribution of the Qumrân Discoveries," 84–91 = *QHBT* 281–88; "Evolution of a Theory," 306–20; W. F. Albright, "New Light on Early Recensions of the Hebrew Bible," *BASOR* 140 (1955): 30–33 = *QHBT* 143–46.

11. Talmon, "Old Testament Text," 193–99 = *QHBT* 35–41; idem, "The Textual Study of the Bible—A New Outlook," in *QHBT* 324–27; E. Tov, "A Modern Textual Outlook Based on the Qumran Scrolls," *Hebrew Union College Annual* 53 (1982): 11–27; idem, *The Text-Critical Use of the Septuagint in Biblical Research* (2nd ed.; Jerusalem Biblical Studies 8; Jerusalem: Simor, 1997), 183–87; idem, *Textual Criticism of the Hebrew Bible*, 160–63, 185–97; see also Trebolle Barrera, *Jewish Bible and the Christian Bible*, 292–95.

12. Cross, "History of the Biblical Text," 296–97 = *QHBT* 192–93.

13. Ibid., 295; cf. 297 = *QHBT* 191, 193.

14. Cross, "Contribution of the Qumrân Discoveries," 86 = *QHBT* 283.

15. Tov, *Textual Criticism of the Hebrew Bible*, 186, 136–37; see also idem, *Text-Critical Use of the Septuagint*, 183–87; idem, "The Septuagint," in *Mikra: Text, Translation, Reading, and Interpretation of the Hebrew Bible in Ancient Judaism and Early Christianity* (ed. M. J. Mulder; Compendia Rerum Iudaicarum ad Novum Testamentum 2/1; Philadelphia: Fortress, 1988), 164–65.

Table 2.1. Textual History of the Old Testament according to F. M. Cross

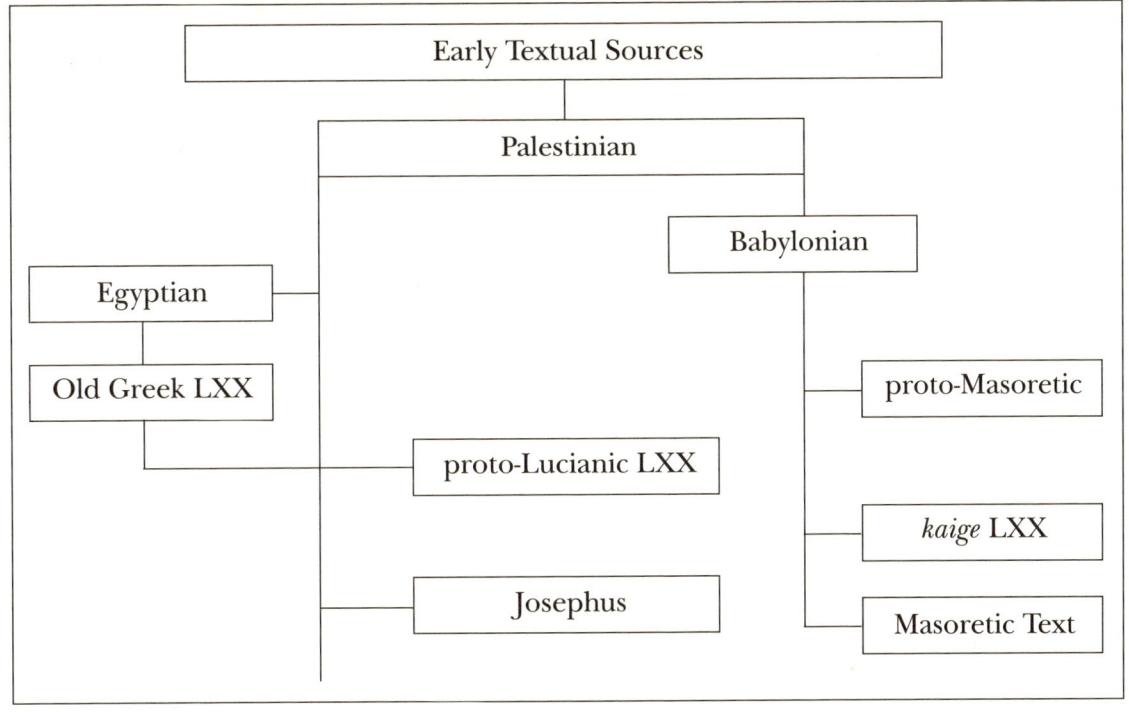

lieved to be represented in the OG sections of Codex Vaticanus, the latter dating to the 4th century C.E.[16]

2.2.1.2. Palestinian Text

Cross identifies the dominant Hebrew text found at Qumran as having its provenance in Palestine:

> By far the majority of the Hebrew witnesses from Qumrân belong to the Palestinian family. The evidence for the identification of the Palestinian family is most easily delineated in Samuel. The three manuscripts of Samuel from Cave IV, while not directly filiated, contain a single textual tradition, known at Qumrân as early as the third century (4QSam^b), the early first century B.C. (4QSam^c), and in the late first century B.C. (4QSam^a). The earliest distinctive witness to a text of the type of these manuscripts is found in the Chronicler. As has been shown elsewhere, the Chronicler, shortly after 400 B.C., cited a text of Samuel which stands in close agreement with the manuscripts of Qumrân, but, as is well known, sharply diverges from the received text. In the second or early first century B.C., the same Palestinian text-form was used to revise the Septuagint: the Proto-Lucianic recension. Finally Josephus at the end of the first century A.D., made use of this Palestinian Greek recension in writing his *Antiquities*.[17]

Elsewhere, Cross writes:

> In studying the text of 4QSam^a, I have been forced to note a series of readings in which the Hebrew of 4QSam^a reflects the so-called Lucianic recension preserved in the Greek minuscules boc$_2$e$_2$, and the Itala [i.e., Old Latin]. In other words, 4QSam^a stands with LXX^L against MT and

---

16. For more on OG origins, see E. Ulrich, *The Dead Sea Scrolls and the Origins of the Bible* (Studies in the Dead Sea Scrolls and Related Literature; Leiden: Brill / Grand Rapids: Eerdmans, 1999), 205–14.

17. Cross, "Contribution of the Qumrân Discoveries," 88 = *QHBT* 285.

LXX[B]. These are proper Proto-Lucianic readings in a *Hebrew* text of the first century B.C., four centuries before the Syrian Father to whom the recension is attributed.[18]

The significance of these comments for the reconstruction of chronology should not be overlooked. Since the L minuscules (except c_2) have the same system of chronological data in 1 Kings as the OG sections of Codex Vaticanus and since the L manuscripts of Samuel go back to a Hebrew *Vorlage* represented by the 1st-century B.C.E. 4QSam[a], we have grounds for expecting that the L text of Kings also derives from the same *Vorlage*, a conclusion with which Shenkel concurs: "Although a proto-Lucian text type that is extensively preserved has not been found among the scanty remains of Hebrew manuscripts for the Books of Kings at Qumran, it is reasonable to suppose that the history of the development of the text for Kings is substantially the same as for the Books of Samuel, considering the intimate relationship of these four books to each other in the Greek text" (*CRD* 10).

2.2.1.3. Babylonian Text

Cross theorizes that a third Hebrew text-type, "distant from both the Egyptian and Palestinian families,"[19] was taken to Babylonia and isolated there during the exile, giving rise to a Babylonian text-type. Reintroduced to Palestine in the Maccabean period, this text-type became dominant by the end of the 1st century C.E.[20] and is now assumed to be the precursor of the MT (i.e., proto-MT), which reached its final form in medieval times.[21]

The proto-MT is reflected in the *kaige* recension, so-called for its characteristic translating of Hebrew גם ('also') with Greek καίγε.[22] The KR was first identified in Dominique Barthélemy's 1963 publication of the Greek Minor Prophets scroll (8ḤevXIIgr) found at Nahal Ḥever in 1952.[23] This KR manuscript is dated to the mid-1st century B.C.E.[24] and is presumed to have brought an earlier Greek text into conformity with the proto-MT.[25] Once widespread,[26] the *kaige* text-type is extant in sections of Samuel and Kings in Codex Vaticanus, Greek manuscripts of Lamentations and Judges, the Theodotionic edition of Exodus, and the Theodotionic additions to the Greek text of Job and elsewhere.[27] The KR was formerly attributed to Theodotion, who lived near the end of the 2nd century C.E., but because the so-called Theodotionic text antedates the historical Theodotion by two centuries, the text is also known as *kaige*-Theodotion or proto-Theodotion.[28]

Only small fragments—none containing chronological data—of the Books of Kings have been found at Qumran. Some are of the proto-MT text-type, while others appear to reflect the

---

18. Cross, "History of the Biblical Text," 292 = *QHBT* 188 (emphasis original).
19. Cross, "Contribution of the Qumrân Discoveries," 90 = *QHBT* 287.
20. Ibid., 91, 95 = *QHBT* 288, 292.
21. Tov, *Textual Criticism of the Hebrew Bible*, 27.
22. Ibid., 145.
23. D. Barthélemy, *Les devanciers d'Aquila: Première publication intégrale du texte des fragments du Dodécaprophéton* (Vetus Testamentum Supplement 10; Leiden: Brill, 1963).
24. Tov, *Textual Criticism of the Hebrew Bible*, 145.
25. For discussion see D. Barthélemy, "Redécouverte d'un chaînon manquant de l'histoire de la Septante," *Revue Biblique* 60 (1953): 18–29 = *QHBT* 127–39; repr. in *Études d'histoire du texte de l'Ancien Testament* (ed. D. Barthélemy; Orbis Biblicus et Orientalis 21; Göttingen: Vandenhoeck & Ruprecht, 1978), 38–49; P. Katz, "Justin's Old Testament Quotations and the Greek Dodekapropheton Scroll," *Studia Patristica* 1 (1957): 343–53, repr. in *Studies in the Septuagint: Origins, Recensions, and Interpretations* (ed. S. Jellicoe; New York: Ktav, 1974), 530–40.
26. Tov, *Textual Criticism of the Hebrew Bible*, 144.
27. K. G. O'Connell, "Greek Versions (Minor)," in *Interpreter's Dictionary of the Bible: Supplementary Volume* (ed. K. Crim; Nashville: Abingdon, 1976), 379; see also Trebolle Barrera, *Jewish Bible and the Christian Bible*, 316.
28. Tov, *Textual Criticism of the Hebrew Bible*, 145; Trebolle Barrera, *Jewish Bible and the Christian Bible*, 314–15.

Vorlage now identified with the proto-L substratum of L.[29] Being based on Hebrew texts that no longer exist, the early Greek manuscripts are vital witnesses to the Hebrew text from which they were translated and, hence, equally vital witnesses to the chronological data contained in the early Hebrew Books of Kings.

2.2.2. Old Greek and *Kaige*

In Samuel–Kings, Codex Vaticanus exhibits the two distinct text-types referred to above: OG and KR. The identification of the OG and KR sections of 1–2 Kings according to text-type is a significant first step in seeking to establish to which recension any given chronological datum belongs. The KR's characteristic translation גם ≈ καίγε was the initial criterion used to differentiate this text-type from the OG. But according to Shenkel (*CRD* 12), more significant characteristics are the KR's greater conformity to the MT away from the OG text-type and "an extreme concern that at least certain important Hebrew expressions receive a uniform rendition into Greek even at the expense of sound Greek usage and idiom."[30] For example, the OG often translates Hebrew verbs with the historical present, whereas the KR uses the aorist.[31] Thus, when Hebrew perfect מלך means "he began to reign" in the regnal formulas, the OG translates it with historical present βασιλεύει, while the KR translates it with aorist ἐβασίλευσεν (*CRD* 50–53). The KR also follows the MT in its sequencing of regnal formulas (see §5.4).

2.2.2.1. Textual Divisions in Codex Vaticanus

Thackeray identifies five sections in Samuel–Kings in Codex Vaticanus according to their textual characteristics and assigns Greek sigla to them (table 2.2).[32] Shenkel (*CRD* 117–20) revised Thackeray's ββ and βγ sections.

Table 2.2. Text-Types in Samuel–Kings in Codex Vaticanus

Text-Type	Siglum	Thackeray's Divisions	Shenkel's Divisions
OG	α	1 Samuel	(same)
OG	ββ	2 Sam 1:1–11:1	2 Sam 1:1–9:13
KR	βγ	2 Sam 11:2–1 Kgs 2:11	2 Sam 10:1–1 Kgs 2:11
OG	γγ	1 Kgs 2:12–21:43	(same)
KR	γδ	1 Kgs 22:1–2 Kgs 25:30	(same)

---

29. Cf. J. Gray, *1 and 2 Kings* (Old Testament Library; London: SCM, 1970), 46–47; Shenkel, *CRD* 122–23 n. 14; De Vries, *1 Kings*, liv.

30. Other characteristics that differentiate the OG and KR have been identified; see Barthélemy, *Les devanciers d'Aquila*, 48–80; M. Smith, "Another Criterion for the καίγε Recension," *Biblica* 48 (1967): 443–45; Shenkel, *CRD* 12–18, 113–16; J. A. Grindel, "Another Characteristic of the *Kaige* Recension: נצח/νικος," *Catholic Biblical Quarterly* 31 (1969): 499–513; E. Tov, "Transliterations of Hebrew Words in the Greek Versions of the Old Testament: A Further Characteristic of the *kaige*-Th. Revision?" *Textus* 8 (1973): 78–92; S. Jellicoe, "Some Reflections on the Καιγε Recension," *VT* 23 (1973): 15–24; O'Connell, "Greek Versions (Minor)," 378–79; Trebolle Barrera, *Jewish Bible and the Christian Bible*, 315–16.

31. H. St. J. Thackeray, *The Septuagint and Jewish Worship: A Study in Origins* (Schweich Lectures, 1920; London: Oxford University Press for the British Academy, 1921; repr. Munich: Kraus-Thomson, 1980), 20–22; cf. Barthélemy, *Les devanciers d'Aquila*, 63–65.

32. H. St. J. Thackeray, "The Greek Translators of the Four Books of Kings," *Journal of Theological Studies* 8 (1907): 262–78; idem, *Septuagint and Jewish Worship*, 16–28.

Thackeray sees the end of the first KR section at 1 Kgs 2:11 with the death of David as evidence of a division between Samuel and Kings earlier than what now appears in the MT.[33] If the change in text-type at 1 Kgs 22:1 to the second KR section indicates where one scroll ended and another began, then 1 Kings 22 was part of the same scroll as 2 Kings, making it, in effect, the first chapter of 2 Kings.

In addition, 1 Kings 20 MT and 1 Kings 21 MT are transposed in the Greek, with 1 Kings 21 coming before 1 Kings 20 (i.e., the last verse of the OG text-type occurs at 20:43 MT = 21:43 Greek). The Greek account of war between Syria and Israel in 1 Kings 21 is then followed by 22:1: "For 3 years Syria and Israel continued without war." The MT placement of Ahab's murder of Naboth in 1 Kings 21 between Ahab's battle with Syria (1 Kings 20) and another battle with Syria (1 Kings 22) exhibits no textual continuity between the last verse of 1 Kings 21 ("I will bring the evil upon his house") and 1 Kgs 22:1. The order of the Greek text is more logical, and the division of the Greek text shown by the change in text-type appears to support an earlier division than is now exhibited by the MT.

While the Hebrew Books of Samuel filled only one scroll, the Greek version of 1–2 Samuel took twice as much space, because the Greek script includes vowels.[34] This raises the question, however, why 2 Samuel exhibits two text-types (both OG and KR) while 1 Samuel, 1 Kings, and 2 Kings each exhibit only a single text-type, roughly corresponding to scroll divisions. The two text-types in 2 Samuel may indicate where one scroll ended and another began. Alternatively, the change may indicate where one copyist stopped and another started, the first copying from an OG scroll, and the second transcribing from a KR scroll.

A similar circumstance could be theorized for the change from OG in section γγ (roughly 1 Kings) to KR in section γδ (roughly 2 Kings). Scrolls of different origins and exhibiting different text-types were subsequently copied and combined to create the great codexes, including Codex Vaticanus, all the while preserving the recensional characteristics of each section.[35] On the other hand, the mixing of two text-types or scrolls may have come about through purely mechanical causes.[36] Not knowing why two recensions were utilized in the compilation of Samuel–Kings leaves unanswered the question whether sections βγ and γδ are the only KR sections ever produced or whether KR versions once existed for sections α, ββ, and γγ—that is, for all of Samuel–Kings.

2.2.2.2. Chronological Data in Codex Vaticanus

Whatever the reason for the two recensions in Samuel–Kings, Codex Vaticanus's exhibiting two different text-types is important for understanding the chronology of the Books of Kings. In fact, the most important feature with regard to chronology in the Books of Kings in Codex Vati-

---

33. Thackeray, "Greek Translators," 262–65.

34. This doubled length likely caused the present division of these books into 1 Samuel and 2 Samuel; see Trebolle Barrera, *Jewish Bible and the Christian Bible*, 97; and Thackeray, "Greek Translators," 265.

35. Trebolle Barrera, *Jewish Bible and the Christian Bible*, 318.

36. E. Tov, "The State of the Question: Problems and Proposed Solutions," in *1972 Proceedings IOSCS and Pseudepigrapha* (ed. R. A. Kraft; Society of Biblical Literature Septuagint and Cognate Studies 2; Missoula, Mont.: Scholars Press, 1972), 5. T. Muraoka proposes that two translators worked side by side on the scrolls and that at a later time βγ and γδ were revised by the KR redactor; "The Greek Texts of Samuel–Kings: Incomplete Translations or Recensional Activity?" in *1972 Proceedings IOSCS and Pseudepigrapha* (ed. R. A. Kraft; Society of Biblical Literature Septuagint and Cognate Studies 2; Missoula, Mont.: Scholars Press, 1972), 90–107, revised in *Abr-Nahrain* 21 (1982–83): 28–49. Barthélemy regards this as improbable; "Prise de position sur les autres communications du colloque de Los Angeles," in *Études d'histoire du Texte de l'Ancien Testament* (ed. D. Barthélemy; Orbis Biblicus et Orientalis 21; Göttingen: Vandenhoeck & Ruprecht, 1978), 257–58.

canus is that 1 Kgs 15:1–21:43 OG contains chronological data that for the most part are at wide variance with the MT data but concur with the L data in boe$_2$ (but not c$_2$). On the other hand, the KR data in section γδ concurs in the majority of instances with the MT data. The OG text is not extant for section γδ but is presumed, consistent with section γγ, to be represented by the data of boe$_2$ where these manuscripts differ from the MT/KR data.[37] And the KR, not being extant in section γγ, is considered to be represented in this section by the MT data, both being derived from a Hebrew proto-MT precursor.

The conflicting chronological data found in the two different recensions of the Books of Kings in Codex Vaticanus may be illustrated by the regnal formula at 1 Kgs 22:41–42. KR and MT both have, "Jehoshaphat son of Asa began to reign over Judah in the 4th year of King Ahab of Israel, . . . and he reigned 25 years." This verse is not extant in OG or L at this position (L does not have 1 Kgs 22:41–51), but appears instead at 16:28a: "In the 11th year of Omri, Jehoshaphat son of Asa began to reign, . . . and he reigned 25 years." These statements are in conflict, and without the expediency of some unattested dating system to explain the difference in accession years, Jehoshaphat's reign cannot have commenced in both Ahab's 4th year and Omri's 11th year.

Jehoshaphat's regnal formula is the only such formula to appear in both the OG and KR text-types in Codex Vaticanus. If the L chronological data in boe$_2$ is representative of the no longer extant OG, then a second example of conflicting regnal data appears in the two text-types at 22:52: KR/MT have, "Ahaziah-I son of Ahab reigned over Israel in Samaria in the 17th year of Jehoshaphat king of Judah and he reigned 2 years"; and L has, "In the 24th year of Jehoshaphat king of Judah, Ahaziah-I son of Ahab began to reign and he reigned 2 years."

A more complex example is the accession synchronism of Joram (2 Kgs 1:17 MT = 1:18a L/KR). The MT and L synchronisms state that Joram became king in Jehoram's 2nd year. The KR says that Joram began to reign in Jehoshaphat's 18th year and repeats this synchronism at 3:1, where it appears also in MT. The MT, therefore, has two synchronisms for the accession of Joram: Jehoram's 2nd year and Jehoshaphat's 18th year.

These three examples—Jehoshaphat, Ahaziah-I, and Joram—are sufficient to show that conflicting data are represented in the OG and KR sections of Codex Vaticanus. Further analysis of the data is required to determine why the OG and KR exhibit variant data, why the respective data in the texts are not internally consistent, and whether any numbers have been altered accidentally or intentionally.

2.2.3. Lucianic Manuscripts

2.2.3.1. Proto-Lucian and Lucian

L is named after its putative author, Lucian of Antioch (ca. 240–311/312 C.E.).[38] Lucian, however, cannot have been the originator of this recension, because it appears as early as the end of

---

37. This applies, however, only to the end of the EDK, which ends with the deaths of Ahaziah-J and Joram at the hands of Jehu (2 Kgs 9:24–28). In the LDK, which commences with the accessions of Athaliah in Judah and Jehu in Israel and ends with the fall of Samaria, there is no difference between the boe$_2$ data and the MT/KR data except for the regnal years for Pekahiah (MT/KR has 2 years; boe$_2$ has 10 years). It is, therefore, in the EDK that the greater number of variants occur between OG/L and MT/KR in Kings.

38. For discussion of the L manuscripts, see the anonymous article "Lucian's Recension of the Septuagint," *Church Quarterly Review* 51 (1900–1901): 379–98; B. M. Metzger, "Lucian and the Lucianic Recension of the Greek Bible," *New Testament Studies* 8 (1961–62), 189–203 = "The Lucianic Recension of the Greek Bible," in *Chapters in the History of New Testament Textual Criticism* (Grand Rapids: Eerdmans, 1963), 1–41; S. P. Brock, "Lucian *Redivivus*: Some Reflections on Barthélemy's *Les devanciers d'Aquila*," *Studia Evangelica* 5 (1968): 176–81; S. Jellicoe, *The Septuagint and Modern Study*

the 1st century C.E. in the writings of Josephus, who used proto-L to construct his Samuel narrative.[39] Moreover, proto-L Samuel appears to derive from a text like the Palestinian Hebrew text (4QSam^a) found at Qumran dating to the 1st century B.C.E. Proto-L is also found in the sixth column of Origen's Hexapla at 2 Sam 11:2–1 Kgs 2:11 (Thackeray's section βγ),[40] in the Old Latin for the Books of Samuel dating from the 2nd century C.E.,[41] in some readings in the Old Testament Peshitta in 1 Samuel, and in other manuscripts of the Old and New Testaments and various church fathers.[42]

Many scholars believe that the substratum used by Lucian was itself a revision of the OG (i.e., the first Greek translation) or of what is now known as proto-L.[43] Other scholars claim that proto-L is either *the* OG[44] or any single OG translation.[45] Depending on the view held, L is seen as a composite text having two or three layers—a composite text that Trebolle Barrera describes as follows:

> It is not easy to determine precisely what was the work Lucian carried out, both in respect of the pre-Hexaplar tradition and in respect of Origen's work. However, the *characteristics of the Lucianic text* are quite obvious: frequent additions, inserted into the text to adapt it to the rabbinic Hebrew text; many duplicate readings in which the old *Septuagint* is juxtaposed to the Hexaplar reading, which in turn is closer to the rabbinic text; grammatical corrections and stylistic improvement of the text; the insertion of explanatory elements, such as proper names, pronouns, articles, etc.; replacement of Hellenistic forms by the Attic equivalents, etc.[46]

2.2.3.2. Lucianic Variants

The L variants are published in the second apparatus of the Larger Cambridge Septuagint beneath the text of Codex Vaticanus.[47] Manuscripts boc$_2$e$_2$, dating from the 10th to 14th

---

(Oxford: Clarendon, 1968), 157–290; Shenkel, *CRD* 8–11; E. Tov, "Lucian and Proto-Lucian: Toward a New Solution of the Problem," *Revue Biblique* 79 (1972): 101–13 = *QHBT* 293–305; N. Fernández Marcos, "The Lucianic Text in the Books of Kingdoms: From Lagarde to the Textual Pluralism," in *De Septuaginta: Studies in Honour of John William Wevers on His Sixty-Fifth Birthday* (ed. A. Pietersma and C. Cox; Mississauga, Ont.: Benben, 1984), 161–74; Trebolle Barrera, *Jewish Bible and the Christian Bible*, 310–11.

39. H. St. J. Thackeray, *Josephus the Man and the Historian* (New York: Jewish Institute of Religion Press, 1929), 82–89; Metzger, "Lucian and the Lucianic Recension," 199 = *Chapters in the History*, 34; E. C. Ulrich, *The Qumran Text of Samuel and Josephus* (Harvard Semitic Monographs 19; Missoula, Mont.: Scholars Press, 1978), 22, 27–28, 257–59.

40. As Cross notes ("History of the Biblical Text," 295 = *QHBT* 191), the sixth column of the Hexapla was normally that of Theodotion, but Adam Mez recognizes that in this section it was proto-L.

41. Trebolle Barrera, *Jewish Bible and the Christian Bible*, 352–53.

42. Metzger, "Lucian and the Lucianic Recension," 196–200 = *Chapters in the History*, 31–35; Tov, "Lucian and Proto-Lucian," 103–5 = *QHBT* 295–97.

43. Cross, "History of the Biblical Text," 295–96 = *QHBT* 191–92; idem, "Evolution of a Theory," 312–15; Ulrich, *Qumran Text of Samuel and Josephus*, 257–59; Fernández Marcos, "Lucianic Text in the Books of Kingdoms," 169–73. C. D. Stanley appears to support the position of a proto-L text: "The Significance of Romans 11:3–4 for the Text History of the LXX Book of Kingdoms," *JBL* 112 (1993): 43–54, esp. 54.

44. Barthélemy, *Les devanciers d'Aquila*, 126–27; cf. idem, "Prise de position," 271–73; D. G. Deboys, *The Greek Text of 2 Kings* (M.Litt. thesis; Oxford University, 1981), 187–89; A. Pietersma, "Proto-Lucian and the Greek Psalter," *VT* 28 (1978): 67.

45. Tov suggests that "the substratum of boc$_2$e$_2$ contains either *the* Old Greek or any single Old Greek translation"; "Lucian and Proto-Lucian," 110 = *QHBT* 302 (emphasis original). See Trebolle Barrera, *Jewish Bible and the Christian Bible*, 310–11.

46. Trebolle Barrera, *Jewish Bible and the Christian Bible*, 310 (emphasis original); see Metzger, "Lucian and the Lucianic Recension," 194–95 = *Chapters in the History*, 25–27.

47. Manuscript r also shows proto-L readings in parts of 2 Kings; see *CRD* 127 n. 39.

Table 2.3. Lucianic Manuscripts

Larger Cambridge Septuagint Siglum	Göttingen Number	Date
b	19 (b')	11th–12th century
	108 (b)	13th–14th century
o	82	12th–13th century
c_2	127	10th century
e_2	93	13th–14th century

centuries,[48] are denoted in the Göttingen Septuagint by numbers (table 2.3).[49]

The agreement of the L chronological data in manuscripts boe_2 with the OG data in section γγ of 1 Kings attests the early pre-Hexaplaric nature of the substratum containing the regnal formulas. The main difference between the chronological data exhibited by L and OG in Vaticanus is at 1 Kgs 16:15. Manuscripts be_2 have a synchronism giving Zimri's accession in Asa's 22nd year and giving to Zimri a reign of 7 days. Codex Vaticanus does not have the synchronism and attributes to Zimri a 7-year reign. The MT has an alternative synchronism giving Zimri's accession in Asa's 27th year, but agreeing with L in giving Zimri a reign of 7 days. Bruce Metzger comments, "Despite the numerous secondary features which Lucian introduced into his recension of the Old Testament, one may expect to find here and there in it certain readings, not extant in the other forms of the Septuagint, which will be useful in ascertaining the most ancient form of the Hebrew text."[50] The unique variant in be_2 giving Zimri's accession in Asa's 22nd year may thus preserve an important witness to a very ancient text not found elsewhere.

On the other hand, specific readings—especially when the Hexaplaric signs are present—show signs of having been conformed to the Greek text in Origen's Hexapla, which was itself conformed to the MT. In the absence of Hexaplaric signs, Shenkel comments, "the coincidence of a reading in the Lucianic text with the reading of the normal hexaplaric witnesses, when such a reading is not found in the Old Greek or the KR, justifies the presumption that the reading in question is an assimilation from the hexaplaric text introduced into the proto-Lucianic text by a later redactor" (*CRD* 19).

For example, at 2 Kgs 1:17 the Larger Cambridge Septuagint provides in its apparatus additional text appearing in $boc_2(*)e_2$: καὶ ἐβασίλευσεν Ἰωρὰμ ὁ ἀδελφὸς Ὀχοζίου ἀντ' αὐτοῦ ὅτι οὐκ ἦν αὐτῷ υἱός (and Joram the brother of Ahaziah-I reigned after him because he did not have a son).[51] This verse in boc_2e_2 does not contain a synchronism, but Hexaplaric minuscules x and y include the synchronism that Joram began to reign in Jehoram's 2nd year. Since the same verse appears in 1:17 MT but not in KR, the synchronism was, according to Shenkel, "inserted into the MT after the KR revision was completed" (*CRD* 74). The absence of the synchronism at 1:17 KR and

---

48. Ulrich, *Qumran Text of Samuel and Josephus*, 21.

49. See Jellicoe, *Septuagint and Modern Study*, 163–64 n. 5, 167; Ulrich, *Qumran Text of Samuel and Josephus*, 19–21; P. K. McCarter, *I Samuel* (Anchor Bible 8; New York: Doubleday, 1980), 9 n. 19.

50. Metzger, "Lucian and the Lucianic Recension," 200 = *Chapters in the History*, 35.

51. Shenkel notes (*CRD* 73–74): "The asterisk after the Lucianic manuscript c_2 shows that this passage was not in the proto-Lucianic stage of the text, but was inserted at a later date to bring the Lucianic text into partial conformity with the MT and the hexaplaric recension, here represented by the text of the two minuscules, x and y."

the asterisk after c_2 showing a Hexaplaric addition at 1:17 indicates that the text and synchronism were not in the *Vorlage* of 1:17 L/KR.

If the position of the datum at 1:17 MT giving Joram's accession in Jehoram's 2nd year is a Hexaplaric addition, what then shall we make of the MT's second synchronism at 3:1 for Joram's accession in Jehoshaphat's 18th year (a synchronism also present in 1:18a KR and 3:1 KR)? Is this an earlier synchronism in an earlier position than that at 1:17? If so, why do L and KR each have Joram's synchronism at 1:18a but with conflicting data? Bearing this in mind we consider the next example of L variation.

L agrees with MT and KR in synchronizing Jehoram's accession in Joram's 5th year (8:16). But this is in conflict with its previous synchronism at 1:18a, in which Joram's accession is synchronized with Jehoram's 2nd year, inferring that Jehoram became king in Ahaziah-I's 2nd year (synchronism not extant). Why does L have a conflict in its data? It could be that the L data in 1:18a and 8:16 belong to different strata of L, one datum from the proto-L stratum and one from the later Hexaplaric stratum in which proto-L has been conformed to the MT. Recognition of which L stratum each datum belongs to may help resolve the enigma of conflicting variants in L.

2.2.4. Aquila, Symmachus, and Theodotion

Three recensions based on the KR originated in the 2nd century: Aquila, Symmachus, and Theodotion occupied the third, fourth, and sixth columns of Origen's Hexapla and together were known as "the Three" (οἱ γ′).[52] Of these, only Theodotion is relevant to my study. The recension formerly attributed to Theodotion of the 2nd century C.E. is related closely to the 1st-century B.C.E. KR.[53] Shenkel notes, however, that "Theodotion's revision can be distinguished from the KR, or proto-Theodotion, by its greater fidelity to the MT" (*CRD* 20; see also 11–12). In other words, the traditional 2nd-century Theodotion cannot be "completely erased from history."[54]

2.2.5. Origen's Hexapla

By the 4th century, three recensions of the LXX were known: Origen, Hesychius, and Lucian.[55] Little is known about Hesychius's edition; Lucian's recension was discussed above. Origen (ca. 185–254) was a scholar of Alexandria who probably composed his Hexapla in Caesarea, completing it in 245.[56] The Hexapla was an enormous six-column volume (hence its name) that contained various Hebrew and Greek texts in its six columns (table 2.4). Unfortunately for text-critical purposes, it is not easy, according to Trebolle Barrera, to determine whether the fifth column

> was the LXX as known by Origen or a text he had already revised which he supplied with the appropriate hexaplaric signs and additions. . . . Origen certainly completed a *later, truly hexaplar edition.* . . . This later edition contained only the text of the LXX; the lacunae in the LXX in respect of the MT (shorter) are completed by the text of Theodotion. As a result, this edition was supplied

---

52. For further information see P. W. Skehan, "Texts and Versions," in *The Jerome Biblical Commentary* (ed. R. E. Brown, J. A. Fitzmyer, and R. E. Murphy; Englewood Cliffs, N.J.: Prentice-Hall, 1968), 571–72; O'Connell, "Greek Versions (Minor)," 378–79; Tov, "Septuagint," 182–84; idem, "State of the Question," 5–7; idem, *Textual Criticism of the Hebrew Bible*, 144–47; Trebolle Barrera, *Jewish Bible and the Christian Bible*, 312–17.

53. Tov, *Textual Criticism of the Hebrew Bible*, 145; Trebolle Barrera, *Jewish Bible and the Christian Bible*, 314–17.

54. Trebolle Barrera, *Jewish Bible and the Christian Bible*, 316. For discussion of the identity of Theodotion, see Barthélemy, *Les devanciers d'Aquila*, 144–57.

55. Trebolle Barrera, *Jewish Bible and the Christian Bible*, 309.

56. Ibid., 309, 311, 528–29.

Table 2.4. Origen's Hexapla

Column	Contents
1	Hebrew text
2	Greek transliteration
3	Aquila
4	Symmachus
5	LXX
6	Theodotion

with the requisite diacritical signs. The hypothesis of this hexaplar edition replaces the other hypothesis, according to which the *fifth* column of the Hexaplar contained the text revised by Origen, marked by asterisks and obeli, the same text later made into the edition of the LXX alone.[57]

"Origen's intention," according to Shenkel, "was to make the Greek text chosen as the basis of his revision conform with the definitively established MT" (*CRD* 18). Accordingly, material added to the LXX from another source was marked with an asterisk (※) at the beginning and a metobelus (∕. or ∕. or ◂) at the end. Material in the LXX not found in the MT was marked with an obelus (− or ⁻ or ÷) at the beginning and again a metobelus at the end. In the course of transmission many of the symbols were deleted or incorrectly transcribed, leading to confusion.[58]

The entire Hexapla was never copied, and the original was lost sometime in the 7th century (except for the Psalms fragments rediscovered by Mercati). The fifth column, however, was widely circulated in Palestine as early as the 4th century.[59] And this text was largely preserved in the Syriac translation of Paul of Tella done in the early 7th century, known as the Syro-Hexaplar, which shows many of the Hexaplaric signs.[60] That the letter *lomadh* (ܠ) is found in the margin of the Syro-Hexaplar beside readings also found in L cursives boe$_2$ indicates that *lomadh* refers to L readings.[61] Tov proposes that Lucian's 4th-century revision of an earlier Greek text is the most important post-Hexaplaric text.[62]

---

57. Ibid., 311 (emphasis original). P. E. Kahle believes that the LXX column did not contain diacritical signs; "The Greek Bible Manuscripts Used by Origen," *JBL* 79 (1960): 116. S. P. Brock argues that the symbols were already in the text appropriated by Origen; *The Recensions of the Septuagint Version of I Samuel* (D.Phil. thesis; Oxford University, 1966), 37–42, cited in his "Origen's Aims as a Textual Critic of the Old Testament," *Studia Patristica* 10 (1970): 215 n. 3, repr. in *Studies in the Septuagint: Origins, Recensions, and Interpretations* (ed. S. Jellicoe; New York: Ktav, 1974), 343 n. 3. Tov notes ("Septuagint," 185–86): "Recently discovered fragments of the *complete* Hexapla, especially the Psalm fragments published by Cardinal Mercati [in *Psalterii Hexapli Reliquiae*], show no Hexaplaric signs in the fifth column. Hence scholars have hypothesized that the original Hexapla did not contain these signs, and that these were inserted subsequently in a separate edition of the fifth column of the Hexapla."

58. See H. B. Swete, *Introduction to the Old Testament in Greek* (2nd ed.; Cambridge: Cambridge University Press, 1914), 59–78; Klein, *Textual Criticism of the Old Testament*, 7–9; Trebolle Barrera, *Jewish Bible and the Christian Bible*, 311–12.

59. Swete, *Introduction to the Old Testament in Greek*, 76.

60. Ibid., 73–78; J. W. Wevers, "Septuagint," in *Interpreter's Dictionary of the Bible* (ed. G. A. Buttrick; New York: Abingdon, 1962), 4:275; Klein, *Textual Criticism of the Old Testament*, 9.

61. Swete, *Introduction to the Old Testament in Greek*, 82–83 (citing 2 Kgs 9:9, 28; 10:24, 25; 11:1; 23:33, 35); cf. Metzger, "Lucian and the Lucianic Recension," 194.

62. Tov, "Septuagint," 186.

Recognizing that the Hexapla was used to bring Greek texts into conformity with the MT has implications for the chronology of the Books of Kings. If Greek chronological data at variance with MT data were replaced by MT data to bring them into conformity, some of the data now found in the Greek texts may actually belong to the MT system. Another result of assimilating OG or proto-L data to the MT data may be that some original data are lost because we have no other extant witnesses of the early Hebrew (Palestinian or Egyptian text-type). If such assimilation took place, not all data having the same accession synchronism or length of reign necessarily reflect the original text. Analyzing the text in conjunction with extrabiblical synchronistic records may determine which data are original, which intermediary, and which Hexaplaric.

2.2.6. Insights from Recensional Development

The above survey reveals some important insights. Understanding the recensional development of the Greek texts is indispensable in evaluating the data for reconstructing the chronology of Israel and Judah. The early Greek manuscripts are important witnesses to Hebrew texts no longer extant. Codex Vaticanus, the earliest witness to Samuel–Kings, contains two text-types: OG and KR. Since the OG chronological data concur with the proto-L data and the KR with the MT data, this divergence causes Vaticanus to exhibit two chronological systems.

Cross's analysis of the Qumran manuscripts and Shenkel's study of the recensional development of the Greek texts of Samuel—which Shenkel presumed also applied to the Books of Kings (*CRD* 3, 11)—leads Shenkel to assert: "Viewed from the perspective of the historical development of the Greek text, it is now evident that the Old Greek chronology, far from being the artificial contrivance of late scribal activity, was the earliest chronology in the Greek textual tradition and was already present in the Hebrew *Vorlage* of the earliest translation of the Books of Kings" (*CRD* 110).

This may be true, but we must determine exactly which OG chronological data is original to the OG text. It is not to be presumed that all data within the OG text necessarily reflect the Greek chronological system. Allowance has to be made for contamination or cross-fertilization of texts over centuries of transmission.[63] Tov views the Qumran texts as showing a multiplicity of texts rather than Cross's tripartite division and notes that the Qumran texts "are primarily a collection of individual texts whose nature is that of all early texts and which relate to each other in an intricate web of agreements and differences. In each text one also notices unique readings, that is, readings found only in one source."[64] This web might have involved transference of chronological data if variants had arisen for some reason in one or another text. Textual corruption, whether accidental or deliberate, can thus be attributed to many causes.[65]

In addition, early Greek texts were revised to bring them into conformity with the proto-MT. The KR data, for example, do not follow the OG/L system but the proto-MT data, now represented by the MT. Later revisions were made to conform the Greek text to the definitive MT— which was one of Origen's aims when he constructed his Hexapla. Subsequent revisions—for example, proto-L—were influenced by Origen's work. The extent to which OG, L, or KR were made to conform to the MT or the extent of cross-fertilization between text-types in the centuries before the stabilization of the MT probably cannot be determined, but analysis of the chron-

---

63. Cf. Cross, "New Qumran Biblical Fragment," 23–24.
64. Tov, *Textual Criticism of the Hebrew Bible*, 160.
65. Ibid., 8–11, 233–85; Trebolle Barrera, *Jewish Bible and the Christian Bible*, 370–76.

ological data may indicate if, or where, data from one text may have been replaced by data from another.

2.3. Thiele's Approach to the Text of Kings

Thiele's first writing on chronology was a 1944 journal article entitled "The Chronology of the Kings of Judah and Israel."[66] The Qumran scrolls had not yet been discovered. Nevertheless, the Vaticanus text of 1–2 Kings had been published in 1930 in the Larger Cambridge Septuagint, with the L variants in its apparatus. Thiele made no reference to the Greek texts, constructing his chronology solely from the MT data and using the same principles that he applied in his later writings (a critique of Thiele's methodology appears in §6.3 and elsewhere). Thiele revised and expanded his journal article into a monograph entitled *The Mysterious Numbers of the Hebrew Kings*, published in three editions and interspersed with a number of journal articles.[67]

In 1951, when Thiele's first edition of *MNHK* was published, only initial discoveries at Qumran had taken place, so the significance of the Dead Sea Scrolls was not known. Thiele does, however, discuss the Greek texts in this edition. After reciting the regnal data and the problems associated with the MT, Thiele notes that

> Already in the third century before the beginning of the Christian era there are indications that the existence of these problems was recognized and that attempts were being made to deal with the problem. The Septuagint, at that time translated from the Hebrew, contains a number of striking variations in the chronological data from those contained in the Massoretic text, variations which it seems were introduced in order to make possible a more harmonious pattern as regards the lengths of reign of the Hebrew kings and the synchronisms. (*MNHK*^{1} 9 = *MNHK*^{2} 11; similarly *MNHK*^{3} 39)

Right at the outset, Thiele acknowledges problems in the chronological data of the Hebrew and Greek texts as early as the 3rd century B.C.E., but he suggests that it is the Greek text into which variants were introduced to correct what were seen as problematic data in the Hebrew text. He did not take into account that it might be the MT, a much later Hebrew text than that from which the Greek was translated, that might be responsible for the variants seen in the extant Hebrew and Greek texts.

Thiele constructed his chronology using the MT data and only then did he turn his attention to the Greek texts. By virtually dismissing the Greek data Thiele not only excluded half of the information available to him in the Books of Kings, but he made a judgment in favor of the MT data without first examining the evidence. The flaw in his method is obvious in light of the complex transmission history reviewed earlier in this chapter.

For his Greek source, Thiele (*MNHK*^{1} 168 n. 2) relied on Burney,[68] giving the MT, LXX, and L data in three columns and explaining, "By 'LXX' we mean the pattern of variations of the early Greek texts as contrasted with the pattern now found in the Massoretic text" (*MNHK*^{1} 169). He is apparently unaware of Thackeray's 1907 observation that Codex Vaticanus exhibits two text-

---

66. E. R. Thiele, "The Chronology of the Kings of Judah and Israel," *Journal of Near Eastern Studies* 3 (1944): 137–86.

67. Other articles by Thiele not previously mentioned include "New Evidence on the Chronology of the Last Kings of Judah," *BASOR* 143 (1956): 22–27; "The Synchronisms of the Hebrew Kings—A Re-evaluation: I," *Andrews University Seminary Studies* 1 (1963): 121–38; "The Synchronisms of the Hebrew Kings—A Re-evaluation: II," *Andrews University Seminary Studies* 2 (1964): 120–37; "Pekah to Hezekiah," *VT* 16 (1966): 83–107; "An Additional Chronological Note on 'Yaw, Son of 'Omri,'" *BASOR* 222 (1976): 19–23.

68. C. F. Burney, *Notes on the Hebrew Text of the Books of Kings* (Oxford: Clarendon, 1903), xli–xliv.

types in 1–2 Kings.[69] Thiele does observe that Ahab's chronological data is the last instance of a regnal formula in which the data in the LXX and L concur and that for the next five kings (Jehoshaphat, Ahaziah-I, Joram, Jehoram, and Ahaziah-J), the L data differ from LXX (*MNHK*[1] 170, 176). But he does not discern that the 1 Kings data in Codex Vaticanus and L belong to the Greek system and that the 2 Kings data belong to the Hebrew system. Failing to distinguish these two text-types, he views the Greek sources of 1 Kings and 2 Kings as one text.

Thiele's analysis of the Greek data, when compared with his dating systems for the Hebrew data, leads him to conclude that the Greek texts used a different dating system, which he calls "inconsequent accession-year reckoning" (*MNHK*[1] 172). Thiele notes that the Greek data, when compared to the MT, were "models of simplicity" (*MNHK*[1] 180). Having already constructed his chronology using the MT data, Thiele then has to explain why he has not used the simpler Greek data, and his answer lay in arguing that the Hebrew data were earlier than the Greek:

> If, however, the Hebrew figures were first, we may well understand how scholars at some early time might have failed to see the basic harmony behind the apparently contradictory figures, and how such a misconception as to the basic nature of the numbers involved could have given rise to an attempt to produce a more harmonious pattern than was considered possible from the Hebrew data. (*MNHK*[1] 182)

Thiele's apparent application of the text-critical principle that a difficult reading is preferred over an easy one fails to take into consideration that the principle is invalidated when the difficult reading is the result of scribal error.[70] Applying the principle to numbers gives even more reason for caution, as numbers are highly prone to corruption,[71] and how numbers were written in non-extant Hebrew manuscripts is subject to debate (see §7.3.6). Thiele does not take into account the late nature of the MT, assumes that the MT data represent the original Hebrew text, and attempts, for example, to illustrate the secondary nature of the LXX over the MT in the EDK:

> In the recorded data in the Massoretic text for this period, the total years for the kings of Judah from Rehoboam to the death of Ahaziah[-J] is ninety-five, whereas the total for Israel from Jeroboam [I] to the death of Joram is ninety-eight. Why should this figure for Judah be three years less than it is for Israel? . . . The increase of the years of Abijam from three to six looks strangely like an attempt at adjustment of a length of reign to make possible the same total of years for Judah in this period as for Israel. (*MNHK*[1] 184)

Thiele proposes that the Greek texts are secondary based on their *agreement* for the regnal totals for Israel and Judah. But, if the Greek texts giving 6 years for the reign of Abijam and a total of 98 years for Israel and Judah are, in fact, correct, no amount of "chronological procedure" will make correct the 3 years given to Abijam in the MT. Thiele was forced to make this proposal to defend his use of the MT data.

In his analysis of the MT data and dating systems, compared with the LXX and L data and dating system, Thiele notes that the simplicity of the Greek numbers is combined with an irregularly applied inconsequent accession-year system, whereas the MT data have a consistent dating system. Thiele concludes, "It seems clear then, that of these three patterns of Hebrew chronology, that of MT. is the earliest and best, that of LXX comes next in points of time and accuracy, and that of Luc. is the latest and the most inaccurate" (*MNHK*[1] 203). Thiele's conclusion is con-

---

69. Thackeray, "Greek Translators," 263. Thiele does not refer to Thackeray's article.
70. Cf. Tov, *Textual Criticism of the Hebrew Bible*, 302–5.
71. J. W. Wenham, "Large Numbers in the Old Testament," *Tyndale Bulletin* 18 (1967): 20–24; J. B. Payne, "The Validity of the Numbers in Chronicles," *Bibliotheca Sacra* 136 (1979): 110.

trary to that proposed later by Shenkel on the basis of his analysis of the Greek texts, which indicated an earlier origin for OG and L than for the MT (*CRD* 18–21).

Thiele's second edition of *MNHK*, published in 1965, removes the chapter on the Greek texts and replaces it with a two-page discussion at the end of the book. After reproducing variants again taken from Burney but leaving out the important datum that Abijam reigned 6 years in the Greek texts and 3 years in the MT (*MNHK*² 198; also *MNHK*³ 209),[72] he writes, "A careful study of these variations reveals the fact that they are not the result of scribal errors but constitute editorial changes made with the object of correcting what were regarded as errors in the early Hebrew text." Thiele makes no mention of the Qumran scrolls, even though initial findings had been published[73] and constituted a threat to Thiele's chronology based on the assumption that the MT exhibited the earliest data.

In 1974 Thiele entered into discussion with Shenkel's *Chronology and Recensional Development in the Greek Text of Kings*, published in 1968.[74] His main point of contention involved the chronology for the Omride period and the identification of the king of Judah in the Moabite campaign (2 Kings 3), an identification that turns on the interpretation given to the variant regnal data for the accessions of Joram and Jehoram. Shenkel's argument is that two variant chronological systems are involved, one exhibiting Greek data and the other Hebrew. Thiele, on the other hand, asserts that the variants show a coregency between Jehoshaphat and Jehoram, and he rejects the explanation that two chronological systems might have been involved.[75]

In the third edition of *MNHK*, published in 1983 well after the discovery of the Qumran scrolls, Thiele continues to utilize the principles he had put into practice in his earlier works. He includes a few pages concerning the Greek data of the Omride period (*MNHK*³ 89–94), but his discussion about Omri's reign claims that the variant data for Jehoshaphat's accession, given twice in Codex Vaticanus (Omri's 11th year in 1 Kgs 16:28a OG/L and Ahab's 4th year in 22:41 KR), reveals that the Greek data are late and artificial (*MNHK*³ 93). Thiele continues to not appreciate what Shenkel had earlier discussed—that the variant data follow two different chronological systems (*CRD* 43–60). Apart from this discussion, Thiele repeats in his third edition the material at the end of the second edition (*MNHK*² 197–99 = *MNHK*³ 209–10).

Thiele's assumption that the MT displays data earlier than the Greek texts gains no support from the transmission history of the Hebrew and Greek texts. The MT text-type is not even found at Qumran.[76] Unfortunately, Thiele never avails himself of the new insight that came to light with the examination and publication of the Qumran Scrolls.

---

72. This table is reproduced with the same omission by Jones, *1 and 2 Kings*, 20.
73. E.g., Albright, "Early Recensions," 27–33 = *QHBT* 140–46; F. M. Cross, *The Ancient Library of Qumran and Modern Biblical Studies* (1st ed.; Garden City, N.Y.: Doubleday, 1958; rev. ed.; Garden City, N.Y.: Anchor Books, 1961); idem, "History of the Biblical Text," 281–99 = *QHBT* 177–95.
74. E. R. Thiele, "Coregencies and Overlapping Reigns among the Hebrew Kings," *JBL* 93 (1974): 174–200.
75. Ibid., 175–86.
76. Cross, "Evolution of a Theory," 314; idem, "Contribution of the Qumrân Discoveries," 95 = *QHBT* 292.

3

Chronological Data

In the Books of Kings the events during a king's reign are usually narrated between an opening formula and a closing formula. The chronological data in the opening formulas consist of an accession synchronism (how that king's accession synchronizes with the neighboring kingdom) and the regnal years or length of each king's reign. Tabulating and analyzing these chronological data—both the regnal years and the accession synchronisms—in the MT, Codex Vaticanus, L minuscules boe$_2$, and Josephus's *Antiquities* helps to identify discrepancies between these texts and make tentative proposals for resolving chronological conflicts.

3.1. Regnal Years in the Divided Kingdom

3.1.1. Regnal Years in the Early Divided Kingdom

The DK began after the death of Solomon with the accessions of Rehoboam to the throne of Judah and of Jeroboam I to the throne of Israel. It ended at the fall of Samaria in Hezekiah's 6th regnal year in Judah and Hoshea's 9th regnal year in Israel (2 Kgs 18:10). Since, therefore, the DK begins and ends at the same time for each kingdom, it stands to reason that the regnal years for Judah and for Israel during the DK should add up to the same total. It is equally reasonable that the MT and OG/L numbers should concur for each EDK king—but they show several variants (indicated in bold in table 3.1).

The variants given for Abijam (MT: 3 years; OG/L: 6 years) and Jehoram (MT: 8 years; L: 10 years) account for the different totals for Judah: 95 or 100 years. The variants given for Jeroboam I (MT: 22 years; OG/L: 24 years) account for the different totals for Israel: 98 or 100 years. OG/L provide the same total (100 years) for both Judah and Israel. The MT, however, has a 3-year discrepancy between the two kingdoms, giving 95 years to Judah and 98 years to Israel. These figures are then either 2 or 5 years less than the OG/L figures. The question we confront is which—if any—of the totals is an accurate indication of the length of the EDK.

We have already seen that the KR chronological data conform with the MT. Here we see evidence of L's being made to conform to the MT in the agreement of the b minuscules with MT's 8 years for Jehoram. While this concurrence must be viewed with caution until the synchronisms are compared to regnal lengths, on the basis of the above information, it is safe to posit that the difference between totals for EDK kings in Judah and Israel is no more than 5 years.

Table 3.1. Regnal Years in the Early Divided Kingdom

Judah	MT	OG/L	Israel	MT	OG/L
Rehoboam (1 Kgs 14:21)	17y	17y	Jeroboam I (1 Kgs 14:20)	**22y**	**24y**[a]
Abijam (1 Kgs 15:2)	**3y**	**6y**	Nadab (1 Kgs 15:25)	2y	2y
Asa (1 Kgs 15:10)	41y	41y	Baasha (1 Kgs 15:33)	24y	24y
Jehoshaphat (1 Kgs 22:42)	25y	25y[b]	Elah (1 Kgs 16:8)	2y	2y
Jehoram (2 Kgs 8:17)	**8y**[c]	**10y**	Zimri (1 Kgs 16:15)	7d	7d[d]
Ahaziah-J (2 Kgs 8:26)	1y	1y	Omri (1 Kgs 16:23)	12y	12y
			Ahab (1 Kgs 16:29)	22y	22y
			Ahaziah-I (1 Kgs 22:52)	2y	2y
			Joram (2 Kgs 3:1)	12y	12y
EDK total	**95y**	**100y**	**EDK total**	**98y 7d**	**100y 7d**

a. OG/L reference is at 15:9. The figure is not actually given; based on associated data it must be either 24 or 25 years with preference being for 24 years.
b. OG/L reference is at 16:28a.
c. L minuscules $b + b'$ (= b) agree with MT in reading 8 years, whereas oe_2 have 10 years. The KR has an anomalous 40 years.
d. OG has 7 years for Zimri.

Table 3.2. Regnal Years in the Late Divided Kingdom

Judah	MT/KR	L	Israel	MT/KR	L
Athaliah[a] (2 Kgs 11:4)	6y	6y	Jehu (2 Kgs 10:36)	28y	28y
Joash-J (2 Kgs 12:2)	40y	40y	Jehoahaz (2 Kgs 13:1)	17y	17y
Amaziah (2 Kgs 14:2)	29y	29y	Joash-I (2 Kgs 13:10)	16y	16y
Azariah (2 Kgs 15:2)	52y	52y	Jeroboam II (2 Kgs 14:23)	41y	41y
Jotham (2 Kgs 15:33)	16y	16y	Zechariah (2 Kgs 15:8)	6m	6m
Ahaz (2 Kgs 16:2)	16y	16y	Shallum (2 Kgs 15:13)	1m	1m
Hezekiah (2 Kgs 18:10)	6y	6y	Menahem (2 Kgs 15:17)	10y	10y
			Pekahiah (2 Kgs 15:23)	**2y**	**10y**
			Pekah (2 Kgs 15:27)	20y	20y
			Hoshea (2 Kgs 17:1)	9y	9y
LDK total	**165y**	**165y**	**LDK total**	**143y 7m**	**151y 7m**

a. Athaliah's regnal years are not stated directly, but she began to reign in the same year as Jehu and was succeeded by Joash-J in Jehu's 7th year (2 Kgs 11:4; 12:2). She must, therefore, have reigned 6+ years (rounded to 6 years).

3.1.2. Regnal Years in the Late Divided Kingdom

The LDK, which ends with the fall of Samaria (2 Kgs 18:10), exhibits only one variant chronological datum (table 3.2). Codex Vaticanus contains the KR text-type in this section, which conforms to the MT, and the Greek text is represented by the L minuscules boe$_2$.

The MT/KR and L figures for LDK Judah are the same: 165 years. The situation is different for Israel: the MT totals 143 years 7 months, and L totals 151 years 7 months. This 8-year difference is found in the reign of Pekahiah, credited with 2 years by MT/KR and 10 years by L.

3.1.3. Total Regnal Years in the Divided Kingdom

The L total for Israel (251+ years) is 14 years less than its total for Judah (265 years) and 9 years less than the MT/KR total for Judah (260 years). The discrepancy between the MT/KR totals for Israel (241+ years) and for Judah (260 years) is 19 years. Some of the regnal figures must, therefore, be discrepant since the DK starts and ends at fixed points—which means that the length of the intervening period should coincide in both kingdoms (table 3.3).

Table 3.3. Regnal Years in the Divided Kingdom

Judah	MT/KR	OG/L	Israel	MT/KR	OG/L
EDK subtotal	95y	100y	EDK subtotal	98y 7d	100y 7d
LDK subtotal	165y	165y	LDK subtotal	143y 7m	151y 7m
DK total	**260y**	**265y**	**DK total**	**241y 7m 7d**	**251y 7m 7d**

The question remains whether the DK kings of Judah reigned 260 (MT) or 265 years (L) or some other figure. This 5-year discrepancy occurs in the regnal years of Abijam and Jehoram, and determining the authentic regnal years for these two kings should supply the correct total for Judah. It might be thought that the synchronism for Abijam's successor could establish which data are more likely correct. Abijam's successor, Asa, according to the natural meaning of the text, came to the throne only after his father died, not as a coregent (1 Kgs 15:8). The datum of his accession synchronism, therefore, theoretically agrees with Abijam's having either a 3-year or a 6-year reign. Unfortunately, the length of reign cannot be resolved so simply, because Asa has *two* alternate accession synchronisms at 1 Kgs 15:9: Jeroboam I's 20th year according to MT, which concurs with Abijam's 3-year reign, and Jeroboam I's 24th year according to OG/L, which agrees with Abijam's 6-year reign. Other evidence, therefore, must be sought to determine if either of the numbers and synchronisms is correct.

The 8 years given to Jehoram by MT and manuscript b versus 10 years in oe$_2$ must likewise be worked out on the basis of the separate chronological systems to which they belong. This is made complex by the absence of Jehoram's accession synchronism in L. Jehoram's accession should synchronize with Ahaziah-I's 2nd year, which is based on the synchronism that Joram began to reign in Jehoram's 2nd year (2 Kgs 1:17 MT; 1:18a L). If Jehoram reigned 12 years beginning in Ahaziah-I's 2nd year and if his successor, Ahaziah-J, began to reign in Joram's 11th year (8:25; 9:29 L), then Jehoram would have an 11-year or 12-year reign not 10.

These two examples (examined in detail in §7.2.2 [Abijam] and §5.4 and §7.2.6 [Jehoram]) illustrate the problems of reckoning the length of the DK. For the present, recall the previous conclusion that proto-L and OG appear to be earlier than the MT and more likely retain original data. The L numbers for EDK Israel and Judah both total 100 years—an agreement suggesting that the L figures of 6 years for Abijam and the accession synchronism of Asa in Jeroboam I's 24th year are more likely to be correct than the MT figures with their 3-year discrepancy. The L figure for Jehoram's regnal years, 10, may likewise reflect a more reliable text.

Even if the Greek texts have retained more reliable data, some plausible explanation is still needed for the appearance of the variant numbers now found in the Greek and Hebrew texts. Why is Abijam given 6 years in OG/L but 3 years in MT, and why is Jehoram given 10 years in two L manuscripts and 8 years in MT and two other L manuscripts? These crucial questions are addressed in the next few chapters.

3.1.4. Thiele's Discussion of Regnal Years

Each of Thiele's three editions of *MNHK* provide the same tables for the regnal years of Israel and Judah given by the MT for the EDK and the LDK.[1] Thiele comments:

> Thus in the first of these two periods that should be identical, we have a total of 98 years and 7 days for Israel as against 95 years for Judah, while in the second there are 143 years and 7 months for Israel as against 166 years for Judah. Compared with Assyrian figures, both of these last figures seem too high. There are only 120 years from 841 B.C., the eighteenth year of Shalmaneser III, when the latter reported having received tribute from Jehu . . . to the accession of Sargon in 722/21, when the latter claimed to have captured Samaria. Compared with Assyrian figures, then, the total of the reigns of kings of Israel for this period seems to be about 23 years too high, while for Judah there seems to be an excess of about 46 years. (*MNHK*³ 37; similarly *MNHK*¹ 6–7 and *MNHK*² 8–9)

Thiele returns to this subject in chapter 9 of his first edition of *MNHK* but leaves it aside in his second and third editions.

In his first edition, in order to reconcile the EDK figures with the supposed length of the EDK, Thiele gives tabulated columns for the kings' regnal years in the MT, LXX, and L—but not all of his figures are found in the texts. Thiele assesses the textual data and derives "actual years" that give both Judah and Israel the same number of years in each text: 90 years in the MT, 93 years in LXX, and 101 years in L (*MNHK*¹ 200).

In the MT, for Judah, using antedating and coregencies, Thiele changes Jehoshaphat's 25 years to 21 years sole reign, and Jehoram's 8 years to 7 years sole reign. For Israel, also using antedating, Thiele changes Jeroboam I's 22 years to 21 years, Nadab's 2 years to 1 year, Baasha's 24 years to 23 years, Elah's 2 years to 1 year, Omri's 12 years to 11 years, Ahab's 22 years to 21 years, Ahaziah-I's 2 years to 1 year, and Joram's 12 years to 11 years. In the LXX, for Judah, Thiele gives Jehoram 3 years sole reign, whereas the datum in 2 Kgs 8:16 is 40 years (which cannot be correct, based on the synchronisms). For Israel, Thiele changes Zimri's 7 days to 1 year, though Vaticanus (OG) gives 7 years, probably in error; he changes Ahaziah-I's 2 years to zero and Joram's 12 years to 6 years sole reign. In L, for Judah, Thiele gives 11 years to Jehoram with a question mark (the representative texts give 10 years, though 11 may be correct) and for Israel changes Elah's 2 years to none, Zimri's 7 days to 3 years sole reign with a question mark, and Ahaziah-I's 1 year to 2 years.

In total, Thiele changes ten reigns in the MT, four in the LXX, and four in L. These years appear calculated to give the MT 90 years, presumably because Thiele assumes (on the basis of synchronizing the Hebrew kings with the AEC) that Rehoboam and Jeroboam I began to reign in

---

1. Thiele's totals are the same as those in my tables 3.1–2, except that I assign Athaliah 6 years for an LDK total of 165 years, whereas Thiele gives Athaliah 7 years, for a total of 166 years (*MNHK*³ 37).

931/930 and that Ahaziah-J and Joram's last year was 842, approximating 90 years. He gives 3 extra years to the LXX (because he argues that Abijam's reign is 3 years in excess) and 101 years to the L data (on the basis of the inconsistently applied inconsequent accession-year reckoning that he himself imposes). Thiele's dubious methods of reconciling the discrepant totals between Judah and Israel for the same period compel further investigation.

3.2 Divided Kingdom Chronological Data

Before examining the regnal years of the DK kings, however, we need to compile the EDK accession-synchronism data for Israel and Judah in 1–2 Kings according to the MT, KR, OG, and L (c_2 data are discussed in chapter 4). Differences in EDK data are shown in bold in table 3.4. Greek equivalents of מלך are given to show how this verb is translated in each accession synchronism in OG, L, and KR (see §5.5 for discussion of this significant feature). The EDK data from Josephus normally concur with the MT data when the OG/L and MT data diverge (e.g., 3 years for Abijam, not 6 as in OG/L). A variant synchronism in Josephus is given for Omri's accession in Asa's 30th year.

In the LDK, beginning with the reigns of Athaliah and Jehu, the Hebrew and Greek chronological data are almost the same (two exceptions involve Jehu's accession and Pekahiah's regnal years). The EDK variants that appeared between OG/L and MT/KR, giving the appearance of two chronological systems, no longer apply. In 2 Kings the verb מלך is normally translated by the aorist in both KR and L (even in the accession synchronisms) and so its Greek translation is not displayed in table 3.5 apart from the exceptional 2 Kgs 10:36+ L. Josephus provides a number of variants for LDK kings.

3.2.1. Accession Synchronisms in the Divided Kingdom

Any reconstruction of DK chronology must accommodate the accession of a king *in* the stated regnal year of his contemporary in the neighboring kingdom, as given by the regnal formulas. Recognizing that a king may die at any time during the year and that his successor would immediately succeed him, a king's final year is rounded to a full year, so that his final year may be somewhat less or more than the number stated. In an effort to accommodate the given accession synchronisms and regnal years for each king's reign, some final years and a successor's first years are positioned in the same square in table 3.6 (pp. 40ff.). The decision whether a final year might be more than or less than a full year depends on the synchronism under study and its associated data. It is acknowledged that this type of alignment is not precisely accurate but should be helpful to define the chronological framework and to identify problem areas.

3.2.2. Accession Synchronisms in the Early Divided Kingdom

No accession synchronism is given for the first DK kings, Rehoboam in Judah and Jeroboam I in Israel, because they began their reigns soon after the death of Solomon. The extant texts do not give an opening regnal formula for Jeroboam I, but 22 regnal years are credited to him in the closing formula at 1 Kgs 14:20 MT. This verse is absent in OG/L, but at 15:8–9 the accession of Asa is synchronized with Jeroboam I's 24th year, which indicates that Jeroboam I reigned at least 24 years. And since Jeroboam I's successor, Nadab, commences his reign in Asa's 2nd year, Jeroboam I reigned no more than 25 years. Asa's synchronism is absent at 15:8 MT but in 15:9 MT his accession is synchronized with Jeroboam I's 20th year (not the 24th year as in OG/L).

Table 3.4. Early Divided Kingdom Chronological Data

Reference	Text-Type	Kingdom	Statement
1 Kgs 14:20	MT	Israel	Jeroboam I reigned **22 years**
1 Kgs 15:8-9	OG L		the **24th year** of Jeroboam I [length of reign not given]
1 Kgs 14:21	MT	Judah	Rehoboam reigned 17 years
	OG L		Rehoboam reigned (ἐβασίλευσεν) 17 years
1 Kgs 15:1-2	MT	Judah	in the 18th year of Jeroboam I, Abijam began to reign; he reigned **3 years**
	OG L		in the 18th year of Jeroboam I, Abijam began to reign (βασιλεύει); he reigned (ἐβασίλευσεν) **6 years**
1 Kgs 15:8	MT	Judah	and Abijam slept with his fathers [**synchronism absent**]
	OG L		and Abijam slept with his fathers in the **24th year** of Jeroboam I [unique synchronism for a king's death]
1 Kgs 15:9-10	MT	Judah	in the **20th year** of Jeroboam I, Asa began to reign; he reigned 41 years
	OG L		in the **24th year** of Jeroboam I, Asa began to reign (βασιλεύει); he reigned (ἐβασίλευσεν) 41 years
1 Kgs 15:25	MT	Israel	Nadab began to reign in the 2nd year of Asa; he reigned 2 years
	OG L		Nadab began to reign (βασιλεύει) in the 2nd year of Asa; he reigned (ἐβασίλευσεν) 2 years
1 Kgs 15:33	MT	Israel	in the 3rd year of Asa, Baasha began to reign; [he reigned] in Tirzah 24 years
	OG L		in the 3rd year of Asa, Baasha began to reign (βασιλεύει); [he reigned] in Tirzah 24 years
1 Kgs 16:8	MT	Israel	in the **26th year** of Asa, Elah began to reign; [he reigned] in Tirzah 2 years
1 Kgs 16:6, 8	OG L		Elah his son reigned (OG: βασιλεύει; L: ἐβασίλευσεν) after him in the **20th year** of Asa; he reigned (ἐβασίλευσεν) 2 years
1 Kgs 16:10	MT	Israel	Zimri killed Elah in the **27th year** of Asa and reigned after him
	OG L		Zimri killed Elah [**no synchronism**] and reigned (ἐβασίλευσεν) after him
1 Kgs 16:15	MT	Israel	in the **27th year** of Asa, Zimri reigned 7 **days** in Tirzah
	OG		[**no synchronism**] Zimri reigned (ἐβασίλευσεν) 7 **years** in Tirzah
	L (be$_2$)		in the **22nd year** of Asa, Zimri reigned (ἐβασίλευσεν) 7 **days** in Tirzah
1 Kgs 16:16	MT	Israel	Omri was king that day[a] (= Asa's **27th year**)
	OG		Omri was king that day [**no synchronism**]
	L		Omri was king that day (= Asa's **22nd year**)

Table 3.4. Early Divided Kingdom Chronological Data (cont.)

Reference	Text-Type	Kingdom	Statement
1 Kgs 16:23	MT	Israel	in the **31st year** of Asa, Omri began to reign 12 years; he reigned 6 years in Tirzah
	OG L		in the **31st year** of Asa, Omri began to reign (βασιλεύει) 12 years; he reigns (βασιλεύει) 6 years in Tirzah
Josephus, *Antiquities* 8.312			in the **30th year** of Asa, Omri reigned 12 years, 6 of them in Tirzah
1 Kgs 16:28a	MT	Judah	[**absent**]
	OG L		in the **11th year** of Omri, Jehoshaphat began to reign (βασιλεύει); he reigns (βασιλεύει) 25 years
1 Kgs 16:29	MT	Israel	Ahab began to reign in the **38th year of Asa**; he reigned 22 years
	OG L		in the **2nd year of Jehoshaphat**, Ahab began to reign (βασιλεύει); he reigned (ἐβασίλευσεν) 22 years
1 Kgs 22:41–42	MT	Judah	Jehoshaphat began to reign in the **4th year** of Ahab; he reigned 25 years
	KR		Jehoshaphat began to reign (ἐβασίλευσεν); in the **4th year** of Ahab, he reigned (ἐβασίλευσεν); 25 years he reigned (ἐβασίλευσεν) in Jerusalem
	L		[**absent**]
1 Kgs 22:52	MT	Israel	Ahaziah-I began to reign in the **17th year** of Jehoshaphat; he reigned 2 years
	KR		Ahaziah-I began to reign (ἐβασίλευσεν) in the **17th year** of Jehoshaphat; he reigned (ἐβασίλευσεν) 2 years
	L		in the **24th year** of Jehoshaphat, Ahaziah-I began to reign (βασιλεύει); he reigned (ἐβασίλευσεν) 2 years
2 Kgs 1:17	MT	Israel	Joram reigned after Ahaziah-I in the **2nd year** of Jehoram [regnal years not stated]
	KR L		[**absent**]
2 Kgs 1:18a	MT	Israel	[**absent**]
	KR		in the **18th year** of Jehoshaphat, Joram began to reign (βασιλεύει) 12 years
	L		in the **2nd year** of Jehoram, Joram began to reign (βασιλεύει) 12 years
2 Kgs 3:1	MT	Israel	Joram began to reign in the **18th year** of Jehoshaphat; he reigned 12 years
	KR		Joram began to reign (ἐβασίλευσεν) in the **18th year** of Jehoshaphat; he reigned (ἐβασίλευσεν) 12 years
	L		Joram reigned (ἐβασίλευσεν) in Israel 12 years [**no synchronism**]
2 Kgs 8:16–17	MT	Judah	in the 5th year of Joram, Jehoram began to reign; he reigned **8 years**

Table 3.4. Early Divided Kingdom Chronological Data (cont.)

Reference	Text-Type	Kingdom	Statement
	KR		in the 5th year of Joram, Jehoram began to reign (ἐβασίλευσεν); he reigned (ἐβασίλευσεν) **40 years**
	L (oe$_2$)		in the 5th year of Joram, Jehoram began to reign (ἐβασίλευσεν); he reigned (ἐβασίλευσεν) **10 years**
	L (b)		in the 5th year of Joram, Jehoram began to reign (ἐβασίλευσεν); he reigned (ἐβασίλευσεν) **8 years**
2 Kgs 8:25–26	MT	Judah	in the **12th year** of Joram, Ahaziah-J began to reign; he reigned 1 year
	KR		in the **12th year** of Joram, Ahaziah-J began to reign (ἐβασίλευσεν); he reigned (ἐβασίλευσεν) 1 year
	L (e$_2$)		in the **11th year** of Joram, Ahaziah-J began to reign (ἐβασίλευσεν); he reigned (ἐβασίλευσεν) 1 year
2 Kgs 8:25	L (b)		in the **11th year** of Joram, Ahaziah-J began to reign (ἐβασίλευσεν) [regnal years not stated]
	L (o)		in the **10th year** of Joram, Ahaziah-J began to reign (ἐβασίλευσεν) [regnal years not stated]
2 Kgs 9:29	MT	Judah	in the 11th year of Joram, Ahaziah-J began to reign [regnal years not stated]
	KR		in the 11th year Joram, Ahaziah-J began to reign (ἐβασίλευσεν) [regnal years not stated]
	L (be$_2$)		in the 11th year of Joram, Ahaziah-J began to reign (ἐβασίλευσεν); he reigned (ἐβασίλευσεν) 1 year
	L (o)		in the 11th year Joram, Ahaziah-J began to reign (ἐβασίλευσεν) [regnal years not stated]

a. "That day" is not part of a formula but supplies the synchronism for Omri, which is inferred from 16:15.

Elah's accession synchronism in OG/L in Asa's 20th year conflicts with the 24 regnal years given to Baasha. Elah could have acceded to the throne in Asa's 20th year only if Baasha reigned only 17 years—not 24. Elah's 2-year reign and his successor's, Zimri's, accession in Asa's 22nd year, found in be$_2$, supports the shorter reign for Baasha. The 24 years credited to Baasha is found in both Hebrew and Greek texts and, therefore, could belong to either system. Omri, who began to reign after Zimri's 7 days, would also have his accession in Asa's 22nd year. According to 1 Kgs 16:23, Omri reigned 12 years: 6 years in Tirzah and 6 years in Samaria. This implies that Omri's move to Samaria occurred in Asa's 27th or 28th year, but Omri's accession synchronism at 16:23 is for Asa's 31st year (30th year according to Josephus). Whence, then, did the 31st year for Omri's accession originate? Based on Elah's synchronism and length of reign, Omri's 12 years ought to have finished with Asa's 33rd year, with Ahab's accession in the 34th year, but this synchronism is not attested.

Abijam came to the throne in Jeroboam I's 18th year, but in MT Abijam is given only 3 years, and Asa's accession is in Jeroboam I's 20th year, not the 24th as in OG/L. Nadab's accession in Asa's 2nd year and Baasha's accession in Asa's 3rd year are not possible if Jeroboam I reigned

Table 3.5. Late Divided Kingdom Chronological Data

Reference	Text-Type	Kingdom	Statement
2 Kgs 10:36	MT KR	Israel	Jehu reigned **28 years**
2 Kgs 10:36+	L		Jehu reigned **28 years**; in the 2nd year of Athaliah, Jehu began to reign (βασιλεύει)
Josephus, *Antiquities* 9.160			Jehu reigned **27 years**
2 Kgs 12:1/2	MT KR L	Judah	in the 7th year of Jehu, Joash-J began to reign; he reigned 40 years
Josephus, *Antiquities* 9.143, 157			in the 7th year of Jehu, Joash-J became king (extrapolated)
2 Kgs 13:1	MT KR L	Israel	in the **23rd year** of Joash-J, Jehoahaz began to reign; he reigned 17 years
Josephus, *Antiquities* 9.173			in the **21st year** of Joash-J, Jehoahaz began to reign; he reigned 17 years
2 Kgs 13:10	MT KR L	Israel	in the 37th year of Joash-J, Joash-I began to reign; he reigned 16 years
Josephus, *Antiquities* 9.177			in the 37th year of Joash-J, Joash-I began to reign; he reigned 16 years
2 Kgs 14:1–2	MT KR L	Judah	in the 2nd year of Joash-I, Amaziah began to reign; [he reigned] 29 years
Josephus, *Antiquities* 9.186, 204			in the 2nd year of Joash-I, Amaziah began to reign; he reigned 29 years
2 Kgs 14:17	MT KR L	Judah	Amaziah lived 15 years after the death of Joash-I
Josephus, *Antiquities* 9.203			Joash-I captured Amaziah and released him in the 14th year of Amaziah
2 Kgs 14:23	MT KR L	Israel	in the 15th year of Amaziah, Jeroboam II began to reign; he reigned **41 years**
Josephus, *Antiquities* 9.205, 215			in the 15th year of Amaziah, Jeroboam II began to reign; [he reigned] **40 years**
2 Kgs 15:1–2	MT KR L	Judah	in the **27th year** of Jeroboam II, Azariah began to reign; he reigned 52 years
Josephus, *Antiquities* 9.216, 227			in the **14th year** of Jeroboam II, Azariah began to reign; he reigned 52 years
2 Kgs 15:8	MT KR L	Israel	in the 38th year of Azariah, Zechariah reigned 6 months
2 Kgs 15:13	MT	Israel	Shallum began to reign in Uzziah's [Azariah's] 39th year; he reigned **1 month** in Samaria
	KR		Shallum began to reign; in the 39th year of Azariah, Shallum reigned **several days** in Samaria
	L		Shallum began to reign in Samaria **a month of days** in the 39th year of Azariah

Table 3.5. Late Divided Kingdom Chronological Data (cont.)

Reference	Text-Type	Kingdom	Statement
2 Kgs 15:17	MT KR L	Israel	in the 39th year of Azariah, Menahem began to reign; he reigned 10 years
2 Kgs 15:23	MT KR	Israel	in the 50th year of Azariah, Pekahiah began to reign; he reigned **2 years**
	L		in the 50th year of Azariah, Pekahiah began to reign; he reigned **10 years**
2 Kgs 15:27	MT KR L	Israel	in the 52nd year of Azariah, Pekah began to reign; he reigned 20 years
2 Kgs 15:30	MT KR	Israel	Hoshea reigned in his stead in the **20th year** of Jotham (cf. 15:32 and 17:1)
	L		[absent]
2 Kgs 15:32-33	MT KR L	Judah	in the 2nd year of Pekah, Jotham began to reign; he reigned 16 years
2 Kgs 16:1-2	MT KR L	Judah	in the 17th year of Pekah, Ahaz began to reign; he reigned 16 years
2 Kgs 17:1	MT KR L	Israel	in the 12th year of Ahaz, Hoshea began to reign; he reigned 9 years
2 Kgs 18:1-2	MT KR L	Judah	in the **3rd year** of Hoshea, Hezekiah began to reign; he reigned 29 years
Josephus, *Antiquities* 9.260			in the **4th year** of Hoshea, Hezekiah began to reign
2 Kgs 18:9-10	MT KR L	Israel	Samaria was captured in the **6th year** of Hezekiah, which was the 9th year of Hoshea
Josephus, *Antiquities* 9.278			Samaria was captured in the 9th year of Hoshea, which was the **7th year** of Hezekiah

only 22 years, as they overlap his last 2 years. The formula gives no hint of coregency: "And he [Jeroboam I] slept with his fathers and his son [Nadab] reigned in his stead" (14:20). Baasha has 24 regnal years in both MT and OG/L, and the accession of his successor, Elah, is synchronized with Asa's 26th year (16:8 MT). Working backward indicates that Baasha's 1st year was in Asa's 3rd year, and Nadab's 1st year in Asa's 2nd year. The conflict remains, therefore, between Jeroboam I's 22 years and the accessions of Nadab and Baasha, which indicates a problem with the MT data. The 24 years credited to Baasha in OG/L and MT caused a conflict in OG/L with the synchronisms given for Elah's accession in Asa's 20th year and Zimri's and Omri's accessions in Asa's 22nd, but these synchronisms are not given by the MT.

If Elah reigned less than 2 full years, it is possible that Zimri's 7 days and Omri's accession at Tirzah occurred in Asa's 27th year, as the MT synchronism states at 16:15. After 6 years on the throne, Omri's move to Samaria ought to have occurred in Asa's 32nd or 33rd year, but the synchronism at 16:23 is for the previous year, the 31st. Although all texts (except Josephus) have Omri's accession in Asa's 31st year, neither the OG/L nor the MT arrangement accommodate this synchronism. It is 4 years too late as a Greek datum, and 1 year too early as a MT datum! This is an area to which I will return, but I note here that the difference between the OG/L and MT

Table 3.6. Divided Kingdom Timeline

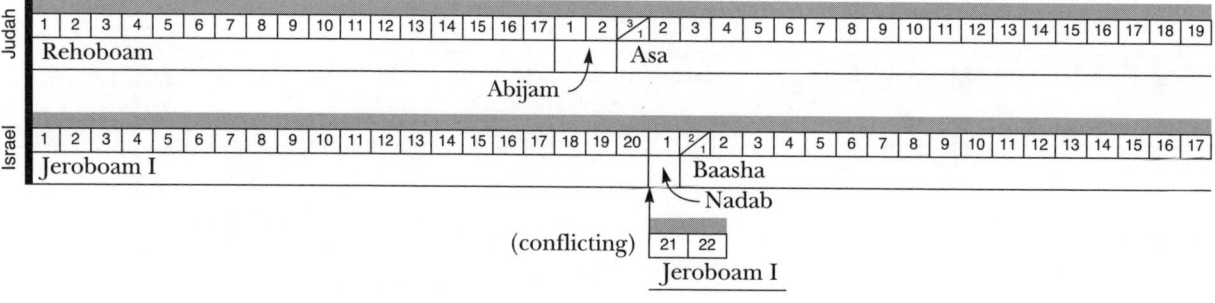

pattern is based on a 6-year discrepancy. If Omri began his 6-year reign in Tirzah in Asa's 22nd year, his move to Samaria would have occurred in Asa's 27th or 28th year. Since the MT reports the 27th year as the synchronism for Omri's accession at Tirzah, this may hold a clue to the conflict in the OG/L and MT data.

If Omri began to reign in Asa's 22nd year, Omri's 6th year aligns with Asa's 27th year. And if Omri reigned 12 years, Ahab, his successor, would be expected to commence his reign in Asa's 34th year. Instead, the synchronism aligns Ahab's accession with Jehoshaphat's 2nd year, Jehoshaphat having begun to reign in the previous year, Omri's 11th year (16:28a). According to the OG/L data, 9 or 10 years should occur from the end of Omri's reign (= Asa's 33rd year) and Ahab's accession in Jehoshaphat's 2nd year, based on 41 years attributed to Asa. The conflicting datum given for Baasha's reign, 24 years as against 17 indicated by the OG/L synchronisms for Elah and Zimri/Omri, is also given in the MT.

The sequence of accessions after Omri's follows a different order in MT and OG/L. In OG/L, Jehoshaphat's accession in Omri's 11th year (16:28a) is followed by Ahab's accession in Jehoshaphat's 2nd year (16:29). But, in the MT, Ahab's accession in Asa's 38th year (16:29) comes before Jehoshaphat's accession in Ahab's 4th year (22:41). The synchronism for Jehoshaphat's reign ap-

Table 3.6. Divided Kingdom Timeline (cont.)

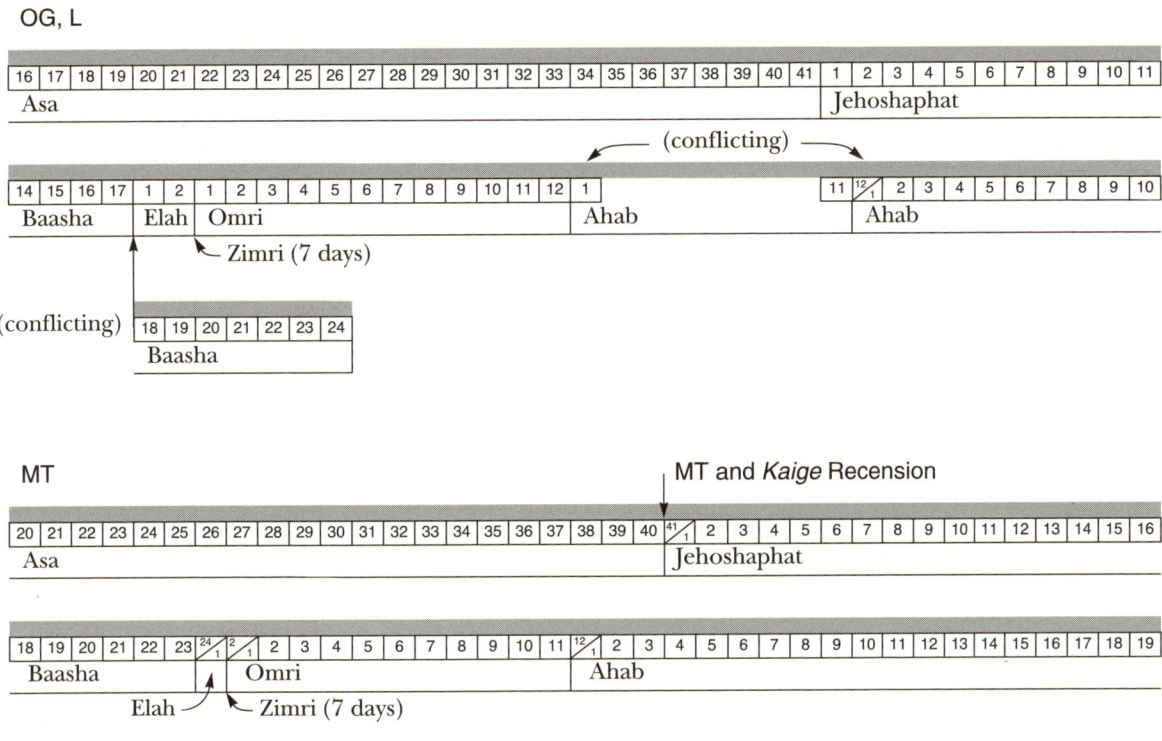

pears at 16:28a–h OG/L; these verses are not present at 16:28 MT but appear at 22:41–51 (but with the MT accession synchronism). The KR also has the narrative at 22:41–51 in accordance with the MT order and its accession synchronism for Jehoshaphat (though 22:47–50 is absent). The two textual traditions placing Jehoshaphat's narrative at different places in their respective texts are responsible for Jehoshaphat's narrative appearing twice in Codex Vaticanus. Neither the MT pattern nor the OG/L pattern explain the datum at 16:23 for Omri's accession in Asa's 31st year. It is evident here that confusing chronological data led to a major textual disruption, which still leaves the original facts in doubt.

The OG/L synchronizes Jehoshaphat's accession with Omri's 11th year and Ahab's accession with Jehoshaphat's 2nd year. Following Ahab's 22-year reign, Ahaziah-I's accession is synchronized with Jehoshaphat's 24th year. Ahaziah-I reigned 2 years, followed by his brother Joram's accession in Jehoram's 2nd year. This is consistent with Jehoshaphat's 25-year reign as given and Jehoram's assuming the throne in that same year, which is aligned with Ahaziah-I's 2nd year. The synchronism for Jehoram is, however, missing from all texts.

Ahaziah-J's accession is synchronized in L to Joram's 11th year (2 Kgs 8:25 be$_2$; 9:29 boe$_2$), which indicates that Jehoram reigned 11–12 years, though L minuscules oe$_2$ give only 10 years

Table 3.6. Divided Kingdom Timeline (cont.)

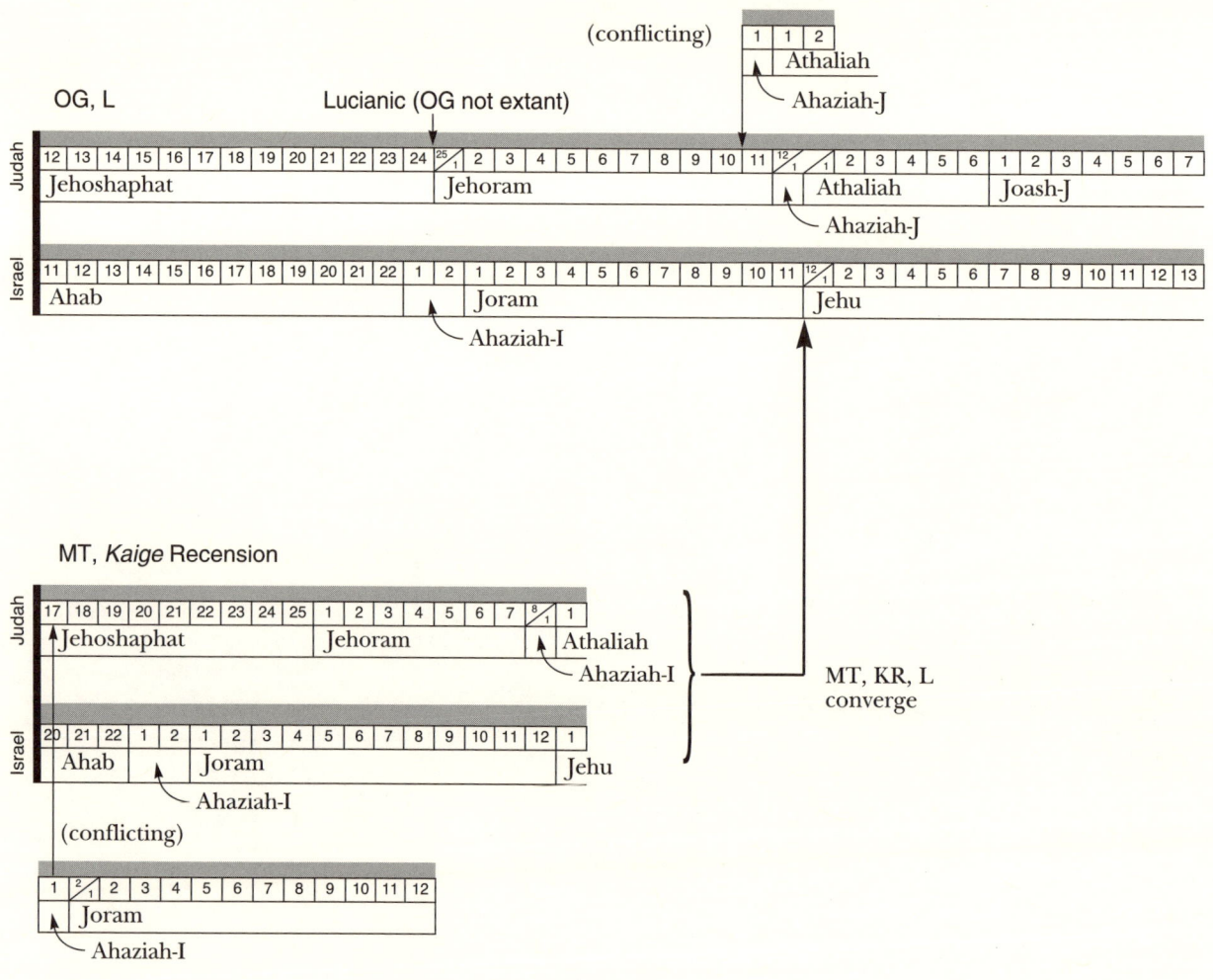

(2 Kgs 8:17).[2] If Ahaziah-J reigned only 1 year beginning in Joram's 11th year, then Ahaziah-J's 1 year extended into Joram's 12th year. The 11 years for Jehoram's reign concur with Joram's having 12 regnal years (2 Kgs 1:18a L), though Joram's last year may not have been a full year. If Jehoram's 12th and final year was partial, Ahaziah-J's 1 year need not have been much more than a full year.

Apart from the absence of an 11th year (and possibly a partial 12th) for Jehoram, OG/L data from Jehoshaphat's accession in Omri's 11th year to the end of the EDK show internal consistency.[3]

---

2. Ἔνδεκα (11) or δώδεκα (12) could have been corrupted to δέκα (10) or perhaps copied from an already corrupt Hebrew text. Minuscule o synchronizes Ahaziah-J's accession with Joram's 10th year (2 Kgs 8:25), consistent with giving Jehoram a 10-year reign, but e_2 has Ahaziah-J's accession in Joram's 11th year, creating a conflict in its data.

3. Two L minuscules, $b + b'$ (= b), give Jehoram 8 years, as does the MT, suggesting that this number was derived from a proto-MT or MT at a late stage of the L textual transmission.

Table 3.6. Divided Kingdom Timeline (cont.)

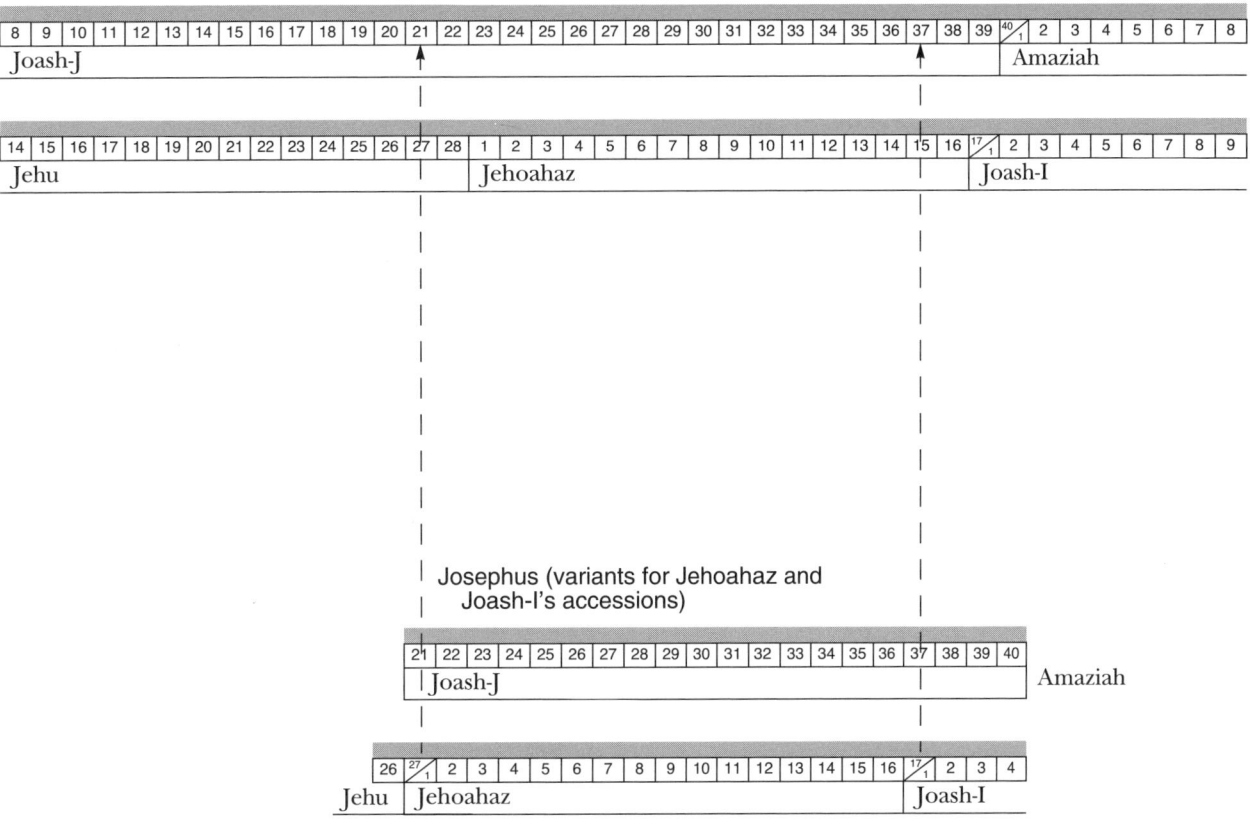

In the MT Ahab has 22 years, but Ahaziah-I's accession needs to be aligned with Jehoshaphat's 20th year, whereas MT/KR synchronizes Ahaziah-I's accession with Jehoshaphat's 17th year. Joram's accession follows the next year in Jehoshaphat's 18th year (2 Kgs 3:1 MT; 2 Kgs 1:18a, 3:1 KR), whereas the anticipated synchronism would be the 22nd. MT 2 Kgs 1:17 provides a second accession synchronism for Joram—during Jehoram's 2nd year—a synchronism also given by 1:18a L,[4] which is consistent with its other data, but not consistent with the MT data.

The synchronism giving Jehoram's accession in Joram's 5th year (2 Kgs 8:16) is consistent with Ahaziah-I and Joram having their accessions in the 20th and 22nd years of Asa, respectively, but these synchronisms do not appear in the MT. Why would the MT synchronize the accessions of Ahaziah-I and Joram with the 17th and 18th years of Jehoshaphat's reign when clearly they do not agree with either the preceding or the following data?

---

4. KR/L have a section designated 2 Kgs 1:18a–d not present in MT. L does not have the synchronism at 3:1.

Table 3.6. Divided Kingdom Timeline (cont.)

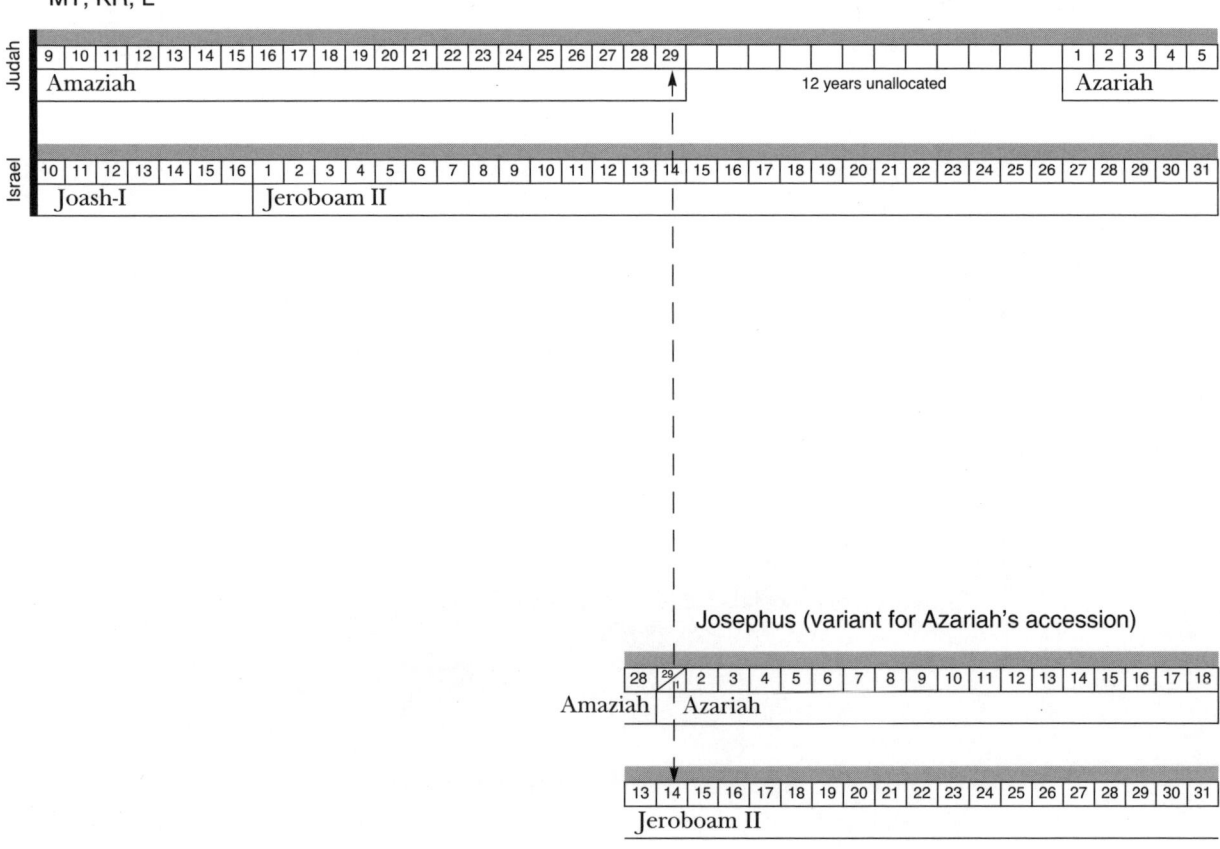

Jehoram's accession in Joram's 5th year gives to him an 8-year reign. His 8 years are followed by Ahaziah-J's 1-year reign, Ahaziah-J's accession being synchronized to Joram's 12th (8:25 MT/KR) or 11th (9:29 MT/KR/L) year. Joram's 12th and last year terminates at the same time as Ahaziah-J's, both being killed by Jehu, bringing the EDK to an end.

The above analysis of the OG/L data shows inconsistency in synchronizing the end of Baasha's reign and the beginning of Omri's reign with Asa. The MT data shows inconsistency in synchronizing the accessions of Nadab and Baasha with Asa's reign and in the accessions of Ahaziah-I and Joram with the reign of Jehoshaphat. OG/L appear to have a more consistent pattern than MT/KR.

3.2.3. Accession Synchronisms in the Late Divided Kingdom

Jehu, usurper to the throne of Israel, killed Ahaziah-J and subsequently caused the death of Joram (2 Kgs 9:24–28). Their successors, Athaliah and Jehu, both began to reign at approximately the same time. But L manuscripts boe$_2$, in an extended passage designated 10:36+ (not found in MT or KR), give Jehu's accession in Athaliah's 2nd year. This may have originated with the oe$_2$

Table 3.6. Divided Kingdom Timeline (cont.)

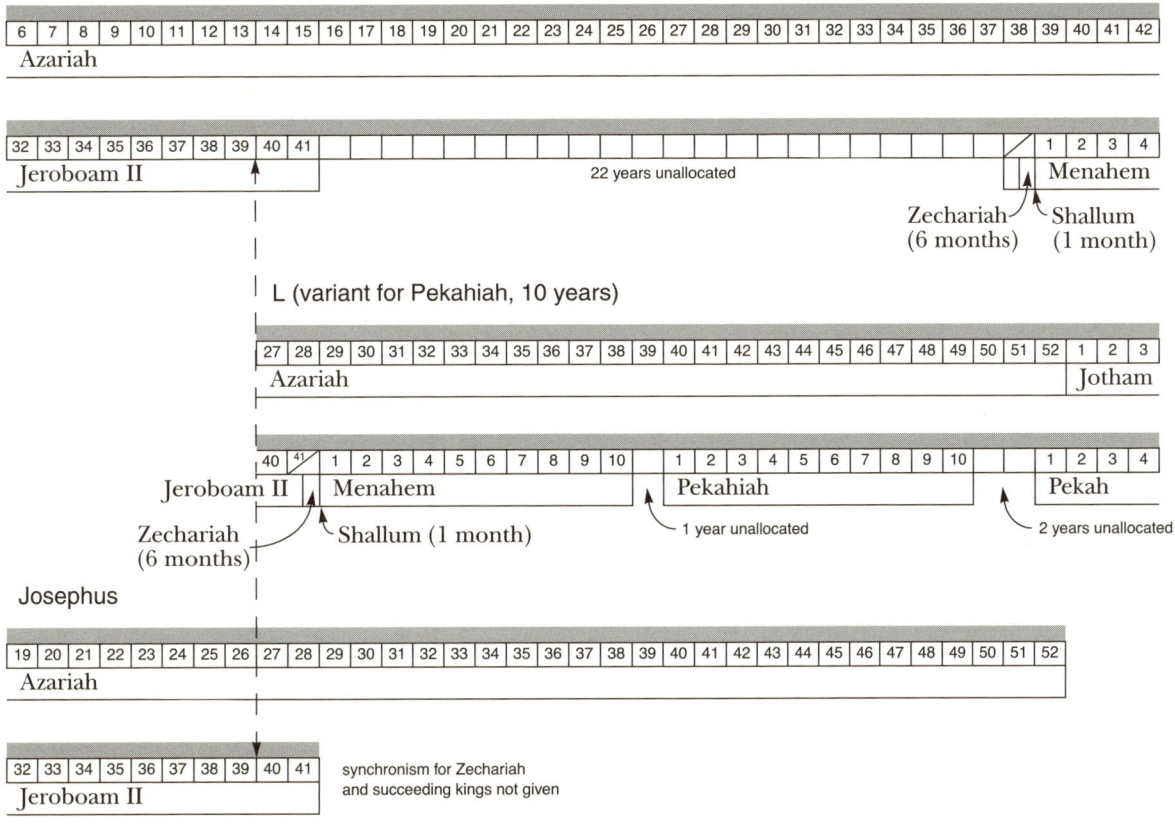

datum that Jehoram reigned 10 years, instead of a probable 11–12.[5] If Ahaziah-J's accession moved up 1 year to synchronize with Joram's 10th year, then Athaliah's accession follows in Joram's 11th year and her 2nd year then becomes Joram's last year and Jehu's 1st year, accounting for the L synchronism at 10:36+. The synchronisms responsible for this arrangement must, however, be secondary, as they conflict with the narrative.

Athaliah's regnal years are not given, but the information that Joash-J began to reign in Jehu's 7th year indicates that Athaliah reigned 6–7 years. Jehu reigned 28 years and was succeeded by Jehoahaz in Joash-J's 23rd year. Jehoahaz reigned 17 years and was succeeded by Joash-I, whose expected accession synchronism would be Joash-J's 39th year—but all the texts give 37th (39th appears only in late Greek manuscripts). The 39th is supported by the next synchronism: after Joash-J had reigned 40 years Amaziah succeeded him in Joash-I's 2nd year. The 37th is probably to be accounted for as a textual error.[6]

---

5. See §3.2.2 n. 2 (p. 42).
6. Acknowledged, e.g., by G. H. Jones, *1 and 2 Kings* (New Century Bible Commentary; Grand Rapids: Eerdmans, 1984), 501; T. R. Hobbs, *2 Kings* (Word Biblical Commentary 13; Waco: Word, 1985), 168.

Table 3.6. Divided Kingdom Timeline (cont.)

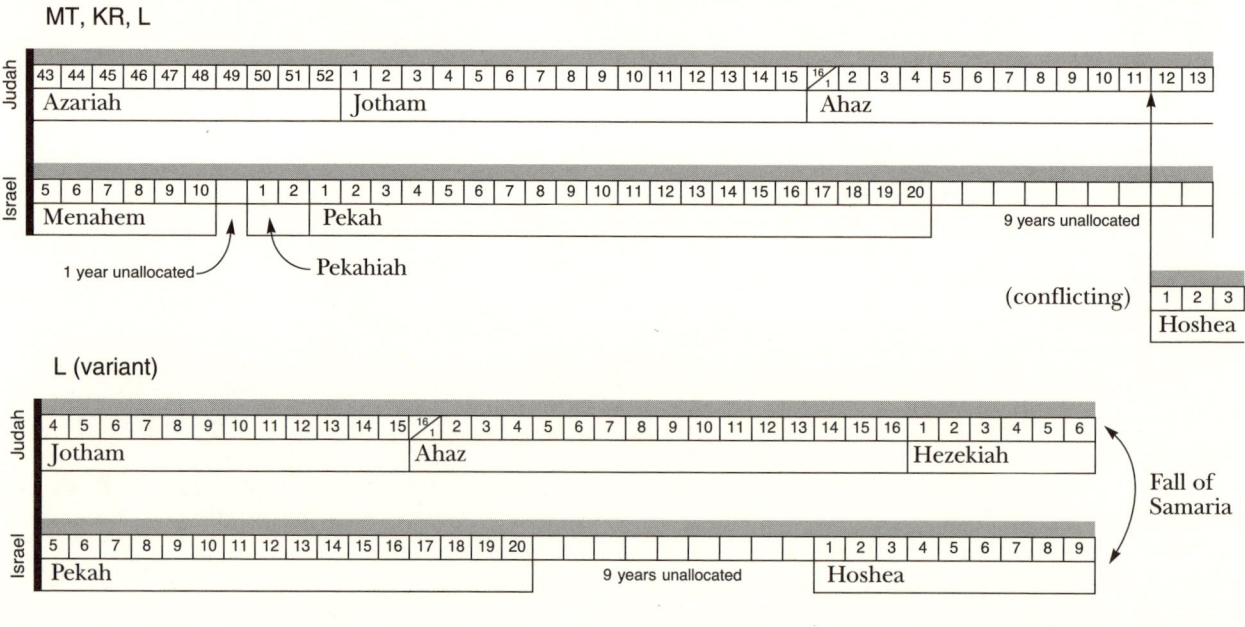

Josephus reduces Jehu's reign from 28 years to 27 and synchronizes Jehoahaz's accession with the 21st year (not 23rd) of Joash-J. After Jehoahaz reigned 17 years he was succeeded by his son Joash-I in Joash-J's 37th year (a discordant synchronism noted at 13:10 MT/KR/L). Josephus's shortening of Jehu's reign may be responsible for synchronizing Joash-I's accession with Joash-J's 37th year, but it is also possible that this synchronism was responsible for bringing into Josephus's text the variants of 27 years for Jehu and Jehoahaz's accession in Joash-J's 21st year. Josephus's variants appear to be secondary and therefore not helpful in reconstructing the chronology.

Since Amaziah reigned 29 years, the accession of his successor, Azariah, is expected in Jeroboam II's 14th or 15th year. The textual datum in 15:1–2, however, gives Jeroboam II's 27th year—12 years later. This can be explained as Amaziah's reigning another 12 years, an interregnum, or an incorrect synchronism. If the 27th is correct we would expect confirmation from the associated data. Instead, we are told that after Jeroboam II reigned 41 years he was succeeded by Zechariah in Azariah's 38th year. This leaves 22 unallocated years between Jeroboam II and Zechariah. There is no accession synchronism for Zechariah's accession in Azariah's 16th year, making dubious the reliability of Azariah's accession in Jeroboam II's 27th year.

Josephus has the variant data of Azariah's accession in Jeroboam II's 14th year. With this accession, Jeroboam II's 41st year then ends in Azariah's 28th year with Zechariah's accession. Josephus does not, however, give any synchronism for Zechariah (nor, indeed, any further synchronisms until the fall of Samaria). The synchronism at 15:8 MT/KR/L shows Zechariah's accession in Azariah's 38th year—not the anticipated 28th. Applying this synchronism to Josephus would leave 9 unallocated years from the end of Jeroboam II's reign to Zechariah's accession. Josephus

Table 3.6. Divided Kingdom Timeline (cont.)

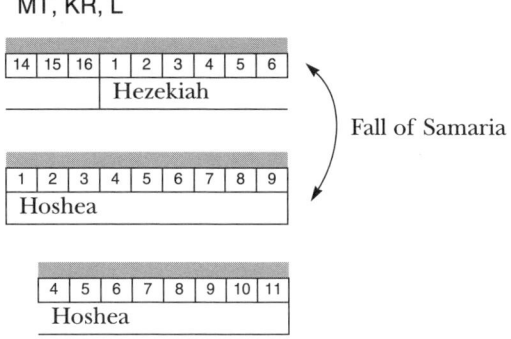

also gives Menahem only 10 years, leaving unallocated a year between Menahem's 10th year in Azariah's 48th year and Pekahiah's accession in Azariah's 50th year (15:23). Pekahiah's 2 years are then followed by Pekah's accession in Azariah's 52nd year (15:27). How can we explain these unallocated years?

An answer may be forthcoming from the L manuscripts, which provide a variant for the reign of Pekahiah. Second Kings 15:23 L gives Pekahiah a 10-year reign, MT/KR give him 2 years, and late Greek texts (Nc₂efmnp*qstwz; *CRD* 26) give him 12 years. Obviously, Pekahiah could not have reigned 10 or 12 years if his accession was in Azariah's 50th year and he was succeeded by Pekah in Azariah's 52nd year. This latter datum is supported by Jotham's accession the following year in Pekah's 2nd year. If, however, Pekahiah's reign is located to span 12 years ending at Azariah's 52nd year, Pekahiah's accession would be in Azariah's 40th year, and Menahem's reign would consequently begin 10 or 11 years earlier (the 11 including the previously unallocated year). This adjustment synchronizes Menahem's accession with Azariah's 29th year and is consistent with Azariah's accession in Jeroboam II's 14th year, as in Josephus's variant. The unallocated years between the end of Jeroboam II's reign and Zechariah's accession are eliminated, as well as the unallocated year between Menahem's 10th year and the accession of Pekahiah. Azariah's accession in Jeroboam II's 14th year seems more plausible than the 27th year given in MT/KR and L. Further analysis may confirm which, if either, is correct.

Jotham's accession in Pekah's 2nd year and his 16-year reign are consistent with Ahaz's accession in Pekah's 17th year. Ahaz, in turn, also reigns 16 years and is followed by Hezekiah's accession in Hoshea's 3rd year. Hezekiah's 4th year synchronizes with Hoshea's 7th and his 6th year with Hoshea's 9th (18:1, 9–10), which implies that most of Hezekiah's 1st year was in Hoshea's 4th year. If most of Hezekiah's 1st year had been in Hoshea's 3rd year the synchronisms for the siege and fall of Samaria would not align. Josephus's variants—otherwise unattested—for Hezekiah's accession in Hoshea's 4th year and the fall of Samaria in Hezekiah's 7th year are mutually exclusive.

Pekah's reign presents many problems. Pekah is given 20 regnal years, which indicates that his successor, Hoshea, ought to have begun to reign in Ahaz's 4th or 5th year, but this synchronism is not given. Instead, Hoshea has two conflicting accession synchronisms: at 15:30 MT/KR (absent in L) Hoshea is reported to have killed Pekah and become king in Jotham's 20th year, and at 17:1 in Ahaz's 12th year. A third contradiction is that if Hezekiah's accession was in Hoshea's 3rd year (18:1), then Hoshea's accession ought to have been in Ahaz's 14th year, not the 12th.

If Pekah reigned 20 years and was not succeeded by Hoshea until Ahaz's 12th or 14th year, 7–9 years are unallocated—which is inexplicable since Pekah was assassinated by Hoshea! Pekah's regnal years must have ended when Hoshea became king, and according to the synchronisms for Hezekiah's accession in Hoshea's 3rd year, this coincides with Ahaz's 14th year. If so, Pekah reigned 29 years. The synchronism for Hoshea's accession in Ahaz's 12th year seems to be a textual error for the 14th, and Pekah's regnal years appear to be incorrectly given as 20 instead of the more probable 29. This gives to Israel the same number of years as to Judah. Pekah's 29-year reign was reduced to 20 years in 15:27 MT/KR/L, which means that Pekah's reign ended in Ahaz's 4th year. But Hoshea's accession in Jotham's 20th year conflicts with the statement that Jotham reigned only 16 years (15:33). If, however, a secondary calculation had been made to give Hoshea an accession after Pekah's reign of only 20 years and not recognizing that Jotham reigned only 16 years and Ahaz had already reigned 4 years, it might have been thought that Jotham was in his 20th year when Hoshea killed Pekah and became king. The synchronism for Hoshea's accession in Ahaz's 12th year further on in the text at 17:1 may not have been noticed. The absence of the synchronism at 15:30 L suggests its secondary nature. (The issues surrounding the length of Pekah's reign and Hoshea's accession synchronism will be discussed again in §6.3.4.7 and §8.2.4.)

The above analyses indicate where the main problems lie in LDK chronology. Inconsistencies are associated with the reigns of Azariah, Jeroboam II, Zechariah, Shallum, Menahem, Pekahiah, and Pekah. Some proposed suggestions might help in reconstructing the chronology. If Azariah's accession is synchronized with Jeroboam II's 14th year, then Zechariah's accession synchronizes with Azariah's 28th year and Shallum's and Menahem's accessions with his 29th—all 10 years earlier than given in 15:8, 13, 17 MT/KR/L. This arrangement then leaves to Menahem an 11-year or 12-year reign (not 10) before Pekahiah's reign synchronizes with the 40th (not 50th) of Azariah. This gives to Pekahiah 12 regnal years (incorporating MT's 2 and L's 10) so that Pekah's accession synchronizes with Azariah's 52nd year as in 15:27 MT/KR/L. Attributing to Pekah 29 years instead of 20 years credits Israel with the same number of years as given to Judah. Further analysis may indicate whether these suggestions are valid.

3.2.4. Thiele's Approach to Accession Synchronisms

Thiele writes:

> In expressing synchronistic years, both Judah and Israel used their own systems for the years of the neighboring kings. Thus in Judah the lengths of reign of Judean kings were at this time expressed in terms of the accession-year system, and the synchronisms with the Israelite kings were also expressed by that system, although in Israel itself the nonaccession-year system was used. In Israel both the synchronisms with Judah and the lengths of reign of Israelite kings were expressed in terms of the nonaccession-year system. The rule was to use the system throughout the history of the two nations. (*MNHK*³ 49)

Table 3.7. Thiele's Chart 3 (*MNHK*³ 82)

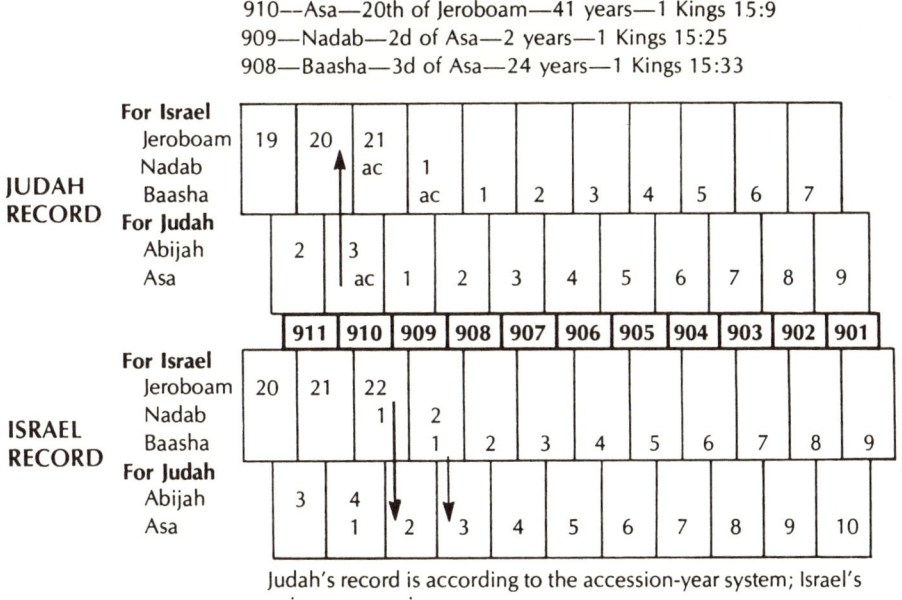

The application of these systems is seen in Thiele's chart 3 (reproduced as table 3.7 here).

Referring to Judah's record, Thiele credits Abijam with 3 years (plus an additional accession year in his predecessor Rehoboam's 17th year), and in his 3rd year Abijam is succeeded by Asa. The portion of year that Asa reigned before the next new year is termed his accession year, so that his 1st year begins with the next new year. Asa's accession year is thus synchronized with Jeroboam I's 20th year (1 Kgs 15:9). Asa has 41 regnal years as in 15:10, but his last three years are overlapped by Jehoshaphat's first 3 coregent years (*MNHK*³ 85 [chart 6, reproduced as my table 6.5, p. 109]).

Though Asa, king of Judah, is attributed his full 41 years (plus his accession year) using Judah's postdating system, the kings of Israel reckoned also by Judah's postdating system have one year deleted from the lengths of their reigns. For example, Jeroboam I is attributed only 21 years (plus an accession year) even though the text gives him 22 years (1 Kgs 14:20); the same applies to Nadab (1 regnal year instead of 2 [15:25]) and Baasha (23 years instead of 24 [15:33]). The synchronisms of Judah's kings with Israel's kings are expressed by Judah's accession-year system—but not their lengths of reign. The difference in length of reign is necessary since the actual date of death of each king had to coincide in each nation's method of reckoning. One year thus had to be deleted from Israel when reckoned according to Judah's record in order for the kings to have died at the same time when reckoned by Israel's system. By contrast, in Israel's system, using non-accession-year reckoning, Jeroboam I, Nadab, and Baasha have their accession year counted as their 1st year and they are given their full number of regnal years. According to this system, Jeroboam I's 22nd year is equivalent to his 21st year in Judah's accession-year system. Thiele's 1-year reduction to the reigns of Jeroboam I, Nadab, and Baasha are not attested in any text.

Looking at Israel's record, Nadab's accession (i.e., his 1st year in the antedating system) synchronizes with Asa's 2nd year, and Baasha's accession synchronizes with Asa's 3rd year. This is made possible only by giving Abijam 4 years (not 3). After Abijam died in his 4th year he was succeeded by Asa, and this portion of year before the next new year is then attributed to Asa's 1st year, regardless of how long or short it was. Israel's antedating system when applied to Judah's kings credits them with 1 year more than given in the text. Abijam thus has 4 years instead of 3, and Asa has 42 not 41 (*MNHK*³ 85)—but these numbers are hypothetical. On the other hand, Israel's system for Israel's kings attributes them the number of years given in the MT: Jeroboam I 22 years, Nadab 2 years, and Baasha 24 years (but their first years are only a portion of a year). In either system, the length of time reigned by each king is the same. It is just the numbering that is different.

Thiele's desire to use the MT data means that he cannot—if Jeroboam I reigned 22 years and Abijam reigned 3 years—merely juxtapose the years of Judah with the years of Israel and have Abijam's accession in Jeroboam I's 18th year, followed by Nadab's in Asa's 2nd year and Baasha's in Asa's 3rd year. Applying this same method (i.e., juxtaposing the years for Israel and Judah) to the OG/L data with its alternative variants accommodates the lengths of reigns and the synchronisms. Thiele devised a method to show Abijam's accession in Jeroboam I's 20th year according to one means of reckoning, and then with the alternate dating method he shows Nadab and Baasha's accessions in Asa's 2nd and 3rd years.

Thiele proposes that the reckoning systems he uses for the MT data were employed throughout the DK. The regnal formulas are to be interpreted according to whether they refer to a king of Israel or Judah. For example, the opening formulas for Abijam (1 Kgs 15:1) and Asa (15:9) are according to the record for Judah using its postdating system. But the opening formulas for Nadab (15:25) and Baasha (15:33) are according to Israel's antedating system. The regnal formulas, however, give no indication to this effect. To these hypothetical dating systems Thiele adds a further unsupported feature that at times Judah or Israel switched from one dating system to the other:

> Israel at the time of the schism followed the nonaccession-year system and continued its use till the close of the ninth century B.C. when under Jehoash [Joash-I] a shift was made to the accession-year system, which continued to be used to the close of Israel's history. Judah at the time of the schism used the accession-year system and continued its use to the middle of the ninth century; from Jehoram to Joash [Joash-J] reigns are reckoned according to the nonaccession-year system; and from Amaziah, at about the beginning of the eighth century, to the close of Judah's history the accession-year system was again in use. (*MNHK*³ 60)

Thiele thus claims that a shift was made from nonaccession-year reckoning in Israel to accession-year reckoning at the commencement of Joash-I's reign. But since there is no textual evidence for this shift, what basis does he have for saying this? Examining Thiele's charts 11–13 (*MNHK*³ 106, 109) may allow us to hazard a guess (reproduced as my tables 3.8–10).

Using nonaccession-year dating for both Israel and Judah, Thiele has Joash-J's 37th year end midway in Jehoahaz's 16th year in 799. But with Jehoahaz having a final 17th year how can Joash-I's accession be aligned with Joash-J's 37th year, as in the MT? Thiele's solution is to propose a shift in dating systems from nonaccession-year to accession-year dating, which results in Joash-J's being attributed a *second* 37th year, which overlaps the first half of Jehoahaz's 17th year according to nonaccession-year dating. Then using accession-year dating, Joash-I's accession year is synchronized with Joash-J's second 37th year in 798. Thiele's proposed shift has to be compared with the earlier analysis that the accession of Joash-I in Joash-J's 37th year could not be accommodated by the associated data, which were otherwise consistent, and that the 37th was

Table 3.8. Thiele's Chart 11 (*MNHK*³ 106)

823–811 B.C.

814—Jehoahaz—23d of Joash—17 years—2 Kings 13:1

	823	822	821	820	819	818	817	816	815	814	813	812	811
JUDAH Joash		14	15	16	17	18	19	20	21	22	23	24	25
ISRAEL Jehu / Jehoahaz	19	20	21	22	23	24	25	26	27	28 / 1	2	3	4

Tishri years for Judah; Nisan years for Israel
Nonaccession-year dating for both Israel and Judah

---

probably a textual error for 39th. If the 37th is an incorrect datum, then Thiele's efforts to explain it in terms of a shift in a nation's dating system lack credibility. Thiele's assertion of other shifts in dating systems during the reign of Jehoram and an opposing switch during the reign of Amaziah are likewise dubious (*MNHK*³ 57–59, 97–101, 105, 215).

Thiele also claims that coregencies were used frequently throughout the DK (see §6.3.4 for further discussion). For example, using the MT data he proposes a coregency to explain the synchronism of Azariah's accession in Jeroboam II's 27th year (2 Kgs 15:1). He theorizes that Amaziah, who reigned 29 years (14:2), had a coregency with his son Azariah for 24 years and only 5 years of sole reign (*MNHK*³ 109–10, 115–19). Since Azariah became king at 16 after the death of his father (14:21), Thiele has Azariah reigning before he was born! His solution is to make Azariah 16 when he became coregent, not when his father died:

> With the throne of Judah vacant when Amaziah was taken to Israel as a prisoner, the people made the sixteen-year-old Azariah king. This item is recorded at 2 Kings 14:21 and 2 Chronicles 26:1–3 as a postscript to the account of Amaziah's reign, but it should more properly have been placed immediately after the account of the war of Jehoash [Joash-I] with Amaziah at 2 Kings 14:8–14 and 2 Chronicles 25:21–24. (*MNHK*³ 119; cf. 109–10)

With no other corroborating evidence, Thiele transposes the text to make it accommodate his coregency theory. But this solution to the problem of Azariah's accession in Jeroboam II's 27th year is not plausible, especially when Josephus's variant has Azariah's accession in Jeroboam II's 14th year (noted by Thiele in chapter 10 of *MNHK*¹). Here again he imposes on Josephus's data his own dating systems: "Reckoning was always according to the accession-year or inconsequent accession-year system" (*MNHK*¹ 211). At the same time as assuming a coregency between Amaziah and Azariah in Judah, Thiele assumes a coregency between Joash-I and Jeroboam II in Israel:

> The simple facts are that when the Massoretic text places Azariah's accession in the twenty-seventh year of Jeroboam [II], it is passing on to us an extremely important bit of chronological information, and that is that there was a coregency in existence at this time between Jeroboam [II] and his father Jehoash [Joash-I]. In Josephus' modification of the figure for this synchronism from the twenty-seventh to the fourteenth year of Jeroboam [II], he cast away this vital evidence of this coregency, and instead of making the problem easier he made it far more difficult, leaving a chronological pattern as to lengths of reign that is widely at variance with the years of contemporary history. (*MNHK*¹ 222; similarly in subsequent editions)

Table 3.9. Thiele's Chart 12 (*MNHK*³ 106)

811–799 B.C.

	811	810	809	808	807	806	805	804	803	802	801	800	799
JUDAH Joash	25	26	27	28	29	30	31	32	33	34	35	36	37
ISRAEL Jehoahaz		4	5	6	7	8	9	10	11	12	13	14	15	16

Tishri years for Judah; Nisan years for Israel
Nonaccession-year dating for both Israel and Judah

Table 3.10. Thiele's Chart 13 (*MNHK*³ 109)

799–788 B.C.

798—Jehoash—37th of Joash—16 years—2 Kings 13:10
796—Amaziah—2d of Jehoash—29 years—2 Kings 14:1–2
793—Jeroboam II—start of coregency
792—Azariah placed on throne by people

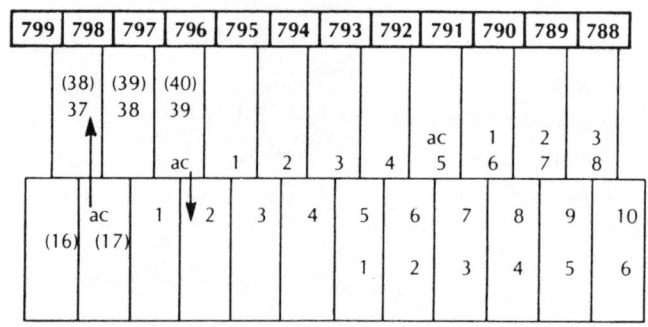

Tishri years for Judah; Nisan years for Israel
Accession-year dating for both Israel and Judah
Nonaccession-year dating in parentheses for Joash in Judah and Jehoahaz in Israel
Dual dating for Jeroboam II in Israel and Azariah in Judah

To the contrary, my analysis indicates that Azariah's accession in Jeroboam II's 14th year is more consistent when considered with the associated data. And since Josephus used proto-L in composing his *Antiquities*, the 14th may be an ancient datum.

Thiele's proposals for synchronisms reflect his use of the MT data. In 1951 he discussed the Greek data and concluded that they were late and inaccurate (*MNHK*¹ 202–3). In 1968 Shenkel urged that the Greek data be taken into account in reconstructing the chronology. But Shenkel's argument, which clearly deserved credence, was treated negatively by Thiele in 1974.[7] And in 1983 Thiele discussed the Greek data only in connection with the Omride period (*MNHK*³ 89–94; see my chapter 7).

---

7. E. R. Thiele, "Coregencies and Overlapping Reigns among the Hebrew Kings," *JBL* 93 (1974): 176–90.

Thiele uses the MT's two variant accession synchronisms for Joram—in Jehoram's 2nd year (2 Kgs 1:17; cf. 1:18a L) and in Jehoshaphat's 18th year (3:1; cf. 1:18a KR and 3:1 KR)—as evidence for his dating systems and explains the MT data as a coregency between Jehoram and Jehoshaphat. Because L omits the synchronism at 3:1 Thiele writes, "Thus the Greek translations have lost this valuable indication that there was a coregency between Jehoram and Jehoshaphat and the precise information regarding the year when it began" ($MNHK^3$ 210).

Thiele also uses the MT's variant accession synchronisms for Ahaziah-J—in Joram's 12th (8:25) and 11th (9:29) years (L has 11th year at both places)—as evidence for a shift in dating systems. Thiele writes, "Lucian lost the valuable clue that at this time a shift had been made in Judah from accession- to nonaccession-year reckoning" ($MNHK^3$ 210). My view is that variant numbers in the MT can be attributed to two textual traditions or systems without need for hypothetical coregencies or switches in dating systems.

4
Chronological Data in Manuscript c_2

According to Eugene Ulrich, manuscript c_2 dates from the 10th century C.E.[1] The other L minuscules (boe_2) date from the 11th to 14th centuries (§2.2.3.2), making c_2 the earliest extant L manuscript. Since in Samuel boe_2 and c_2 share readings with 4QSam^a, a 1st-century B.C.E. Hebrew text from Qumran (§2.2.1.2), we may analogously assume that the boc_2e_2 text in Kings derives from a similar *Vorlage*. L readings appear in Josephus's *Antiquities*, antedating Lucian by four centuries, indicating that these L minuscules exhibit a proto-L substratum.

Manuscript c_2 frequently exhibits chronological data that differ from that in the MT and boe_2. Shenkel's analysis of the c_2 data leads him to assert,

> The data of this manuscript are not to be accorded equal status with the chronological data of the other Lucianic manuscripts (boe_2) that for the most part preserve the Old Greek chronology. The chronological data of c_2 contribute nothing in fact to the determination of the early development of the Greek text. Apart from its late and artificial chronological system, however, c_2 is ordinarily a reliable witness to the Lucianic text, especially where it agrees with boe_2. (*CRD* 31)

Notwithstanding Shenkel's negative criticism, it is necessary to conduct my own analysis of the c_2 data (as listed in the apparatus of the Larger Cambridge Septuagint) to determine its contribution to DK chronology.

4.1. Regnal Years in the Divided Kingdom according to c_2

The EDK regnal years given in c_2 for Judah and Israel are set out in table 4.1. When MT and OG/L agree with each other, c_2 concurs with these text-types. When MT and OG/L differ, c_2 twice agrees with MT—3 years for Abijam (1 Kgs 15:2) and 22 years for Jeroboam I (14:20)—and once with L minuscules oe_2—10 years for Jehoram (2 Kgs 8:17). c_2 has 12 years for Joram at 1:18a in agreement with KR/L (MT is absent at 1:18a–d), and 11 years at 3:1, whereas MT/KR/L have 12 years, making 12 the better attested number.

In c_2 both Judah and Israel total 97 regnal years during the EDK if Joram is given 11 years. If Joram is given 12 years, then Israel has 98 years in c_2, which agrees with MT (table 3.1). On the other hand, OG/L total 100 years for both Judah and Israel during the EDK. The 3 additional years for Judah are accounted for by Abijam's having 6 years not 3 as in MT and c_2; and the 3 additional years for Israel are accounted for in 2 extra years given to Jeroboam I (24 not 22) and 1 extra year to Joram (12 not 11). The 97 years that c_2 gives to Judah is 2 years more than the 95 years in MT, a difference that is accounted for in c_2's giving Jehoram 10 years (MT has 8 years).

---

1. E. C. Ulrich, *The Qumran Text of Samuel and Josephus* (Harvard Semitic Monographs 19; Missoula, Mont.: Scholars Press, 1978), 21.

Table 4.1. Regnal Years in the Early Divided Kingdom according to c_2

Judah		Israel	
Rehoboam	17y	Jeroboam I	22y
Abijam	3y	Nadab	2y
Asa	41y	Baasha	24y
Jehoshaphat	25y	Elah	2y
Jehoram	10y	Zimri	7d
Ahaziah-J	1y	Omri	12y
		Ahab	22y
		Ahaziah-I	2y
		Joram	12y (or 11y)
EDK total	**97y**	**EDK total**	**98y (or 97y) 7d**

The LDK regnal years given in c_2 are set out in table 4.2. The number of years for Israel and Judah (to the fall of Samaria) are the same in c_2 (165 years), and c_2 gives the same number of years to each individual king of Judah as do MT/KR and L (table 3.2). For Israel, c_2 matches MT/KR and L for the first six kings (Jehu through Shallum), but the regnal years differ for the next three kings: Menahem has 12 years in c_2 (not 10), Pekahiah has 12 years (not 2 as in MT/KR or 10 as in L), and Pekah has 30 years (not 20). The c_2 data for Hoshea (9 years) matches MT/KR and L.

Table 4.2. Regnal Years in the Late Divided Kingdom according to c_2

Judah		Israel	
Athaliah	6y	Jehu	28y
Joash-J	40y	Jehoahaz	17y
Amaziah	29y	Joash-I	16y
Azariah	52y	Jeroboam II	41y
Jotham	16y	Zechariah	6m
Ahaz	16y	Shallum	1m
Hezekiah	6y	Menahem	12y
		Pekahiah	12y
		Pekah	30y
		Hoshea	9y
LDK total	**165y**		**165y 7m**

The chronology arising from Azariah's accession in Jeroboam II's 27th year seems discordant (see §3.2.3) and requires the 14th year given by Josephus (*Antiquities* 9.216), noted as 15th by c_2. This synchronism requires Menahem to have reigned 10–12 years, Pekahiah 12 years, and Pekah 29 years if the years of Israel are to match those of Judah. The agreement between MT/KR/L and

Table 4.3. Regnal Years in the Divided Kingdom according to c_2

	Judah	Israel
EDK subtotal	97y	98y (or 97y) 7d
LDK subtotal	165y	165y 7m
DK total	**262y**	**263y (or 262y) 7m 7d**

c_2 in Judah's regnal years suggests that c_2's figures should not be dismissed as late and artificial, as Shenkel does. If the Judahite figures are correct, the kings of Israel must, therefore, have reigned the same number of years. My proposed reconstruction of the data for Israel (§3.2.3) is supported by the data given by c_2. In fact, the c_2 figures for LDK Israel appear to indicate a deficiency in MT (143 years 7 months) and L (151 years 7 months). The totals for Judah in c_2 are 263 or 262 years (table 4.3)—not the MT's 260 or L's 265—and reflect the variants observed already in the EDK.

It does not necessarily follow that because Israel's regnal years equate with those of Judah in c_2 that all of c_2's numbers are authentic, for regnal years in c_2 variously concur with the MT data or L data. One could not expect the combination of two diverging systems to provide a correct chronology without further examination. The question still remains, which of the data given by MT/KR, OG, and boc_2e_2 are original?

4.2. Accession Synchronisms in the Divided Kingdom according to c_2

The DK regnal years and accession synchronisms given in c_2 are set out in table 4.4 (in exact alignment with that given by Shenkel in *CRD* 29–30). Manuscript c_2 synchronizes Abijam's 1st year with Jeroboam I's 18th year and gives Jeroboam I a 22-year reign in agreement with 15:1 MT. Nadab's accession, however, is synchronized with Asa's 3rd year, not the 2nd as in 15:25 MT/OG/L. Asa's accession in c_2 is synchronized with Jeroboam I's 21st year, not the 20th as in 15:9 MT or 24th in 15:9 OG/L. In c_2, after Nadab's 2-year reign, his successor, Baasha's 1st year is synchronized with Asa's 4th year at 15:28 and with Asa's 5th year at 15:33 (the 5th year is shown on table 4.4 [p. 58], which conforms to the preceding and subsequent synchronisms).

The synchronisms for Asa's accession in Jeroboam I's 21st year, Nadab's accession in Asa's 3rd year, and Baasha's accession in Asa's 5th year are unique to c_2 and indicate how its chronology was compiled. A regnal year of a king of Judah was matched with a regnal year of a king of Israel (or vice versa). Thus, Rehoboam's 17 years are aligned with Jeroboam I's first 17 years; and Abijam's 3 years are aligned with his 18th, 19th, and 20th years. Asa's 1st year is then aligned with Jeroboam I's 21st year, Nadab's 1st year is matched with Asa's 3rd year, and Baasha's 1st year with Asa's 5th year. In other words, the compiler reckoned the kings' years as rounded or full regnal years, even final years that are not normally full years (unless the king died on the same date as his accession)—in contrast to the texts presented in the previous chapter, where kings began their reigns *in* the regnal year of the king with which their accession synchronized and recognizing partial final years. This artificial alignment of matching regnal years, year by year, for each DK king seems to be responsible for c_2's unique synchronisms (it remains to be seen how the compiler dealt with reigns of less than a full year).

Following this practice, Baasha's 24-year reign (15:33) is followed by Elah's 1st year, which is aligned with Asa's 29th year (16:6) and thus creates another synchronism unique to c_2. Elah is given 2 full years (16:8) so that Zimri's 7 days and Omri's 1st year are aligned with Asa's 31st year (16:23).[2]

Asa's 41-year reign (15:10) is followed by Jehoshaphat's 1st year, which is aligned with Omri's 12th (11th at 16:28a OG/L; not in MT). Omri's final year was his 12th, so Ahab, his successor, begins his reign in Jehoshaphat's 2nd year (16:29 OG/L). Ahab reigns 22 years (16:29), and his successor, Ahaziah-I, has his reign aligned with Jehoshaphat's 24th year (22:52 L; 17th year in MT).

Jehoshaphat reigns 25 years (16:28a OG/L, including c_2; 22:42 MT), so that Ahaziah-I's 2 regnal years end at the same time as Jehoshaphat's reign. This creates another unique c_2 synchronism that aligns the first years of Jehoram and Joram, whereas the other L minuscules synchronize Joram's 1st year with Jehoram's 2nd year (2 Kgs 1:18a). Jehoram's 1st year thus begins in Ahaziah-I's 2nd year, but this synchronism is absent from all texts. Its counterpart at 8:16 MT/c_2 has Jehoram's accession in Joram's 5th year, but Joram's 5th year cannot be accommodated to c_2's other data and therefore cannot have originated with c_2.

The alignment of Joram's 1st year with Jehoram's 1st year creates problems for subsequent alignments. Extrapolating the L data for Jehoram's reign means that Jehoram should have reigned 11–12 years (§3.2.2). Now that Joram's and Jehoram's reigns begin at the same time, however, Jehoram's reign has to be reduced to 10 years if Ahaziah-J's accession is to synchronize with Joram's 11th year (8:25 and 9:29 in other L manuscripts; MT has 12th at 8:25 and 11th at 9:29). One year later Ahaziah-J and Joram both die at the hands of Jehu, bringing the EDK to an end. The reduction of the reign of Jehoram from 11 to 10 years has its counterpart in Joram's reign being reduced from 12 to 11 years, since no year is allotted in Judah to correspond with Joram's 12th year—a reduction that creates c_2's unique variant of 11 years for Joram at 3:1.

After Athaliah's 6-year reign, Joash-J's accession is aligned with Jehu's 7th year (as in 12:1/2 MT/KR/L), followed by Jehoahaz's accession in Joash-J's 23rd year (13:1) and Joash-I's accession in Joash-J's 40th and last year (13:10). MT/KR/L synchronize this last accession with Joash-J's 37th year, which seemed erroneous because the next synchronism, Amaziah's accession in Joash-I's 2nd year, requires Joash-I's accession to be previously synchronized with Joash-J's 39th year. The difference of 1 year downward in c_2 (from 39th to 40th) can be attributed to partial final years being reckoned as full years. This alignment then allows c_2 to synchronize Amaziah's accession with Joash-I's 2nd year (as in 14:1 MT/KR/L), which implies that Joash-J's 40th year was not a full year. By aligning Amaziah's accession at the same time as the *beginning* of Joash-I's 2nd year, when it should have been during ("*in* the 2nd year of"), other secondary synchronisms emerge: Jeroboam II's synchronism in Amaziah's 15th year (14:23 MT/KR/L) is moved down 1 year in c_2 to Amaziah's 16th year; and in turn this aligns Azariah's accession with Jeroboam II's 15th year when the 14th (Josephus, *Antiquities* 9.216) would have been appropriate.

Azariah's accession in MT/KR/L synchronizes with Jeroboam II's 27th year, an erroneous synchronism because it agrees neither with previous nor subsequent synchronisms. Concurring with its previous synchronism of Azariah's accession in Jeroboam II's 15th year, c_2 aligns the accession of Zechariah with Azariah's 28th year. Zechariah's 6-month reign is followed by Shallum's accession still in Azariah's 28th; and after Shallum's 1-month reign, Menahem's accession is also

---

2. In §3.2.2 I queried how Asa's 31st year could have originated as an accession synchronism for Omri (1 Kgs 16:23). In c_2 Omri's accession is synchronized with Asa's 31st year because of c_2's alignment practice. While the alignment does not explain why the 31st appears in MT and OG/L with their different associated data, the c_2 alignment may suggest a possible origin for this datum. I return to this issue in §7.2.3.

Table 4.4. Divided Kingdom Timeline according to c_2

[Timeline chart showing regnal years of Judah and Israel kings]

Judah: Rehoboam (1-17) | Abijam (1-3) | Asa (1-18...)
Israel: Jeroboam I (1-22) | Nadab (1-2) | Baasha (1-14...)

Judah: Jehoshaphat (17-25, 1-10) | Jehoram (1-10) | Ahaziah-J (1) | Athaliah (1-6) | Joash-J (1-12...)
Israel: Ahab (16-22) | Ahaziah-I (1-2) | Joram (1-11) | Jehu (1-18...)

Judah: Amaziah (9-29) | Azariah (1-17...)
Israel: Joash-I (10-16) | Jeroboam II (1-31...)

Judah: Jotham (5-16) | Ahaz (1-16) | Hezekiah (1-6...) — Fall of Samaria
Israel: Pekah (6-30) | Hoshea (1-9)

aligned with Azariah's 28th year.[3] This arrangement may be compared with that of MT/KR/L, which positions the accessions of these kings 10 years later.

c_2 credits Menahem with a 12-year reign, not 10 years (15:17 MT/KR/L). The accession of his successor, Pekahiah, is synchronized with Azariah's 40th year, not the 50th (15:23 MT/KR/L), and his reign ends after 12 years (cf. MT's 2 and L's 10). Pekah's accession is then synchronized with Azariah's 52nd year (15:27 MT/KR/L), so that at this point the texts again concur. This agreement is short-lived, however, as Pekah is credited with a 30-year reign in c_2, not 20 years as in MT/KR/L. The 30 years does, however, match year for year the reigns of Jotham and Ahaz, taking

---

3. The c_2 redactor took into account that the reigns of Zechariah and Shallum consisted only of months and did not attribute to them separate years.

Table 4.4. Divided Kingdom Timeline according to c_2 (cont.)

19	20	21	22	23	24	25	26	27	28	29	30	31	32	33	34	35	36	37	38	39	40	41	1	2	3	4	5	6	7	8	9	10	11	12	13	14	15	16
Asa																							Jehoshaphat															

15	16	17	18	19	20	21	22	23	24	1	2	1	2	3	4	5	6	7	8	9	10	11	12	1	2	3	4	5	6	7	8	9	10	11	12	13	14	15
Baasha										Elah		Omri												Ahab														

↑ Zimri (7 days)

13	14	15	16	17	18	19	20	21	22	23	24	25	26	27	28	29	30	31	32	33	34	35	36	37	38	39	40	1	2	3	4	5	6	7	8	9	10	11
Joash-J																												Amaziah										

19	20	21	22	23	24	25	26	27	28	1	2	3	4	5	6	7	8	9	10	11	12	13	14	15	16	17	1	2	3	4	5	6	7	8	9	10	11	12
Jehu										Jehoahaz																	Joash-I											

18	19	20	21	22	23	24	25	26	27	28	29	30	31	32	33	34	35	36	37	38	39	40	41	42	43	44	45	46	47	48	49	50	51	52	1	2	3	4
Azariah																																			Jotham			

32	33	34	35	36	37	38	39	40	41	1	2	3	4	5	6	7	8	9	10	11	12	1	2	3	4	5	6	7	8	9	10	11	12	1	2	3	4	5
Jeroboam II										Menahem												Pekahiah												Pekah				

↑ ↑
Zechariah Shallum
(6 months) (1 month)

into account Ahaz's 1-year displacement, in that his 1st year is aligned with Ahaz's 18th year instead of the 17th (16:1 MT/KR/L).

The 20 years credited to Pekah in MT/KR/L do not span the corresponding period attributed to the kings of Judah, which requires 29 years for Pekah. The 1-year downward displacement attributed to Ahaz's accession accounts for the 30 years that c_2 gives to Pekah, instead of the proposed 29. It appears that c_2's method was applied to an earlier 29, which gives some support to its being original.

In c_2 Hoshea's accession is aligned with Ahaz's 14th year (not the 12th), a synchronism proposed in §3.2.3 on the basis of the associated data.[4] Hezekiah's accession is aligned with Hoshea's 4th year (also in Josephus, *Antiquities* 9.260), not the 3rd. c_2's alignment agrees with the following MT/KR/L synchronisms (18:9–10) that the siege against Samaria began in Hezekiah's 4th year (= Hoshea's 7th year) and that Samaria fell in Hezekiah's 6th year (= Hoshea's 9th year). Unexpectedly, c_2 gives Ahaz's 10th year instead of Hezekiah's 6th year, which is clearly impossible and must be explained as scribal error.[5]

---

4. An alternative synchronism in 15:30 MT/KR for Hoshea's accession in Jotham's 20th year is not given by c_2 or the other L manuscripts.

5. c_2 has δεκάτῳ τοῦ Ἀχάζ instead of ἕκτῳ τῷ Ἐζεκίᾳ.

4.3. Conclusions concerning c_2 Data

The above analysis shows that the c_2 redactor juxtaposed the years of Judah and Israel on a year-for-year basis but did not take into account that final years should be calculated as partial years. He used the MT regnal years for Abijam (3) and Jeroboam I (22), which caused new synchronisms for the accessions of Asa, Nadab, Baasha, Elah, Zimri/Omri, and Jehoshaphat. The alignment for Jehoshaphat's accession in Omri's 12th year is displaced downward by only 1 year from the OG/L synchronism for Omri's 11th year. The next synchronism, Ahab's accession in Jehoshaphat's 2nd year, matches the OG/L datum. From here to the end of the EDK, c_2 concurs with the data of the other L synchronisms for Jehoshaphat, Ahab, Ahaziah-I, and Ahaziah-J, but for Joram and Jehoram in the manner previously described.

During the LDK, MT/KR and L exhibit the same data for the reigns of Judah, and c_2 matches them year for year for the reigns of Israel (in MT/KR/L more years are credited to Judah than to Israel), except for the *faux pas* of c_2's final synchronism (the fall of Samaria in Ahaz's 10th year).

My analysis of the chronological data in chapter 3 resulted in almost the same chronology displayed by c_2 (even if the displacement of some of the reigns and synchronisms by 1 year in c_2 causes minor differences). It may be that c_2 is the sole witness to data that have been lost from MT/KR/L. Further analysis is needed to determine if the actual regnal years of the kings have been retained or whether some may be secondary.

4.4. Scholarly Discussion of c_2

The chronological data of c_2 are discussed by Thiele, Shenkel, Galil, and others.[6] I now consider their conclusions in the light of my above analysis.

4.4.1. Thiele and Shenkel

Thiele's first edition of *MNHK* copied the Greek variants from Burney's *Notes on the Hebrew Text of the Book of Kings*.[7] Burney did not recite the c_2 numbers, and Thiele consequently omitted reference to them in *MNHK*[1] and *MNHK*[2]. Shenkel, however, discusses c_2 in treating the chronological data in the Books of Kings (*CRD* 27–35), and Thiele responds to him in his article "Coregencies and Overlapping Reigns among the Hebrew Kings."[8]

Shenkel notes that although c_2 is normally "characterized by its assimilation to the hexaplaric recension, [it] has a unique and highly artificial chronological system" (*CRD* 27). Seeking to find a dating system for the c_2 data, he compares c_2's method with antedating and postdating, which he says were "in use not only in Israel, but in the other kingdoms of the ancient Near East as well" (*CRD* 28). He then proposes that c_2 had a different method known as "inconsequent accession-year dating" (*CRD* 28), a term used by Thiele in *MNHK* to describe the dating system he applied to the Greek texts.[9] Shenkel too applies this dating method to the kings in two principles that he believed were followed by c_2:

---

6. E.g., W. R. Wifall, "The Chronology of the Divided Monarchy of Israel," *Zeitschrift für die alttestamentliche Wissenschaft* 80 (1968): 319–37; J. Hughes, *Secrets of the Times: Myth and History in Biblical Chronology* (Journal for the Study of the Old Testament Supplement 66; Sheffield: JSOT Press, 1990), 119–21.

7. C. F. Burney, *Notes on the Hebrew Text of the Books of Kings* (Oxford: Clarendon, 1903), xli–xliv. See *MNHK*[1] 169.

8. E. R. Thiele, "Coregencies and Overlapping Reigns among the Hebrew Kings," *JBL* 93 (1974): 174–200.

9. Thiele notes that a similar method had been earlier proposed by scholars to help clear up chronological difficulties (*MNHK*[1] 172 n. 3). See also Galil, *CKIJ* 130–31 n. 14.

The artificial character of the inconsequent accession-year method of dating is evident. Unless every king were to die precisely on New Year's Day (whenever that may have been in the respective kingdoms) there would have been an interregnum after the death of every king during the unfulfilled part of his last year because the accession year of the new king is identical with the first full year of the new king and begins with the royal New Year.

Once this system of inconsequent accession-year dating has been set in motion by the redactor of c_2 on the basis of initial data supplied by the MT, it is carried out with absolute consistency. As a result the occasional agreements of c_2, now with the other Lucianic manuscripts, now with B, now with the MT, or finally, with other late Greek chronological systems, are purely coincidental. (*CRD* 28)

Shenkel then diagrams c_2's regnal years for Judah and Israel in two parallel rows and states that this diagram "illustrate[s] the inconsequent accession-year method of reckoning" (*CRD* 29). He does not identify which synchronisms agree "now with the other Lucianic manuscripts, now with B, now with the MT, or finally, with other late Greek chronological systems." According to my analysis, c_2 initially follows the MT data for the regnal years of Abijam and Jeroboam I, creating its unique synchronisms for Nadab through Omri. From the accessions of Ahab and Jehoshaphat to the end of the EDK it follows the OG/L pattern, adjusting as necessary for its year-for-year approach. During the LDK the L data cannot be distinguished from MT data except for Pekahiah's regnal years, and in this period Vaticanus (= KR) is the same as MT. c_2 has its own variant data for the reigns of Zechariah, Shallum, Menahem, Pekahiah, and Pekah. Shenkel's statement, therefore, seems to be based on an inadequate analysis of the c_2 data.

The c_2 data suggest that they are based on a *Vorlage*, such as Josephus used, possibly L, that had Azariah's accession in Jeroboam II's 14th year. The c_2 data for Zechariah, Shallum, Menahem, Pekahiah, and Pekah — seen as late and artificial by Shenkel (*CRD* 31) and others — may have come from this *Vorlage* also. My analysis shows that the c_2 data are not the result of an inconsequent accession-year method of dating but arise from a year-for-year alignment based predominantly on L data where L differs from the MT; this alignment is not "purely coincidental." c_2's unique data may be valuable witnesses to the original chronology.

Shenkel's assertion that the c_2 data were based on the inconsequent accession-year method was subsequently used by Thiele to buttress his prior argument that the Greek chronological pattern was "a late, artificial, and highly deceptive contrivance."[10] But, Shenkel makes a distinction between the status of OG/boe$_2$ and c_2, arguing that the former "far from being the artificial contrivance of late scribal activity, was the earliest chronology in the Greek textual tradition" (*CRD* 110).

4.4.2. Galil

Gershon Galil's 1996 comments about c_2 are pertinent to our discussion:

The author of c_2 attempts to confirm, as much as possible, all the data in MT relating to years of reign, while modifying them to conform to the above-mentioned synchronistic system. Thus, e.g., in order to resolve the discrepancy of three years between the count of the years of Israelite kings from the coronation of Omri to the rebellion of Jehu (48) and the count of the Judahite kings in this period (45), he shortened Joram's reign from 12 to 9 years, while extending the reign of Jehoram of Judah by two years, from 8 to 10. (*CKIJ* 131)

Contrary to Galil, c_2 was not using MT data throughout. The only specific MT data not also shared by OG/L (or only L if OG is not present) in c_2 are the years attributed to Abijam (3) and

---

10. Thiele, "Coregencies and Overlapping Reigns," 182.

Jeroboam I (22). Data that differ from MT are either based on OG/L or, having no other attested source, may be considered as sole witnesses to a nonextant *Vorlage* or as variants unique to c_2.

Galil attributes to c_2's modification of the MT data the shortening of Joram's reign from 12 to 9 years. But since Joram has 12 regnal years in 2 Kgs 1:18a KR/L (MT being absent) and at his second regnal formula in 3:1 c_2 gives him 11 years, Galil's comment appears to be unsubstantiated (he does not provide a reference for the 12-year to 9-year variant). Galil also asserts that c_2 extended Jehoram's reign from 8 years to 10, but c_2 is not the only manuscript with 10 years (also oe_2). As proposed earlier, 8 years follows the MT datum, and 10 years the L data, but the OG datum requires at least 11 years (*CRD* 77, 82). In this case, Jehoram's reign has not been extended by 2 years, but has been *reduced* by 1 year. If the Greek data are earlier than the MT, then the MT has reduced 11 years to 8 and not the other way around. Galil's comments seem to be based on an inadequate understanding of the c_2 and other L data, while showing a preference for the MT data.

Another point by Galil concerns the discrepancy between Judah's 165 years during the LDK and Israel's 143 years 7 months. "In order to bridge this gap," Galil writes, "c_2 extends the reigns of three Israelite kings: Menahem, Pekahiah, and Pekah. He allots 12 years to Menahem, instead of the 10 in MT; 12 years to Pekahiah (MT: 2); and 30 years to Pekah (MT: 20)" (*CKIJ* 131). Galil's statement that c_2 *extended* the years for these three kings does not acknowledge that the MT might be deficient. Galil's assumption is probably explained by a footnote concerning the reign of Pekahiah:

> The most striking difference between the data of MT and those in the Septuagint for the period from the rebellion of Jehu to the conquest of Samaria is the count of the years of Pekahiah. MT and MS. B count 2 years for him; the Lucianic manuscripts boe_2 and MS. Agr, 10 years; and c_2 and many other manuscripts, 12 years. It is inconceivable, however, that Pekahiah ruled 10 or 12 years. These data contradict not only other data stated by these same manuscripts, but also the Assyrian chronological data which indicate that Menahem, the father of Pekahiah, offered tribute to Assyria also in 738, and that Hoshea gave tribute in the city of Sarabanu in 731. Consequently, Pekahiah and Pekah could not have ruled more than 7 years. (*CKIJ* 129 n. 10)

Galil's first point, that a 10-year or 12-year reign for Pekahiah contradicts the other data, can be said just as forcefully in reverse. As shown in the year-for-year alignment, Pekahiah's reign requires 12 years in order to agree with the years given for Judah. This concurs with c_2's previous attribution of Azariah's accession in Jeroboam II's 15th year rather than the 27th (as in 2 Kgs 15:1 MT/KR/L), but the 27th does not agree with the synchronism of Jeroboam II's accession in Amaziah's 15th year (14:23). This in turn places the accession of Zechariah, Shallum, and Menahem in Azariah's 28th year, not the 38th/39th as in 15:8, 13, 17 MT. This arrangement allows Menahem 11–12 years, Pekahiah 12 years, and Pekah 29–30 years, whereas the MT still has a 22-year deficit for Israel (143 years) as against Judah (165 years).

But the crux of Galil's argument lies in his second point: that the years of Pekahiah and Pekah cannot be made to synchronize with Menahem's offering tribute to Assyria in 738 and Hoshea's giving tribute in 731 (the latter being Galil's date for Hoshea's accession year; *CKIJ* 82). These dates are not proven and remain open to debate. Like Thiele, Galil assumes that Menahem paid tribute to Tiglath-pileser III (745–727).[11] This assumption requires that at least one or more years of Menahem's reign, all of Pekahiah's reign (2 years according to Galil, using the MT datum), and all of Pekah's reign must fit between 745 and 731, a space of 14 years. Obviously, the years given

---

11. See §1.3.4 for the reason Menahem is considered to be a contemporary of Tiglath-pileser III.

by c_2 to Menahem, Pekahiah, and Pekah will not allow this, so Galil assumes that c_2's regnal years for Pekah must be erroneous.[12] Yet 2 Kings 15 gives no indication that Menahem was contemporary to Tiglath-pileser III (15:29 mentions that Pekah and Tiglath-pileser were contemporary). If Menahem is not contemporaneous with Tiglath-pileser III, there is no need to assume that the c_2 figures for Pekahiah and Pekah are impossible. Galil's assertion (*CKIJ* 65) that Pekahiah and Pekah could not have reigned more than 7 years (2 and 5 years respectively) contradicts even the MT datum that credits Pekah with a 20-year reign. Galil's reconstruction of the text is far more presumptive than c_2, about which he says, "The chronology of c_2 is undoubtedly lacking any historical value" (*CKIJ* 133).

4.4.3. Significance of c_2

Manuscript c_2 provides important insights to consider when reconstructing DK chronology. Its special significance lies in the variant regnal years and synchronisms it gives for Israel during the troubled LDK period. In addition, c_2 has the same number of years for Israel as for Judah in the LDK, and the total for Judah in all texts is 165 years. At least this Judahite part of the c_2 data cannot, therefore, be singled out as being "late and artificial."

c_2 is the only extant text to give synchronisms and regnal years that provide an internally consistent chronology for this period. The accession synchronism for Azariah in Jeroboam II's 15th year is 1 year later than Josephus's datum, and Ahaz's accession in Pekah's 18th year is 1 year later than the datum in MT/KR and L, but both are caused by c_2's year-for-year alignment. The intermediate synchronisms of Zechariah's, Shallum's, and Menahem's accessions in Azariah's 28th year and Pekahiah's in Azariah's 40th year are the only extant textual representatives of these data. c_2's chronology concurs again with MT/KR/L at the accession of Pekah in Azariah's 52nd year and Jotham's accession a year later in Pekah's 2nd year. c_2 also witnesses to the variant of Hoshea's accession in Ahaz's 14th year, given as the 12th in the other texts.

The matching regnal years and synchronisms given for the kings of Israel and Judah may well derive from an early Greek (formerly Hebrew) text. That c_2 "is ordinarily a reliable witness to the Lucianic text, especially where it agrees with boe$_2$" (*CRD* 31) should caution us against dismissing its data too readily as not having any chronological value. Even if these variant data are late efforts at harmonization, they at least illustrate one way to reconstruct the regnal years in Israel to agree with those in Judah.

---

12. Elsewhere Galil writes, "Pekah undoubtedly did not reign for 20 years as a sole monarch, since ca. 7 years elapsed between the giving of tribute by Menahem (year 8 of Tiglath-pileser III – 738) and by Hoshea in year 15 of Tiglath-pileser III (731)" (*CKIJ* 65).

5

Regnal Formulas

The narratives in the Books of Kings attest to having been collated from earlier records that were apparently in existence when 1–2 Kings was composed: "Are they not written in the Book of the Chronicles/Annals of the kings of Israel/Judah?" Such annals functioned as official registers of details about the monarchy and contained significant events pertaining to a king's reign, including accession, death, and succession. The compiler of the Books of Kings thus had sources with established and recognized credibility from which to copy regnal data and narrative material. These separate annals for Judah and Israel provided the author(s) of Kings with the historical data from which to compose theological narrative.[1]

Analyzing the regnal formulas—both opening and closing—may reveal information about the original compositions that will help determine which data are original and which are secondary in the Hebrew and Greek texts. Investigation of supplementary material contained within or between closing and opening formulas will help place the formulas within the original compilation and determine their conformity to the books' literary framework (i.e., inconsistent or irregular positioning of an opening and closing formula may indicate an area of reworked and secondary text). Evaluating the sequence of the reigns in Israel and Judah in the Hebrew and Greek narratives will help determine which sequence is most likely original. And observation of how the Hebrew verb מלך was translated in the regnal formulas in OG, L, and KR may also yield clues about which data are primary or secondary.

5.1. Patterns of Opening and Closing Formulas

Examining the regnal formulas to determine what patterns, if any, can be isolated may help identify primary and secondary text. E. Ulrich asks,

> How can we explain the variety in the text and how unravel or determine the "authentic" text? Or in other words, among the myriad variants displayed by our witnesses to the text of the OT are there *patterns* discernible which can provide the intelligibility for the development of the text? Are there *patterns* discernible which can provide the link between the earliest texts and our presently varying witnesses?[2]

---

1. See M. Haran, "The Books of the Chronicles 'of the Kings of Judah' and 'of the Kings of Israel': What Sort of Books Were They?" *VT* 49 (1999): 162–64.
2. E. Ulrich, "Horizons of Old Testament Textual Research at the Thirtieth Anniversary of Qumran Cave 4," *Catholic Biblical Quarterly* 46 (1984): 620 (emphasis original).

5.1.1. Opening Formulas

Two patterns of opening formulas can be distinguished in the Books of Kings (*CRD* 48–50). Each formula typically consists of three components: accession statement, duration statement, and assessment statement (table 5.1).

Table 5.1. Opening Formulas

	Pattern 1	Pattern 2
Accession Statement	now in the 18th year of King Jeroboam I son of Nebat, Abijam began to reign over Judah	Nadab son of Jeroboam I began to reign over Israel in the 2nd year of King Asa of Judah
Duration Statement	he reigned for 3 years in Jerusalem	and he reigned over Israel 2 years
Assessment Statement	and he walked in all the sins that his father did before him	he walked in all the way of Asa his father

In pattern 1, represented by Abijam's opening formula at 1 Kgs 15:1-2, the accession synchronism always precedes the name of the king whose formula is being given. Sometimes, the age of the king of Judah at accession is cited (e.g., Jehoshaphat at 1 Kgs 16:28a OG/L; Jehoram at 2 Kgs 8:17; Joash-J at 12:1 MT; and all subsequent kings of Judah to the fall of Jerusalem). The name of the king's mother is usually given for Judah (Ahaz is an exception in 2 Kgs 16:1-2), but not for Israel. Pattern 1 ends with an assessment of the king's reign, whether good or evil, etc.[3] In pattern 2, represented by Nadab's formula at 1 Kgs 15:25, the accession synchronism always follows the name of the acceding king. But neither their age at accession nor their mother's name is given for kings of Israel.

Patterns 1 and 2 are fairly similar, with the main difference being the position of the accession synchronism: pattern 1 places the synchronism to the regnal year of the neighboring king before the name of the acceding king; pattern 2 has the acceding king's name before the synchronism. Pattern 2 occurs far less frequently than pattern 1 (see table 5.5) and for only one king of Judah (Jehoshaphat at 1 Kgs 22:42 MT/KR). Whichever pattern commences a king's account, the narrative itself consists of selected events from his reign, typically including accounts of various wars, prophetic denunciations of evil kings, and excerpts from the ministries of prophets like Elijah and Elisha. The account may be no more than a paragraph or two (e.g., Nadab at 1 Kgs 15:27-30; Pekahiah at 2 Kgs 15:25), or it may extend over several chapters (e.g., Ahab at 1 Kgs 16:31-22:38; Joram at 2 Kgs 3:4-8:15).

---

3. For discussion of regnal formulas, see S. R. Bin-Nun, "Formulas from Royal Records of Israel and of Judah," *VT* 18 (1968): 414-32; R. D. Nelson, *The Double Redaction of the Deuteronomistic History* (Journal for the Study of the Old Testament Supplement 18; Sheffield: JSOT Press, 1981), 29-36; W. H. Barnes, *Studies in the Chronology of the Divided Monarchy of Israel* (Harvard Semitic Monographs 48; Atlanta: Scholars Press, 1991), 138-40; A. F. Campbell, *Of Prophets and Kings: A Late Ninth-Century Document (1 Samuel 1-2 Kings 10)* (Catholic Biblical Quarterly Monograph Series 17; Washington, D.C.: Catholic Biblical Association of America, 1986), 139-68; M. A. O'Brien, *The Deuteronomistic History Hypothesis: A Reassessment* (Orbis Biblicus et Orientalis 92; Göttingen: Vandenhoeck & Ruprecht, 1989), 180-85; B. Halpern and D. S. Vanderhooft, "The Editions of Kings in the 7th-6th Centuries B.C.E.," *Hebrew Union College Annual* 62 (1991): 183-203; B. O. Long, *1 Kings with an Introduction to Historical Literature* (Forms of Old Testament Literature 9; Grand Rapids: Eerdmans, 1984), 160-61.

5.1.2. Closing Formulas

The account of a king's reign is usually followed by a closing regnal formula. Judah has one basic pattern (pattern A), and Israel has two (pattern A and pattern B [in two varieties: pattern B1 and pattern B2]).

5.1.2.1. Pattern A

Pattern A (table 5.2), represented for Judah by Abijam's closing formula at 1 Kgs 15:7–8 and for Israel by Omri's closing formula at 16:27–28, begins with a referral notice indicating sources: "Now the rest of the acts of *x* are they not written in *y*?" This may be followed by a supplementary notice, and the formula then concludes with the death, burial, and succession notices. Each king is succeeded by a son, with one exception: Ahaziah-J was succeeded by his mother, Athaliah. Only Athaliah has no opening or closing formula, and Ahaziah-J has no proper closing formula.[4]

Table 5.2. Closing Formula: Pattern A (Kings of Judah and Israel Succeeded by a Son)

	Judah	Israel
Referral Notice	now the rest of the acts of Abijam and all that he did, are they not written in the Book of the Chronicles of the Kings of Judah?	now the rest of the acts of Omri which he did, and the might he showed, are they not written in the Book of the Chronicles of the Kings of Israel?
Supplementary Notice	and there was war between Abijam and Jeroboam I	—
Death Notice	and Abijam slept with his fathers [OG/L add: in the 24th year of Jeroboam I]	and Omri slept with his fathers
Burial Notice	and they buried him in the city of David	and they buried him in Samaria
Succession Notice	and Asa his son reigned after him	and Ahab his son reigned after him

The supplementary notice—found in pattern A only for Judahite kings—gives a short explanatory comment about a king's reign. Jehoram (2 Kgs 8:23–24), Azariah (15:6–7), and Ahaz (16:19–20) do not have supplementary notices in their closing formulas. A slight change occurs in pattern A for three kings[5] who were killed in battle or palace conspiracies (Ahaziah-J in 9:27–28, Joash-J in 12:21–22, and Amaziah in 14:19–20): their death and burial notices are combined: "buried *x* with his fathers in the city of David." The words *slept with his fathers* are not applied to Ahaziah-J or Joash-J, but 14:22 applies the phrase to Amaziah when noting that Azariah built and restored Elah to Jerusalem after "the king [Amaziah] slept with his fathers."

---

4. After Athaliah had ruled 6 years, she was slain, and Joash-J, 7-year-old son and heir of Ahaziah-J, was placed on the throne (2 Kgs 11:1–12:1). Ahaziah-J does not have a proper closing formula at 9:28. The referral, supplementary, and succession notices are absent, and only the death and burial notices appear.

5. Jeroboam I of Israel is an exception at 1 Kgs 14:20 MT (absent in OG/L). His regnal years, 22, are included as a supplementary notice in his closing formula because he has no opening formula.

The death notice in 1 Kgs 15:8 OG/L that Abijam died in Jeroboam I's 24th year is the only instance of a king's year-of-death synchronism in pattern A. The presence of the synchronism in 15:8 may have been prompted by the absence in OG/L of the opening regnal formula for Jeroboam I, which appears in 14:19–20 MT (where the length is 22 years), which is absent in OG/L. Or, the synchronism may be a dittograph brought up from the next verse: "in the 24th year of Jeroboam I" (15:9 OG/L). The absence of other synchronisms like this for Judah suggests that the death notice in 15:8 OG/L is not part of the original text.

For Israel, the referral notice comes first, followed by the death notice ("slept with his fathers").[6] The burial notice may be absent, as for Jeroboam I (1 Kgs 14:20), Jeroboam II (2 Kgs 14:29), and Menahem (15:22). The succession notice ("his son reigned after him") comes last. Pattern A is used whether the king died of natural causes or from injury. Ahab, for example, died from wounds received in battle (1 Kgs 22:35–37) but the closing formula follows pattern A, except that the burial notice is absent in 22:40, having already been given in 22:37 after the account of the king's death. Ahab "slept with his fathers" and was succeeded by his son Ahaziah-I.[7]

5.1.2.2. Pattern B

Israel's pattern B applies to assassinated kings who were not succeeded by a son and to Zimri, who committed suicide to avoid being killed by Omri's troops (1 Kgs 16:17–20). In pattern B the formulas begin with the death notice, which relates that the king was killed. But death is not indicated by the phrase *he slept with his fathers* as in pattern A. The death notice is followed by the succession notice ("reigned in his place"; but not for Zimri). The succession notice may be followed by a supplementary notice, but the burial notice is absent. Pattern B concludes with a referral notice ("now the rest of the acts of *x*"), and an additional supplementary notice may then appear.

Pattern B has two versions (table 5.3). Pattern B1 applies to the reigns of two assassinated kings: Nadab (1 Kgs 15:28–31) and Elah (16:10–14), and to Zimri. The referral notice is presented as a question (as in pattern A).

In pattern B1 the death notice appears first. In 1 Kgs 15:28 all texts have a death synchronism for Nadab, but at 16:10 the death synchronism for Elah appears only in the MT ("in the 27th year of Asa" is absent in OG/L). In MT the same 27th year is used as an accession synchronism for Zimri's reign at 16:15; but L (be$_2$) has a conflicting accession synchronism for Zimri in Asa's 22nd

---

6. The instances are Jeroboam I (1 Kgs 14:20), Baasha (16:6), Omri (16:28), Ahab (22:40), Jehu (2 Kgs 10:35), Jehoahaz (13:9), Joash-I (14:16), Jeroboam II (14:29), and Menahem (15:22).

7. Maxwell Miller argues that the phrase *slept with his fathers* refers only to kings of Israel who met a natural death. He seeks to identify the anonymous king of Israel who went with Jehoshaphat to fight the Syrian army at Ramoth-gilead and was slain (1 Kgs 22:1–38) as Jehoahaz, not Ahab. Miller states "the deuteronomist was apparently unaware that Ahab met an untimely death"; "The Elisha Cycle and the Accounts of the Omride Wars," *JBL* 85 (1966): 444–45. Halpern and Vanderhooft concur with Miller's argument ("Editions of Kings," 230–33). See also S. L. McKenzie, *The Trouble with Kings: The Composition of the Book of Kings in the Deuteronomistic History* (Vetus Testamentum Supplement 42; Leiden: Brill, 1991), 88–93; Galil, *CKIJ* 34–36 and n. 4. Amaziah also met a violent death, was succeeded by his son, and "slept with his fathers" (2 Kgs 14:19–22). Josiah was killed by Pharaoh Neco, and his son Jehoahaz succeeded him (23:29–30), but it is not said of Josiah that "he slept with his fathers." Jehoiakim also *slept with his fathers* (2 Kgs 24:6) but suffered a violent death (2 Chr 36:6; Jer 22:18–19; 36:30–31; Ezek 19:8–9). It seems that the phrase merely indicates that the king died and may be used of kings who died by natural or violent means. Since most of the kings of Judah died natural deaths, their deaths are indicated by the phrase *he slept with his fathers*. To claim, as Miller does, that Ahab was not the king of Israel at the battle of Ramoth-gilead merely on the basis that he "slept with his fathers" and therefore did not die a violent death is to press unwarranted meaning into a regnal formula phrase.

Table 5.3. Closing Formula: Pattern B1 (Assassinated Kings of Israel Not Succeeded by a Son)

	Nadab	Elah
Death Notice	so Baasha killed [Nadab] in the 3rd year of King Asa of Judah	Zimri came in and struck [Elah] down and killed him [MT only: in the 27th year of King Asa of Judah]
Succession Notice	and reigned in his place	and reigned in his place
Supplementary Notice	[15:29–30 relates that Baasha killed all the house of Jeroboam I]	[16:11–13 relates that Zimri destroyed the house of Baasha]
Referral Notice	now the rest of the acts of Nadab and all that he did, are they not written in the Book of the Chronicles of the Kings of Israel?	now the rest of the acts of Elah and all that he did, are they not written in the Book of the Chronicles of the Kings of Israel?
Additional Supplementary Notice	there was war between Asa and Baasha all their days [15:32 MT]	—

year (OG omits the synchronism). The death notice is followed by the succession notice, which in turn is followed by a supplementary notice and the referral notice. The referral notice concludes the closing formula for Elah (16:14 OG/L/MT), but 15:32 MT (OG/L is absent) has an additional supplementary notice about war between Asa and Baasha after Nadab's closing formula and before Baasha's opening formula at 15:33.

Pattern B2 applies to four kings in 2 Kings 15 (Zechariah, Shallum, Pekahiah, and Pekah) and is represented by Zechariah's closing formula at 15:10–12 (table 5.4).

Table 5.4. Closing Formula: Pattern B2 (Assassinated Kings of Israel Not Succeeded by a Son)

Death Notice	Shallum son of Jabesh conspired against [Zechariah] and struck him down at Ibleam and killed him
Succession Notice	and reigned in his place
Referral Notice	now the rest of the acts of Zechariah, behold, they are written in the Book of the Chronicles of the Kings of Israel
Supplementary Notice	[15:12 relates the promise the Lord gave to Jehu]

In pattern B2 the death notice appears first, followed by the succession notice. Unlike pattern B1 in 1 Kgs 15:28 MT and 16:10 MT, pattern B2 does not include a synchronism for the year of death but concurs instead with 16:10 OG/L in *not* having a year-of-death synchronism in a succession notice. One B2 accession synchronism that could also be interpreted as a year-of-death synchronism appears after Pekah's succession notice before his referral notice at 2 Kgs 15:30: "Hoshea . . . slew him and reigned in his place in the 20th year of Jotham" (this MT synchronism is absent in L; OG is not extant). Hoshea has another conflicting accession synchronism ("in the 12th year of Ahaz") in its expected place at 17:1 at the beginning of the opening formula. The synchronisms found only in 1 Kgs 16:10 MT and 2 Kgs 15:30 MT with their variant data seem dubious as part of the original regnal formulas pattern. The only closing formula in OG/L (and MT) in pattern B that has a death synchronism in the death notice is Nadab's at 1 Kgs 15:28. Again, its irregularity implies its addition to all texts. The absence in OG/L of these death (or accession) synchronisms in death notices increases doubt about their inclusion in the original compilation.

In pattern B2 the referral notice is a statement (הנם כתובים), not a question (הלא־הם כתובים), and applies to Zechariah (15:11), Shallum (15:15), Pekahiah (15:26), and Pekah (15:31), whereas the other kings in 2 Kings 15 follow pattern A (Azariah in 15:6, Menahem in 15:21, and Jotham in 15:36). The predominance of pattern A referral notices throughout 1–2 Kings suggests that the pattern B2 referral notices in 2 Kings 15 are the work of another hand.[8]

In pattern B2 some supplementary notices appear after the referral notice: Zechariah (15:12) and Shallum (15:16), but not Pekahiah (15:26) and Pekah (15:31). The absence of supplementary notices in some closing formulas in pattern B2 and their differing distribution where they do appear in patterns B1 and B2 also raises doubt that supplementary notices were part of the original pattern.

Ahaziah-I's closing regnal formula (2 Kgs 1:17–18) does not fall into either pattern A or B. Ahaziah-I injured himself falling from an upstairs room and, because he had no son, was succeeded by his legitimate heir and brother, Joram. Joram's accession seems to warrant a pattern A formula but the formula more closely conforms to pattern B (death notice, succession notice, and referral notice) even though Ahaziah-I was not assassinated—at least not that we know (cf. 1:16). Perhaps the unusual circumstances of Ahaziah-I's death dictated the use of the pattern B closing formula. On the other hand, the two-pattern presentation of closing formulas may be based more on literary style than on intention to distinguish two groups of successors. Whatever the reason, since Ahaziah-I's is the only formula to differ from the two observed patterns, we cannot be sure that this regnal formula remains in its original format. As we will see in §5.3.7, this formula has been reworked to include a synchronism for Joram's accession.

The closing regnal formula of Joram is absent in all texts. Since Joram was killed by Jehu (2 Kgs 9:23–24), who succeeded him, the expected closing formula, if present, would follow pattern B1 or B2.

Patterns B1 and B2 are not dissimilar. If (a) the referral notices of B2 are retroverted to a question as in pattern B1, (b) the year-of-death notices are removed from the MT closing formulas (and 1 Kgs 15:28 OG/L), and (c) the supplementary notices are recognized as additions to the original pattern, then patterns B1 and B2 appear to derive from a single template applied to kings who were assassinated.

5.2. Distribution of Opening Formulas

The distribution of opening regnal formulas throughout 1–2 Kings is displayed in table 5.5 (where L refers to manuscripts boe_2 [i.e., excluding c_2]). Pattern 1 (beginning with the accession synchronism) predominates, with pattern 2 (beginning with the name of the acceding king) occurring for only six kings but in seven positions:

1. 1 Kgs 15:25 MT/OG/L gives Nadab's accession in Asa's 2nd year.
2. 1 Kgs 22:41 MT/KR has Jehoshaphat's accession in Ahab's 4th year, whereas 16:28a OG/L has pattern 1 and synchronizes Jehoshaphat's accession to Omri's 11th year.

---

[8]. The referral notice is also a statement at 1 Kgs 14:20 MT (absent in OG/L) for Jeroboam I, but in a pattern A formula.

Table 5.5. Distribution of Opening Regnal Formulas

Reference	Text-Type			Pattern	Statement
1 Kgs 15:1	MT	OG	L	1	in the 18th year of Jeroboam I, Abijam began to reign
1 Kgs 15:9	MT			1	in the 20th year of Jeroboam I, Asa began to reign
		OG	L	1	in the 24th year of Jeroboam I, Asa began to reign
1 Kgs 15:25	MT	OG	L	2	Nadab began to reign in the 2nd year of Asa
1 Kgs 15:33	MT	OG	L	1	in the 3rd year of Asa, Baasha began to reign
1 Kgs 16:6		OG	L	1	in the 20th year of Asa, Elah began to reign
1 Kgs 16:8	MT			1	in the 26th year of Asa, Elah began to reign
1 Kgs 16:15	MT			1	in the 27th year of Asa, Zimri began to reign
		OG		-	[absent]
			L (be$_2$)	1	in the 22nd year of Asa, Zimri began to reign
1 Kgs 16:23	MT	OG	L	1	in the 31st year of Asa, Omri began to reign
1 Kgs 22:41	MT	KR		2	Jehoshaphat began to reign in the 4th year of Ahab
1 Kgs 16:28a		OG	L	1	in the 11th year of Omri, Jehoshaphat began to reign
1 Kgs 16:29	MT			2	Ahab began to reign in the 38th year of Asa
		OG	L	1	in the 2nd year of Jehoshaphat, Ahab began to reign
1 Kgs 22:52	MT	KR		2	Ahaziah-I began to reign in the 17th year of Jehoshaphat
			L	1	in the 24th year of Jehoshaphat, Ahaziah-I began to reign
2 Kgs 1:17	MT			*	Joram reigned after him in the 2nd year of Jehoram
2 Kgs 1:18a		KR		*2	Joram began to reign over Israel 12 years in the 18th year of Jehoshaphat
			L	*2	Joram began to reign over Israel 12 years in the 2nd year of Jehoram
2 Kgs 3:1	MT	KR		2	Joram began to reign in the 18th year of Jehoshaphat
			L	-	[absent]
2 Kgs 8:16	MT	KR	L	1	in the 5th year of Joram, Jehoram began to reign
2 Kgs 8:25	MT	KR		1	in the 12th year of Joram, Ahaziah-J began to reign
			L	1	in the 11th year of Joram, Ahaziah-J began to reign
2 Kgs 9:29	MT	KR	L	1	in the 11th year of Joram, Ahaziah-J began to reign
2 Kgs 10:36+			L	1	in the 2nd year of Athaliah, Jehu began to reign
2 Kgs 12:1/2	MT	KR	L	1	in the 7th year of Jehu, Joash-J began to reign
2 Kgs 13:1	MT	KR	L	1	in the 23rd year of Joash-J, Jehoahaz began to reign
2 Kgs 13:10	MT	KR	L	1	in the 37th year of Joash-J, Joash-I began to reign
2 Kgs 14:1	MT	KR	L	1	in the 2nd year of Joash-I, Amaziah began to reign

Table 5.5. Distribution of Opening Regnal Formulas (cont.)

Reference	Text-Type			Pattern	Statement
2 Kgs 14:23	MT	KR	L	1	in the 15th year of Amaziah, Jeroboam II began to reign
2 Kgs 15:1	MT	KR	L	1	in the 27th year of Jeroboam II, Azariah began to reign
2 Kgs 15:8	MT	KR	L	1	in the 38th year of Azariah, Zechariah reigned 6 months
2 Kgs 15:13	MT			2	Shallum began to reign in Uzziah's [Azariah's] 39th year; he reigned 1 month
		KR		*2	Shallum began to reign; in the 39th year of Azariah, Shallum reigned several days
			L	*2	Shallum began to reign in Samaria a month of days in the 39th year of Azariah
2 Kgs 15:17	MT	KR	L	1	in the 39th year of Azariah, Menahem began to reign
2 Kgs 15:23	MT	KR	L	1	in the 50th year of Azariah, Pekahiah began to reign
2 Kgs 15:27	MT	KR	L	1	in the 52nd year of Azariah, Pekah began to reign
2 Kgs 15:32	MT	KR	L	1	in the 2nd year of Pekah, Jotham began to reign
2 Kgs 16:1	MT	KR	L	1	in the 17th year of Pekah, Ahaz began to reign
2 Kgs 17:1	MT	KR	L	1	in the 12th year of Ahaz, Hoshea began to reign
2 Kgs 18:1	MT	KR	L	1	in the 3rd year of Hoshea, Hezekiah began to reign

* Denotes irregular patterns.

3. 1 Kgs 16:29 MT has Ahab's accession synchronism in Asa's 38th year, whereas 16:29 OG/L has pattern 1 and synchronizes Ahab's accession to Jehoshaphat's 2nd year.
4. 1 Kgs 22:52 MT/KR gives Ahaziah-I's accession in Jehoshaphat's 17th year, but 22:52 L uses pattern 1 to synchronize Ahaziah-I's accession to Jehoshaphat's 24th year.
5. 2 Kgs 3:1 MT/KR (L is absent) gives Joram's accession in Jehoshaphat's 18th year, which matches the synchronism in 1:18a KR. On the other hand, 1:17 MT and 1:18a L give an alternative synchronism for Joram's accession in Jehoram's 2nd year. The irregular patterns at 1:18a KR/L (absent in MT) begin with the name of the king, also suggesting conformity to the MT pattern 2 at 3:1.
6. 2 Kgs 15:13 MT gives Shallum's accession in Azariah's 39th year. KR and L give the same synchronism using an irregular pattern 2. L also gives Azariah's 39th year, but uses a formula that shows partial conformity to the MT.

The predominance of pattern 1 over pattern 2 suggests that pattern 1 is more likely original. Of the six occurrences of pattern 2 in MT, only the first (Nadab at 1 Kgs 15:25) and last (Shallum at 2 Kgs 15:13) have the same accession synchronism in OG/L. The other four synchronisms show variation between MT/KR (KR is not extant at 1 Kgs 16:29) and OG/L (L alone where OG is not extant). Since Joram's accession at 2 Kgs 3:1 has pattern 2 and shows evident reworking of text at

1:18a KR/L, giving alternative synchronisms, then we must consider that Shallum's synchronism at 15:13 may also have been reworked in KR and L toward conformity with the MT and might earlier have exhibited pattern 1 with an alternative synchronism.

If in fact Shallum's synchronism was altered from the original, then Nadab's synchronism remains the only pattern 2 in OG/L with the same data as the MT. Since pattern 2 is normally associated with MT/KR data, its occurrence in 1 Kgs 15:25 OG/L for Nadab's accession gives evidence that Nadab's accession in Asa's 2nd year is secondary, having been altered from the original (not now extant) to conform with the MT. Since the year-of-death synchronism for Nadab in Asa's 3rd year appears in a closing formula that was also suspect, it is possible that both Nadab formulas contain secondary text.[9] And if the synchronisms for Nadab and Shallum are incorrect, any following synchronisms that depend on them may also be suspect (e.g., Menahem's accession in Azariah's 39th year; 2 Kgs 15:17).

5.3. Supplementary Notices

After examining the patterns and distribution of regnal formulas in 1–2 Kings, it is appropriate to return to the question of whether supplementary notices that occur within or between closing and opening formulas were part of the original compilation of the Books of Kings.

5.3.1. Rehoboam

The first example of a supplementary notice in a closing regnal formula exclusive of 1 Kgs 14:20 MT previously noted in §5.1.2.1 (n. 5, p. 66) appears in 1 Kgs 14:30 MT/OG/L between Rehoboam's referral notice and death notice: "There was war between Rehoboam and Jeroboam I all the days." This comment is repeated in 15:6 MT (OG/L is absent), which adds "of his life," but it is inappropriate there because it comes under Abijam's narrative and Rehoboam has already died.[10] The appropriate supplementary notice for Abijam appears in his closing formula at 15:7 between his referral and death notices: "There was war between Abijam and Jeroboam I." The absence of a reference to Rehoboam and Jeroboam I in 15:6 OG/L and the presence of a reference to Abijam and Jeroboam I in 15:7 suggests that 15:6 MT is secondary.

A similar supplementary notice appears after Nadab's closing formula in 15:32 MT (absent in OG/L): "There was war between Asa and King Baasha of Israel all their days." At 15:16 MT/OG/L the same notice appears to introduce the war between Asa and Baasha, but here it is not in a regnal formula. The absence of 15:32 OG/L and the presence of all three texts at 15:16 suggests that 15:32 MT is an addition to Nadab's closing formula. Without this addition, the referral notice in 15:31 concludes Nadab's closing formula and Baasha's opening formula immediately follows, as it still does in OG/L. No death notice ("slept with his fathers") follows the referral notice in 15:32 because the assassination of Nadab by Baasha was recounted at 15:28 (pattern B1). Since

---

9. Bin-Nun writes ("Formulas from Royal Records," 426), "It stands to reason that the records of a king, whether annals or entries in a king-list, began with the king's name or with his regnal year, but not with the name and year of a neighbouring king, not even if they were on friendly terms. The parallel phrasing of all synchronisms for the kings of Judah and nearly all the kings of Israel and their place at the head of the formulas disclose a later hand, that attempted to bring all the kings of both states under a common frame." She regards the pattern for the five kings of Israel and Jehoshaphat of Judah as "more authentic" (427). My analysis indicates that pattern 1 (synchronism first) is most likely the pattern used by the compiler of Kings and that pattern 2 (acceding king's name first), with alternative chronological data, is secondary.

10. The supplementary notice appears in late Greek manuscripts; in the Syro-Hexaplar, it is under the Hexaplaric asterisk and attributed to the version of Aquila.

15:32 is in the same relative position as in Rehoboam's closing formula at 14:30 and Abijam's closing formula at 15:7, one might argue for the original positioning of the supplementary notice at 15:32, but the absence of 15:6 and 15:32 in OG/L makes one wonder whether 14:30, 15:6, 15:7, 15:16,[11] and 15:32 are all additions after the initial compilation of the text of 1 Kings.

5.3.2. Asa

A supplementary notice about Asa's diseased feet appears between the referral and death notice in his closing formula at 1 Kgs 15:23 MT/OG/L.[12]

5.3.3. Nadab and Elah

Nadab's closing formula at 1 Kgs 15:29–30 MT/OG/L contains a supplementary notice that Baasha killed all the house of Jeroboam I. Elah's closing formula at 16:11–13 MT/OG/L contains a similar supplementary notice that Zimri destroyed the house of Baasha. Both of these supplementary notices separate a death notice from a referral notice.

5.3.4. Baasha

Similar to the supplementary notices for Nadab and Elah, Baasha's closing formula at 1 Kgs 16:6–8 MT/OG/L contains a lengthy intrusion (v. 7) recording the prophet Jehu's denunciation of Baasha: "Moreover the word of the Lord came by the prophet Jehu son of Hanani against Baasha and his house, both because of all the evil that he did in the sight of the Lord, provoking him to anger with the work of his hands, in being like the house of Jeroboam I, and also because he destroyed it." Examination of Baasha's closing formula (table 5.6) may throw light on whether the supplementary notices in 15:29–30 and 16:11–13 are original.

If 16:7 MT were absent, Baasha's closing formula would be followed immediately by Elah's opening formula: "And Elah his son reigned after him; in the 26th year of King Asa of Judah, Elah son of Baasha began to reign over Israel." In contrast to my above analysis of closing and opening formulas, which found that the succession notice is the last element of a closing formula and that the accession synchronism is the first element in an opening formula, OG/L conflate into a single sentence Baasha's succession statement and Elah's accession statement: "Elah his son reigned after him in the 20th year of King Asa of Judah" (OG omits "of Judah"). OG/L's conflated succession/accession statement (16:6b) is also separated from Elah's opening duration statement (16:8) by the intrusion of Jehu's denunciation of Baasha (16:7). This insertion is obviously responsible for separating the accession synchronism into two parts (now 16:6 and 16:8), for 16:7 is located *within* Elah's accession statement, causing the first part of the statement containing the accession synchronism to follow Baasha's succession statement as though it was part of his closing formula. If Jehu's denunciation of Baasha was originally in the text at 16:7, the accession synchronism in 16:8 could not have become transposed to 16:6 because the presence of 16:7 would have prevented this happening; 16:7 was, therefore, added after the original text was compiled.

What might have caused 16:7 to be positioned within the accession statement in OG/L? In a typical set of opening and closing formulas, the succession statement in a closing formula ("his

---

11. This verse conflicts with 2 Chr 15:19: "There was no war until the 35th year of Asa." If 1 Kgs 15:16 is not original it might resolve the conflict with 2 Chr 15:19. A further problem is the mention of Asa's 35th year and his 36th year in the following verse (2 Chr 16:1); see §7.3.5.

12. The parallel account at 2 Chr 16:12–13 gives additional information that Asa's feet became diseased in his 39th year and he died in his 41st year (MT; 40th in Vaticanus).

Table 5.6. Baasha's Closing and Elah's Opening Formulas (1 Kgs 16:6–8 MT/OG/L)

MT	Baasha's Closing Succession Notice	and Elah his son reigned after him
	Baasha's Supplementary Notice	moreover the word of the Lord came . . . against Baasha . . . he destroyed it
	Elah's Opening Accession Statement	in the 26th year of King Asa of Judah, Elah son of Baasha began to reign over Israel
	Elah's Opening Duration Statement	2 years in Tirzah
OG	Baasha's Closing Succession Notice	and Elah his son reigned (βασιλεύει) after him
	Elah's Opening Accession Synchronism	in the 20th year of King Asa
	Baasha's Supplementary Notice	moreover the word of the Lord came . . . against Baasha . . . he destroyed it
	Elah's Opening Duration Statement	and Elah son of Baasha reigned (ἐβασίλευσεν) over Israel 2 years in Tirzah
L	Baasha's Closing Succession Notice	and Elah his son reigned (ἐβασίλευσεν) after him
	Elah's Opening Accession Synchronism	in the 20th year of King Asa of Judah
	Baasha's Supplementary Notice	moreover the word of the Lord came . . . against Baasha . . . he destroyed it
	Elah's Second Opening Accession Synchronism	in the [ ] King Asa of Judah
	Elah's Opening Duration Statement	and Elah son of Baasha reigned (ἐβασίλευσεν) over Israel 2 years in Tirzah

son Elah reigned after him") is followed by the accession ("in the 20th year of King Asa of Judah, Elah son of Baasha began to reign over Israel") and duration ("and he reigned 2 years in Tirzah") statements in an opening formula. In other words, we expect the typical formula in the Hebrew text to contain three instances of the verb מלך (italicized in table 5.7).

In 16:6–8 MT, where we expect to find three verbs, there are only two; the third occurrence of מלך has been omitted, so that "2 years in Tirzah" appears without a verb (English translations may not reflect this omission). This produces the rendering "Baasha began to reign over Israel 2 years in Tirzah," which is incongruent. If the Hebrew *Vorlage* of OG/L also omitted the third מלך, it would have been easier for 16:7 to intrude into the accession statement in these text-types.

Normally, in the OG section of 1 Kings (in which 16:6–8 is found), OG and L translate the second מלך (began to reign) with the historical present βασιλεύει and the third instance of מלך (he reigned *x* years) with the aorist ἐβασίλευσεν (*CRD* 51). In 16:8 OG/L the anomalous single מלך is translated with the aorist and placed in the duration statement, consistent with its normal usage. Thus "Elah son of Baasha began to reign over Israel" is replaced by "and Elah son of Baasha reigned over Israel 2 years in Tirzah," at least producing a complete sentence. As a result, Elah's accession synchronism no longer made sense at the beginning of this sentence: "In the 20th year of King Asa, Elah son of Baasha began to reign over Israel 2 years in Tirzah." It made more sense at the end of Baasha's closing formula: "His son Elah succeeded him in the 20th year of Asa."

The attachment of Elah's accession synchronism to Baasha's succession notice at the end of Baasha's closing formula, followed by a new sentence starting with Elah's duration of reign statement, seems to have been the arrangement of the text prior to the insertion of the supplemen-

Table 5.7. Hypothetical Original of 1 Kgs 16:6–8 according to the Typical Format

Closing Succession Notice	and Elah his son *reigned* after him.
Opening Accession Statement	In the 20th year of King Asa of Judah, Elah son of Baasha *began to reign* over Israel
Opening Duration Statement	and he *reigned* 2 years in Tirzah

tary notice about Jehu's denunciation of Baasha. The supplementary notice was entered between what appeared to be two consecutive sentences so that 16:7 now intrudes into the middle of an opening formula in OG/L.

The MT arrangement is not typical either. The MT places Jehu's denunciation of Baasha (16:7) after his succession statement and before Elah's accession synchronism, thus separating the opening formula from the closing formula, which is nonetheless better placed than in OG/L. The accession synchronism that Elah acceded the throne in Asa's 26th year is at variance with OG/L's 20th year. One (or both) of these accession synchronisms must be secondary.

With wording that combines MT and OG, the L text is also peculiar. L duplicates Elah's accession statement at 16:6 and 16:8 (though here the year is left blank)[13] and then begins a new sentence (as in OG) with "and Elah son of Baasha reigned over Israel 2 years in Tirzah." The duplicate accession synchronism in 16:8 may have been added at a late stage of transmission in order to bring L into conformity with MT. But since MT's 26th year conflicted with L's own 20th year, already stated in 16:6, the year may have been omitted in 16:8. If this analysis is correct, the OG/L datum for Elah's accession in the 20th year more likely reflects the original than MT's 26th year. In conformity with my preliminary findings, 16:8 MT is suspected of having changed its data rather than OG/L (though here pattern 1 is used in all text-types). By analogy, therefore, similar supplementary notices in Nadab's closing formula at 15:29–30 and Elah's at 16:11–13 may not form part of the original compilation of the narratives in Kings.

5.3.5. Omri

A supplementary notice explaining how Omri became king (1 Kgs 16:21–22) separates Zimri's closing formula (16:20) and Omri's opening formula (16:23): "And Tibni died *and Jehoram his brother at that time*, and Omri reigned *after Tibni*" (italic type indicates OG/L's longer text). Reworking has occurred, but we cannot tell whether in MT or OG/L. As in previous cases, without the supplementary notice the closing formula of one king would be followed immediately by the opening formula of the next king.

5.3.6. Jehoshaphat

Jehoshaphat's narrative and regnal formulas appear in 1 Kgs 16:28a–h OG/L and 22:41–51 MT. Between his referral and death notices, a supplementary notice recounts his extermination

---

13. Concerning the MT rendering of the accession synchronism at 16:8, S. J. De Vries writes, "G^B omits; G^L 'in the (reign) of Asa of Judah.' G^L attempts awkwardly to supply the omission seen in G^B, which cannot be regarded as original vis-à-vis MT because its aorist rendering (ἐβασίλευσεν 'reigned') for MT מלך is not in conformity with G^B's normal and undoubtedly original Gr., the OG historical pres, seen in 15:1, 9, 25, 33, 16:28 (βασιλεύει 'reign')"; *1 Kings* (Word Biblical Commentary 12; Waco: Word, 1985), 196. Contrary to De Vries, my analysis shows that the omission should be filled with the synchronism, not the word *reign*. In addition, the use of the aorist is correct when it refers to the duration statement in OG/L, which is its use in 16:8, as discussed above. See *CRD* 51–52.

of cult prostitutes, the absence of the Edomite king, and Jehoshaphat's boat-building enterprise (16:28d–g OG/L = 22:47–50 MT). The supplementary notice is absent, however, in KR so that Jehoshaphat's referral notice in 22:46 is immediately followed by his death, burial, and succession notices in 22:51 and Ahaziah-I's opening formula at 22:52.

Shenkel attributes the absence of this material to the KR redactor "because he was interested only in reworking the seven verses containing the essential elements of the introductory and concluding regnal formula and then transposing them to a place in the text consonant with the Hebrew chronology" (*CRD* 58–59). In his view, the notice concerning the absence of a king in Edom during the reign of Jehoshaphat conflicted with the MT/KR chronology and may be the reason this material was omitted by KR. Since, however, both chronological systems accommodate the presence of the deputy Edomite king, the KR redactor had no need to leave out the verses.

If Shenkel is correct that the KR redactor deleted 22:47–50, then one might consider that regnal formulas without supplementary notices indicate deleted text, which is contrary to my previous observations that supplementary notices within regnal formulas are later additions to the original text. KR without the supplementary notice may, therefore, represent the text that came from the compiler of Kings. This conclusion that the supplementary notices at 16:28d–g (OG/L) and 22:47–50 (MT) were not part of Jehoshaphat's original regnal formula is supported by other closing formulas that contain no internal supplementary notices between the referral notice and death notice: Omri (1 Kgs 16:27–28), Jehoram (2 Kgs 8:23–24), Jehu (10:34–35), Joash-I (13:12–13 and 14:15–16), and Ahaz (16:19–20). Shenkel notes that the Larger Cambridge Septuagint attributes the four verses (22:47–50) to Codex Alexandrinus, the Armenian version, and the Sryo-Hexaplar, the latter crediting them to the version of Aquila. But 16:28a–h, including the supplementary notices at d–g, exhibit the usual OG/L characteristics (*CRD* 46, 57–59).

From 1 Kings, I need to note the occasions when a closing formula is immediately followed by an opening formula with no intervening supplementary notice: Abijam (1 Kgs 15:8) and Jeroboam I (15:9), Asa (15:24) and Nadab (15:25), Elah (16:14) and Zimri (16:15), Omri (16:28) and Jehoshaphat (16:28a OG/L) or Ahab (16:29 MT), and Ahab (22:40) and Jehoshaphat (22:41 MT/KR) or Ahaziah-J (22:41 L). Thus, whether OG/L or MT has the original sequence for Jehoshaphat, the pattern observed for his reign is that a closing formula was followed immediately by an opening formula.

5.3.7. Ahaziah-I

An accession synchronism for Joram appears at 2 Kgs 1:17 MT, which by comparison with 1:17–18 KR/L (table 5.8) suggests that the synchronism at 1:17 MT is an insertion in the form of a supplementary notice.

In 1:17–18 MT, Ahaziah-I's succession notice ("became king in his place")—an element that normally ends a closing formula—is continuous with Joram's accession synchronism ("in the 2nd year of Jehoram son of King Jehoshaphat of Judah"). The formula then gives the continuation of Ahaziah-I's succession notice ("because he had no son") and concludes with his referral notice ("now the rest of the acts of Ahaziah-I"). Neither KR nor L have Joram's accession synchronism at 1:17. Shenkel points out that L's closing succession notice ("Joram his brother became king in his place because Ahaziah-I had no son") is under the Hexaplaric asterisk in c_2, indicating that it was not in the proto-L stage of c_2 but a later insertion (late Greek minuscules xy include the synchronism, thus showing their conformity to the MT and Hexaplaric recension; *CRD* 73–74). From this it seems that neither L nor KR had the accession synchronism and succession notice at 1:17, which suggests that it is also secondary in MT. In any case, MT's separating the two parts of

Table 5.8. Ahaziah-I's Closing Formula (2 Kgs 1:17–18 MT/KR/L)

MT	Ahaziah-I's Closing Death Notice	and [Ahaziah-I] died according to the word of the Lord that Elijah had spoken
	Ahaziah-I's Closing Succession Notice	Joram his brother became king in his place
	Joram's Opening Accession Synchronism	in the 2nd year of Jehoram son of King Jehoshaphat of Judah
	Ahaziah-I's Continued Closing Succession Notice	because he had no son
	Ahaziah-I's Closing Referral Notice	now the rest of the acts of Ahaziah-I . . . that he did, are they not written in the Book of the Chronicles/Annals of the Kings of Israel?
KR	Ahaziah-I's Closing Death Notice	and [Ahaziah-I] died according to the word of the Lord that Elijah had spoken
	Ahaziah-I's Closing Referral Notice	now the rest of the acts of Ahaziah-I . . . that he did, are they not written in the Book of the Chronicles/Annals of the Kings of Israel?
	Joram's Opening Accession Statement	and Joram son of Ahab reigns over Israel
	Joram's Opening Duration Statement	in Samaria 12 years
	Joram's Opening Accession Synchronism	in the 18th year of King Jehoshaphat of Judah
	Joram's Opening Assessment Statement	and he did evil . . . house of Ahab
L	Ahaziah-I's Closing Death Notice	and Ahaziah-I died according to the word of the Lord that Elijah had spoken
	Ahaziah-I's Closing Succession Notice	and Joram the brother of Ahaziah-I became king in his place because he had no son
	Ahaziah-I's Closing Referral Notice	now the rest of the acts of Ahaziah-I . . . that he did, are they not written in the Book of the Chronicles/Annals of the Kings of Israel?
	Joram's Opening Accession Statement	and Joram son of Ahab reigns over Israel
	Joram's Opening Duration Statement	in Samaria 12 years
	Joram's Opening Accession Synchronism	in the 2nd year of Jehoram son of King Jehoshaphat of Judah, Joram son of Ahab reigned in Samaria
	Joram's Opening Assessment Statement	and he did evil . . . house of Ahab

its closing succession notice with an opening accession synchronism shows its radical irregularity. We may, therefore, suppose that 1:17 originally had only the words *and he died according to the word of the Lord that Elijah had spoken*, as now appears in KR. However, this would leave Ahaziah's closing formula without the customary succession notice before the referral notice, suggesting that the asterisk after the c_2 passage is incorrectly inserted. If so, v. 17 originally had the succession notice (but not the accession synchronism), as now appears in boe$_2$, indicating that KR has omitted the succession notice.

According to the pattern observed in 1 Kings, a closing formula ought to be followed immediately by an opening formula, but the MT has no opening formula after Ahaziah-I's closing formula in 1:18, and 2 Kings 2 (which is not a supplementary statement but a prophetic narrative normally positioned between the opening and closing formulas of a king's reign) follows without being under any king's opening formula. KR and L, however, give Joram's opening formula in 1:18a–d, but they disagree about the synchronism for his accession: in Jehoshaphat's 18th year (KR) or Jehoram's 2nd year (L, as in 1:17 MT). The second accession synchronism at 3:1 MT/KR (absent in L) for Joram's accession in Jehoshaphat's 18th year is not preceded by a closing formula, nor is Joram's narrative concluded with a closing formula at 8:15 before Jehoram's opening formula at 8:16. The absence of an orthodox opening formula at 1:18a MT and the duplication of text at 1:18a KR and 3:1 KR indicates reworking.

5.3.8. Joash-J

Athaliah is succeeded by Joash-J, 7-year-old son of Ahaziah-J.[14] A supplementary statement about his death in a conspiracy is found in his closing formula at 2 Kgs 12:20–22 between his referral and death notices.

5.3.9. Joash-I

Jehoahaz's closing formula (2 Kgs 13:8–9) is immediately followed by Joash-I's opening formula (13:10–11), which in turn is immediately followed in 13:12–13 MT/KR by his closing formula without any narrative separating them, contrary to the expected practice (L omits the closing formula). Moreover, Joash-I's closing formula is irregularly worded ("and Jeroboam II sat upon his throne") and not followed in 13:14 with Jeroboam II's opening formula. The appropriately worded closing formula for Joash-I is found instead at 14:15–16 but after Amaziah's opening formula and narrative (14:1–14) and before Amaziah's closing formula (14:18–22)! The appropriate place for Joash-I's closing formula is 13:25 after the narrative applicable to his reign; it is not found there in MT/KR, but is in L, where its position preceding Amaziah's opening formula (14:1) is appropriate and where it contains the historical present θάπτεται.[15] That the closing formulas at 13:13 and 14:16 are not followed by Amaziah's opening formula suggests their secondary positioning.

---

14. Joash-J's age of accession is given in 12:1 MT = 11:21 KR before the synchronism of his accession (v. 2). L has the usual order, giving the king's age after the synchronism and before the duration of reign statement at 12:1. (L omits 11:21.)

15. D. W. Gooding notes that this passage contains a historical present that Shenkel regards as proof that a passage belongs to the OG. Gooding writes, "Is this passage not a survival of the Old Greek? Hardly! It is all mixed up with what Montgomery calls 'invented midrash.' . . . But if it is not, the criterion has failed again" (review of *CRD* in *Journal of Theological Studies* 21 [1970]: 129).

5.3.10. Amaziah

Amaziah's irregularly worded closing formula (2 Kgs 14:18-22) contains two supplementary notices: the conspiracy that killed Amaziah (14:19) and his building of Elath (14:22).

5.3.11. Jeroboam II

Jeroboam II's closing formula (2 Kgs 14:28-29) has a supplementary notice as part of the referral notice: "He recovered Damascus for Israel" (14:28).

5.3.12. Zechariah

Zechariah's closing formula (2 Kgs 15:10-11) is separated from Shallum's opening formula (15:13) by a supplementary notice about the fulfillment of the prophecy that Jehu's royal line would last four generations (15:12).

5.3.13. Menahem

Shallum's closing formula (2 Kgs 15:15) and Menahem's opening formula (15:17) are separated by a supplementary notice about Menahem's battles (15:16).

5.3.14. Hoshea

Pekah's closing formula (2 Kgs 15:30-31) contains a supplementary notice about Hoshea in the form of an accession synchronism between the succession notice and the referral notice (pattern B2): "In the 20th year of Jotham son of Azariah." That an alternative accession synchronism (17:1) for Hoshea's accession in Ahaz's 12th year uses pattern 1 suggests that 17:1 is the original position for the synchronism.

5.3.15. Jotham

Jotham's closing formula (2 Kgs 15:36-38) contains a supplementary notice (15:37) about Rezin and Pekah between the referral notice and death notice (pattern A).

5.3.16. Conclusion

The preceding analysis leads to the conclusion that the original compilation of 1–2 Kings did not place supplementary notices within a closing formula or between a closing formula and an opening formula. This narrative arrangement of a king's closing regnal formula immediately followed by the next king's opening formula constitutes the framework of the Books of Kings.[16] Deviations from this pattern—for example, an opening formula not preceded by a closing formula (e.g., Joram at 2 Kgs 3:1), an inappropriately positioned formula (e.g., Joram at 1:17 MT or Joash-I at 13:12-13 and 14:15-16), or the addition of supplementary notices (enumerated above)—indicate reworked or additional text that was not part of the original compilation of the Books of Kings.

5.4. Sequence of Reigns in the Books of Kings

Having observed that the narratives of the kings of Israel and Judah constitute the framework of the Books of Kings, I now turn to the order in which their reigns appear in the Greek and Hebrew texts. Their chronological sequence is explained by S. R. Driver:

---

16. Cf. J. Skinner, *I and II Kings* (Century Bible; Edinburgh: Jack, 1904), 10-13.

In the arrangement of the reigns of the two series of kings a definite principle is followed by the compiler. When the narrative of a reign (in either series) has once begun, it is continued to its close, — even the contemporary incidents of a prophet's career, which stand in no immediate relation to public events, being included in it: when it is ended, the reign or reigns of the other series, which have synchronized with it, are dealt with; the reign overlapping it at the end having been completed, the compiler resumes his narrative of the first series with the reign next following, and so on.[17]

The first sequence variation occurs with Jehoshaphat and Ahab. According to the MT, Ahab ascended the throne in Asa's 38th regnal year (1 Kgs 16:29). In 16:28a OG/L (absent in MT), however, the last king of Israel to ascend the throne during Asa's reign was Omri, Ahab's father; and the next king of Judah is Jehoshaphat, who began to reign in Omri's 11th year. In OG/L Ahab's accession is synchronized with Jehoshaphat's 2nd year, indicating that Jehoshaphat began to reign before Ahab; whereas in 22:41 MT/KR Jehoshaphat's accession is synchronized with Ahab's 4th year, indicating that Jehoshaphat began to reign after Ahab.[18] Asa's death thus occurs either 2 years before Omri's death (OG/L) or 3–4 years after Omri's death (MT). Whatever the reason for the divergent synchronisms in OG/L and MT, it is obvious that the alternative synchronisms for Jehoshaphat and Ahab in the Hebrew and Greek texts determine the sequence of the following kings' reigns. Since MT/KR exhibit the secondary pattern 2 (with the acceding king's name first) in this section and since the data for these kings' reigns are therefore also likely secondary, the OG/L sequence more likely represents the original sequence.

Ahaziah-I's accession is next (22:52) — in Jehoshaphat's 17th (MT/KR) or 24th (L) year. L's synchronism concurs with its previous synchronism for Ahab's accession in Jehoshaphat's 2nd year and Ahab's 22-year reign (16:29). The MT/KR synchronism giving Ahab's accession in Asa's 38th year and Asa's 41-year reign (15:10) followed by Ahab's 22-year reign means that Ahaziah-I's expected synchronism is Jehoshaphat's 20th year — not 3 years earlier in the 17th. MT/KR follow Ahaziah-I's 2-year reign with Joram's accession only 1 year later in Jehoshaphat's 18th year (2 Kgs 3:1; also 1:18a KR), though the 21st or 22nd would be expected.

L's synchronizing of Ahaziah-I's accession in Jehoshaphat's 24th year and Ahaziah-I's 2-year reign (1 Kgs 22:52) is followed 2 years later by Joram's accession in Jehoram's 2nd year. The accession of Jehoram, who succeeded Jehoshaphat after his 25-year reign, should have been in Ahaziah-I's 2nd year, but this synchronism does not appear in any text, even though it is implied from 2 Kgs 1:17 MT and 1:18a L, which give the expected synchronism for Joram's accession in Jehoram's 2nd year.

The appropriate place for the now-missing synchronism for Jehoram's accession in Ahaziah-I's 2nd year is in an opening formula following Ahaziah-I's closing formula at 2 Kgs 1:18. Instead, Joram's accession appears in 1:18a KR/L, but with different synchronisms (KR has Jehoshaphat's 18th year and L has Jehoram's 2nd year). If Jehoram's opening formula had been at 1:18a, his narrative section would include 8:19–22 and 2 Kings 2 about Elijah and Elisha.[19] Jehoram's closing formula would then have followed at the end of 2 Kings 2 before Joram's opening formula at 3:1,

---

17. S. R. Driver, *An Introduction to the Literature of the Old Testament* (6th ed.; Edinburgh: Clark, 1897), 189; Shenkel, *CRD* 23–24.

18. Because the text-type in Codex Vaticanus abruptly switches from OG to KR at 1 Kgs 21:43, this Greek manuscript contains two accession synchronisms for Jehoshaphat: in Omri's 11th year (16:28a OG) and Ahab's 4th year (22:41 KR).

19. It could be argued that the prophetic narrative was not part of the original composition but, even if so, this does not alter the argument that Jehoram's narrative would be expected after Ahaziah-I's closing formula at 1:18 and before Joram's accession at 3:1.

where it now appears for the second time. According to the L sequence, the synchronism would have been for Jehoram's 2nd year, not Jehoshaphat's 18th year, which is found here because this is the MT synchronism, and the MT sequence does not have Jehoram's narrative between Ahaziah-I's and Joram's.

If the L sequence is original, Jehoram's 2nd year was replaced by Jehoshaphat's 18th year at 3:1. The insertion of Joram's accession synchronism into Ahaziah-I's closing formula at 1:17 MT, where it is out of place, supports the suggestion that Joram's opening formula was originally at 3:1. Joram's opening formula at 3:1 employs pattern 2, which is indicative of secondary text. The opening formula for Joram at 1:18a KR/L is similar to pattern 2 (i.e., with the name of the acceding king first), although the duration-of-reign statement (12 years) comes before the accession statement with the synchronism, followed by the assessment statement.

We may speculate that proto-MT once had the OG/L (formerly Hebrew) datum for Ahaziah-I's accession in Jehoshaphat's 24th year (at 1 Kgs 22:52 MT/KR/L), because Joram's accession in Jehoram's 2nd year derives from it. When the proto-MT datum for Ahaziah-I's accession changed from the 24th to 17th year (a reason for this will be discussed in §7.3.6), Joram's accession had to change to comply. Joram's accession synchronism was changed in 2 Kgs 3:1 proto-MT from Jehoram's 2nd year to Jehoshaphat's 18th year, and the king's name was placed before the synchronism. The original synchronism was preserved by being awkwardly inserted into Ahaziah-I's closing formula at 1:17. And the regnal formulas and narrative for Jehoram were (at some stage) transposed from their original position after 1:18 to 8:16–24, leaving Ahaziah-I's closing formula at 1:18 without a following opening formula (as in MT).

The KR does not have Joram's accession at 1:17, implying that it was not in its *Vorlage*,[20] but it does have the MT synchronism at 3:1. The KR redactor copied the proto-MT by giving the king's name first and translating מלך with the aorist ἐβασίλευσεν at 3:1. KR may also at this time have transposed Jehoram's regnal formulas and narrative from after 1:18 to 8:16–24 to conform to the sequence of kings' reigns now exhibited by the MT. Unlike the MT, however, the KR has 1:18a–d giving Joram's opening regnal formula, presumably to provide an opening formula after Ahaziah's closing formula at 1:18, as is the usual practice.

Shenkel asserts that "the four verses in II Kings 1:18[a–d] are the only surviving remnants of the Old Greek translation in II Kings" (*CRD* 69–70; see p. 86 n. 31 below; and Shenkel's criteria, p. 82 below). On the other hand, the opening formula begins with the name of the acceding king, indicative of pattern 2, and has the secondary synchronism and is in a secondary position, which are not OG characteristics. What accounts for the presence of OG characteristics at 1:18a–d? Shenkel observes: "If a passage in the old text corresponds to nothing in the proto-Masoretic text, then there is no need for revision. The old text is left as it is but is not excised from the revised text. As 1:18[a–d] corresponds to nothing in the developed Hebrew text, it was left unrevised by the KR redactor" (*CRD* 73). But he notes that the synchronism was changed. It may be that when the KR redactor (or later editor) removed Jehoram's regnal account to 8:16–24 he retained the opening formula and, in conformity with the proto-MT's secondary pattern, put the acceding king's name first, substituted Jehoram's name with Joram's, and changed the accession synchronism, but otherwise retained the OG characteristics.

---

20. Shenkel (*CRD* 74) notes that Hexaplaric manuscripts x and y have the synchronism at 1:17: "This can only mean that the synchronism here was inserted into the MT after the KR revision was completed.... The KR was made on the basis not of the definitive MT but of a Hebrew text very close to the latter, designated as proto-Masoretic."

At some stage, L was also conformed to the MT/KR sequence by inserting Joram's regnal formula at 1:18a–d, while keeping its own synchronism for Joram's accession in Jehoram's 2nd year. L did not retain the original synchronism at 3:1, which according to pattern 1 would have read: "In the 2nd year of King Jehoram of Judah, Joram son of Ahab became king (βασιλεύει) over Israel in Samaria and he reigned (ἐβασίλευσεν) 12 years." The KR has: "And Joram son of Ahab reigned (ἐβασίλευσεν) over Israel in the 18th year of King Jehoshaphat of Judah and he reigned (ἐβασίλευσεν) 12 years." The L text now reads: "And Joram son of Ahab reigned (ἐβασίλευσεν) over Israel [*synchronism absent*] 12 years"—which is identical to the KR without the synchronism. L has adapted pattern 1, leaving out the synchronism and expressing Joram's duration of reign in the aorist according to its usual practice. The absence of the synchronism from 3:1 and the transposition of Jehoram's reign from after 1:18 to 8:16–24, where it now conflicts with its own regnal sequence, shows L's undoubted conformity to the MT/KR sequence of reigns.

Contrary to the above analysis, Shenkel concludes that Joram's accession always stood in the text at 1:18a–d, as witnessed by KR and L, but that MT transposed the regnal formula to 2 Kings 3 (*CRD* 74, 82–83). Furthermore, he maintains that Jehoram's reign (which comes before Joram's in the OG/L sequence) was always at 8:16–24, whereas it now appears after Joram's in all texts (*CRD* 77). He argues that Joram's opening formula in 1:18a–d KR belonged to the OG text-type, though the synchronism conforms to the MT datum at 3:1. Shenkel recognizes the historical present βασιλεύει in 1:18a as a criterion of the OG text, whereas the aorist ἐβασίλευσεν is used in 3:1. He also notes that at 3:1 "the name of the king is characteristically in the dative, the sign of the KR, whereas the Old Greek practice of employing the genitive is evidenced by the text at 1:18ᵃ" (*CRD* 71). Furthermore, in 1:18b ביני (in the eyes of) is translated with ἐνώπιον and in 3:2 with ἐν ὀφθαλμοῖς (*CRD* 70–72). Shenkel comments that "characteristic rendition of certain phrases by 1:18ᵃ⁻ᵈ demonstrates that it belongs to the Old Greek translation, and is the older of the two regnal formulae of Joram under comparison" (*CRD* 72).

In his *Journal of Theological Studies* review of Shenkel's book, D. W. Gooding challenges Shenkel's assertion that 1:18a–d represents the older OG text and that 3:1–3 represents the later KR. Gooding points out that ἐνώπιον is used in 3:2 L, "which shows that the Old Greek once had the Joram regnal introduction standing in ch. iii, which in turn would seem to ruin a major part of Shenkel's thesis."[21] The presence of ἐνώπιον at 3:2 reinforces the proposal that Joram's opening formula was originally at 3:1–3. But this does not ruin Shenkel's overall thesis that the OG/L chronology is older than that of MT/KR, because the synchronism at 3:1–3 would originally have been the OG/L synchronism for Joram's accession in Jehoram's 2nd year, not the MT's "18th of Jehoshaphat."

If, for the sake of argument, Joram's opening formula was originally at 1:18a as Shenkel asserts, the expected place for Joram's closing formula would be the end of 2 Kings 2, but it does not appear there—probably because it would have then preceded his second *opening* formula at 3:1. In the MT sequence, Joram's closing formula was appropriate after 8:15 at the end of his narrative, but it does not appear there either. Joram's closing formula is absent in all texts, which suggests that it was deleted in the reworking of his regnal formulas and transposition of the text. My conclusion is that Joram's opening formula was originally at 3:1–3, not 1:18a–d.

One outcome of the different sequencing in MT/KR and L for the reigns of Jehoram and Joram is that in the OG/L sequence Jehoram was the king of Judah who accompanied Joram to fight the Moabites early in Joram's reign (2 Kings 3). In the current MT/KR sequence, this king

---

21. Review of *CRD*, 129–30.

of Judah is Jehoshaphat. Some scholars propose, however, that these kings were probably anonymous in the original version of 2 Kings 3 and only subsequently named.[22] MT/KR has "the king Joram" once (3:6) and "the king of Israel" six times (3:9, 10, 11, 12, 13 [twice]). L names Joram four times (3:6, 7, 8, 9), "King Joram of Israel" twice (3:6, 9), and "the king of Israel" elsewhere, as in MT/KR (except 3:9). In MT/KR neither name nor title are given at 3:7 and 3:8. For Judah, MT/KR name Jehoshaphat five times (3:7, 11, 12 [twice], 14) and "the king of Judah" once (3:9). L names Ahaziah-J as the king of Judah in the Moabite campaign three times (3:7 [twice], 9) and "the king of Judah" elsewhere (3:11, 12 [twice], 14).

L's naming of Ahaziah-J in the Moabite campaign is unexpected because Ahaziah-J was contemporary with Joram for only 1 year at the end of Joram's reign (2 Kgs 8:25–26; 9:24–29) and the Moabite campaign occurred toward the beginning of Joram's reign, within a few years of Ahab's death (1:1; 3:5–6) (the 2-year reign of Ahaziah-I intervened). In L's sequence of reigns, Jehoram was reigning at the time of the Moabite campaign, and consequently the naming of Ahaziah-J is contradictory.

Shenkel asserts that in L's chronology the king of Judah could have been either Jehoram or Ahaziah-J, claiming that the elapsed time between the death of Ahab and the Moabite campaign is not explicit in either 2 Kings or the Mesha Stela (*CRD* 93–94; see §7.2.4). He also argues that there was *no* king of Edom during the reign of Jehoshaphat (*CRD* 102–4). The reference to a deputy (1 Kgs 16:28e OG/L and 22:48 MT) is understood to refer to a deputy of Jehoshaphat—not a king of Edom.[23] He argues that since there was a king of Edom in the Moabite campaign, the king of Judah could not have been Jehoshaphat, but Jehoram or Ahaziah-J.

Other interpretations of 22:48 explain the verse to mean a deputy king of Edom during the reign of Jehoshaphat. This king, possibly a vassal,[24] would be the king of Edom mentioned in 2 Kings 3.[25] The people of Edom revolted from Judah in the reign of Jehoram and set up their own king (2 Kgs 8:20–22; 2 Chr 21:8–10), implying that they replaced their former king.[26] Ahaziah-J could not have accompanied the king of Edom in the Moabite campaign, as Judah and Edom were no longer allies in his reign. That leaves Jehoram as the king of Judah in 2 Kings 3 according to the L sequence of reigns.[27]

---

22. See Shenkel, *CRD* 98–101; R. W. Klein, *Textual Criticism of the Old Testament: The Septuagint after Qumran* (Philadelphia: Fortress, 1974), 38–40; A. R. Green, "Regnal Formulas in the Hebrew and Greek Texts of the Books of Kings," *Journal of Near Eastern Studies* 42 (1983): 175–80.

23. *CRD* 103, citing a proposal by B. Stade, "Miscellen," *Zeitschrift für die alttestamentliche Wissenschaft* 4 (1884): 178. Galil (*CKIJ* 141) states that "Shenkel's reconstruction is inconceivable." But Galil's further assertion (*CKIJ* 142–43) that "the name 'Jehoshaphat' was replaced by that of Ahaziah[-J] so that the narrative would conform to the BL system" is not accurate. Codex Vaticanus (= Galil's B) contains the KR text in 2 Kings 3, which has Jehoshaphat as the king of Judah, whereas L has Ahaziah-J. Furthermore, Ahaziah-J as king of Judah in 2 Kings 3 does not conform to the L system any more than it conforms to the MT/KR system!

24. G. H. Jones, *1 and 2 Kings* (New Century Bible Commentary; Grand Rapids: Eerdmans, 1984), 394; Galil, *CKIJ* 141–42 and n. 43.

25. See M. Cogan and H. Tadmor, *II Kings: A New Translation with Introduction and Commentary* (Anchor Bible 11; Garden City, N.Y.: Doubleday, 1988), 44 n. 9; cf. D. W. Gooding, "A Recent Popularisation of Professor F. M. Cross' Theories on the Text of the Old Testament," *Tyndale Bulletin* 26 (1975): 128; Green, "Regnal Formulas," 176.

26. Josephus (*Antiquities* 9.97) says the Idumeans revolted from Judah, killed their former king, who had been subject to Jehoram's father, and "set up a king of their own choosing."

27. Green makes the surprising assertion that "the textual material does not support a third possibility of Joram [Jehoram] of Judah as the identification of that king." Having ruled out Ahaziah-J and having accepted a deputy as king of Edom during the days of Jehoshaphat, Green writes, "One can conclude only that the identification of Jehoshaphat as king of Judah in 2 Kings 3 in the MT is probably correct" ("Regnal Formulas," 180).

The naming of Ahaziah-J in L seems therefore to be an editorial error and serves to support the proposal that the kings were originally anonymous in the prophetic narratives. MT/KR subsequently named Jehoshaphat as the king of Judah in accordance with their sequence of reigns. The presence of the "king of Edom" did not preclude this identification, presumably because he was understood to be the vassal king contemporary with Jehoshaphat.

A letter supposedly sent from Elijah to Jehoram warning him that he would die of bowel disease because of evil acts he had already committed (2 Chr 21:12–15) conflicts with the chronology that places Elijah's departure by whirlwind *early* in the reign of Jehoram (in the OG/L sequence, Elijah's ascension in 2 Kings 2 comes within the narrative section for Jehoram). Elisha had replaced Elijah as prophet prior to the Moabite campaign (3:11–20), and so Elisha—not Elijah—must have sent the letter to Jehoram. A. R. Green comments: "Only the two final consonants of the prophet's name need to be altered, and such mistaken identity could easily have arisen from a simple scribal error."[28]

Returning to the main argument: Joram's opening formula at 3:1–3 is followed by the narrative of his reign ending at 8:15, where his closing formula would be expected. As noted above, his closing formula is absent here and elsewhere, attesting to disturbance in his regnal formulas. Instead, the opening formula for Jehoram's accession in Joram's 5th year appears at 8:16, followed by a short narrative and his closing formula at 8:24. According to the L sequence, Jehoram's opening regnal formula would have been at the end of 2 Kings 1, his narrative would have included 2 Kings 2 and 8:16–24, before his closing formula at the end of 2 Kings 2.

Shenkel recognizes that the OG/L chronology places Jehoram's reign ahead of Joram's, but he argues that Jehoram's narrative was always at 8:16–24, coming after Joram's reign, even though Joram's accession took place a year earlier in Jehoram's 2nd year (1:17 MT; 1:18a L). Shenkel notes the presence of two historical presents in Jehoram's narrative: ἀθετεῖ in oc_2 or ἀθέτη in be_2 (he revolts) in 8:22, and θάπτεται (is buried) in 8:24, which according to him, "can only mean that L, and hence the proto-Lucian text, already had the regnal formula at 8:16–24 before the KR revision was made in II Kings" (*CRD* 77). To support the positioning of Jehoram's narrative at 8:16–24, Shenkel proposes an analogy with the reigns of Athaliah and Jehu and resorts to assumed dating systems. He proposes that Athaliah's accession year was counted as her 1st year using nonaccession-year dating (antedating), making her 1st *full* year her 2nd year. Jehu's reign, however, is based on accession-year dating (postdating) so that his accession year is not counted, and his 1st full regnal year is counted as his 1st year, which synchronizes it with Athaliah's 2nd year. He then says that this is a perfect analogy with the reigns of Joram and Jehoram because Athaliah's narrative is placed after Jehu's, even though Jehu began to reign in Athaliah's 2nd regnal year (*CRD* 78–79).

Shenkel's argument is actually based on an aberrant synchronism in 10:36+ L (see §3.2.3). According to the narrative, Jehu's and Athaliah's accessions would have taken place almost at the same time, rendering Jehu's accession synchronism in Athaliah's 2nd year inadmissible as an original synchronism. Shenkel's analogy based on an errant datum does not prove Jehoram's narrative was always at 8:16–24, and his dating methods for Athaliah and Jehu are also unconfirmed. The historical presents at 8:22 and 8:24 did not need to be changed to aorists when the text was transferred from 2 Kgs 1:18ff., and their presence does not necessarily indicate the original position of the verses. The L sequence indicates that Jehoram's reign would have followed the end of

---

28. "Regnal Formulas," 176.

2 Kings 1 and would have included the Elijah/Elisha narrative of 2 Kings 2 — if it was in the text at the time of the transfer[29] — which is now under Joram's reign in KR and L.

In the L sequence, Ahaziah-J's opening formula would immediately follow Joram's now-missing closing formula at 8:16. As it now appears, L has Jehoram's regnal formulas and narrative at 8:16–24 in conformity with the MT sequence. Ahaziah-J's opening formula now appears at 8:25, and his accession is synchronized in L with Joram's 11th year, while MT/KR have Ahaziah-J's accession synchronized with Joram's 12th year. Ahaziah-J's death and burial are recounted at 9:27–28, but his closing formula does not end in the usual referral notice (see p. 66 n. 4 above). Unexpectedly, Ahaziah-J has a second opening formula synchronizing his accession to Joram's 11th year at 9:29 — after his death and burial notices in 9:28! Second Kings 9:29 would be an appropriate place for Jehu's opening formula, before his narrative commences in 9:30, but his opening formula is absent in all texts (though his length of reign is found after his closing formula at 10:36).

The sequence of the remaining kings is the same in all texts.

A king whose reign has already been narrated, including his death in his closing formula, may be mentioned again in a subsequent narrative pertaining to the reign of his contemporary in the other kingdom. Jehoshaphat's reign, for example, is narrated at 1 Kgs 16:28a–h OG/L, but his alliance with Ahab against the Syrians at Ramoth-gilead is told in 1 Kings 22 under Ahab's narrative. The reason for this narrative in Ahab's reign seems to be because Ahab, not Jehoshaphat, was the principal participant. Shenkel (*CRD* 43–64) proposes that the OG/L sequence with Jehoshaphat's reign before Ahab's (1 Kgs 16:28a–h) was original — not the MT sequence, which gave Ahab's reign before Jehoshaphat's (16:29–22:40). Gooding objects that OG/L had only a summary at 16:28a–h, whereas, if OG/L had the original sequence, it should have had a full account of Jehoshaphat's reign before the summary. Jehoshaphat's narrative at 22:41–51 MT/KR (the same summary as at 16:28a–h) seemed to sum up what had been recounted in 22:1–40, making the MT sequence more feasible in Gooding's opinion.[30] The recognition that narratives are placed with the main participant when two kings are involved in one event counters Gooding's objection to Shenkel's proposal that the OG/L text and sequence was earlier than MT.

Further to our discussion, in the MT/KR sequence, Jehoshaphat accompanies Joram in the battle against the Moabites, though Jehoshaphat's death has already been recounted in 22:51 MT/KR. In the OG/L sequence, Jehoram accompanied Joram to fight the Moabites (2 Kings 3). Although not now extant, Jehoram's regnal formulas, narrative, and death would have appeared after 1:18 and before Joram's narrative at 3:1. Thus it appears that in either the OG/L or MT/KR sequence the king whose death has been recorded is mentioned again in the narrative of Joram's reign.

Pekah is another example of a king's reappearance subsequent to the report of his death. Pekah's opening formula is at 2 Kgs 15:27, his assassination by Hoshea at 15:30, and his closing formula at 15:31; but Pekah is mentioned again in 16:5–7 when he joins with Rezin of Syria in attacking Ahaz and Jerusalem. This event is narrated under Ahaz's reign (16:1–20), not Pekah's, since Ahaz has the predominant role. Another example: Hoshea is the main participant in the fall of Samaria recounted at 17:1–6, and his name is mentioned again in 18:9–10 where his regnal years are synchronized with Hezekiah's for the siege and fall of Samaria. Hezekiah did not,

---

29. See S. L. McKenzie, *The Trouble with Kings: The Composition of the Book of Kings in the Deuteronomistic History* (Vetus Testamentum Supplement 42; Leiden: Brill, 1991), 95–99.

30. Gooding, review of *CRD*, 119, 125–26; idem, *Current Problems and Methods in the Textual Criticism of the Old Testament: An Inaugural Lecture Delivered before the Queen's University of Belfast on 10 May 1978* (New Lecture Series 118; Belfast: Queen's University, 1979), 17.

however, actively participate in the fall of Samaria, so the main account of the fall of Samaria is in Hoshea's narrative. From these examples it can be seen that when a king of Israel or Judah participated in one event, the fuller record of the event may be placed with the main participant.

The above analysis makes it probable that the OG/L sequence giving Jehoshaphat's reign at 1 Kgs 16:28a–h before Ahab's at 16:29 is original. Jehoshaphat's reign after Ahab's in 22:41–51 MT/KR is secondary. The L sequence—where Jehoram began to reign in Ahaziah-I's 2nd year (synchronism missing) before Joram began to reign in Jehoram's 2nd year (2 Kgs 1:17 MT; 1:18a L)—is the original order. Consequently, Joram's reign was followed immediately by Ahaziah-J's at 8:16—not Jehoram's. In 2 Kings, L shows its conformity to the MT order so that the L sequence is all but lost in our extant texts. Enough of the L chronology remains, however, to enable us to deduce what its synchronisms and sequence would have been. The OG/L sequence appears to be earlier than the MT/KR and probably exhibits a greater number of the original data.

5.5. Translation of מלך

The translation of Hebrew מלך (he reigned) in the opening regnal formulas of the Greek texts has bearing on our study of patterns in the Books of Kings. מלך is variously translated by historical present βασιλεύει and aorist ἐβασίλευσεν throughout in 1–2 Kings (table 5.9; see also Shenkel's helpful study in *CRD* 43–86, esp. 50–52 of the translation practice of OG/L and KR with respect to verb tenses).

In the OG/L section of 1 Kings, when the verb מלך refers to the king's accession "in the *x*th year of King A, King B *began to reign*," it is always translated by the historical present βασιλεύει (*CRD* 50–52). In the KR section, beginning with Jehoshaphat's accession in 1 Kgs 22:41, מלך is always translated by aorist ἐβασίλευσεν —except Joram's accession in 2 Kgs 1:18a, as in L (see #3 below for explanation). In L in the section corresponding to the KR, the historical present has survived at 1 Kgs 22:52, 2 Kgs 1:18a, 10:36+, and 12:1 (bc$_2$ only). L's change from the historical present to the aorist in 2 Kings probably shows its conformity to the MT, a conformity also evidenced in the data given by two L manuscripts (*b* + b′ = b) for Jehoram's accession in Joram's 5th year and crediting him with 8 years (8:16–17). The aorist is also used at 8:16 oe$_2$, which also have the MT accession synchronism but credit Jehoram with 10 regnal years (8:17). L also has the aorist for the regnal formulas for Ahaziah-J at 8:25 and 9:29, where both texts give Joram's 11th year according to the Greek chronology, whereas MT has 12th year at 8:25, but 11th year at 9:29—the latter probably indicating the earlier synchronism. It is evident that the historical present has been replaced by the aorist in L, showing its assimilation to the KR (*CRD* 52).

An exception to L's using the aorist in 2 Kings occurs at 10:36+ in text not found in MT/KR, where Jehu's accession is synchronized with Athaliah's 2nd year. This is not an original synchronism because it conflicts with the narrative and, coming after Jehu's closing formula, seems out of its original position. The text has two historical presents: βασιλεύει in the accession synchronism and θάπτουσιν (they bury) (*CRD* 78, 133 n. 22), which are consistent with L usage in 1 Kings. This passage may reflect an early text that was altered to include a secondary synchronism, or the passage may be a late addition.[31] Either way, the historical presents have escaped assimilation to the aorist in 2 Kings.

---

31. The presence of two historical presents at 10:36+ causes Gooding to criticize Shenkel's assertion that the only surviving remnant of OG is 1:18a–d. Shenkel says the historical present at 10:36+ "attests the antiquity of this supplementary material in L" (*CRD* 78). Gooding writes (review of *CRD*, 128), "Is 'antiquity' the same as 'Old Greek'? Actually the passage is a summary of material culled from viii.26–ix.28. It is therefore secondary, in position at least." On the

When מלך refers to the number of years the king reigned it is normally translated by aorist ἐβασίλευσεν in OG, KR, and L. There are, however, three exceptions where βασιλεύει is used for the duration of reign statement:

1. At 1 Kgs 16:23 מלך is translated with the historical present: "In the 31st year of Asa, Omri began to reign (βασιλεύει) over Israel 12 years; he reigns (βασιλεύει) 6 years in Tirzah." As noted previously, this is the sole occasion where one king is given three accession synchronisms (or four if counting Josephus's variant 30th year). The other variants are inferred from 16:10, 15-16: 27th year (MT) and 22nd year (be₂). The unusual occurrence of these two features (i.e., the historical present for duration of reign and three accession synchronisms in this one verse) indicates reworked text, which if restored to the original would aid in reconstructing the chronology.
2. The accession synchronism at 1 Kgs 16:28a uses the historical present for the duration of reign: "In the 11th year of Omri, Jehoshaphat son of Asa began to reign (βασιλεύει) . . . and he reigns (βασιλεύει) 25 years in Jerusalem." The section designated 16:28a-h OG/L is absent in the MT because the MT sequence places Ahab's reign ahead of Jehoshaphat's, with Ahab's opening formula being at 16:29. Previous discussion led me to consider that the OG/L sequence is more likely the earlier sequence. If the OG/L sequence reflects the original, it would have been translated from a Hebrew text that had Jehoshaphat's reign ahead of Ahab's. The translation βασιλεύει for the duration of reign in OG/L is unexpected, but by itself not sufficient to indicate alteration of the original synchronism. It may simply be attributable to the same person who wrote βασιλεύει in Omri's opening formula at 16:23.
3. A third irregular use of βασιλεύει comes at 2 Kgs 1:18a KR for Joram's accession: "Joram son of Ahab began to reign (βασιλεύει) over Israel in Samaria 12 years in the 18th year of Jehoshaphat." Normally using the aorist, the KR here shows deviation from its normal practice. If the duration of reign, 12 years, is put in its usual position at the end of the verse, the verse reads, "Joram son of Ahab began to reign (βασιλεύει) over Israel in Samaria in the − − − and he reigned 12 years." This is the expected usage of βασιλεύει (see #1 above) in OG/L formulas when it refers to a king's accession, but the synchronism should come before the king's name in pattern 1 (see §5.1.1 and §5.2).

The accumulative evidence of the above analyses of regnal formulas indicates that the occurrence of exceptions to the normal patterns are the result of original data being substituted by secondary data in the reworking of the text. The data and deductions discussed above will be considered again in reconstructing the chronology. It is apparent that all texts considered above have been subject to reworking in various ways and a careful analysis of the evidence is required to ascertain the original chronological data.

5.6. Thiele's Analysis of Regnal Formulas' Patterns

Thiele does not analyze the patterns found in opening and closing regnal formulas in the Books of Kings. He does, however, notice that the Hebrew text (Thiele's term for the MT) and the Greek text (his term for the LXX and L) present a different sequence for two sets of kings.

---

originality of this passage, see Julio Trebolle [Barrera], "Redaction, Recension, and Midrash in the Books of Kings," *Bulletin of the International Organization for Septuagint and Cognate Studies* 15 (1982): 21-22; McKenzie, *Trouble with Kings*, 71-73.

Table 5.9. Translation of מלך by βασιλεύει (= HP) and ἐβασίλευσεν (= A)

Reference	Meaning of מלך	KR	OG	L
1 Kgs 14:21	years reigned		A	A
1 Kgs 15:1–2	began to reign		HP	HP
	years reigned		A	A
1 Kgs 15:9–10	began to reign		HP	HP
	years reigned		A	A
1 Kgs 15:25	began to reign		HP	HP
	years reigned		A	A
1 Kgs 15:33	began to reign/years reigned*		HP	HP
1 Kgs 16:6, 8	began to reign/reigned after him		HP	A
	years reigned		A	A
1 Kgs 16:15	years reigned		A	A
1 Kgs 16:23	began to reign		HP	HP
	years reigned		HP	HP
1 Kgs 16:28a	began to reign		HP	HP
	years reigned		HP	HP
1 Kgs 16:29	began to reign		HP	HP
	years reigned		A	A
1 Kgs 22:41	began to reign	A		
	years reigned	A		
1 Kgs 22:52	began to reign	A		HP
	years reigned	A		A
2 Kgs 1:18a	began to reign/years reigned*	HP		HP
2 Kgs 3:1	began to reign	A		—
	years reigned	A		A
2 Kgs 8:16–17	began to reign	A		A
	years reigned	A		A
2 Kgs 8:25–26	began to reign	A		A
	years reigned	A		A
2 Kgs 9:29	began to reign	A		A
	years reigned			A
2 Kgs 10:36	years reigned	A		A
2 Kgs 10:36+	began to reign			HP
	years reigned			A

Table 5.9. Translation of מלך by βασιλεύει (= HP) and ἐβασίλευσεν (= A) (cont.)

Reference	Meaning of מלך	KR	OG	L
2 Kgs 12:1/2	began to reign	A		HP/A
	years reigned	A		A
2 Kgs 13:1	began to reign/years reigned*	A		A
2 Kgs 13:10	began to reign/years reigned*	A		A
2 Kgs 14:1-2	began to reign	A		A
	years reigned	A		A
2 Kgs 14:23	began to reign	A		A
	years reigned	—		A
2 Kgs 15:1-2	began to reign	A		A
	years reigned	A		A
2 Kgs 15:8	began to reign/years reigned*	A		A
2 Kgs 15:13	began to reign	A		A*
	years reigned	A		—
2 Kgs 15:17	began to reign/years reigned*	A		A
2 Kgs 15:23	began to reign/years reigned*	A		A
2 Kgs 15:27	began to reign/years reigned*	A		A
2 Kgs 15:32-33	began to reign	A		A
	years reigned	A		A
2 Kgs 16:1-2	began to reign	A		A
	years reigned	A		A
2 Kgs 17:1	began to reign/years reigned*	A		A
2 Kgs 18:1	began to reign	A		A
	years reigned	A		A

* Only one Greek verb covers both meanings.

Thiele notes (*MNHK*[3] 90-94) that in the Hebrew text Ahab's reign precedes Jehoshaphat's (1 Kgs 16:29) and in the Greek text Jehoshaphat's reign precedes Ahab's (16:28).[32] He asserts that the Hebrew text predated the Greek because the Greek has an additional account of Jehoshaphat's reign at 16:28. Thiele attributed to the Greek only one verse and to the MT ten verses, not realizing that the Greek had the parallel account at verses designated 28a-h (*MNHK*[3] 91). Arguing that the Greek text's two accounts show it to be "utterly inconsistent," Thiele explains that the second account was placed at 16:28 because of the Greek's "own divergent synchronism" giving Jehoshaphat's accession in Omri's 11th year (*MNHK*[3] 91). Thiele's work does not reflect the LXX's two text-types in Codex Vaticanus (OG and KR) or Shenkel's proposal (*CRD* 7) that they

---

32. Cf. E. R. Thiele, "Coregencies and Overlapping Reigns among the Hebrew Kings," *JBL* 93 (1974): 178-82.

represent "two stages in the recensional development of the text: original translation and subsequent recension." Thiele does not recognize that the KR section of Vaticanus exhibits the MT chronological data and not that of the Greek, nor does he point out that L does not have Jehoshaphat's narrative at 22:41–51, which means that it does not have a second account "in the Greek." Thiele's attempt to dismiss "the Greek" as being secondary because of its two accounts for Jehoshaphat displays inadequate understanding of the textual issues involved, even though he had some acquaintance with Shenkel's book.[33]

With regard to the two accession synchronisms for Joram, Thiele writes, "The eighteenth year of Jehoshaphat's reign was the second year of Jehoram's coregency" ($MNHK^3$ 99). Thiele also notes that if Jehoram began to reign 2 years before Joram, Jehoram should have preceded Joram in 2 Kings. Because L has the Greek synchronism for Joram's reign in Jehoram's 2nd year but follows the Hebrew sequence with Joram before Jehoram, Thiele writes, "Such an inconsistency in the Greek gives evidence of its dependence on an earlier Hebrew text. Again, this is positive proof that the Hebrew preceded the Greek" ($MNHK^3$ 99). Joram's synchronisms arise from two divergent chronological systems—one in OG/L and the other in MT/KR—not from an unattested coregency. Thiele does not consider the possibility that the L text was made to conform to the MT, particularly in 2 Kings, which accounts for its reigns following the Hebrew sequence. Thiele is also not aware ($MNHK^3$ 99, 209) that the LXX and L synchronisms for Joram's reign in 2 Kings 1 are found in 1:18a, not 1:17, where the MT alone has inserted the synchronism. Thiele shows no firsthand acquaintance with the Greek text of 1–2 Kings in the Larger Cambridge Septuagint, relying solely on Burney's tabulation of variants and not on the text itself.[34]

---

33. Ibid., 176–89.
34. $MNHK^3$ 90 n. 6, 209 n. 5, citing C. F. Burney, *Notes on the Hebrew Text of the Books of Kings* (Oxford: Clarendon, 1903), xli–xliv.

6

Reconstructing Chronology

6.1. Establishing Relative Chronology

6.1.1. Methodology for Reconstructing Chronology

The chronological data in the Books of Kings should be understood within their own context—the regnal formulas. As chapter 5 revealed, the regnal formulas are stereotypical statements expressing the length of a king's reign, his accession synchronism, and upon his death the name of his successor. The methodological factors in constructing chronology should be obtained from the regnal formulas or, if a wider context is required, from the Books of Kings before going to an outside source. In defining methodology, I first address a series of questions:

1. *From what time of year were regnal years reckoned?* As noted in chapter 5, the only time reference in the regnal formulas is the notation that a king began to reign when his predecessor died, synchronized to a regnal year of the contemporary king in the other kingdom ("in the xth year of King y of [Judah/Israel]"). A king's accession does not appear to be dated to the beginning of the calendar year in either Judah or Israel or aligned with the beginning of the regnal year of the king of the other kingdom. A king might, perchance, die on New Year's Day, in which case his successor would also accede on New Year's Day or shortly thereafter, but a king likely died on some other day in the year. The regnal formulas do not indicate that the partial year remaining after the death of one king and before the next new year began was reckoned either by accession-year or nonaccession-year dating of the new king's reign. Instead, a king's 1st year was reckoned from the time his predecessor died and each regnal year thereafter was dated from this point (this is analogous to the way the years of our lives are reckoned from birthday to birthday or years of employment from their starting date). On these considerations, it is irrelevant to determine whether kings' reigns were reckoned from Nisan or Tishri and whether they used antedating or postdating. My methodology reckons a king's reign from the time his predecessor died, synchronized to the regnal year of the contemporary king in the other kingdom. Likewise, since there is no indication in the regnal formulas that a throne may have been vacant between the death of one king and the accession of the next, interregnums are not used in my methodology. Finally, coregencies also are eliminated from my reconstruction (see §6.3.4).

2. *Were reigns in Israel and Judah calculated according to the same system?* It seems self-evident that whatever dating data were originally contained in the individual annals of Judah

and Israel, a compiler of a composite account such as 1–2 Kings adapted his sources to create a coherent and unified system suited to his purposes. That the compiler of 1–2 Kings did not design a complex system is seen in the use of the same regnal formulas for both Israel and Judah. The same dating system recorded the synchronizations between Judah and Israel; if not, explanations would have been added to the regnal formulas to indicate what system was being used, in which nation, and at what time. Since these indications are not given, I conclude that the same dating system is used for both Israel and Judah.

3. *What was the system used for calculating the length of each king's reign?* Except for kings who reigned less than a year, the reigns of all DK kings are stated in terms of full years. Rounding must, however, have taken place, for it is unlikely that all of these DK kings ruled full years to the day. Examples of rounding are found elsewhere in the Bible: (a) David reigned 7 years 6 months at Hebron and 33 years in Jerusalem, which is rounded to 40 years (2 Sam 5:4–5). (b) Solomon built his temple in 7 years 6 months (the foundation was laid in Ziv, the 2nd month of his 4th year [1 Kgs 6:1, 37], and the temple was finished in Bul, the 8th month of the 11th year [6:38]), which is rounded to 7 years in 6:38. (c) Rehoboam and Jeroboam I began to reign in the same year, Rehoboam probably coming to the throne of Judah before Jeroboam I returned from Egypt to assume the throne of Israel (1 Kings 12). Rehoboam is said to have reigned 17 years (14:21) but the accession of his successor, Abijam, is synchronized with Jeroboam I's 18th year (15:1), seeming to indicate that Rehoboam reigned somewhat more than 17 years, but rounded down to 17 years. (d) Zedekiah, the last king of Judah, reigned 10 years 3 months 9 days (he was captured on the 9th day of the 4th month of his 11th year; 2 Kgs 25:2–7; Jer 39:2; 52:6), yet his regnal formula in 2 Kgs 24:18 rounds his reign to 11 years. Other examples are lacking, but one can infer that the kings' reigns were given in terms of rounded years in the regnal formulas, even though their last year was not a full year. The actual length of an event may have been shorter (e.g., Zedekiah) or longer (e.g., David, Solomon's Temple, Rehoboam) than the round number. It thus seems likely that round numbers were used to state regnal years during the DK without recording the precise number of months and days in the final year.

4. *How can the length of the final year be calculated?* The length of the final year can be calculated, if only approximately, by synchronizing the kings' reigns. For a synchronism of a king to fall in the stated year of the neighboring king, the length of a final year must be adjusted. If more than the due amount is reckoned to final years of several consecutive kings, the synchronisms will soon occur a year after the stated year (a similar observation was made in §4.2 about c_2's year-for-year alignment for Joram and Jehoram), with the result that the regnal years eventually fall ahead of the synchronisms. The opposite effect occurs if insufficient time is credited to final years of consecutive kings. In my reconstructed chronology, the length of the king's final year is determined by the king's reign ending close to the rounded year stated and his successor's synchronism falling in the stated year of the contemporary king of the other kingdom. The correct synchronization of reigns requires that the data be based on the original reign lengths and synchronisms. Recognition of the data that make up the original chronology must then be derived from text that, on analysis of several criteria, points to being the primary text. If synchronisms do not concur with regnal

years (and vice versa) an incorrect datum may have entered the text. This procedure may also provide a clue to the original number.

5. *How can one calculate the total number of calendar years by the stated DK regnal years?* This question is answered by table 7.1, which aligns calendar years and regnal years.

6.1.2. Methodology for Identifying Original Numbers

As in §6.1.1, a series of questions about the methodology of identifying original numbers is appropriate:

1. *How can original numbers be recognized from secondary?* On the assumption that the compiler of 1–2 Kings wrote a synchronistic record using preexisting annals of Judah and Israel, one expects that the original regnal years and accession synchronisms were internally consistent and coherent. If, through centuries of transmission, an error occurred in a number, the alteration would affect the congruency of an otherwise consistent system. If the many variant numbers presently found in the OG/L and MT/KR derive from an originally consistent record, we may infer that inconsistent variants are secondary. Numbers that do not agree with associated data may be useful in pointing out where a text has diverged and may lead to the recovery of an original figure that has been replaced by a secondary datum. In seeking to determine an original number, recall that MT and OG/L may share the same data for several reasons: (a) they may both have some of the same original data; (b) early errors may have entered the Hebrew text and subsequently translated into Greek texts; or (c) some of the data of the Greek texts may have been made to conform to the MT data after the divergency in the chronological data was noticed. For example, the regnal data in boe$_2$ are composed of a proto-L substratum dating back to about the 2nd century B.C.E., but this data may have been affected by Origen's practice in the 4th century C.E. of correcting the Greek text toward conformity with the MT. Another example: the phrase *in the 5th year of Joram* at 2 Kgs 8:16 MT/KR/L belongs to the MT/KR system because of its consistency with the associated MT data but not with the associated L data. Examination of other data may surface further examples where the L (or OG) data have been made to conform to the MT. Differentiating original data from secondary data is a complex task. If, however, we can identify possible reasons for the variants and how they might have affected subsequent data, we may well be on our way to recovering the original chronology.

2. *How can we account for variant numbers in the texts?* Not all problematic numbers should be viewed as accidental changes. For example, Abijam's 6 regnal years in OG/L and 3 years in MT may be due to a copyist's error. Whatever the reason, a change in Abijam's years causes the associated synchronism for his successor's accession to fall at a different time from the original. Consequently, the accession of Asa, given as Jeroboam II's 24th year in OG/L and his 20th year in MT (both at 1 Kgs 15:9), probably indicates that one of these is an intentional change to make Asa's accession concur with the length of Abijam's reign, whether 6 years or 3 years. This situation, if followed through, would cause alterations to take place in subsequent regnal years and/or accession synchronisms. And such differences are found in 1 Kgs 16:28a–29 for the data following Omri's reign and the different sequence for Ahab and Jehoshaphat. These alterations attest deliberate reworking in OG/L or MT; for example, Joram's

accession synchronism in Jehoram's 2nd year (2 Kgs 1:17 MT and 1:18a L) or in Jehoshaphat's 18th year (1:18a KR and 3:1 MT/KR) is inexplicable as inadvertent error. One text has been altered to accommodate Joram's accession and to concur with its associated data. This alteration probably reflects a desire to correct an apparent error. Perhaps a scribe noticed an inconsistency and "corrected" what he saw as a mistake by changing the synchronism or number of regnal years instead of reverting the incorrect number back to the original number.

3. *How were numbers written in early manuscripts no longer extant?* At least four ways have been proposed: (a) in words as they now appear in extant Hebrew manuscripts; (b) in the letters of the Hebrew alphabet in which every consonant or combination of consonants had its own value;[1] (c) in a series of signs or horizontal hooks for digits and vertical strokes for tens (see §7.3.6); and (d) as abbreviations, using the initial letters of the Hebrew words for numbers.[2] Option b is especially prone to error, for confusion between graphically similar Hebrew letters is well documented;[3] if these letters were used for numbers, then confusion in numbers could have occurred. Derek Kidner's comment on the list of returning exiles in Ezra 2:2–35 and Neh 7:7–38 is pertinent, for it points out the startling contrast between the transmission of names and numbers: "The names in the two lists show only the slightest variations whereas half the numbers disagree, and do so apparently at random. The fact that the two kinds of material in the one document have fared so differently lends the weight of virtually a controlled experiment to the many other indications in the Old Testament that numbers were the bane of copyists."[4] In other words, the high proportion of divergence in numbers between these lists seems to indicate that names and numbers were not written in the same way. Since names were written as words, numbers may have been indicated by some other method, which might explain why some variants entered the text (discussed further in §7.3.6).

4. *How can we establish if chronological data within their own text-type are congruent?* To establish whether the synchronisms and regnal years concur within each text-type, I have constructed a table consisting of parallel rows for Israel and Judah. Table 7.1 shows whether it is possible for the regnal years and synchronisms to concur in each text-type. Comparisons can also be made between text-types. If the data of a text-type are not internally consistent, the presence of variance might be indicated. Further analysis might explain why the variant arose and what number it might have replaced.

---

1. E. Kautzsch, *Gesenius' Hebrew Grammar* (2nd ed.; trans. A. E. Cowley; Oxford: Clarendon, 1910), §5k; J. W. Haley, *Alleged Discrepancies of the Bible* (repr. Grand Rapids: Baker, 1977), 20–24, 380; C. F. Keil, *The Books of the Chronicles* (trans. A. Harper; Biblical Commentary on the Old Testament 7; repr. Grand Rapids: Eerdmans, n.d.), 44–45; O. Zöckler, *The Books of the Chronicles* (trans. J. G. Murphy; Lange's Commentary on the Holy Scriptures 7; repr. Grand Rapids: Zondervan, 1960), 25; G. R. Driver, "Abbreviations in the Massoretic Text," *Textus* 1 (1960): 126; G. L. Archer, *Encyclopaedia of Bible Difficulties* (Grand Rapids: Zondervan, 1982), 226.

2. Driver, "Abbreviations in the Massoretic Text," 125–26; idem, "Once Again Abbreviations," *Textus* 4 (1964): 82–86.

3. S. R. Driver, *Notes on the Hebrew Text and the Topography of the Books of Samuel* (Oxford: Clarendon, 1960), lxv–lxvii; J. Gray, *1 and 2 Kings* (Old Testament Library; London: SCM, 1970), 51–53; L. C. Allen, *The Greek Chronicles* Part 2: *Textual Criticism* (Vetus Testamentum Supplement 27; Leiden: Brill, 1974), 109–23; P. K. McCarter, *Textual Criticism: Recovering the Text of the Hebrew Bible* (Philadelphia: Fortress, 1986), 44–49; E. Tov, *Textual Criticism of the Hebrew Bible* (2nd ed.; Minneapolis: Fortress, 2001), 243–49.

4. D. Kidner, *Ezra and Nehemiah* (Tyndale Old Testament Commentaries; Leicester: Inter-Varsity, 1979), 38.

6.2. Establishing Absolute Chronology

6.2.1. Establishing a Starting Date for the Divided Kingdom

The establishment of a reliable starting date for Israel and Judah depends on synchronizing a year of the reign of one or more kings with a date that can be determined by the Julian calendar. One such date is provided in the reign of Assyrian King Ashur-dan III, when a solar eclipse was recorded in the month Siwan in his 9th year, noted against the eponym of Bur-Saggile in the AEC.[5] This eclipse has been verified by astronomers as having occurred on 15/16 June 763 B.C.E.[6]

Dates in the AEC for each king's reign after 763 B.C.E. are verified by comparing them with the reigns of the Babylonian kings indicated in the Canon of Ptolemy. Ptolemy (second century C.E.), a famous Greek scholar and astronomer in Alexandria, compiled a list of rulers from 747 B.C.E. onward, beginning with Babylonian kings and giving the length and dates of the kings' reigns in terms of the years of the Nabonassar era (*Almagest*, 466).[7] Where applicable, Ptolemy stated in which year of a king's reign a lunar eclipse occurred, and these now establish the dates for the kings (*MNHK*³ 70–71, 229). Since the histories of Babylonian and Assyrian kings are interwoven, the dates that follow the year 763 B.C.E. can be established fairly accurately. For the years preceding 763 B.C.E., however, no records of solar or lunar eclipses or other data exist by which the dates can be verified. Even the dates for Egypt's 22nd Dynasty, during which Shishak (Shoshenq I) campaigned in Judah in Rehoboam's 5th year (1 Kgs 14:25–27; 2 Chr 12:2–4, 9–10), is set by Kitchen in dependence on Thiele's date of 925,[8] which is itself dependent on the AEC.[9]

The years of reign of Assyrian kings were recorded by eponyms (Akkadian *limmu*). The name (eponym) of the king or one of his high officials who assumed the office associated with cultic responsibilities was assigned to each year consecutively.[10] The resulting eponym lists served to number the years of the kings' reigns.[11] Some lists were composed only of eponyms, while others included the title of the official and a significant occurrence in the year (often a campaign or religious event) or the notation that the king "stayed in the land."[12]

---

5. A. Ungnad, "Eponymen," in *Reallexikon der Assyriologie* (ed. E. Ebeling and B. Meissner; Berlin: de Gruyter, 1938), 2:412–37; A. R. Millard, *The Eponyms of the Assyrian Empire 910–612 B.C.* (State Archives of Assyria Studies 2; Helsinki: Neo-Assyrian Text Corpus Project, 1994), 1–62, esp. 58.

6. Millard, *Eponyms of the Assyrian Empire*, 2 and n. 6

7. See Leo Depuydt, "'More Valuable than All Gold': Ptolemy's Royal Canon and Babylonian Chronology," *Journal of Cuneiform Studies* 47 (1995): 97–117.

8. K. A. Kitchen, *The Third Intermediate Period in Egypt (1100–650 B.C.)* (2nd ed; Warminster: Aris & Phillips, 1986), 72–76.

9. Cf. K. A. Kitchen, "The Basics of Egyptian Chronology in Relation to the Bronze Age," in *High, Middle, or Low? Acts of an International Colloquium on Absolute Chronology Held at the University of Gothenburg, 20th–22nd August 1987* (ed. P. Åström; Gothenburg, 1987), 1.38.

10. Millard, *Eponyms of the Assyrian Empire*, 1–14; idem, "Observations from the Eponym Lists," in *Assyria 1995: Proceedings of the 10th Anniversary Symposium of the Neo-Assyrian Text Corpus Project, Helsinki, September 7–11, 1995* (ed. S. Parpola and R. M. Whiting; Helsinki: Neo-Assyrian Text Corpus Project, 1997), 207–8; J. K. Kuan, *Neo-Assyrian Historical Inscriptions and Syria-Palestine* (Jian Dao Dissertation Series 1; Hong Kong: Alliance Bible Seminary, 1995), 7–8.

11. For Akkadian transliteration, showing the various lists, see Ungnad, "Eponymen," 412–57. For collation with transliteration and English translation, see Millard, *Eponyms of the Assyrian Empire*, 23–62. For collated lists in English, see G. Smith, *The Assyrian Eponym Canon* (London: Bagster, 1875), 57–71; *ARAB* 2: §§1194–98; Thiele, *MNHK*³ 221–26; E. W. Faulstich, *History, Harmony, and the Hebrew Kings* (Spencer, Iowa: Chronology Books, 1986), 265–73. For other publications, see also review of Millard, *Eponyms of the Assyrian Empire* by T. C. Mitchell, *BASOR* 297 (1995): 93–94.

12. Millard, *Eponyms of the Assyrian Empire*, 4–5; Kuan, *Neo-Assyrian Historical Inscriptions*, 8–9.

Table 6.1. Assyrian Eponym Canon for Shalmaneser IV and Ashur-dan III

Year	Eponym	Title of Official	Annotation
774	Ishtar-duri	governor of Nisibin	to Namri
773	Mannu-ki-Adad	governor of Raqmat	to Damascus
772	Ashur-belu-usur	governor of Kalah	to Hatarikka
		[ ] years, Shalmaneser, king of Assyria	
771	Ashur-dan [III]	king of Assyria	to Gananati
770	Shamshi-ilu	commander	to Marad
769	Bel-ilaya	of Arrapha	to Itu'a
768	Aplaya	of Zamua	in the land
767	Qurdi-Ashur	of Ahizuhina	to Gananati
766	Mushallim-Ninurta	of Tille	to Media
765	Ninurta-mukin-nishi	of Habruri	to Hatarikka; plague
764	Sidqi-ilu	of Tushhan	in the land
763	Bur-Saggile	of Guzana	revolt in the citadel; in Siwan the sun had an eclipse
762	Tab-belu	of Amedi	revolt in the citadel
761	Nabu-mukin-ahi	of Nineveh	revolt in Arrapha

The section of the AEC from the final years of Shalmaneser IV's reign and the first 11 years of Ashur-dan III's reign is reproduced in table 6.1 following Millard (who added the dates).[13]

The horizontal line that often appears before the eponym of a king[14] seems to indicate that the king held the 1st eponymate of his reign, but on occasion a king held the office of eponym in his 2nd regnal year (e.g., Shalmaneser III and Tiglath-pileser III), with his 1st full regnal year being the year preceding the horizontal line.[15] From the time of Shalmaneser V (727–722) a different procedure seems to have been in place, as Shalmaneser V and the succeeding kings Sargon II and Sennacherib (the last king named in the extant portion of the AEC) do not hold the office of eponym in either their 1st or 2nd regnal years.[16] Regarding kings' reigns preceding Shalmaneser V, scholars debate whether the king's eponym indicates the 1st or 2nd year of his reign.[17] The answer is important in determining the number of years and the dates assigned to each king's

---

13. Millard, *Eponyms of the Assyrian Empire*, 58.

14. Ibid., 12–13.

15. The rule for Tiglath-pileser III is before his accession year in some lists and after his 1st regnal year in others (Millard, *Eponyms of the Assyrian Empire*, 43, 59). Eponyms from the reign of Shalmaneser III downward may be viewed in the tables in chapter 9.

16. Millard, *Eponyms of the Assyrian Empire*, 13; S. Zawadzki, "The Question of the King's Eponymate in the Latter Half of the 8th Century and the 7th Century B.C." in *Assyria 1995*, 383–89.

17. A. Poebel, "The Assyrian King List from Khorsabad," *Journal of Near Eastern Studies* 2 (1943): 71–78; P. van der Meer, *The Chronology of Ancient Western Asia and Egypt* (Leiden: Brill, 1955), 3–4; Millard, *Eponyms of the Assyrian Empire*, 13; Kuan, *Neo-Assyrian Historical Inscriptions*, 9–18.

reign. An even more important issue, however, is whether all the years of the kings' reigns are represented by the eponyms that now comprise the extant portion of the AEC.

6.2.2. Reliability of the Assyrian Eponym Canon

Eponyms documenting the last 300 years of Assyrian history are found on tablets and inscriptions, including "nineteen manuscripts list[ing] the officials in order . . . although none now extend beyond 649 B.C."[18] The lists—apparently copied in the 7th century B.C.E.[19]—are inscribed on tablets and have been found in ruins at Nineveh, Ashur, and Sultantepe. Where one list is broken away, one or more other lists appear to overlap it, yielding a composite list of 261 or 262 eponyms.[20] If the list is complete, its extant portion extends back to 911 or 910 B.C.E.[21] Despite uncertainties, the reliability of the AEC appears to be confirmed from the restoration of the Assyrian King List, itself composed from several king lists.[22] Referring to the Assyrian King List, Millard writes,

> There the length of each reign is stated and the figures agree with the years allotted by the Eponym Lists as described above in every case. Although the King Lists and the Eponym Lists may be generically related, that still serves to confirm the figures as handed down from one generation of scribes to another, and so indicates the reliability of these sources for the Neo-Assyrian period, when correctly understood.[23]

The reliability of Assyrian, Hebrew, Egyptian and related chronologies depends upon the tenuous—and unverifiable—assumption that the lists copied in the 7th century B.C.E. were then complete and without error. Despite Millard's confident assertion, the king lists cannot be used as a definite confirmation since they may incorporate whatever faults their *Vorlage(n)* contained. Furthermore, the reliability of a composite list collated from fragments has been questioned in at least two places: (1) scholars acknowledge confusion among the eponyms for Adad-nirari III's reign; and (2) aligning the reign of Joash-I with Adad-nirari III, to whom Joash-I paid tribute, is problematic.

6.2.2.1. Reign of Adad-nirari III

The section of confused eponyms during Adad-nirari III's reign is set out in table 6.2 (following Gurney's arrangement).[24] The eponyms are dated in the AEC to the years 788–783 if Balatu and Nabu-sharru-usur share the year 786 (discussed below).[25]

---

18. Millard, *Eponyms of the Assyrian Empire*, 4.
19. Ibid., 4.
20. See the following discussion of the eponyms of Balatu and Nabu-sharru-usur.
21. Ungnad, "Eponymen," 418–29; Millard, *Eponyms of the Assyrian Empire*, 4, 55–62.
22. For discussion of king lists, see Poebel, "Assyrian King List," 71–90; I. J. Gelb, "Two Assyrian King Lists," *Journal of Near Eastern Studies* 13 (1954): 209–30; see also "The Babylonian King List A" in *ANET* 272; "The Synchronistic Chronicle" in *ANET* 272–74; and "The Assyrian King List" in *ANET* 564–66.
23. Millard, *Eponyms of the Assyrian Empire*, 13.
24. O. R. Gurney, "The Sultantepe Tablets," *Anatolian Studies* 3 (1953): 21. Gurney begins C^a3 1 year ahead of the other lists.
25. The eponyms come from four eponym lists designated C^a6, C^b2, C^c, and C^a3 by Ungnad ("Eponymen") and two Sultantepe tablets numbered 150 and 18 by Gurney ("Sultantepe Tablets," 19–21) and STT 1 47 and STT 1 46 + 2 348 by J. A. Brinkman ("A Further Note on the Date of the Battle of Qarqar and Neo-Assyrian Chronology," *Journal of Cuneiform Studies* 30 [1978]: 174, written in reply to W. H. Shea, "A Note on the Date of the Battle of Qarqar," *Journal of Cuneiform Studies* 29 [1977]: 240–42). Millard (*Eponyms of the Assyrian Empire*, 17–21) redesignates these sigla as follows: C^a6 = A6; C^b2 = B2; C^c = A7; C^a3 = A3; Sultantepe 150 = A8; and Sultantepe 18 = B10.

Table 6.2. Eponyms during Adad-nirari III's Reign
according to the Assyrian Eponym Canon

C^{a}6, C^{b}2, C^c	C^{a}3	Sultantepe 150 (STT 1 47)	Sultantepe 18 (STT 1 46 + 2 348)
	Adad-mushammer		
Adad-mushammer	Sil-Ishtar	Adad-mushammer	Adad-mushammer
Sil-Ishtar	Balatu	Sil-Ishtar	Sil-Ishtar
Nabu-sharru-usur	Adad-uballit	Nabu-sharru-usur	Adad-uballit
Adad-uballit	Marduk-sharru-usur	Nergal-uballit	Marduk-sharru-usur
Marduk-sharru-usur	Nabu-sharru-usur	Nergal-sharru-usur	Adad-mushammer
Ninurta/Marduk-nasir	Ninurta-nasir	Ninurta-nasir	Ninurta-nasir

The first and second names on all lists are the same: Adad-mushammer and Sil-Ishtar. Ungnad and Millard assign to the last 3 years the names Adad-uballit, Marduk-sharru-usur, and Ninurta-nasir. They equate Nergal-uballit and Nergal-sharru-usur in Sultantepe 150 with Adad-uballit and Marduk-sharru-usur respectively of the other lists. Nabu-sharru-usur in C^{a}3 is seen as a variant and repetition of the previous Marduk-sharru-usur.[26] Concerning the repetition of Adad-mushammer in the fifth place in Sultantepe 18, Gurney comments, "The repetition of Adad-mušammir in Sultantepe 18 is unlikely to be correct, since he would hardly have been designated for a second term of office only four years after his first term."[27]

Implementing the above suggestions means that Adad-uballit becomes the fourth name in all lists except Sultantepe 18, where he is the third name. The other lists have Nabu-sharru-usur as the third name, with the exception of C^{a}3, which has an otherwise unattested Balatu, and Sultantepe 18, which has neither Nabu-sharru-usur nor Balatu in third position. Gurney, however, asserts that Nabu-sharru-usur should be placed between Sil-Ishtar and Adad-uballit in Sultantepe 18 and notes that the AEC comment for the eponym Adad-uballit for 785, "the great god went to Dêr," is dated to the same year shown in Sultantepe 18 but with the eponym Marduk-sharru-usur, the name following Adad-uballit in the list. This shows that Nabu-sharru-usur has been omitted between the two eponyms.[28] Nabu-sharru-usur should, therefore, be reinstated to Sultantepe 18 between Sil-Ishtar and Adad-uballit. By analogy, Nabu-sharru-usur ought also to be reinstated to C^{a}3 after the name Sil-Ishtar. This leaves the eponym Balatu in C^{a}3 between Nabu-sharru-usur and Adad-uballit. Ungnad,[29] followed by Thiele (*MNHK*^{3} 73–76, 223), gives 1 year (786) to both Balatu and Nabu-sharru-usur. Millard notes the name as an eponym for the year 786[30] but in the reconstructed list assigns the year solely to Nabu-sharru-usur.[31]

Instead of assigning Nabu-sharru-usur and Balatu to the same year or omitting Balatu, the positioning of the names may be explained by proposing a disruption in the lists, as illustrated by the horizontal rule in table 6.3.

---

26. Ungnad, "Eponymen," 422; Millard, *Eponyms of the Assyrian Empire*, 37, 58. On variant spellings, see also Gurney, "Sultantepe Tablets," 18; Brinkman, "Further Note," 174–75.
27. Gurney, "Sultantepe Tablets," 21.
28. Ibid., 21.
29. Ungnad, "Eponymen," 422.
30. Millard, *Eponyms of the Assyrian Empire*, 8, 37, 87.
31. Ibid., 58.

Table 6.3. Reconstruction of Eponyms during Adad-nirari III's Reign

C^{a}6, C^{b}2, C^c	C^{a}3	Sultantepe 150 (STT 1 47)	Sultantepe 18 (STT 1 46 + 2 348)
Adad-mushammer	Adad-mushammer	Adad-mushammer	Adad-mushammer
Sil-Ishtar	Sil-Ishtar	Sil-Ishtar	Sil-Ishtar
Nabu-sharru-usur	[Nabu-sharru-usur]	Nabu-sharru-usur	[Nabu-sharru-usur]
	Balatu		
Adad-uballit	Adad-uballit	Nergal-uballit	Adad-uballit
Marduk-sharru-usur	Marduk-sharru-usur	Nergal-sharru-usur	Marduk-sharru-usur
Ninurta-nasir	Ninurta-nasir	Ninurta-nasir	Ninurta-nasir

In this arrangement Nabu-sharru-usur is the third name on all lists. Supposing a break in the lists after Nabu-sharru-usur, C^{a}3 begins one name earlier in the next section with the name Balatu, not mentioned in the other lists, which begin instead with the next name, Adad-uballit. In C^{a}6, C^{b}2, C^c, and Sultantepe 150, a possible break appears between Nabu-sharru-usur and Adad-uballit, in C^{a}3 between Sil-Ishtar and Balatu, and in Sultantepe 18 between Sil-Ishtar and Adad-uballit. The very possibility of names missing from one area of the collated AEC means that the years afforded to the AEC prior to 763 B.C.E. cannot be confirmed as correct. The credibility of the Assyrian, Hebrew, and Egyptian chronologies dependent on the accuracy of AEC dates before 763 B.C.E. cannot, therefore, be unequivocally upheld while the accuracy of the AEC remains suspect. If eponyms have dropped from the lists between Nabu-sharru-usur and Balatu at a presumed year 786, any number of years could be missing in this section of eponyms. If so, their number needs to be determined, and new Julian dates reassigned to the AEC.

6.2.2.2. Tribute by Joash-I

The AEC exhibits another inconsistency between Assyrian and biblical records, again during Adad-nirari III's reign. The problem concerns the synchronization of Adad-nirari's 5th year with the payment of tribute by Joash-I. In current chronologies Joash-I is not contemporaneous with Adad-nirari's 5th year. Briefly, the situation is as follows. The Assyrian Tell al-Rimah Stela records a western campaign by Adad-nirari undertaken in a single year in which Mari' of Damascus, Jehoash of Samaria (i.e., Joash-I), and the king of Tyre and Sidon paid him tribute.[32] The Saba'a Stela attributes to Adad-nirari's 5th year a western campaign and submission of rebel kings, as

---

32. For discussion about Joash-I and the Tell al-Rimah Stela, see S. Page, "A Stela of Adad-nirari III and Nergal-Ereš from Tell al Rimah," *Iraq* 30 (1968): 139–53; idem, "Joash and Samaria in a New Stela Excavated at Tell al Rimah, Iraq," *VT* 19 (1969): 483–84; idem, "Adad-nirari III and Semiramis: The Stelae of Saba'a and Rimah," *Orientalia* 38 (1969): 457–58; A. Cody, "A New Inscription from Tell al-Rimāḥ and King Jehoash of Israel," *Catholic Biblical Quarterly* 32 (1970): 325–40; A. Jepsen, "Ein Neuer Fixpunkt für die Chronologie der Israelitischen Könige?" *VT* 20 (1970): 359–61; J. A. Soggin, "Ein Ausserbiblisches Zeugnis für die Chronologie des Jᵉhô'āš/Jô'āš, König von Israel," *VT* 20 (1970): 366–68; A. Malamat, "On the Akkadian Transcription of the Name of King Joash," *BASOR* 204 (1971): 37–39; H. Tadmor, "The Historical Inscriptions of Adad-nirari III," *Iraq* 35 (1973): 141–44; W. H. Shea, "Adad-nirari III and Jehoash of Israel," *Journal of Cuneiform Studies* 30 (1978): 101–2, 106–11; idem, "Israelite Chronology and the Samaria Ostraca," *Zeitschrift des Deutschen Palästina-Vereins* 101 (1985): 10–13; Miller and Hayes, *HAIJ* 288 (photograph of Tell al-Rimah Stela), 293, 299 (translation); Kuan, *Neo-Assyrian Historical Inscriptions*, 78–81, 93–106.

Table 6.4. Nonsynchronization of Adad-nirari III's 5th Year with the Regnal Years of Joash-I

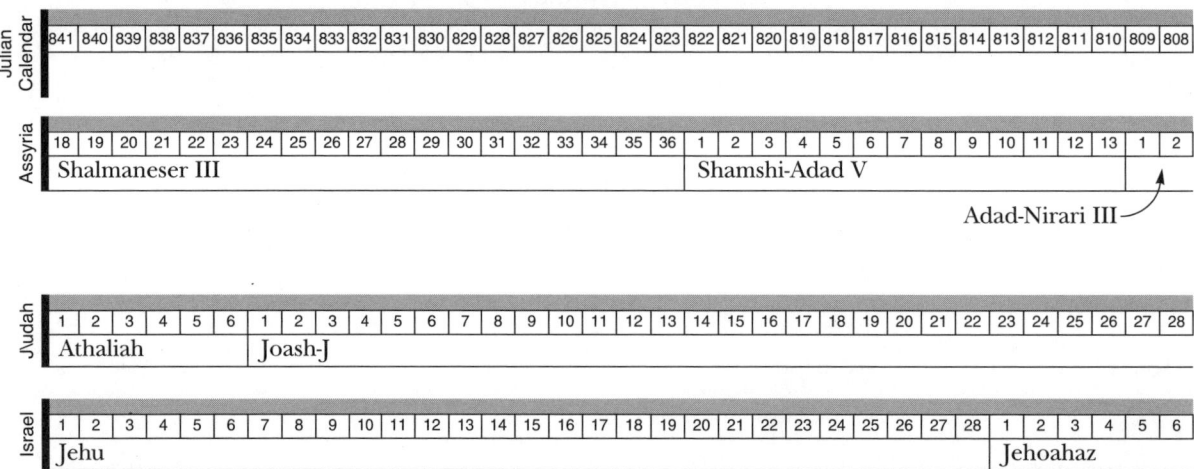

well as payment of tribute by Mariʾ of Damascus.[33] Other evidence from the Calah Slab,[34] the Sheikh Hammad Stela (British Museum 131124),[35] and the Scheil and Millard fragment[36] seems to indicate that Adad-nirari suppressed a coalition of northern Syrian kings led by Artashumki of Arpad in the same year that he received tribute from Mariʾ of Damascus, Joash-I, and the king of Tyre and Sidon, which equates the "single year" campaign with the "fifth year" campaign.[37] In the AEC the year 809 has the eponym Adad-nirari. The 5th eponym, for the year 805, has the annotation "to Arpad," signifying a campaign in northern Syria that year.[38] Joash-I's regnal year, when he paid tribute to Adad-nirari, is neither noted in the inscriptions nor mentioned in the Bible.

---

33. *ARAB* 1: §§732–37; *ANET* 282; H. Tadmor, "A Note on the Sabaʾa Stele of Adad-nirari III," *Israel Exploration Journal* 19 (1969): 46–48; idem, "Historical Inscriptions of Adad-nirari III," 144–48; Cody, "New Inscription from Tell al-Rimāḥ," 327–37; W. Schramm, "War Semiramis Assyrische Regentin?" *Historia* 21 (1972): 514–19; A. R. Millard, "Adad-nirari III, Aram, and Arpad," *Palestine Exploration Quarterly* 105 (1973): 161–62; Shea, "Adad-nirari III and Jehoash," 105–8; Miller and Hayes, *HAIJ* 291–93; Kuan, *Neo-Assyrian Historical Inscriptions*, 84–87, 93–106.

34. *ARAB* 1: §§738–41; *ANET* 281–82; Cody, "New Inscription from Tell al-Rimāḥ," 327–37; Tadmor, "Historical Inscriptions of Adad-nirari III," 148–49; Shea, "Adad-nirari III and Jehoash," 109; Kuan, *Neo-Assyrian Historical Inscriptions*, 81–84, 93–106.

35. A. R. Millard and H. Tadmor, "Adad-Nirari III in Syria: Another Stele Fragment and the Dates of His Campaigns," *Iraq* 35 (1973): 57–60; Millard, "Adad-nirari III, Aram, and Arpad," 162–63; Tadmor, "Historical Inscriptions of Adad-nirari III," 141; Shea, "Adad-nirari III and Jehoash," 104, 109–11; Kuan, *Neo-Assyrian Historical Inscriptions*, 87–89, 93–106.

36. First published by V. Scheil in *Revue d'Assyriologie* 14 (1917): 159–60; text reproduced in Millard and Tadmor, "Adad-nirari III in Syria," 60–61; see also Millard, "Adad-nirari III, Aram, and Arpad," 162–63; Shea, "Adad-nirari III and Jehoash," 102, 104; Kuan, *Neo-Assyrian Historical Inscriptions*, 88–89, 93–106.

37. Artashumki of Arpad is mentioned in the Sheikh Hammad Stela, the Scheil and Millard fragment, the Pazarcik Stela, and the Zakkur Stela (Kuan, *Neo-Assyrian Historical Inscriptions*, 87–93). For the Pazarcik Stela, see V. Donbaz, "Two Neo-Assyrian Stelae in the Antakya and Kahramanmaraş Museums," *Annual Review of the Royal Inscriptions of Mesopotamia Project* 8 (1990): 8–10.

38. That the 5th eponym "to Arpad" is in agreement with the stelas seems to confirm that the campaign to Arpad was in Adad-nirari's 5th year, yet a number of scholars (see p. 96 n. 17 above) think that the eponym of the king refers to his 2nd regnal year, in which case the 5th-year campaign refers to Mannai, a country east of Assyria, thus conflicting with the stelas. See Kuan, *Neo-Assyrian Historical Inscriptions*, 97–98.

Table 6.4. (cont.)

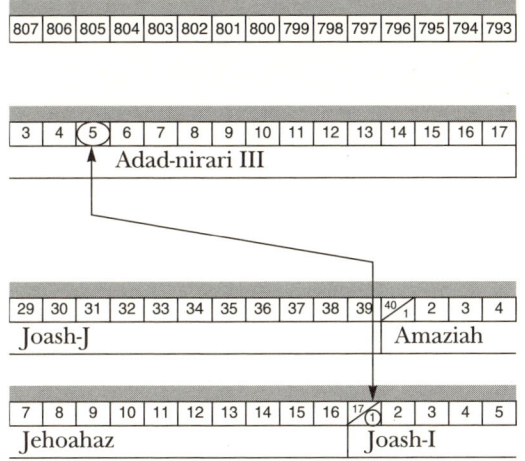

Adad-nirari III's 5th year falls short of Joash-I's reign by 8 years

The overall time frame is determined by Shalmaneser's 18th year, dated to 841 in the AEC, this date being attributed to Jehu's 1st year on the grounds that *Iaúa* equals Jehu (though this identification is not proven) and that Jehu gave tribute in that year.

Since Joash-I paid tribute in Adad-nirari's 5th year, 805 in the AEC, Joash-I's reign could not have started after 805 and probably began before 805. Accordingly, the 36 years between Shalmaneser's 18th year and Adad-nirari's 5th year should be compatible with Joash-I's reign beginning no later than 805. In this period, Jehu's 28 years (2 Kgs 10:36) are followed by Jehoahaz's 17 years (13:1) and at least 1 year of Joash-I, indicating a minimum of 45–46 years between Jehu's 1st year and Joash-I's 1st year. This shows a deficiency of at least 8 years in the AEC—and more if the tribute was paid in a later year of Joash-I's reign. If the biblical record is correct (and in this period there is a discrepancy of only 2 years in the texts, as previously discussed in §3.2.3) and the Assyrian record of Joash-I's payment of tribute to Adad-nirari in the latter's 5th year is correct, then the AEC must be incorrect in having only 36 years between Shalmaneser's 18th year and Adad-nirari's 5th year (table 6.4). The Assyrian records of Adad-nirari's reign do not agree with the number of years attributed to the AEC.

Thiele's chronology proposes that Joash-I reigned from 798 to 782, which does not include Adad-nirari's 5th year in 805 according to the AEC. Thiele (and other scholars) attribute Joash-I's payment to a later western campaign, the only year for such a campaign being the year 796, when there was a campaign "against Manṣuate."[39] The year 796 falls within Thiele's dates for Joash-I. Thiele writes, "The evidence presently available points to this as having been at Manṣuate in 796. Beyond that we need not go" (*MNHK*³ 113). Thiele refers to the Tell al-Rimah Stela found in

---

39. For discussion, see E. Lipiński, "The Assyrian Campaign to Manṣuate, in 796 B.C., and the Zakir Stela," *Annali dell' Instituto Orientale di Napoli* 31 (1971): 393–99; Tadmor, "Historical Inscriptions of Adad-nirari III," 146; Millard and Tadmor, "Adad-nirari III in Syria," 61–64; Millard, "Adad-nirari III, Aram, and Arpad," 161–64; Thiele, *MNHK*³ 112–13; Miller and Hayes, *HAIJ* 291–93, 298; W. T. Pitard, *Ancient Damascus* (Winona Lake, Ind.: Eisenbrauns, 1987), 161–65; M. Cogan and H. Tadmor, *II Kings: A New Translation with Introduction and Commentary* (Anchor Bible 11; Garden City, N.Y.: Doubleday, 1988), 151–52 and nn. 4–6; J. Hughes, *Secrets of the Times: Myth and History in Biblical Chronology* (Journal for the Study of the Old Testament Supplement 66; Sheffield: JSOT Press, 1990), 196–98; Galil, *CKIJ* 53–56; Kuan, *Neo-Assyrian Historical Inscriptions*, 93–106.

1967 and says, "The year when Jehoash [Joash-I] paid tribute to Adad-nirari III is not specifically mentioned on the new stele, but the eponym canon provides the following possible dates" (*MNHK*³ 112). Thiele does not mention that the Saba'a Stela records a western campaign by Adad-nirari in his 5th year in which he subjugated rebellious kings and received tribute from Mari' of Damascus, though Thiele cites articles that refer to this event and he mentions the stela by name (*MNHK*³ 112 n. 3, 113). Thiele thus declines to provide all the relevant information at his disposal. To have done so affords more years to the Assyrian chronology than Thiele allowed based on the AEC and indicates a serious discrepancy in his chronology. Manṣuate is not mentioned in the above records pertaining to the north Syrian campaign.

The problem of only 36 years in the AEC between Shalmaneser's 18th year and Adad-nirari's 5th year points to the AEC's deficiency in this area of eponyms. Any missing eponyms must have fallen from either the end of Shalmaneser III's reign or some time during the reign of Shamshi-Adad V.[40] The 1st to 5th eponyms of Adad-nirari's reign are reasonably certain since his 5th-year campaign "to Arpad" occurs against the 5th eponym of his reign. The 36 years of Shalmaneser's reign seem assured because in his 30th eponym[41] the king again has an eponymate followed by those of his chief officials. Unless eponyms fell from Shalmaneser's reign after his 36th year, they must have fallen from the reign of Shamshi-Adad V.

Records from the reign of Shamshi-Adad V indicate that he deported Babylonian King Marduk-balatsu-iqbi to Assyria, followed a year later by his successor Baba-aha-iddina. Brinkman dates these two campaigns to around 813–812,[42] that is, Shamshi-Adad's 11th and 12th regnal years of a supposed 13-year reign. Shamshi-Adad then returned to Babylonia, received tribute from the Chaldeans, and reestablished the borders between Assyria and Babylonia.[43] According to Brinkman, Shamshi-Adad's inscriptions "claimed for him the title 'king of Sumer and Akkad'—which represents an assertion of suzerainty over Babylonia."[44] There seems to have been a "kingless period" in Babylon following the deposition of Baba-aha-iddina. The eponym record for

---

40. Shalmaneser's 18th-year campaign is collated from various inscriptions. For the annalistic fragment known as III R 5,6 (= H. C. Rawlinson, *The Cuneiform Inscriptions of Western Asia* [London: British Museum, 1875], 3: pl. 5, no. 6), see *ARAB* 1: §671 and §672; *ANET* 280; K. L. Younger, *Ancient Conquest Accounts: A Study in Ancient Near Eastern and Biblical History Writing* (Journal for the Study of the Old Testament Supplement 98; Sheffield: JSOT Press, 1990), 106–7; Kuan, *Neo-Assyrian Historical Inscriptions*, 51–52. For the Marble Slab Inscription, see W. F. Albright, "The New Assyro-Tyrian Synchronism and the Chronology of Tyre," *Annuaire de l'Institut de Philologie et d'Historie Orientales et Slaves* 13 [Mélanges Isidore Levy] (1953): 1–9; Cogan and Tadmor, *II Kings*, 334; H. J. Katzenstein, *The History of Tyre* (Jerusalem: Schocken Institute for Jewish Research, 1973), 134, 175; Younger, *Ancient Conquest Accounts*, 105–6; Kuan, *Neo-Assyrian Historical Inscriptions*, 55, 61–62. For the Black Obelisk Inscription, see *ARAB* 1: §590; *ANET* 281; Miller and Hayes, *HAIJ* 286–87; Kuan, *Neo-Assyrian Historical Inscriptions*, 62–63. For the Bull Inscription and Kurba'il Statue, see Younger, *Ancient Conquest Accounts*, 108–10.

41. Millard writes, "Thirty years evidently marked a cycle, which we may, speculatively, consider a generation, requiring some renewal or reaffirmation of the old king's authority" (*Eponyms of the Assyrian Empire*, 14).

42. J. A. Brinkman, *A Political History of Post-Kassite Babylonia, 1158–722 B.C.* (Analecta Orientalia 43; Rome: Pontifical Biblical Institute Press, 1968), 51; cf. Poebel, "Assyrian King List," 80.

43. Collated from Poebel, "Assyrian King List," 80; Chronicle 21, iii rev. lines 6–9; iv obv. lines 1–14, in *ABC* 167–69; A. K. Grayson, "Assyria: Ashur-dan II to Ashur-nirari V (934–745 B.C.)," in *Cambridge Ancient History*, vol. 3/1: *The Prehistory of the Balkans; and the Middle East and the Aegean World, Tenth to Eighth Centuries B.C.* (ed. J. Boardman et al.; Cambridge: Cambridge University Press, 1982), 269–71; Brinkman, *Political History of Post-Kassite Babylonia*, 72–73, 205–13; idem, "Babylonia, *c.* 1000–748 B.C.," in *Cambridge Ancient History*, vol. 3/1: *The Prehistory of the Balkans; and the Middle East and the Aegean World, Tenth to Eighth Centuries B.C.* (ed. J. Boardman et al.; Cambridge: Cambridge University Press, 1982), 307–9.

44. Brinkman, "Babylonia, *c.* 1000–748 B.C.," 309.

Shamshi-Adad's last year has him "in the land," that is, in Assyria. Was Shamshi-Adad king over Babylon for only 1 year? Two reconstructed lines of Babylonian Chronicle 24 (rev. lines 7–8) seem to indicate that, following the deposing of Marduk-balatsu-iqbi of Babylon: "For *x* years there was no king in the land" (*ABC* 182). The number of years was originally stated but the reading is now uncertain. Brinkman sees the sign for at least a 2, possibly indicating 12 or more years.[45] Poebel suggests 12 though he says it could also be 33, 35, or 10 written over an erased 30.[46] Whatever the reading, there were at least 4 years, as another text mentions a 4th year with no king in the land.[47]

Referring to Babylonian King List A, Brinkman cites a problem in interpreting the summary in line iv 6, which concerns the period between Baba-aha-iddina and Ninurta-apl?-[x], during which time no available sources attest to any kings ruling Babylon. Brinkman writes, "Most summary lines which give dynastic totals in Kinglist A read: '*x* (years), *x* kings(s), dynasty of GN.' This line [iv 6 in Kinglist A], however, reads simply '*x*, dynasty of GN'; and it is unspecified whether the *x* is to be interpreted as the number of years or the number of kings."[48] Brinkman notes that the number can be read as 22 or 12,[49] but he observes that this could not refer to the total number of years for the dynasty and should refer to the number of kings; the space in king list A could not, however, accommodate 22 kings, and 12 kings would interrupt the sequence of known kings. He reaches no certain conclusion about the meaning of the summary line.[50]

It may be suggested that the summary number in king list A refers to the years of the "kingless period" of Babylonian Chronicle 24. Both records refer to the same time period and both may be read as either 12 or 22 years. Grayson suggests that during the interregnum "Babylon was in the hands of some rival faction, probably the Assyrians or Arameans" (*ABC* 217). The kingless period may then have been due to Shamshi-Adad's assumption of sovereignty over Babylonia after the deposition of Baba-aha-iddina, the reason there was no local king of Babylon during these years.[51] If so, more years must be attributed to Shamshi-Adad's reign from the time he went "to Babylon" in his 12th regnal year until his last year, when he was "in the land," that is, Assyria. As noted, the reconciliation of the biblical record with the Assyrian record requires at least another 8 years if *Ia-ú-a mār Ḫu-um-ri-i* who paid tribute to Shalmaneser in the latter's 18th year is equated with Jehu (and this is not certain; see §7.2.7 and §9.3.1) and if Joash-I's payment of tribute to Adad-nirari occurred no later than his 1st year. More than 8 years are required if *Iaúa* refers to an earlier king (such as Joram, as suggested by McCarter)[52] and if Joash-I's payment of tribute to Adad-nirari occurred later than his 1st year.

This discussion raises serious doubts about the reliability of the AEC before 763 B.C.E. Even the possibility, let alone the proof, that the AEC has eponyms missing from the reigns of Shamshi-Adad V and his successor Adad-nirari III, means that the AEC should not be used as a reliable chronological indicator for dating the Assyrian kings or kings of other nations for the period prior to 763. With no synchronism coming before 763 to provide a Julian date for Israel and

---

45. Brinkman, *Political History of Post-Kassite Babylonia*, 213 and n. 1327.
46. Poebel, "Assyrian King List," 80–81 and n. 293.
47. Brinkman, *Political History of Post-Kassite Babylonia*, 213.
48. Ibid., 52.
49. Ibid., 53, 58.
50. Ibid., 58.
51. Other interregnums in Babylon were times when Assyrian kings ruled there: Tiglath-pileser III (729–727), Shalmaneser V (727–722), Sargon II (709–705), and Sennacherib (703–702 and 687–680).
52. P. K. McCarter, "'Yaw, Son of 'Omri': A Philological Note on Israelite Chronology," *BASOR* 216 (1974): 5–7.

Judah, it remains for a date to be found after 763. Such a date from the AEC/Canon of Ptolemy after 763 could be synchronized with a year of a king of Israel and/or Judah. Working back from such a date would then provide earlier dates for the preceding Hebrew kings.

Despite their problems, the chronologies of Israel and Judah provide a dual set of records that are deliberately pegged to each other. This appears to supply an account intrinsically more reliable before 763 B.C.E. than a single listing of consecutive eponyms of dubious reliability such as the AEC.

6.3. Thiele's Methodology

Having discussed components of Thiele's methodology in previous chapters, I here reiterate the main points and further explain Thiele's coregency hypothesis.

6.3.1. Using MT Data in Preference to the Greek

Thiele's chronology is built upon the MT data in preference to the Greek (see §2.3): "Greek variants came into being because of a failure to understand the meaning of the Hebrew data and from an effort to correct supposed errors" (*MNHK*³ 90). Thiele did not use the same dating systems for the Greek data that he proposes for the MT data. Instead he imposes on the Greek texts what he calls the inconsequent accession-year method: "In this system the year when a ruler is set forth as having begun his reign is actually the year after his reign began" (*MNHK*³ 93). Thiele cites c_2 as an example of the inconsequent accession-year method (following Shenkel, *CRD* 28–30), and he uses it to support his hypothesis that "the late Lucianic redactors were under the impression that the regnal data in the Hebrew text of the Books of Kings were in need of revision" (*MNHK*³ 94). He does not point out that c_2 does not represent the data of the other L manuscripts. After imposing his own hypothetical system on to the Greek texts, Thiele writes, "There is no consistency in methods of chronological procedure . . . only a haphazard jumping back and forth from one system to another, and often the resort is to an utterly fallacious system" (*MNHK*³ 93). Rather than admit that his system does not do justice to the data Thiele disparages the data for not fitting into his system. He keeps attention on the MT data, for which he had hypothesized a system that "works" (*MNHK*³ 60; cf. 211).

By contrast, my methodology seeks to take into consideration all the chronological data appearing in the Hebrew and Greek texts under discussion.

6.3.2. Using Postdating and Antedating

When Thiele formulated his chronology he did not go to the regnal formulas of the Hebrew kings to determine how their reigns were reckoned. Instead, he notes how the surrounding nations reckoned their years:

> In Assyria, Babylon, and Persia when a king first came to the throne, the year was usually called the king's *accession* year, but not till the first day of the first month of the next new year did the king begin reckoning events in his own first year. This system of reckoning is called the *accession-year system*, or *postdating*. In other places a king began to reckon his first year from the day he first came to the throne. This method of reckoning is known as the *nonaccession-year system*, or *antedating*. It will be noticed that any particular year of a king's reign according to the nonaccession-year system is always one year higher than according to the accession-year method. Thus the first year according to the accession-year system would be called the second year according to the nonaccession-year system, and so on. (*MNHK*³ 43–44 [emphasis original]; similarly 47–48)

Thiele does not offer evidence that these dating systems were used in Israel and Judah, yet he employs them as the basis of his chronology. Nor does he explain why the compiler of the composite account in 1–2 Kings would retain unmodified, disparate systems in his sources, if such was the case. Thiele gives no explanation why he does not date kings' accessions "in the *x*th year" of the contemporary king of the other kingdom, even though this was the regular wording of the regnal formulas.

Antedating and postdating systems date a king's reign from the New Year's Day following the accession of the king (noted above), which means that Thiele needed to ascertain which month was the first month of the year. He notes, "Most biblical chronologists have followed a Nisan-to-Nisan year in dealing with the Hebrew kings" (*MNHK*³ 51 and n. 3); but he also writes, "Many of the best modern students of chronology follow a Tishri-to-Tishri reckoning for both Judah and Israel." He continues, "The difficulty with the above systems, however, is that they do not succeed in clearing up the discrepancies in the synchronisms" (*MNHK*³ 51).[53]

6.3.3. Using Tishri Years for Judah, Nisan Years for Israel

1. Thiele argues that there is evidence for a Tishri-to-Tishri year in Judah on the basis of the dates for the building of Solomon's temple. He notes that the foundation was laid in Ziv, the 2nd month of Solomon's 4th year (1 Kgs 6:1, 37), and the temple was finished in Bul, the 8th month of Solomon's 11th year (6:38), but these $7\frac{1}{2}$ years are reckoned as 7 years in 6:38. Ziv is the 2nd month of a year beginning in Nisan. Thiele proposes that if the years were reckoned from Nisan the time taken for the building of the temple would have amounted to 8 years, which conflicts with the stated 7 years. Therefore, he equates the 2nd month of the 4th year not with Ziv but with the month after Tishri, that is, Bul, and the 8th month of the 11th year, not with Bul but with Ziv (seen in *MNHK*³ 52 [diagram 5])! This is completely opposite to what is stated in 6:1, 37–38, but serves Thiele's purpose in reducing 8 years to 7 years to argue for a year beginning in Tishri: "The figure of seven years . . . can be secured only when regnal years are computed from Tishri-to-Tishri but with a Nisan-to-Nisan year used for the reckoning of ordinary events and the ecclesiastical year" (*MNHK*³ 52). Thiele's continued argument for regnal years beginning in Tishri in Judah cannot be sustained. The 7 years are obviously intended as a round number (see §6.1.1 #3).

2. Thiele seeks to find further support for a Tishri-to-Tishri year from the reign of Josiah and the repair of the temple (in the single kingdom). Thiele notes that in Josiah's 18th year the repair of the temple was ordered (2 Kgs 22:3) and Passover was held (23:23). Since Passover is observed on Nisan 14, there would not have been time for the repairs to have been carried out if Josiah's 18th year started in Nisan. Thiele concludes, therefore, that the reckoning must have been from Tishri (*MNHK*³ 51–53). If, however, as I propose, the king's regnal years are dated from his accession and not from either Tishri or Nisan, it could be that Josiah came to the throne well in advance of Nisan 14, which still allowed Passover to be observed within his 18th year.

3. Thiele also argues from Neh 1:1 and 2:1 that Kislev and the following Nisan were both in King Artaxerxes of Persia's 20th year. Thiele infers from this that the year started in Tishri, though he recognizes that the custom was for the year to start in Nisan in Persia

---

53. See also the discussion by D. J. A. Clines, "Regnal Year Reckoning in the Last Years of the Kingdom of Judah," *Australian Journal of Biblical Archaeology* 2 (1972): 9–34; idem, "The Evidence for an Autumnal New Year in Pre-exilic Israel Reconsidered," *JBL* 93 (1974): 22–40; G. H. Jones, *1 and 2 Kings* (New Century Bible Commentary; Grand Rapids: Eerdmans, 1984), 15–17.

(*MNHK*³ 53). Again, it is possible that the king's years were dated from his accession and that Nisan and Kislev were both in Artaxerxes' 20th regnal year. Hugh Williamson cites Bickerman's view:

> He argues that in court circles, in which Nehemiah moved, it would not have been unusual to follow the regnal rather than the calendar year, and he cites an independent example from Thucydides (8:58) to support this claim. In addition, he maintains that Artaxerxes ascended the throne in the month of Ab (22 July–20 August). In a regnal year based on this date, Kislev would be the fifth month and Nisan the ninth. Thus 1:1 would refer to December 446 B.C. and 2:1 to the following spring.[54]

    Bickerman's view supports a regnal year dating system, not a Nisan or Tishri year system.

4. Thiele's proposals for a Judahite Tishri-to-Tishri year requires an explanation of Jer 36:22: "It was the ninth month and the king was sitting in the winter house and there was a fire burning in the brazier." The 9th month was a winter month, inferring that the first month was Nisan, in the spring. This seems to counter Thiele's argument that Judah followed a Tishri-to-Tishri year, at least for the last kings of Judah.

5. Regarding Nisan years in Israel, Thiele comments, "For Israel there seems to be no direct scriptural evidence as to the time of the beginning of the regnal year. However, when a Nisan-to-Nisan regnal year is used for Israel together with a Tishri-to-Tishri year for Judah, the perplexing discrepancies disappear" (*MNHK*³ 53).

I conclude that Thiele's "perplexing discrepancies" have not disappeared at all and that evidence is absent from the biblical record to support antedating or postdating or years starting in Tishri in Judah and Nisan in Israel. Thiele's utilization of four dating systems to cope with the MT chronological data (*MNHK*³ 54–57) cannot be sustained. Separate dating systems were not used and recorded independently in Israel and Judah, nor were there switches in dating systems. Thiele's assertions that the MT data can be synchronized only when changes in dating systems are invoked, without supporting evidence, emphasizes the precarious methodology on which his chronology rests.

6.3.4. Using Coregencies

Another principle Thiele uses to bring the MT data into "harmony" is an assumption of coregencies,[55] that is, "when a son sits on the throne with his father" (*MNHK*³ 231).[56] Thiele explains further:

> Concerning the regnal data for coregencies and rival reigns, it is vital to know that in five of the nine such reigns the datum for the length of reign is the number of years from the beginning of the period of overlap to the end of the sole reign, but the synchronism of accession marks the end of the overlap and the commencement of the sole reign. This I term *dual dating*. Failure to under-

---

54. H. G. M. Williamson, *Ezra, Nehemiah* (Word Biblical Commentary 16; Waco: Word, 1985), 170, citing E. J. Bickerman, "En Marge de l'Écriture, I: Le comput des années de règne des Achéménides (Néh., i,2: ii,1 et Thuc., viii,58," *Revue Biblique* 88 (1981): 19–23.

55. See also E. R. Thiele, "The Question of Coregencies among the Hebrew Kings," in *A Stubborn Faith: Papers on the Old Testament and Related Subjects Presented to Honor William Andrew Irwin* (ed. E. C. Hobbs; Dallas: Southern Methodist University Press, 1956), 39–52; idem, "Coregencies and Overlapping Reigns among the Hebrew Kings," *JBL* 93 (1974): 174–200.

56. Thiele's definition is not strictly applied by him because he claims a coregency between Pekahiah and Pekah, but Pekah was Pekahiah's army captain (2 Kgs 15:25) not his son. See *MNHK*³ 63, 121 (diagram 17), 129.

stand this practice more than anything else has been responsible for the confusion and bewilderment that has arisen concerning the data in Kings. (*MNHK*³ 55 [emphasis original])

Note what Thiele says: the length of reign of a king whose reign commences as a coregent includes both the period of coregency and the subsequent period of sole reign. But accession synchronisms are pegged not to the commencement of a reign as coregent, but to the commencement of a subsequent sole reign. Unless the length of the overlap is known, the data of the regnal formulas cannot be used to determine the length of a king's sole reign. This runs contrary to the apparent intention of the compiler(s) of the regnal formulas to state accurately the length of each king's reign, which they reinforced by supplying accession synchronisms.

Thiele's examples show that a king may have a period of overlap at both the beginning and end of his reign (e.g., Jehoshaphat and Azariah). Coregencies may also occur concurrently in both nations, so that two kings are ruling in Israel while two kings are ruling in Judah. I will briefly consider the proposed coregencies in the order they occur, to examine how Thiele utilizes them in his chronology.

6.3.4.1. Tibni and Omri (Israel)

Thiele's first dual-dating example is Omri's coregency with Tibni (*MNHK*³ 61, 88–94).[57] According to Thiele, using the MT datum for Zimri's accession at 1 Kgs 16:15, Omri began to reign from Asa's 27th year. He also uses Asa's 27th year to date Omri's supposed coregency with Tibni, with Omri's sole reign commencing in Asa's 31st year (16:23) after Tibni died in battle. The 12 years that Omri reigned (16:23) are reckoned from the coregency beginning in Asa's 27th year and ending in Asa's 38th year, when Omri was succeeded by Ahab (16:29 MT) (*MNHK*³ 61–62, 88–92).

Thiele claims that "the Greek editor could not understand how a reign of twelve years for Omri that began in the thirty-first year of Asa could terminate in the thirty-eighth year of Asa with Ahab at that time coming to the throne." So, Thiele concludes, "The Greek editor began the twelve years of Omri, not in the twenty-seventh year of Asa when Omri was first elevated to the kingship at the elimination of Zimri (1 Kings 16:15–18), but in the thirty-first year of Asa" (*MNHK*³ 92). He hypothesizes that the Greek ends the 12 years reign of Omri in Ahab's 2nd year (1 Kgs 16:29) and not Asa's 38th year (16:29 MT) because the Greek editors did not understand dual-dating (*MNHK*³ 92–93).

In Thiele's third edition of *MNHK*, he does not discuss Zimri's accession in Asa's 22nd year, appearing in L manuscripts be$_2$ (16:15). Because Zimri reigned only 7 days, Omri also began to reign in Asa's 22nd year. Thiele ignores this datum, though he tabulates Zimri's accession year at the end of his book (*MNHK*³ 209). Three accession synchronisms to Asa's reign are given for Omri: the 22nd (16:15 be$_2$), the 27th (16:15 MT), and the 31st (16:23 MT/OG/L). Thiele attributes the 31st year synchronism to "the Greek arrangement" (*MNHK*³ 92), while at the same time using it as the commencement of Omri's sole reign in the MT. Since there is already both a Greek synchronism (22nd year) and a MT synchronism (27th year), on what grounds is the 31st year a Greek synchronism?[58] The origin of the three synchronisms for Omri's accession in Asa's

---

57. See also Thiele, "Coregencies and Overlapping Reigns," 175–83, 190.

58. Thiele is not alone in understanding 31st as a Greek synchronism. Even scholars who note that be$_2$ give Zimri's accession in Asa's 22nd year assume 31st is a Greek synchronism. See Shenkel, *CRD* 36–41, 84; D. W. Gooding, review of *CRD* in *Journal of Theological Studies* 21 (1970): 123–25; A. R. Green, "Regnal Formulas in the Hebrew and Greek Texts of the Books of Kings," *Journal of Near Eastern Studies* 42 (1983): 170; Galil, *CKIJ* 136–38; cf. J. M. Miller, "Another Look at the Chronology of the Early Divided Monarchy," *JBL* 86 (1967): 281–84.

22nd, 27th, or 31st year needs to be explained before a coregency between Omri and Tibni can be considered.

The narrative of 16:15–24 relates that after Zimri's death a battle took place between the troops of Omri and Tibni over who would replace Zimri. Tibni died in the skirmish, so Omri became king.[59] Tibni is not credited with an accession synchronism or any regnal years, even though Zimri's accession and short reign of 7 days is recorded. This seems to indicate that Tibni never ruled.

I conclude that the synchronisms given for Omri's reign in OG/L and MT are better understood as an example of textual divergency rather than a coregency between Omri and Tibni.

6.3.4.2. Asa and Jehoshaphat (Judah)

Thiele's next example of a dual-dating coregency is Asa and Jehoshaphat (*MNHK*³ 63, 83, 85–87, 97–98).[60] Thiele states that Jehoshaphat's 25 regnal years actually started in Asa's 39th year when Asa became diseased in his feet (2 Chr 16:12), not after Asa died in his 41st year (1 Kgs 15:10).[61] According to Thiele, the synchronism giving Jehoshaphat's accession in Ahab's 4th year (1 Kgs 22:41 MT/KR) marked his sole reign after the 3 years overlap with Asa (see *MNHK*³ 85 [chart 6, reproduced as my table 6.5]). To understand why Thiele finds this coregency necessary, we need to examine the synchronism for Ahaziah-I's accession after Ahab died. Ahab's reign began in Asa's 38th year, and he died in his 22nd regnal year (16:29 MT), when Ahaziah-I succeeded him. Ahaziah-I's accession is noted in 1 Kgs 22:52 MT/KR as Jehoshaphat's 17th year, but the actual year by calculation has to be 3 years later, in Jehoshaphat's 20th year (table 3.6). In order to make Jehoshaphat's 17th year coincide with Ahaziah-I's accession, Thiele posits a 3-year coregency between Jehoshaphat and Asa in Asa's 39th through 41st years, so that what was Jehoshaphat's 20th coregent year becomes his 17th sole-reign year (see *MNHK*³ 97 [chart 8, reproduced as my table 6.6]). This hypothesis takes care of a 3-year excess in Jehoshaphat's reign.

I noted in chapter 5 that Jehoshaphat's accession in Ahab's 4th year (22:41) is the MT/KR synchronism using pattern 2, indicating its probable secondary nature. The alternative OG/L chronology, which has Ahab's accession in Jehoshaphat's 2nd year (16:29 OG/L) and Ahaziah-I's accession in Jehoshaphat's 24th year (22:52 L) after Ahab had reigned 22 years is perfectly consistent, whereas the MT's synchronism of Ahaziah-I's reign in Jehoshaphat's 17th year is inconsistent. In the OG/L chronology there is no cause to resort to coregency to explain the data. I conclude, therefore, that a coregency between Asa and Jehoshaphat is not warranted by the evidence.

6.3.4.3. Jehoshaphat and Jehoram (Judah)

Thiele's third example of a coregency (not dual-dated) is Jehoshaphat and Jehoram (*MNHK*³ 55, 63, 98–100).[62] Thiele notes the MT's two accession synchronisms for Joram—Jehoram's 2nd

---

59. The Greek has an addition at 16:22 that states that Omri reigned "after (μετά) Tibni." Some scholars see this as meaning after Tibni reigned, whereas the preceding event is Tibni's death to which it must refer. See J. M. Miller, "So Tibni Died (1 Kings xvi 22)," *VT* 18 (1968): 394; Shenkel, *CRD* 40; Galil, *CKIJ* 22 n. 23.

60. See also E. R. Thiele, "The Chronology of the Kings of Judah and Israel," *Journal of Near Eastern Studies* 3 (1944): 151; idem, "The Synchronisms of the Hebrew Kings—A Re-evaluation: I," *Andrews University Seminary Studies* 1 (1963): 136; idem, "Coregencies and Overlapping Reigns," 190–91.

61. This information is not given in the equivalent verse in 1 Kgs 15:23.

62. See also Thiele, "Chronology of the Kings," 149–51; idem, "Question of Coregencies," 41–43; idem, "Synchronisms of the Hebrew Kings—A Re-evaluation: I," 137–38; idem, "Coregencies and Overlapping Reigns," 184–86.

Table 6.5. Thiele's Chart 6 (*MNHK*³ 85)

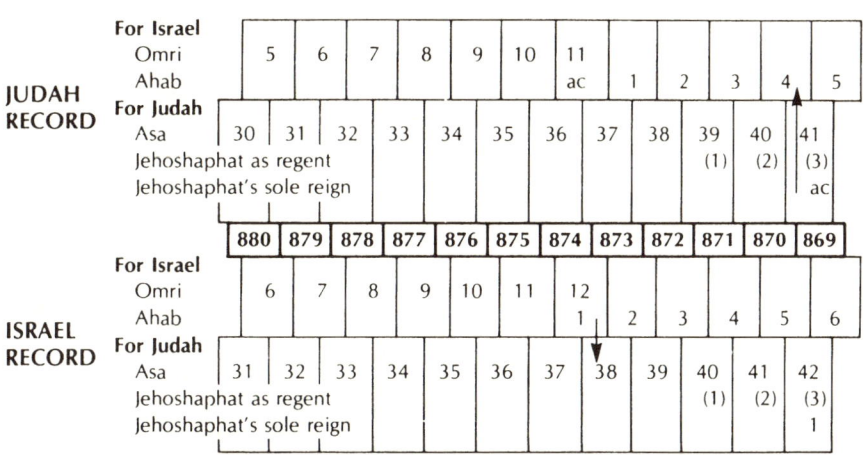

year at 2 Kgs 1:17 and Jehoshaphat's 18th year at 3:1 — and writes, "This undoubtedly points to a coregency between Jehoshaphat and his successor Jehoram, a coregency that is again referred to in 2 Kings 8:16" (*MNHK*³ 55).[63] Thiele assumes that Jehoram's 2nd year must coincide with Jehoshaphat's 18th year, implying a coregency.

According to Thiele, Ahaziah-I's accession occurred in Jehoshaphat's 17th sole-reign year. Ahaziah-I's 2nd year and Joram's 1st sole-reign year correspond to Jehoshaphat's 18th sole-reign year (i.e., after the death of Asa),[64] which is also Jehoram's 2nd year as coregent with Jehoshaphat (see *MNHK*³ 97–98, 101 [charts 8–9 and diagram 12, reproduced as my tables 6.6–8]). Jehoram is coregent with Jehoshaphat for another 4 years, to Jehoshaphat's 24th (coregent) year. And Jehoshaphat's final year is equivalent to Joram's 5th year, at which point Jehoram begins his sole reign in accordance with the synchronism at 2 Kgs 8:16.

---

63. 2 Kgs 8:16 KR has "in the 5th year of Joram, ... Jehoshaphat being then king of Judah ... Jehoram began to reign." Thiele acknowledges in *MNHK*² 181–82 (= *MNHK*³ 199) that this was based on an editorial misunderstanding since "it was not at that time that Jehoshaphat was king of Judah, for that was the year of his death and the commencement of Jehoram's sole reign in the fifth year of Joram of Israel. The statement ... should properly have gone with a synchronism of the commencement of Jehoram's coregency, which began before Joram's accession in Israel." He writes elsewhere, "It is only when the number eight is recognized as the length of Jehoram's sole reign, rather than the total including his coregency, that harmony in the chronological data of this period is possible" (*MNHK*² 199 = *MNHK*³ 210). See Shenkel, *CRD* 81, 133 n. 26; W. H. Barnes, *Studies in the Chronology of the Divided Monarchy of Israel* (Harvard Semitic Monographs 48; Atlanta: Scholars Press, 1991), 20–21; Hughes, *Secrets of the Times*, 106; Galil, *CKIJ* 40.

64. They are not actually sole-reign years, as Jehoram is coregent from Jehoshaphat's 17th year.

Table 6.6. Thiele's Chart 8 (*MNHK*³ 97)

858–847 B.C.

853—Ahaziah—17th of Jehoshaphat—2 years—1 Kings 22:51
853—Jehoram—start of coregency
852—Joram—2d of Jehoram—2 Kings 1:17
    —18th of Jehoshaphat—2 Kings 3:1
    —12 years—2 Kings 3:1
848—Jehoram—5th of Joram—8 years—2 Kings 8:16–17

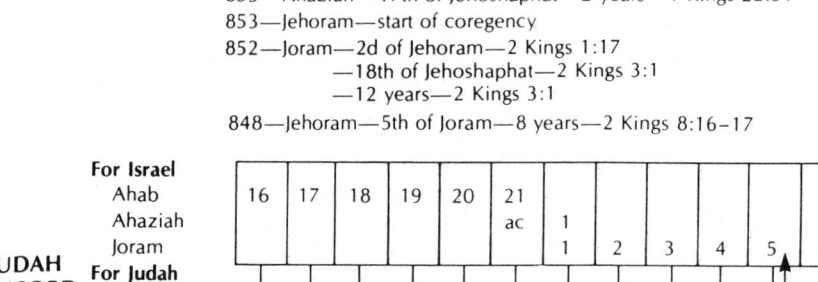

In accord with the practice up to this time, Jehoshaphat in Judah used accession-year reckoning for both Judah and Israel. But with his successor Jehoram, who married Athaliah, the daughter of Ahab and Jezebel of Israel, Judah shifted to the nonaccession-year system used in Israel. Judah followed this system for the reigns of Jehoram, Ahaziah, Athaliah, and Joash, and then shifted back to accession-year reckoning. The years of Jehoshaphat in parentheses are from the beginning of his coregency. Dual-dating procedure was followed for the regnal data of Jehoshaphat. The years of Joram in parentheses are in accord with accession-year reckoning.

Jehoram is credited with 8 regnal years (8:16) but Thiele does not include in this number the years of coregency with Jehoshaphat. Altogether Jehoram is credited with a 14-year reign! If Jehoram's reign had been reckoned by Thiele in the same manner as he reckoned Jehoshaphat's reign, then Jehoram ought to have been reckoned with 14 years at 8:16. Jehoshaphat's 25 years include the 3-year overlap with Asa, but Jehoram's 8 years do not include the 6-year overlap with Jehoshaphat. Why not? Because if Jehoram had a 6-year coregency reign he would have had only 2 years of sole reign, ending in Joram's 7th year. Jehoram's reign being followed by Ahaziah-J's 1 year would mean that Ahaziah-J was killed in Joram's 8th year. But Joram died at the same time as Ahaziah-J after a 12-year reign (3:1) or an 11-year reign according to Thiele's nonaccession-year reckoning (*MNHK*³ 99), so Ahaziah-J and Joram cannot have died 4 years apart! Thiele admits that he has to reckon the 8 years from the end of Jehoshaphat's reign (see p. 109 n. 63 above).

Joram's accession synchronism at 2 Kgs 1:17 MT for Jehoram's 2nd year is based on L data that previously synchronized Ahaziah-I's reign with Jehoshaphat's 24th year (1 Kgs 22:52). This synchronism also appears in 2 Kgs 1:18a L. The synchronism at 3:1, "the 18th year of Jehoshaphat," is an MT/KR datum based on the previous MT/KR synchronism that Ahaziah-I began to reign in Jehoshaphat's 17th year (1 Kgs 22:52). The two synchronisms for Joram's accession can

Table 6.7. Thiele's Chart 9 (*MNHK*³ 101)

847–835 B.C.

841—Ahaziah—11th year of Joram—2 Kings 9:29
—12th year of Joram—2 Kings 8:25
—1 year—2 Kings 8:26
841—Athaliah—regnal data not given
841—Jehu—28 years—2 Kings 10:36
835—Joash—7th of Jehu—40 years—2 Kings 12:1

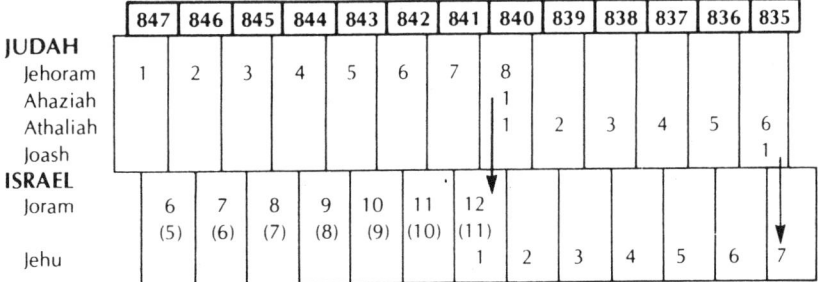

Tishri years for Judah; Nisan years for Israel.
Nonaccession-year reckoning used in both Israel and Judah.
The years of Joram in parentheses are according to accession-year reckoning.

Table 6.8. Thiele's Diagram 12 (*MNHK*³ 98)

874–841 B.C.

```
      874  872      869        853      852      848          841
JUDAH
      Asa 38        41
                 Jehoshaphat      (17)     (18)      25
                 regent       sole reign
                              Jehoram   2                       8
                              regent              sole reign  Ahaziah
                                                              Athaliah
ISRAEL
      Ahab         4          22
                              Ahaziah   2
                                        Joram    5           11 accession-year
                                                                reckoning
                                                             12 nonaccession-year
                                                                reckoning
```

be understood to reflect the divergence between the Greek and Hebrew texts; they are not evidence for a coregency between Jehoshaphat and Jehoram.

6.3.4.4. Joash-I and Jeroboam II (Judah)

Thiele's third example of a dual-dating coregency is Joash-I and his son Jeroboam II (*MNHK*³ 62, 106–16).[65] Thiele notes that Jeroboam II's accession is synchronized with Amaziah's 15th year

---

65. See Thiele, "Question of Coregencies," 43–47; idem, "Coregencies and Overlapping Reigns," 191–93.

Table 6.9. Thiele's Diagram 16 (*MNHK*³ 118)

841–740 B.C.

```
     841  835  814      798  796  792  782  767  753      752      750  742  740

JUDAH
Athaliah
       Joash  23        37        40
                              Amaziah   15        29
                                   Azariah              38   39   39        50   52
                                                                       Jotham
ISRAEL
Jehu   7    28
             Jehoahaz  17
                     Jehoash  2         16
                              Jeroboam II    27   41
                                         Zechariah
                                              Shallum
                                              Menahem
                                                    Pekah  2
                                                       Pekahiah 2
```

(2 Kgs 14:23) and that Amaziah lived 15 more years after Joash-I died (14:17). This means that Amaziah's son, Azariah, should have begun to reign in Jeroboam II's 14th or 15th year. Azariah's accession, however, is given for Jeroboam II's 27th year (15:1). Thiele accounts for the discrepancy by claiming that Jeroboam II had a 12-year coregency with Joash-I, so that Jeroboam II's 41 years included 12 years of overlap and 29 years of sole reign.

In previous discussion (§3.2.3,) I noted that a variant of Jeroboam II's 14th year for Azariah's accession (Josephus, *Antiquities* 9.216) is consistent with the preceding data. If the 14th is the correct datum, then the 27th is secondary, and Thiele's assumption of a coregency between Joash-I and Amaziah is without basis.

6.3.4.5. Amaziah and Azariah (Judah)

Thiele's fourth example of a dual-dating coregency is Amaziah and Azariah (*MNHK*³ 63–64, 108–11, 113–20; see previous discussion in §3.2.3),[66] beginning only 2 years after his proposed coregency of Joash-I and Jeroboam II in Israel. Thiele claims that Azariah was coregent with his father Amaziah for 24 of his father's 29 years, Azariah himself ruling for 52 years (2 Kgs 15:2). Following Thiele's argument, if Azariah began ruling in Jeroboam II's 27th year and reigned 52 years, he should have died 14 years after Jeroboam II. Jeroboam II reigned 41 years (14:23). If Jeroboam II's 27th year coincides with Azariah's 1st year, Jeroboam II's 41st year and the accession of Zechariah occurred 14–15 years later, and the expected date would have been in Azariah's 15th/16th year (see table 3.6 above, pp. 44–45, and *MNHK*³ 118 [diagram 16, reproduced as my table 6.9]). The accession synchronism for Zechariah is, however, in Azariah's 38th year (15:8), which is 23–24 years later. Thiele proposes that the extra 24 years is to be accounted for as a period of coregency between Amaziah and Azariah and that the remaining 28 years is the period of sole reign, the data being explicable in terms of dual-dating.

---

66. See Thiele, "Question of Coregencies," 43–50; idem, "Coregencies and Overlapping Reigns," 191–93.

The proposal that Azariah ruled 24 years before Amaziah died causes a problem for Thiele because Azariah was only 16 years old when the people made him king after his father died in a conspiracy (2 Kgs 14:21). How then could Azariah have reigned 24 years before his father died — 8 of them before he, Azariah, was born? Thiele explains that when Joash-I captured Amaziah he took him to Samaria and the vacant throne in Jerusalem caused the people to make 16-year-old Azariah king. Thiele asserts that the account at 14:21 of Azariah's accession placed after the death of his father Amaziah is a postscript that "should more properly have been placed immediately after the account of the war of Jehoash [Joash-I] with Amaziah at 2 Kings 14:8–14 and 2 Chronicles 25:21–24" (*MNHK*³ 119).

Second Kgs 14:13–14 states that Joash-I captured Amaziah at Bethshemesh and took him to Jerusalem, whereupon Joash-I broke down the walls and took hostages and treasures back to Samaria. It does not say that Amaziah was taken to Samaria and that Judah's throne was vacant. According to Josephus, Joash-I captured Amaziah outside Jerusalem and was threatened with death unless he persuaded the Jerusalemites to open the city gates. Amaziah complied and Joash-I released him. This took place in Amaziah's 14th year (*Antiquities* 9.200–203). Joash-I, however, must have died soon after this victory, because in Amaziah's 15th year, Jeroboam II son of Joash-I began to reign in Israel (14:23). Only after we learn of Amaziah's death (coming 15 years after Joash-I died [14:17]) are we told of Azariah's accession. Thiele's method alters the meaning of the text to fit a coregency into his chronology, then alleges the insertion of an editorial postscript in the wrong place to justify his alteration.

If Azariah's accession is synchronized with Jeroboam II's 14th year, as in Josephus's variant, Jeroboam II's final (41st) year ends in Azariah's 28th year, not the 38th, when Zechariah came to the throne (2 Kgs 15:8). I discussed this in §3.2.3 and will return to it in the next chapter. Suffice it to say here that I find no evidence for a coregency between Amaziah and Azariah.

6.3.4.6. Pekah and Menahem/Pekahiah (Israel)
6.3.4.7. Azariah and Jotham (Judah)

Thiele's next two coregencies need to be considered together (*MNHK*³ 63, 120, 124, 128–37, 199–200).[67] Thiele's fifth example of a dual-dating coregency is Pekah coreigning first with Menahem (10 years) and then with Pekahiah (2 years), followed by 8 years of sole reign for a total reign of 20 years (2 Kgs 15:27). Thiele's second example of coregency not employing dual dating — which took place concurrently with Pekah's two coregencies in Israel — is Azariah and his son Jotham in Judah. After contracting leprosy, Azariah lived in a house by himself and Jotham took charge of the royal household and governed the people (2 Kgs 15:5). Thiele and other scholars use this biblical example for validating coregency as a legitimate method (*MNHK*³ 55, 64).[68] But, as Hughes points out, "2 Kings 15.5f. is the one clear situation in Kings that might have called for a coregency, with Azariah being unable to carry out his royal duties, and yet the text of Kings plainly indicates that a coregency was not created. This must make it extremely doubtful that coregencies ever existed as a possible form of government in Israel or Judah."[69]

---

67. See also E. R. Thiele, "The Synchronisms of the Hebrew Kings — A Re-evaluation: II," *Andrews University Seminary Studies* 2 (1964): 126–33; idem, "Pekah to Hezekiah," *VT* 16 (1966): 83–107; idem, "Coregencies and Overlapping Reigns," 194–200.

68. S. J. De Vries, "Chronology of the OT," in *Interpreter's Dictionary of the Bible* (ed. G. A. Buttrick; New York: Abingdon, 1962), 1:587; J. Gray, *1 and 2 Kings* (Old Testament Library; London: SCM, 1970), 57; Tadmor, "Chronology of the First Temple Period," 53, 57; Galil, *CKIJ* 59–60.

69. Hughes, *Secrets of the Times*, 104–5.

Table 6.10. Thiele's Diagram 18 (*MNHK*³ 130)

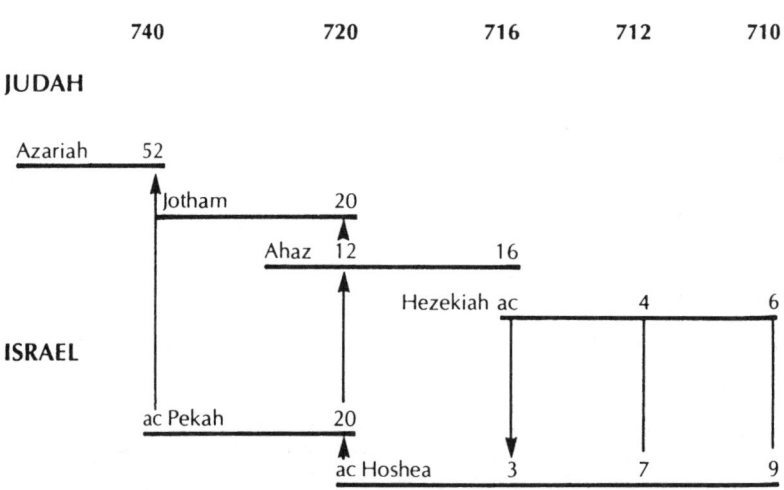

When Thiele first reconstructed the reigns of the kings under consideration, he did not assume a coregency for Pekah with Menahem and Pekahiah or for Jotham with Azariah (see *MNHK*³ 130 [diagram 18, reproduced as my table 6.10]). He had already dated Azariah's 52nd and last year to 740 on the basis of constructing the kings' reigns according to his dating systems and coregencies, with the initial dates of Ahab's last year falling in 853 and Jehu's 1st year falling in 841. Jotham succeeded Azariah in Pekah's 2nd year (15:32) so that Jotham and Pekah began to reign within a year of each other, approximately 740. Pekah's 20th (supposedly final) year coincided then with Jotham's 20th year (15:30 conflicts with the 16 years of 15:33), which meant that both of their successors, Hoshea and Ahaz respectively, should have begun to reign about 720. Since a second synchronism for Hoshea places his accession in Ahaz's 12th year (17:1), Thiele overlaps Ahaz's reign with Jotham's by 12 years to synchronize Jotham's 20th with Ahaz's 12th. This gives Ahaz 4 years of sole reign, equivalent to Hoshea's first 3 years, before Hezekiah succeeded Ahaz in Hoshea's 3rd year (18:1) in 716. The fall of Samaria, dated to Hezekiah's 6th year and Hoshea's 9th year (18:10) occurred in 710.

However, Thiele realizes that his chronology places the reigns of Hoshea and Ahaz 12 years later than can be allowed (*MNHK*³ 135–36). The accession of Hoshea, who killed Pekah, apparently at the instigation of Tiglath-pileser III of Assyria (see §8.3.3), must fall in 732[70] because, according to the AEC dates and notations, Tiglath-pileser III came to Damascus in 733/732.

Thiele hypothesizes a new arrangement for Judah in which Jotham's reign is thrust back 12 years to overlap with Azariah's, and for Israel Pekah's is thrust back 12 years to overlap with Menahem and Pekahiah. Thiele states (see *MNHK*³ 121 [diagram 17, my table 6.11]):

> In 750, the second year of Pekah, Jotham began his reign of sixteen official years (fifteen actual years) in a coregency with Azariah (2 Kings 15:32–33). In 735, the end of the sixteen official years of Jotham, Ahaz took the throne of Judah in the seventeenth year of Pekah (2 Kings 16:1).

---

70. Thiele, *MNHK*³ 125; idem, "Pekah to Hezekiah," 86.

Table 6.11. Thiele's Diagram 17 (*MNHK*³ 121)

752-701 B.C.

```
              752   750  742      740  735    732      723    716/15      701

JUDAH
Azariah         39        50       52
                   Jotham      ↑   ↑  16      20
                                     Ahaz                      16
                                                           Hezekiah  14
ISRAEL
Menahem        ac         10
                     Pekahiah  2
Pekah          ac    2              17       20
                                          Hoshea    9
```

Regnal years in diagram 17 are actual years since the data for both Israel and Judah are in accord with the accession-year system. The data for Pekah are in accord with dual-dating procedure.

Although not on the throne, Jotham continued to 732, his twentieth year (2 Kings 15:30). Then Ahaz began sixteen years of rule that terminated in 716/15 when Hezekiah came to the throne. That brings us to the fourteenth year of Hezekiah in 701, a date firmly established in Assyrian chronology by the attack of Sennacherib on Hezekiah that year. (*MNHK*³ 120, similarly, 124–25)

Regarding Israel, Thiele writes,

In the pattern that begins Pekah's reign in 740 he is twelve years beyond his true position, and so also are Jotham and Hoshea. When Hoshea is in his true position, his reign is over before that of Hezekiah begins. Also, Hoshea begins his nine years in 732 when the sixteen years of Ahaz begin. Thus it is only when the synchronisms of 2 Kings 17 and 18 are seen as late and artificial that the true picture of Hebrew history of this important time can be reconstructed. (*MNHK*³ 136)

Notice that Thiele asserts that the synchronism at 17:1 giving the opening regnal formula of Hoshea's reign synchronized with Ahaz's 12th year is "late and artificial," as are the synchronisms in 2 Kings 18 that the siege began in Hezekiah's 4th year and Hoshea's 7th year and that the fall of Samaria occurred in Hezekiah's 6th year and Hoshea's 9th year (18:9–10).[71] Thiele seeks to prove that "the Old Testament is silent about any contacts between Hezekiah and Hoshea" (*MNHK*³ 168).[72] The synchronisms do not fit his chronology even when he imposes coregencies. Rather than admit that his chronology cannot reconcile the data, Thiele blames the editors of Kings instead: "Failure to recognize dual dating for Pekah threw him and Hoshea twelve years beyond their true positions in history. This misunderstanding was responsible for the synchronisms in 2 Kings 17 and 18" (*MNHK*³ 137; similarly 130, 134, 136).

The hypothesized coregency between Pekah and Pekahiah is problematic for Thiele because Pekahiah was not the son of Pekah (2 Kgs 15:25) and, therefore, as a rival, could not have sat on

---

71. Similarly, Cogan and Tadmor, *II Kings*, 195.
72. For Galil's criticism of this expediency, see *CKIJ* 86–87.

the same throne. Thiele seeks to validate his idea of two rival reigns in Israel, with Pekah ruling from Gilead, from the King James Version of Hos 5:5: "Therefore shall Israel and Ephraim fall in their iniquity" (*MNHK*³ 63, 129–30).[73] This is merely a case of Hebrew parallelism with the *waw* between Israel and Ephraim indicating apposition ("even, indeed") — not that Israel had been divided into two kingdoms.[74] In fact, 2 Kgs 15:27 records that Pekah was king of Israel in Samaria, not in Gilead. The idea of two rival northern kingdoms is predicated on the need for a coregency, not on the observation that two kingdoms merited two kings. Two rival kingdoms would not have been theorized unless a coregency was imposed to give the kings their "correct" dates.

I previously discussed the synchronisms for Hoshea's accession (§3.2.3, §5.1.2.2, §5.3.14) at 2 Kgs 15:30: "Hoshea made a conspiracy against Pekah . . . and struck him down and slew him and reigned in his stead in the 20th year of Jotham." The phrase *in the 20th year of Jotham* is an exception to the normal practice of ending a closing formula with the succession statement and not an accession synchronism. Furthermore, the synchronism conflicts with 15:33 in stating that Jotham reigned 16 years and with the synchronism at 17:1 that Hoshea began to reign in Ahaz's 12th year.

The synchronism at 15:30 seems to be based on the earlier datum that Pekah reigned 20 years (15:27), which is likely an error for Pekah's 29th or 30th year (§3.2.3).[75] This caused Pekah's 20th year to end in Ahaz's 4th, which would have been Jotham's 20th year if Jotham had actually lived 20 years (16 + 4). Jotham's 20th year at 15:30 does not take into account that Jotham reigned only 16 years, the datum that appears at 15:33. The shortening of Pekah's reign from 29/30 to 20 years seems responsible for the secondary addition at 15:30 recording Pekah's assassination by Hoshea "in the 20th year of Jotham." The opening regnal formula for Hoshea remains at its original position at 17:1. A coregency to explain the two synchronisms is unwarranted.

6.3.4.8. Jotham and Ahaz (Judah)

Thiele's eighth example of a coregency, and the third not dual-dated, is Jotham and his son Ahaz (*MNHK*³ 64, 121, 132–33, 136, 199). With Jotham's reign beginning in 750, his 16-year reign would have ended in 735 when Ahaz succeeded him in Pekah's 17th year (2 Kgs 16:1). Thiele, however, asserts that Jotham did not die at that time but was allowed to live till 732 (see *MNHK*³ 121 [diagram 17]). This credits Jotham with his 20th year when Hoshea killed Pekah (15:30). Ahaz is credited with 16 years (15:33); if his reign began in 735, he should have died in 720/719. However, his successor, Hezekiah, did not begin to reign until 716/715 because, according to Thiele's understanding, Hezekiah's 14th year was in 701, for him a fixed date. This left 4 years between the death of Ahaz and the accession of Hezekiah. Thiele's solution was to give Ahaz a 4-year overlap with Jotham's 16th–20th years (though not on the throne) and count Ahaz's 16 years from 732 not 735. Thus Jotham and Ahaz had a coregency from 735 to 732. Thiele seeks to justify this coregency thus: "The combined attack on Jerusalem by Rezin of Aram and Pekah of Israel is mentioned in the account of Ahaz at 2 Kings 16:5–7 and also in a postscript to the account of Jotham at 2 Kings 15:37. That clearly points to an overlap between Jotham and Ahaz. If the attack had come when Jotham was in full control, it would have been reported only in the account of his reign" (*MNHK*³ 132). The "overlap" is not at all clear. The texts recount that Rezin

---

73. See discussion by Hughes, *Secrets of the Times*, 101–2.

74. D. Stuart, *Hosea–Jonah* (Word Biblical Commentary 31; Waco: Word, 1987), 93, where he also notes "the verb in the plural is not surprising." For a contrary opinion see H. J. Cook, "Pekah," *VT* 14 (1964): 127–35.

75. Galil asserts that Pekah could not have reigned for 20 years because Menahem gave tribute to Tiglath-pileser III in 738 and Hoshea gave tribute in 731. Pekah's reign could have been only about 7 years (*CKIJ* 65). Both of these dates are assumptions that I discuss further in §8.2.4.

and Pekah began attacking Judah while Jotham was king. After his death they intensified their efforts by besieging Jerusalem. This does not call for a coregency. Thiele posits a coregency to account for the absence of 4 years in his chronology of Judah.

6.3.4.9. Hezekiah and Manasseh (Judah)

Thiele's ninth and final example of a coregency (and the fourth not dual-dated) is Hezekiah and his son Manasseh (*MNHK*³ 64, 174, 176–77). While this does not occur during the DK, I mention it here because it impinges on the date of Hezekiah's accession. Thiele writes, "During his last ten years (696–686), Hezekiah associated Manasseh with him as regent" (*MNHK*³ 176). This 10-year coregency is necessary because of "the excess of ten years in the reigns of the kings of Judah from the death of Hezekiah in 686 to the accession of Jehoiachin in 597" (*MNHK*³ 177). Thiele dates Sennacherib's attack on Judah in Hezekiah's 14th year (2 Kgs 18:13) to the year 701, about which he says, "Full confidence can be placed in 701 as the fourteenth year of Hezekiah, and complete confidence can be placed in any other dates for either Israel or Judah reckoned from that date in accord with the requirements of the numbers in Kings" (*MNHK*³ 174). If Thiele's date for Hezekiah's 14th year is a textual error for his 24th year as some scholars suggest,[76] then no reason exists to posit a coregency to delete 10 excess years from the chronology. (The date of the fall of Samaria and the years of Hezekiah's reign are discussed in §8.3.)

6.3.4.10. Summary

Thiele's attempt to shorten the Hebrew chronology by overlapping the reigns of kings highlights the problem of chronology bound to the AEC years between 853 (supposedly Ahab's last year) and 701. If indeed years are missing from the AEC collation, additional years not currently recognized can be allowed to the Hebrew chronology for the entire length of the DK.

In none of the nine examples of coregency discussed above is one certain coregency elicited from the text. Thiele uses coregencies for several reasons: to explain the presence of more than one accession synchronism for a king; to explain conflicting and otherwise irreconcilable data; to remove unwanted excess years from the chronology. I conclude that the biblical text does not warrant the assumption of even one coregency.

6.3.5. Using the AEC to Establish a Starting Date

The last major issue of Thiele's methodology concerns the establishment of a starting date for the chronology of the Hebrew kings. As mentioned previously, Thiele dates the Hebrew kings' reigns to the AEC on the basis that Ahab's last year was Shalmaneser's 6th, which coincided with the battle of Qarqar, commonly dated to 853. *Iaúa*'s tribute to Shalmaneser in the latter's 18th year is attributed to Jehu's 1st year, 12 years after 853, therefore 841. To make only 12 years between the 6th and 18th years of Shalmaneser III entails reducing Ahaziah-I's 2-year reign to 1 year and Joram's 12 years to 11 years using the nonaccession-year dating system (*MNHK*³ 76–78). But there is no indication in regnal formulas or elsewhere that the 14 years should be 12 years, that the battle of Qarqar occurred in 853, or that *Iaúa* gave tribute in 841. Based on these dates

---

76. G. Smith, "On a New Fragment of the Assyrian Canon Belonging to the Reigns of Tiglath-pileser and Shalmaneser," *Transactions of the Society of Biblical Archaeology* 2 (1873): 323, 327; J. A. Montgomery, *A Critical and Exegetical Commentary on the Books of Kings* (ed. H. S. Gehman; International Critical Commentary; Edinburgh: Clark, 1951), 483; H. H. Rowley, "Men of God," in *Studies in Old Testament History and Prophecy* (London: Nelson, 1963), 113; E. J. Young, *The Book of Isaiah* (New International Commentary on the Old Testament; Grand Rapids: Eerdmans, 1969), 2:541–42; Archer, *Encyclopaedia of Bible Difficulties*, 207, 211; Jones, *1 and 2 Kings*, 25.

Thiele fixes the beginning of the DK to 931/930 (*MNHK*³ 78–80). No corroboration of these dates exists in extrabiblical sources. The result of shortening the Hebrew chronology to fit the AEC is seen toward the end of the DK when the reigns of the last kings will not fit into the years remaining before Hezekiah's 14th year in 701. This forces Thiele to posit coregencies to make the reigns concur with the AEC dates. The method cannot be recommended.

6.4. Taking up Thiele's Challenge

At the end of his book, Thiele asserts, "This chain [the chronological evidence of the MT data] we believe to be complete, sound, and capable of withstanding any challenge that historical evidence may bring to it. It is only proper that the dates we have given here for the rulers of Israel and Judah should be subjected to every possible test" (*MNHK*³ 211–12). Since Thiele therefore invites challenge to his chronology, in following chapters I propose a reconstruction based on the Hebrew and Greek data, consonant with the regnal formulas of the Books of Kings.

I hypothesize one original Hebrew text of the Books of Kings that recorded with an accuracy appropriate to its religious and historical purposes the lengths and accession synchronisms in Israel and Judah. From this the first and subsequent generations of texts derived their data. The variant data that now exist in the earliest extant Hebrew and Greek texts (MT/KR, OG/L) suggest that some original data have been replaced with secondary data. I hope to recover enough of the original data by textual analysis to reconstruct the chronology.

The methodology to determine whether accession synchronisms and regnal years are internally consistent employs the following principles in constructing the tables in the following chapters:

1. Only one dating system was employed by the compiler(s) of 1–2 Kings to record the reigns in Israel and Judah.
2. The dating system remained constant throughout the DK.
3. Kings began to reign upon the death of their predecessor from whatever date this occurred in the civil calendar.
4. A king's 1st regnal year was reckoned from his accession and dated by the compiler of 1–2 Kings to the regnal year of the contemporary king of the neighboring kingdom. Subsequent years were counted from the accession date.
5. The regnal years of each king were reckoned as rounded years, whether up or down, unless the king ruled less than a year, then in months or days.
6. Each year of a king's reign was reckoned as a full year except his last.
7. The approximate length of the final year is estimated by keeping consecutive synchronisms and regnal years in step with each other.
8. Coregencies are not considered, being witnessed neither by the regnal formulas nor any other textual evidence.

While verification of the chronology will be sought from extrabiblical sources, the reliability of the AEC prior to 763 B.C.E. will not be assumed. Indeed, common assumptions about the AEC will be challenged by new proposals based on other evidence.

7

Relative Chronology of the Early Divided Kingdom

7.1. Explanation of Table 7.1

Table 7.1 represents the reigns of the EDK kings of Israel and Judah and gives their accession synchronisms and regnal years (for the method employed, see §6.1.1). This table gives a comparative overview of the data in the OG/L, the MT, and a hypothetical pre-MT (the pre-MT data ends with the accessions of Jehoshaphat and Ahab).[1] Calendar years are noted at the top of the table and numbered consecutively from year 1 at the beginning of Rehoboam's reign. Each year of a king's reign is a full year, except his last, which is often part of a year. The total number of years attributed to a king's reign is rounded up or down. If rounded up, the reign ends before the final year is complete and is numbered on the table. Or, if rounded down, the reign extends into the next year, in which case the partial year is not numbered but left blank.

The adjusted data shown in the OG/L register of table 7.1 represent the original chronology of the EDK. This conclusion arises from the following discussion of textual variants in the OG/L, MT, and a hypothetical pre-MT.

7.2. Explanation of Early Divided Kingdom Chronology

7.2.1. Rehoboam (Judah); Jeroboam I (Israel)

Rehoboam reigned 17 years (1 Kgs 14:21).[2] His son, Abijam, began to reign in Jeroboam I's 18th year (15:1). Consistent with my methodology that a final year of a king's reign may be somewhat more or less than the round number stated, Rehoboam has 17 full years plus additional months in his 18th year. This enables Abijam's accession (immediately following his father's death in accordance with my stated methodology) to synchronize with Jeroboam I's 18th year.

Jeroboam I's reign begins slightly later than Rehoboam's since Jeroboam I was in Egypt when Rehoboam became king (12:2–3a, 20). An estimated 1–2 months has been allowed for Jeroboam I's return journey before he became king of Israel. Apart from this starting point, the positioning of the kings' reigns occur without reference to the commencement of a calendar year.

---

1. The term *pre-MT* is used to avoid associating this text with a proto-MT as a forerunner of the MT. Whether the data arose in a proto-MT or another text-type cannot be known; hence the vague designation "pre-MT."

2. Codex Vaticanus at 1 Kgs 12:24a (not present in MT) states that Rehoboam was 16 years old when he began to reign and he reigned 12 years. At 12:24a boc$_2$e$_2$ state that Rehoboam was 41 years when he began to reign and he reigned 17 years, concurring with 14:21 MT/OG/L. The variant data of Vaticanus at 12:24a conflict with the following synchronisms. For comment on variant numbers see §7.3.6.

Table 7.1. Early Divided Kingdom Chronology

7.2.2. Abijam and Asa (Judah); Nadab and Baasha (Israel)

Abijam is accorded 6 regnal years in OG/L but 3 years in MT — a major difference that has many connected effects. Abijam's 6 years in OG/L requires that Asa's accession be synchronized with Jeroboam I's 24th year (1 Kgs 15:9 OG/L). But Abijam's 3 years in MT make Asa's accession synchronize with Jeroboam I's 20th year (15:9 MT). Jeroboam I's regnal years are not stated in OG/L, though the next synchronism, Nadab's accession in Asa's 2nd year (15:25), indicates that Jeroboam I reigned either 24 or 25 years. To determine which is preferred, note that Nadab's 2-year reign (15:25 all texts) is followed by Baasha's accession in Asa's 3rd year (15:28, 33 all texts). If Baasha began to reign in Asa's 3rd year, then Nadab's prior accession would be expected to synchronize with Asa's 1st year if Jeroboam I reigned 24 years. But the 2nd is also possible in OG/L if Jeroboam I reigned 25 years and Baasha's accession occurred at the end of Asa's 3rd year. If Jeroboam I reigned 25 years, Nadab's 2nd (and final) year is less than a full year, but still conforms to my methodology. Jeroboam I's reign in OG/L is thus either 24 or 25 years in length — two options that can be resolved by the following considerations.

Table 7.1. Early Divided Kingdom Chronology (cont.)

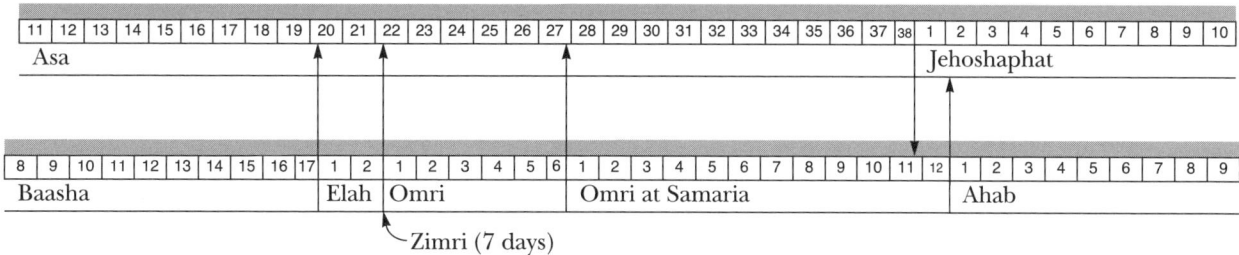

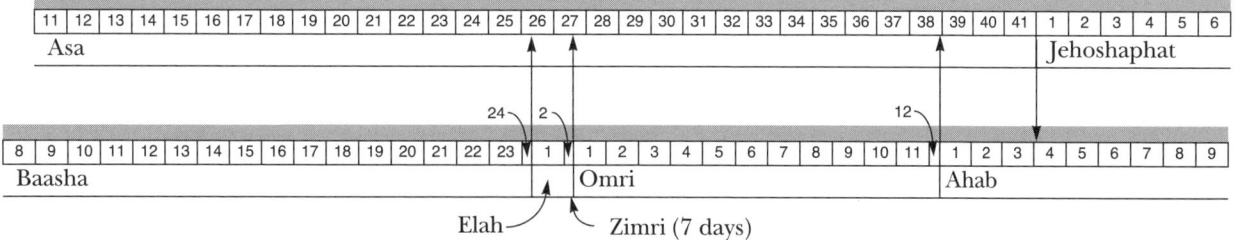

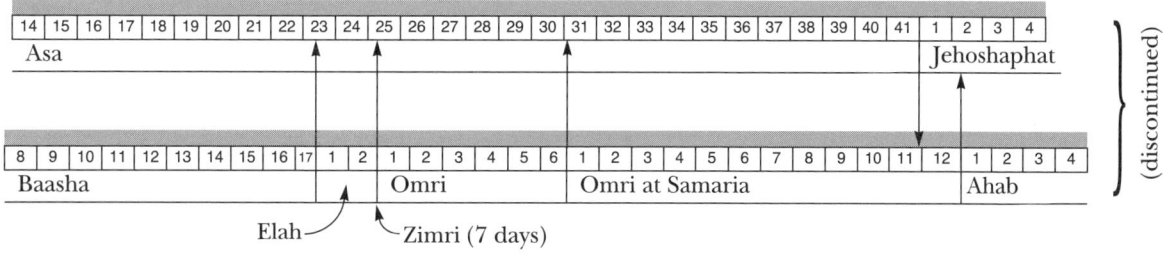

Nadab's accession synchronism belongs to pattern 2 of opening regnal formulas (king's name first), whereas Baasha's regnal formula follows pattern 1 (synchronism first). I concluded in §5.2 that the presence of pattern 2 indicates reworked text and that apart from this one occasion in OG/L (and its irregular occurrence in L alone at 2 Kgs 1:18a and 15:13) pattern 2 occurs only in the MT or KR. If, therefore, Nadab's accession in Asa's 2nd year is not an original synchronism, what might account for its presence? The MT credits Jeroboam I with 22 years (1 Kgs 14:20) and synchronizes Nadab's accession with Asa's 2nd year (15:25). Nadab's accession in Asa's 1st year— a distinct possibility in the OG/L arrangement—is not possible in the MT. As it is, Jeroboam I's 22nd year has to be very short in order to accommodate Nadab's accession in Asa's 2nd year, and Nadab's 2nd year can consist of only a few months if Baasha's accession is to synchronize with Asa's 3rd year.

Nadab's accession in Asa's 2nd year is questionable because it employs pattern 2. In OG/L the preferred length of reign for Jeroboam I is 24 years, not 25, because 24 years concurs better with Baasha's accession in Asa's 3rd year, which employs pattern 1. This consideration indicates that

Table 7.1. Early Divided Kingdom Chronology (cont.)

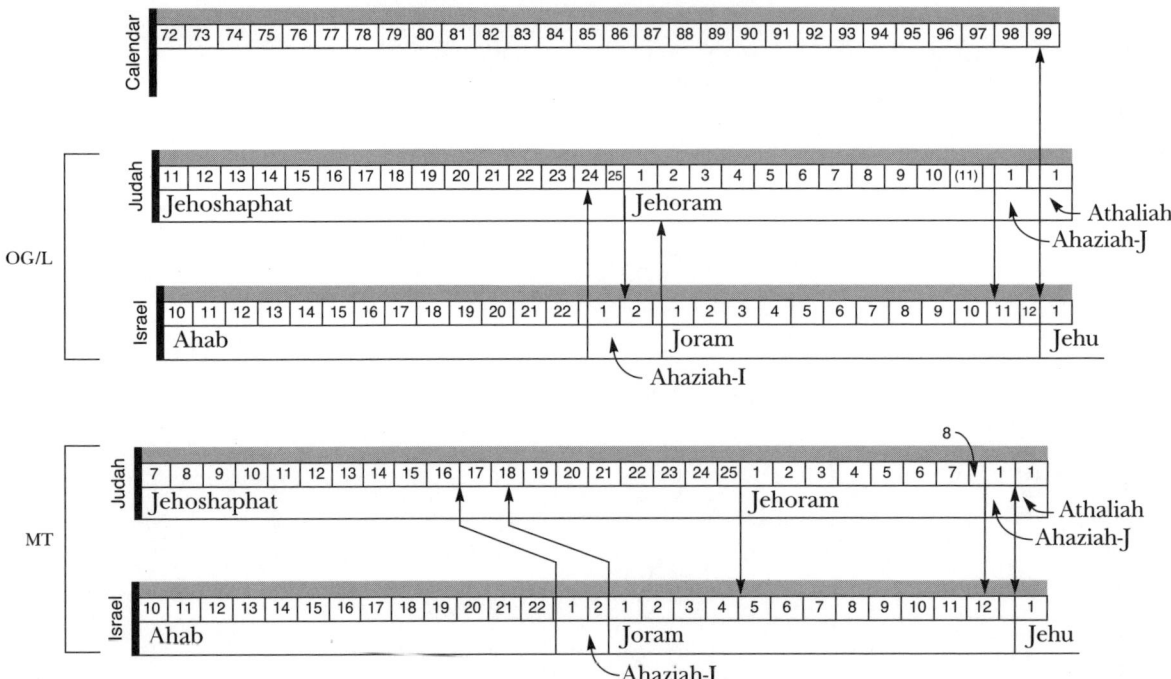

Nadab's original accession in Asa's 1st year was changed to the 2nd. The change was required by the MT after Jeroboam I's reign was shortened from 24 to 22 years,[3] because Nadab's accession no longer synchronized with Asa's 1st year. In MT, Asa's accession was synchronized with Jeroboam I's 20th year, and Nadab's accession with Asa's 2nd year. In OG/L, Jeroboam I's 24 years and Nadab's 2 years synchronize easily with Asa's 1st and 3rd years respectively, while in MT Jeroboam I's 22 years and Nadab's 2 years can scarcely meet the synchronisms except by positing very short final years for both Jeroboam I and Nadab. If these had been the original years, it seems more likely for Jeroboam I to have been credited 21 years and Nadab 1 year.[4]

---

3. It could be proposed that Jeroboam I's reign was mistakenly reduced from 24 years to 22, causing a reduction of Abijam's reign to accommodate Jeroboam I's shortened reign. My reconstruction of the hypothetical pre-MT has 3 years for Abijam while at the same time having 24 years for Jeroboam I (explained later), which indicates that Abijam's reign was changed to 3 years at an early stage.

4. Analysis of the overall reconstruction shows that final years noted in the text do not consist of only a few weeks, but a substantial part of a year.

The above factors lead me to conclude that Nadab's original accession was changed from Asa's 1st year to the 2nd in what was presumably a proto-MT,[5] to fit the arrangement required by reducing Abijam's 6-year reign to 3 years, the synchronism being reworked to pattern 2 when the change to Nadab's datum occurred. It appears that OG/L were made to conform to MT (or proto-MT) at a later time, since Nadab's accession in Asa's 2nd year is the sole instance of pattern 2 in OG/L text and is inconsistent with OG/L's other data.

The synchronism for Baasha's accession in Asa's 3rd year comes 3 years earlier in the MT than it does in OG/L because of the reduction of 3 years to Abijam's reign and the reduction of 2 years to the reign of Jeroboam I. Realigning Baasha's accession to fall at the beginning of Asa's 3rd year permits the following MT synchronisms to be demonstrated, as shown on table 7.1.

7.2.3. Asa (Judah); Baasha, Elah, Zimri, Omri (Israel)

Having established Baasha's accession in Asa's 3rd year, new problems are presented in the length of his reign and the accession of Elah, Baasha's successor. Previous discussion in §3.2.2 noted the problem of reconciling the length of Baasha's reign with the synchronisms of accession given variantly for Elah and for Omri's accession at Tirzah and Samaria, found in OG/L and MT.

OG/L and MT assign Baasha 24 years, indicating that his reign should end in Asa's 26th or 27th year. Elah's accession is synchronized with Asa's 20th year in 1 Kgs 16:6 OG/L and with Asa's 26th year in 16:8 MT. In all texts Elah is assigned 2 years. The accession of his successor, Zimri, is synchronized with Asa's 22nd year at 16:15 be$_2$ (the synchronism is absent in OG). The OG/L synchronism for Elah indicates that Baasha reigned only 17 years, not 24. On the other hand, the MT synchronism for Elah's accession in Asa's 26th year (16:8) and Zimri's accession in Asa's 27th year (16:15), seeming to concur with 24 years for Baasha, allows Baasha little more than 23 years and Elah little more than 1 year. Baasha's 17 years followed by Elah's 2 years concur with the L accessions for Elah and Zimri, but Baasha's 24 years followed by Elah's 2 years scarcely concur with the MT accessions for Elah and Zimri.

Previous discussion (§5.3.4) concerning Elah's opening formula (16:6–8) noted that 16:7 (Jehu's denunciation of Baasha) in OG/L intruded between the accession synchronism of the opening formula (in 16:6) and the remainder of the opening formula (in 16:8). Both OG and L have Elah's accession in Asa's 20th year at 16:6, but L repeats the beginning of the opening formula again in 16:8, where it is found in MT, and omits the year of the synchronism. L presumably did not include the MT synchronism in 16:8 for "the 26th year of Asa" because it would have conflicted with its prior synchronism for the 20th in 16:6.

In 16:10 MT (but not OG/L), a synchronism for the year of Elah's death appeared in a supplementary notice: "the 27th year of Asa." My analysis indicates that "year-of-death" synchronisms were probably not in the original compilation (see §5.1.2.1, §5.1.2.2). This same MT synchronism reappears for Zimri's accession in Asa's 27th year at 16:15, while the be$_2$ synchronism at 16:15 is Asa's 22nd year. If Zimri's accession in Asa's 27th year at 16:15 MT is not correct, then Baasha's reign given as 24 years in MT is also incorrect.

Further, if Zimri reigned only 7 days (16:15 be$_2$; OG has 7 years; see §7.4.2), Omri would also have begun his reign at Tirzah in Asa's 22nd year. Omri's move to Samaria after 6 years would have occurred in Asa's 27th, 28th, or 29th year depending on the length of Omri's 6th year (rounded up or down). The 27th year is the MT synchronism at 16:15, where it applies to his

---

5. The proto-MT is assumed because the datum now appears in the MT.

accession in Tirzah, but according to the L synchronism it should have applied to his accession at Samaria, which is the synchronism expected at 16:23. The datum at 16:23, however, is for Asa's 31st year. If Asa's 22nd year is the correct datum at 16:15 and if the 27th is correct at 16:23, the L and MT data concur. These data infer 17 years, not 24, for Baasha's reign—a difference of 7 years. Within the overall matrix, the difficulty of fitting these 7 years between the 20th and 26th years of Asa's reign (Elah's accession in MT), means that Baasha's 24 years amounted to little more than 23 full years. The 24 years could not extend to Asa's 27th year as this was Zimri's/Omri's accession year at Samaria, and Elah's 2-year reign had to be fitted in before the 27th, which allowed little more than 1 year for Elah's 2-year reign in Asa's 26th–27th year.

The difficulty of attributing 24 years to Baasha is seen in the MT's attempt to accommodate the regnal years to the synchronisms. The OG/L chronology—which gives 17 years to Baasha, 2 full years to Elah, and nearly 6 years to Omri's reign at Tirzah before his move to Samaria in the 27th year—has no such problem. It becomes preferable to conclude that Baasha reigned 17 years, even though all texts attribute to him 24 years. The change to 24 years in the MT caused an alteration to Elah's accession. No longer possible in Asa's 20th year, it was relocated to the 26th. This meant that Zimri's and Omri's accessions could no longer be synchronized with the 22nd, so this synchronism was probably deleted in the proto-MT. The OG was subsequently brought into conformity with the proto-MT, shown by the absence of a synchronism for Zimri or Omri at 16:15, but the be$_2$ texts escaped this revision. The question now is, why was the synchronism for Omri's accession at Samaria in Asa's 27th year not left at 16:23? Where did the 31st year at 16:23 come from?

First Kings 16:23 MT reads מלך עמרי על־ישראל שתים עשרה שנה בתרצה מלך שש־שנים (Omri reigned over Israel 12 years; he reigned 6 years in Tirzah), which seems to mean that the 12 years included the 6 years at Tirzah. As noted in §5.5, this verse in OG/L uses the historical present βασιλεύει in the duration of reign statement, contrary to the normal practice of using the aorist. This and the anomaly of Omri's three accession synchronisms make this verse suspect. In the MT Asa's reign was synchronized with Jeroboam I's 20th year, instead of the 24th as in OG/L, indicating his accession 3 years earlier in MT (recall that the MT credits Abijam with only a 3-year reign, whereas OG/L credited him with 6 years). This means that Asa's 27th year, in a text that gives Abijam 6 years, now becomes the 31st year in this new arrangement, which gives Abijam only 3 years.[6] The 31st year was entered at 16:23 in what I call the pre-MT. As shown in table 7.1, Omri's accession at Samaria is in Asa's 27th year in OG/L and MT, but in the 31st year in the pre-MT.

It appears, then, that the 31st datum derived from a pre-MT and was subsequently entered into 16:23 OG/L and MT. In the MT the (presumed) original synchronism for Omri's move to Samaria in the 27th year was moved back to 16:15. First Kings 16:15 may have lacked the synchronism for Zimri's accession, which was already deleted after Baasha's reign was extended from 17 to 24 years. The OG does not have a synchronism for Zimri's accession at 16:15, nor does OG have Omri's move to Samaria in the 27th year at 16:23, the 27th having been replaced by the 31st. The be$_2$ texts keep the synchronism for the 22nd at 16:15, but it seems that when the 31st was entered at 16:23, the 27th was deleted. OG/L no longer have the 27th in their texts.

---

6. An alternative arrangement appears in c$_2$ (see table 4.4), in which Asa's 31st year also appears as Omri's year of accession at Samaria and Asa is credited with 41 years. The main difference between the two arrangements is that in c$_2$ Baasha is allocated 24 years, whereas in the hypothetical pre-MT arrangement in table 7.1 he is assigned 17 years.

I conclude from this analysis that Omri began to reign from Tirzah in Asa's 22nd year, which means that Elah began his 2-year reign in Asa's 20th year, which in turn indicates that Baasha reigned 17 years not 24. The question now is how long did Asa and Omri reign in their respective kingdoms?

7.2.4. Asa and Jehoshaphat (Judah); Omri and Ahab (Israel)

In §3.2.2 I discussed the problem of aligning Omri's supposed 12 years with Asa's 41 years. OG/L appear to miss 9–10 years between Omri's death in his 12th year and Ahab's accession in Jehoshaphat's 2nd year (1 Kgs 16:29 OG/L). The MT recognizes no gap between the reigns of Omri and Ahab, but places Ahab's accession in Asa's 38th year (16:29 MT), not Jehoshaphat's 2nd year (see table 3.6).

My conclusion that Omri began his reign in Tirzah in Asa's 22nd year and after 6 years moved to Samaria in Asa's 27th year invokes the question of the length of Omri's reign in Samaria. The MT, beginning Omri's reign in Asa's 27th year, gives him 12 years and synchronizes Ahab's accession with Asa's 38th year. OG/L, however, locate Ahab's accession in Jehoshaphat's 2nd year, implying a 15-year reign of Omri from Samaria. A 12-year reign from Samaria beginning in Asa's 27th year leaves 3 of the 15 years unaccounted for. These remaining years could be explained by proposing that Asa reigned only 38 years and not 41. A 38-year reign for Asa concurs with synchronisms for Jehoshaphat's accession in Omri's 11th year, followed by Ahab's accession in Jehoshaphat's 2nd year. The OG/L arrangement then approximates the same calendar years as in the hypothetical pre-MT arrangement, except that in the latter Asa has 41 years.

The reason the hypothetical pre-MT arrangement has 41 years and not 38 may be explained by my earlier conclusion that pre-MT gave Abijam 3 regnal years instead of 6, while Jeroboam I's regnal years remained 24. This caused Abijam's accession to synchronize with Jeroboam I's 20th year instead of the 24th. The advance of Asa's accession by 3 years affects the length of Asa's reign and Jehoshaphat's accession. If Asa's reign remains 38 years, Jehoshaphat's accession could also be advanced by 3 years, requiring a new synchronism for his successor; or an unallocated period of 3 years could fall between the end of Asa's reign and the accession of Jehoshaphat in Omri's 11th year; or Asa's reign could be extended by 3 years to meet the accession synchronism. My analysis indicates that the pre-MT extended the reign of Asa from 38 years to 41 to compensate for the shortfall of 3 years in Abijam's reign. The OG/L texts, by providing 6 years for Abijam, have Jehoshaphat's accession in Omri's 11th year and Ahab's accession in Jehoshaphat's 2nd year, indicating Asa reigned 38 years. The 41 years now present in OG/L incurs a 3-year overlap of Asa's 39th to 41st years with Jehoshaphat's first 3 years.

The MT also attributes 41 years to Asa (1 Kgs 15:10). However, the 41 years occurs 3 years later in the MT arrangement than it does in pre-MT. This shows that the MT (or its *Vorlage*) originally had 6 years for Abijam, confirmed by Baasha's accession being correctly synchronized with Asa's 3rd year (15:33) (discussed in §7.2.2). Allowing 6 years for Abijam and 41 years for Asa meant that Jehoshaphat's accession could no longer be synchronized with Omri's 11th year. Instead of reverting Asa's reign to 38 years from 41, Jehoshaphat's accession was synchronized with Ahab's 4th year, and then Ahab's prior accession was synchronized with Asa's 38th year. The secondary nature of these MT synchronisms is evidenced by Omri's not having a 12-year reign from Asa's 27th year before Ahab's accession in the 38th; Omri's reign is little more than 11 years. The OG/L texts, however, comfortably assign Omri 12 years commencing from Asa's 27th year, followed by Ahab's accession in Jehoshaphat's 2nd year.

The OG/L texts with Jehoshaphat's accession in Omri's 11th year and Ahab's accession in Jehoshaphat's 2nd year show the original sequence of reigns. The addition of 3 years to the reign of Asa in MT necessitated a repositioning of the narrative for Jehoshaphat's reign. Jehoshaphat's reign precedes Ahab's in 16:28a–h OG/L, but Ahab's now precedes Jehoshaphat's at 16:29–22:40 MT, with Jehoshaphat's narrative appearing at 22:41–51 (discussed in §5.4). I noticed previously (§5.2) that the accession formulas for Ahab and for the next three kings in MT/KR (Jehoshaphat, Ahaziah-I, Joram) employ pattern 2, which appears to indicate reworked text. These kings have different regnal data in MT/KR from that of OG/L, which continue to employ pattern 1. A presumed original 38 years at 15:10 was changed in OG/L and MT to 41 years. It appears that the OG/L texts were brought into conformity with a pre- or proto-MT, the arrangement shown in table 3.6, but prior to that the OG/L manifested the chronology shown in table 7.1.

The preceding analysis proposes that Omri reigned 6 years in Tirzah from Asa's 22nd year and an *additional* 12 years in Samaria to Jehoshaphat's 2nd year, when Ahab's reign commenced (1 Kgs 16:29 OG/L). An 18-year reign thus appears to be the intention of 16:23; Omri's 12 years do *not* include his 6 years at Tirzah.

Pertinent to the discussion is a reference from the Moabite Stone, lines 7–8:

וירש עמרי את ארץ מהדבה וישב בה ימה וחצי ימי בנה ארבען שת

Earlier scholars translated these lines as follows:

> (Now) Omri had occupied the land of Medeba, and (Israel) had dwelt there in his time and half the time of his son (Ahab), forty years.[7]

André Lemaire's recent translation reads:

> And Omri had taken possession of the land of Medeba. And he dwelt in it in his days and the *sum* of the days of his sons: 40 years.[8]

Scholars have translated בנה in both singular and plural:[9] the earlier translation as "his *son*" infers that the occupation ended midway through Ahab's reign,[10] whereas Lemaire's translation uses the plural, referring to a 40-year occupation of Medeba by Omri and his *sons*. The translation of וחצי is also uncertain, being translated "half" in earlier translations, "period" by Galling,[11] and "sum" by Lemaire.

---

7. Translation by W. F. Albright, "The Moabite Stone," in *ANET* 320; similarly, E. Lipiński, "North Semitic Texts from the First Millennium B.C.," in *Near Eastern Religious Texts Relating to the Old Testament* (ed. W. Beyerlin; trans. J. Bowden; Philadelphia: Westminster, 1978), 238; S. Herrmann, *A History of Israel in Old Testament Times* (Philadelphia: Fortress, 1981), 215.

8. A. Lemaire, "'House of David' Restored in Moabite Inscription," *Biblical Archaeology Review* 20/3 (1994): 33. The italicized word *sum* indicates the uncertainty of the translation.

9. Herrmann, *History of Israel*, 215, 219 n. 37; J. C. L. Gibson, "Inscriptions in Moabite," in *Textbook of Syrian Semitic Inscriptions*, vol. 1: *Hebrew and Moabite Inscriptions* (Oxford: Clarendon, 1971), 79.

10. For discussion see W. H. Bennett, *The Moabite Stone* (Edinburgh: Clark, 1911), 18–22; J. Liver, "The Wars of Mesha, King of Moab," *Palestine Exploration Quarterly* 99 (1967): 14–31, esp. 18–20; Shenkel, *CRD* 93–94; Gibson, "Inscriptions in Moabite," 71–84; M. Miller, "The Moabite Stone as a Memorial Stela," *Palestine Exploration Quarterly* 106 (1974): 9–18; S. H. Horn, "The Discovery of the Moabite Stone," in *The Word of the Lord Shall Go Forth* (ed. C. L. Meyers and M. O'Connor; Winona Lake, Ind.: Eisenbrauns, 1983), 497–505; idem, "Why the Moabite Stone Was Blown to Pieces," *Biblical Archaeology Review* 12/3 (1986): 50–61; A. R. Green, "Regnal Formulas in the Hebrew and Greek Texts of the Books of Kings," *Journal of Near Eastern Studies* 42 (1983): 178–79; Lipiński, "North Semitic Texts," 237–40; G. Garbini, *History and Ideology in Ancient Israel* (trans. J. Bowden; London: SCM, 1988), 33–37; Lemaire, "House of David," 30–37.

11. K. Galling (cited by Herrmann, *History of Israel*, 219 n. 37): "and the period of the reign of his sons—forty years."

Second Kings 1:1 and 3:4–5 state that Moab rebelled after the death of Ahab. The sequence of events of Joram's reign indicates that the Moabite campaign occurred at the beginning of his reign, not midway or at the end (see §9.3.1).[12] If Omri reigned 18 years and Ahab 22 years (1 Kgs 16:23, 29), their reigns amount to the 40-year occupation and place Moab's rebellion after Ahab's death. On the other hand, a 12-year reign for Omri followed by half of Ahab's 22 years cannot be reconciled with a 40-year occupation; nor does a 12-year reign for Omri followed by 22 years for Ahab, 2 years for Ahaziah-I, and 12 years for Joram (Omri's son and grandsons) amount to 40 years.

A translation that attributes the 40-year occupation to the sum of the reigns of Omri and his son (singular) concurs with the chronology indicated by OG/L synchronisms that Omri reigned 18 years and Ahab 22 years. If a 40-year occupation during the reigns of Omri and Ahab is the correct interpretation of the Moabite Stone, then 18 years for Omri is confirmed.

The incorrect attribution of 24 years to Baasha's reign combined with a 3-year reduction to Abijam's reign and followed by the extension of 3 years to Asa's reign accounts for the problems discussed in the preceding chronology. The effects of Asa's 3 additional years in the MT continue in the following EDK chronology.

7.2.5. Jehoshaphat (Judah); Ahab, Ahaziah-I, and Joram (Israel)

Beginning with the reign of Ahab, the sequence of reigns in OG/L and MT differs. Also, MT now employs pattern 2 for the accession synchronisms of Ahab and the next three consecutive kings and supplies them with data different from OG/L: Ahab's accession in Asa's 38th year (1 Kgs 16:29), Jehoshaphat's in Ahab's 4th year (22:41), Ahaziah-I's in Jehoshaphat's 17th year (22:52), and Joram's in Jehoshaphat's 18th year (2 Kgs 3:1).[13] The KR is not extant at 1 Kgs 16:29, but concurs with MT for the last three kings. OG is not extant for the last three kings, where L alone represents the OG chronology. L normally employs pattern 1 except where it has been made to conform to the MT sequence and data (commented on below).

Ahaziah-I's accession, synchronized with Jehoshaphat's 24th year in 22:52 L[14] and employing pattern 1, is consistent with Ahab's prior accession in Jehoshaphat's 2nd year and Ahab's 22-year reign (16:29). Ahaziah-I reigns 2 years (22:52 L) and the accession of his brother, Joram, is synchronized with Jehoram's 2nd year (2 Kings 1:18a L). This infers that Jehoram began to reign the previous year in Ahaziah-I's 2nd year (synchronism not extant), which is consistent with Jehoshaphat's 25-year reign (1 Kings 16:28a OG/L; 22:42 MT/KR).

According to the MT, Jehoshaphat accedes to the throne in Ahab's 4th year (22:41) at calendar year 65. Ahab reigns 22 years, making Ahaziah-I's accession align with Jehoshaphat's 20th year (year 84). But in the MT Ahaziah-I's accession is synchronized with Jehoshaphat's 17th year (22:52). This is 3 years earlier than expected if Ahab reigned 22 years. That Ahab reigned 22 years is shown by the synchronization of Jehoram's accession with Joram's 5th year (2 Kgs 8:16). If Ahab had not reigned 22 years the synchronism for Jehoram would not appear. Why then is Ahaziah-I's accession synchronized with Jehoshaphat's 17th year in MT, when the alignment requires the 20th, and L has the 24th? The L text was consistent with its data, giving Jehoshaphat's

---

12. Contrary to Shenkel's analysis in *CRD* 93–94.

13. Pattern 2 is secondary and most likely contains secondary chronological data. That is, these four MT synchronisms are likely secondary; see discussion in §5.2 and §5.4.

14. S. J. De Vries gives the number as the 27th, which is unattested; *1 Kings* (Word Biblical Commentary 12; Waco: Word, 1985), 275.

24th year as the accession synchronism of Ahaziah-I, and this may hold the reason that MT gives the 17th instead.

Recall that Baasha's 17 regnal years may have been incorrectly transcribed as 24 years (1 Kgs 15:33). Here, at 22:52, the reverse may have occurred: 24th written as 17th. It seems likely that the original Hebrew text had the 24th year—the datum still appearing in L—for Ahaziah-I's accession. L records the number correctly, whereas the MT number has been altered, probably unintentionally, through confusion of graphically similar letters, that is, the consonants for 10 and 20 and for 4 and 7 (see §7.3.6).

The reason that Ahaziah-I's accession is aligned with the 20th and not Jehoshaphat's 24th year is because Jehoshaphat's accession is previously incorrectly aligned with Ahab's 4th year in the MT instead of Omri's 11th year as in OG/L. The extra 3 years assigned to Asa's reign when extended from 38 years to 41, combined with the discrepant year when Ahab's accession was synchronized with Asa's 38th year when the 39th would have been more appropriate, caused Jehoshaphat's 24th year to fall 4 years later in MT/KR than in L. This caused Ahaziah-I's accession to be aligned with the 20th instead of the 24th, now incorrectly given as the 17th. The discrepancy between the 20th and 24th is again a repercussion of Abijam's reign being reduced from 6 years to 3 years and of Asa's reign being extended from 38 years to 41 years to compensate. But in a pre-MT the 6 years of Abijam were followed by the 41 years of Asa, which causes an excess of 3 years. According to the MT arrangement a new synchronism was required for Ahaziah-I's accession in Jehoshaphat's 20th year. For some reason the alteration was not made, perhaps because there was already an inconsistency in the text, that is, the 17th year instead of the 24th.

In the MT, Ahaziah-I's 2-year reign is followed by Joram's accession in Jehoshaphat's 18th year (2 Kgs 3:1), though 1:17 MT also has Joram's accession in Jehoram's 2nd year, concurring with 1:18a L. It is evident from my discussion in §5.3.7 and §5.4 that Ahaziah-I's accession was correctly synchronized with Jehoshaphat's 24th year and that MT's 17th year is a corruption. It follows then that the MT/KR synchronism for Joram's accession in Jehoshaphat's 18th year must also be incorrect and secondary. Unlike Ahaziah-I's accession, which may be explained as a confusion between look-alike Hebrew letters, the accession of Joram in Jehoshaphat's 18th year cannot be inadvertent error for Jehoram's 2nd year. Joram's accession in Jehoshaphat's 18th year probably arose from an effort to make Joram's accession comply with Ahaziah-I's prior accession in Jehoshaphat's 17th year.

7.2.6. Jehoram and Ahaziah-J (Judah); Joram (Israel)

In the MT the extension of Asa's reign caused Jehoshaphat's reign to begin and end 4 years later than in L. This in turn caused a change in the sequence, not only in the reigns of Jehoshaphat and Ahab, but also for the reigns of Jehoram and Joram. Jehoram's reign comes a year before Joram's in L (Ahaziah-I's 2nd year extrapolated), but 4 years after Joram's in MT.

The change in the sequence of reigns caused great confusion in the MT, particularly in 2 Kgs 1:17–18, when the original order of reigns was adjusted to the secondary order. In the L order, Jehoram's accession would have synchronized with Ahaziah-I's 2nd year but is lacking in all texts. In the MT Jehoram's accession in Ahaziah-I's 2nd year would have been impossible due to Jehoshaphat's reign ending 4 years later in MT than in L. The original synchronism was excised and replaced by Joram's accession in Jehoshaphat's 18th year in dependence on the prior synchronism for Ahaziah-I's accession in Jehoshaphat's 17th year. In the MT Joram accedes to Israel's throne before Jehoram accedes to Judah's throne. Joram's accession is appropriate at 3:1 according to the MT order of sequence, but the datum is incorrect. The positioning of Joram's accession at 3:1 is also appropriate in the L order, as L would have had Jehoram's accession at 1:18a in accord with its own sequence of reigns. But it has been replaced by Joram's accession synchronism, which though correct for Jehoram's 2nd year, is incorrectly positioned. KR replaced Jehoram's accession at 1:18a with Joram's accession in Jehoshaphat's 18th year which, although correctly positioned at 3:1, in both places contains incorrect synchronisms.

The MT inserted Jehoram's accession synchronism at 8:16, synchronized with Joram's 5th year. The L text also has Jehoram's accession in Joram's 5th year at 8:16. This synchronism brought the L text into conformity with the MT at the expense of consistency with its other data. Because L now follows the MT sequence of reigns, it too omits the accession synchronism proper to its sequence for Jehoram's accession in Ahaziah-I's 2nd year. It has, however, retained its original synchronism for Joram's accession in Jehoram's 2nd year at 1:18a. The original position would have been at 3:1 where it is now omitted (see §5.4).

The repercussions of extending Asa's reign by 3 years continue in the MT synchronism for Jehoram's accession. Even though the accessions of Ahaziah-I and Joram are synchronized 3 years earlier than their actual alignment with Jehoshaphat's reign, Jehoram's accession has been calculated on the basis that Ahaziah-I's accession was in Jehoshaphat's 20th year, and Jehoshaphat's reign was 25 years long (1 Kgs 22:42). Jehoram's accession was then caused to fall in Joram's 5th year (2 Kgs 8:16), which meant that Jehoram's reign began 4 years later in MT than in L. MT must now shorten Jehoram's reign by the same amount for the 1-year reign of Ahaziah-I to conclude simultaneously with the end of Joram's 12-year reign when both were killed in the same coup led by Jehu.

Jehoram is credited with 7 years, though the actual length cannot be much more than $7\frac{1}{2}$ years if Ahaziah-J's accession is to synchronize with Joram's 12th year and allow Ahaziah-I his 1-year reign. Jehoram's allocation of 8 years in MT does not allow Ahaziah-J's accession to synchronize with Joram's 11th year as in 8:25 L and 9:29 L, though MT states this at 9:29. The MT modified Joram's 11th year to the 12th at 8:25 in accord with its secondary arrangement. In L, Ahaziah-J's 1-year reign ends in Joram's 12th year, but in MT, Ahaziah-J's reign ends in Joram's 13th (unattested) year because of the way the synchronisms have been secondarily calculated.

Ahaziah-J's accession in Joram's 11th year (2 Kgs 8:25; 9:29 L) indicates that Jehoram reigned 11 years if commencing in Ahaziah-I's 2nd year (as extrapolated). L manuscripts oe_2 accord Jehoram only 10 years at 8:17, but the synchronism shows this is defective. The 10 years could be a scribal error, ἕν having been accidentally omitted from ἕνδεκα. Or, it may have been a late alteration to bring it into conformity with c_2, which gives Jehoram 10 years according to its year-for-year alignment. The other L minuscules b + b' (= b) assign Jehoram 8 years in conformity with the MT. The KR gives Jehoram 40 regnal years, which is impossible. Perhaps 40 years resulted from a scribal lapse that added Jehoram's age of 32 years to the 8 regnal years the MT attributed to him (8:17) or from confusion between 8 and 40 when written as the letters ח and מ in the *Vorlage* of the KR. Otherwise the Greek data for the reigns of Jehoshaphat, Jehoram, and Ahaziah-J are consistent with the data for the reigns of Ahaziah-I and Joram.

The EDK terminates with the deaths of Ahaziah-I and Joram at the same time. In OG/L, this is in the middle of year 99, as shown on table 7.1. Altogether the EDK lasted $98\frac{1}{2}$ years.

7.2.7. Identity of *Iaúa*

I now turn to the identity of *Ia-ú-a mār Ḫu-um-ri-i*, who is mentioned in Assyrian inscriptions in a context of paying tribute to Shalmaneser III in the latter's 18th year (see §6.3.5, §9.3.1). Scholars usually identify *Ia-ú-a mār Ḫu-um-ri-i* with Joram's successor: Jehu "son of Omri." Since

Jehu was not a "son of Omri," scholars point out that Israel was known as *Bīt Ḫumrî* (the house/dynasty of Omri) by the Assyrians until the days of Tiglath-pileser III and Sargon II.[15] The reference to Jehu as "son of Omri" is thus understood to mean that Jehu was of the dynasty of Omri. Significantly, Thiele uses antedating to attribute 1 year to Ahaziah-I and 11 years to Joram in order to synchronize Shalmaneser III's 6th year with Ahab's last year and Shalmaneser's 18th year with Jehu's 1st year. This enables him to identify *Iaúa* with Jehu. Ahab is understood to have been at the battle of Qarqar in Shalmaneser's 6th year. By Shalmaneser's 18th year Ahab had been succeeded by *Ia-ú-a mār Ḫu-um-ri-i*. On philological and chronological grounds, McCarter argues that Joram was *Ia-ú-a mār Ḫu-um-ri-i*, asserting that Joram was indeed the "son of Omri," that is, the grandson of Omri.[16] Thiele argues against McCarter on chronological grounds.[17] Weippert, Halpern, and Hughes also argue against McCarter on phonetic grounds, claiming that *Iaúa* must be Jehu not Joram.[18]

Text-critical analysis of the chronological data makes identification of *Iaúa* with Jehu simply untenable. The synchronisms of the period, even though varying in MT and L, are based on the data that Ahaziah-I reigned 2 years and Joram 12. The only possible candidate is Joram, grandson of Omri. Joram's designation as "son of Omri" is not only valid but also differentiated him from his contemporary, Jehoram son of Jehoshaphat. Moreover, since Jehu "slew all that remained to Ahab" (2 Kgs 10:17), he would hardly be known as "son of Omri."[19] Joram was recognized as the grandson of Omri at the time he paid tribute to Shalmaneser, and Israel was later known as the "land of Omri" after its former illustrious ruler.

7.3. Textual Solutions for Early Divided Kingdom Chronology

In the EDK several textual changes account for the differences in the chronology now found in the OG/L and MT.

7.3.1. Abijam's Reign Changed from 6 Years to 3 Years

The adjustment from the 6 years given to Abijam in OG/L to the 3 years given in 1 Kgs 15:2 MT has the greatest overall impact upon EDK chronology. It resulted in Asa's accession being moved from Jeroboam I's 24th year in OG/L to the 20th in MT (15:9). Thus Nadab's original synchronism in Asa's 1st year (OG/L by extrapolation) was no longer possible. Baasha's original synchronism in Asa's 3rd year was, however, retained. In order to sustain this synchronism, Jeroboam I's 24-year reign was reduced to 22 years, and Nadab's accession was synchronized with Asa's 2nd year. The reduction of Abijam's reign placed Asa's accession 3 years earlier in MT than in OG/L. But because MT retained the original synchronism for Baasha's accession in Asa's 3rd year, the OG/L and MT aligned again at the same calendar year. This introduced a gap in the MT chronology by the absence of the 4th–6th years of Abijam and of the 23rd and 24th years of Jeroboam I.

---

15. M. Cogan and H. Tadmor, *II Kings: A New Translation with Introduction and Commentary* (Anchor Bible 11; Garden City, N.Y.: Doubleday, 1988), 106; J. Hughes, *Secrets of the Times: Myth and History in Biblical Chronology* (Journal for the Study of the Old Testament Supplement 66; Sheffield: JSOT Press, 1990), 183 n. 55.

16. P. K. McCarter, "'Yaw, Son of 'Omri': A Philological Note on Israelite Chronology," *BASOR* 216 (1974): 5–7.

17. E. R. Thiele, "An Additional Chronological Note on 'Yaw, Son of 'Omri,'" *BASOR* 222 (1976): 19–23.

18. M. Weippert, "Jau(a) mār Ḫumrî—Joram oder Jehu von Israel?" *VT* 28 (1978): 113–18; B. Halpern, "Yaua, Son of Omri, Yet Again," *BASOR* 265 (1987): 81–85; Hughes, *Secrets of the Times*, 183 n. 55.

19. T. Schneider's suggestion that Jehu "son of Omri" may have been related to Omri is no longer relevant if *Iaúa* is Joram not Jehu; "Did Jehu Kill His Own Family?" *Biblical Archaeology Review* 25/1 (1995): 26–33, 80; idem, "Rethinking Jehu," *Biblica* 77 (1996): 100–107.

If the MT had retained the correct accession year for Nadab, the remainder of the chronology might have synchronized but for the following incident: Asa's reign was extended from 38 to 41 years. Copyists of a pre-MT appear to have noticed that if Abijam's 3-year reign was followed by Asa's 38 years a gap of 3 years was created between the end of Asa's reign and the synchronism for his successor, Jehoshaphat. Accordingly, they added 3 years to Asa's 38 years, giving him 41 years. Jehoshaphat's accession now synchronized with Omri's 11th year (1 Kgs 16:28a OG/L). But because the years were not added to the correct reign (i.e., Abijam's), Asa's reign still began 4 years ahead of the actual time, that is, in the 20th year of Jeroboam I, not the 24th. Consequently, Asa's 27th year, when Omri moved from Tirzah to Samaria, became the 31st. This synchronism replaced Asa's 27th year at 16:23, and Asa's 41 years replaced his 38 years at 15:10.

Subsequently, it must have been noticed that if Abijam reigned 6 years followed by Asa's 41-year reign, Jehoshaphat's accession would not coincide with Omri's 11th year (16:28a OG/L). Jehoshaphat's accession was recalculated to fall in Ahab's 4th year, and Ahab's accession was recalculated for Asa's 38th year (16:29), even though these synchronisms meant that Omri reigned from Samaria only 11 years, not 12.

The excess 3 years in Asa's reign in the proto-MT caused a change in the sequence of the kings' reigns so that Ahab's reign was reported before Jehoshaphat's. This caused Jehoshaphat's narrative at 1 Kgs 16:28a–h OG/L to be transferred to 22:41–51 following Ahab's narrative at 16:29–22:40. Subsequently, Jehoram's narrative—which would have appeared after Ahaziah-I's and before Joram's at 2 Kings 2 in the original sequence (shown by the extrapolated OG/L order)—was transferred to 8:16–24. These alterations were probably made to a proto-MT. The MT shows the secondary nature of this arrangement with the absence of closing regnal formulas before Joram's opening formula at 3:1 and before Jehoram's opening formula at 8:16.

The addition of 3 years to the reign of Asa not only changed Ahab's and Jehoshaphat's accessions, but also required alteration to the accession years of kings who were synchronized with Jehoshaphat's reign, that is, Ahaziah-I and Joram. Ahaziah-I's accession aligned with Jehoshaphat's 20th year, though the MT synchronized his reign with the 17th, a corruption of the 24th. Joram's accession was consequently synchronized with Jehoshaphat's 18th year even though it aligned with Jehoshaphat's 22nd year. Jehoshaphat's 25-year reign ended 3 years later in MT than it does in L (OG not extant), and instead of Jehoram's accession synchronizing with Ahaziah-I's 2nd year (by extrapolation), it was synchronized with Joram's 5th year. This caused the last 4 years of Jehoshaphat's reign to coincide with Joram's first 4 years, thus wrongly identifying Jehoshaphat as the Judahite king who was Joram's ally in the Moabite campaign (2 Kings 3 MT). In the OG/L order Judah's king in the Moabite campaign would rightly be identified as Jehoram.

Since Ahaziah-J and Joram died at the same time, Jehoram's reign had to be reduced by 3 years. Consequently his 11 years (L extrapolated) became 8 years in MT. Finally, Ahaziah-J's reign was synchronized with Joram's 12th year (2 Kgs 8:25) instead of the 11th as at 9:29 (also 8:25 and 9:29 L). At 8:16 the L text also has Jehoram's accession in Joram's 5th year, and two L manuscripts ($b + b' = b$) gave Jehoram's regnal years as 8, having been made to conform to the MT.

The above changes all arise from Abijam's reign being changed from 6 years to 3 years, Asa's reign being changed from 38 years to 41 years to compensate, and then the figure 41 (instead of 38) being introduced into a text that already had 6 years for Abijam's reign. Drastic consequences were the result.

7.3.2. Baasha's Reign Changed from 17 Years to 24 Years

The change from an original 17 regnal years for Baasha to 24 years (1 Kgs 15:33) was quite independent of changes associated with the reduction of Abijam's reign from 6 years to 3 years.

Instead of Baasha's reign terminating after 17 years and Elah's accession being synchronized with Asa's 20th year, as in 16:6 (OG/L), the MT now contained 7 excess years. Omri's reign at Samaria began in Asa's 27th year, so Elah's reign was synchronized with Asa's 26th year (16:8). which reduced it from 2 years to 1 year. Zimri's original accession in Asa's 22nd year at 16:15 (attested now only in be$_2$) was probably deleted in MT (OG does not have the synchronism). In MT, 16:15 was later interpolated with Asa's 27th year, when the 27th was replaced by the 31st at 16:23. Consequently, in the MT, Omri appeared to have reigned only 12 years—6 in Tirzah and 6 in Samaria. The actual situation is attested by the be$_2$ manuscripts, which give Omri's accession at Tirzah in Asa's 22nd year, showing that Omri reigned 18 years altogether. These 18 years are corroborated by the Moabite Stone, which speaks of the 40 years that Israel occupied Moab, that is, Ahab's 22 followed by Omri's 18.

7.3.3. Ahaziah-I's Accession Changed from Jehoshaphat's 24th Year to 17th Year

The third independent change in the Hebrew text is Ahaziah-I's accession being changed from Jehoshaphat's 24th year to 17th year. The L text retained the 24th year at 1 Kgs 22:52, whereas MT/KR have the 17th. This change is significant for showing that the Hebrew text had Ahaziah-I's accession in Jehoshaphat's 24th year, subsequently incorrectly recognized as the 17th. The Greek texts as well as the MT had the 24th synchronism for Ahaziah-I's accession, showing that they once had a common chronology (i.e., the Greek was a translation of a yet earlier Hebrew *Vorlage*). This inadvertent change caused the following synchronism, Joram's accession in Jehoram's 2nd year (2 Kgs 1:18a L and 1:17 MT), to be changed to Jehoshaphat's 18th year (1:18a KR and 3:1 MT/KR [repeated]).

7.3.4. Summary of Textual Solutions

All three of these alterations to the original text produced the divergencies now seen in the OG/L and MT/KR. The explanations given above for the reconstruction of the chronology account for the data now appearing in these texts. The majority of divergencies are found in the MT. Conflicting and inconsistent data that appear in OG/L also appear in the MT. The absence of any inherent reason for the appearance of these conflicting data in OG/L leads me to assume that at some stage the original data was replaced to make the text conform to data now found in the MT. These extraneous data are Nadab's accession in Asa's 2nd year (instead of the 1st, extrapolated) at 1 Kgs 15:25; 24 years credited to Baasha (15:33) instead of 17; 41 years assigned to Asa (15:10) instead of 38; Asa's 31st year replacing the 27th (16:23); Jehoram's accession in Joram's 5th year (2 Kgs 8:16) instead of in Ahaziah-I's 2nd year; and the attribution to Jehoram of 8 regnal years (8:17 L [b]) instead of 11. If the secondary data were replaced with the data suggested, the OG/L texts would exhibit a perfectly synchronous chronology. For some reason not all the OG/L data were brought into conformity with the proto-MT. Unlike OG/L, the proto-MT utilized the erroneous 24 years of Baasha and the 41 years of Asa, causing textual upheaval, producing new synchronisms to replace the old, and introducing a new sequence for the kings' narratives.

7.3.5. Two Additional Matters regarding Numbers

In addition to the three main changes involving numbers described above, two other matters require attention.

Second Chronicles 15:19–16:1 reads, "And there was no more[20] war until the thirty-fifth year of the reign of Asa. In the thirty-sixth year of the reign of Asa, Baasha king of Israel went up

---

20. The word *more* is not in the Hebrew or Greek.

against Judah" (RSV).²¹ Baasha's accession was in Asa's 3rd year. Since Baasha reigned only 17 years, dying in Asa's 20th year, how could he have attacked Judah in Asa's 35th and 36th years? Second Chronicles 13:23–14:7 MT indicates that the first 10 years of Asa's reign were peaceful. Then Israel celebrated a victory over the Ethiopians and Libyans (14:8–14 MT; 16:8) in the 3rd month of Asa's 15th year (15:10–11). As Asa's 15th year corresponds to Baasha's 12th/13th year and Baasha reigned only 17 years, it seems likely that the 35th and 36th years are scribal errors for 15th and 16th, and that 10 and 30 were confused while 5 and 6 of the original were undisturbed (see further comments in §7.3.6).

If Asa reigned only 38 years as claimed above, we have to account for 2 Chr 16:12–13: "In the 39th year of his reign Asa was diseased in his feet. . . . Then Asa slept with his fathers, dying in the 41st year of his reign." First Kings 15:23–24 merely says, "But in his old age he was diseased in his feet. Then Asa slept with his ancestors and was buried." The addition in 2 Chr 16:12–13 suggests that the difference of 38 or 41²² years for Asa's reign was understood by assuming that the 3 extra years referred to the period of the disease, and 16:12–13 was adjusted to effect this.

7.3.6. Suggested Explanation for Changes in Numbers

The ways that numbers could have been written in early Hebrew manuscripts was introduced in §6.1.2 #3. Two divergent systems of numbers arose after the translation of the Hebrew into Greek about the 2nd century B.C.E. and before the writing of the KR around the 1st century B.C.E. The scripts in use in Israel and Judah in this period were the paleo-Hebrew and Aramaic (also known as Assyrian square), which the exiles brought back with them from Babylon.²³ My analysis of the chronological data shows examples (some by extrapolation) of 6 becoming 3 (1 Kgs 15:2), 24 interchanged with 17 (15:33), 17 interchanged with 24 (22:52), and 15 and 16 becoming 35 and 36 (2 Chr 15:19–16:1). Two further examples from the LDK (to be discussed in §8.2.2, §8.3.2) show 14 interchanging with 27 (2 Kgs 15:1), and 24 becoming 14 (18:13). Apparently, the interchange occurred due to confusion in the script or notational system used. The recurrence of the number 4 in these examples is quite striking.

Notational systems used in Israel/Judah seem to fall into four categories: (1) in words, as written on the Moabite Stone and some Samaria Ostraca; (2) in Egyptian hieratic symbols, as found on ostraca mainly from Arad and Samaria used for recording weights and measures and possibly documentation of military conscripts;²⁴ (3) in horizontal hooks and vertical strokes using an early Phoenician notational system dating back to an ancient proto-Canaanite script; and (4) (more circumstantially) in letters of the Hebrew alphabet.

If numbers are written as words, it is difficult to see how they could have changed accidentally because the spelling of the words (involving several letters) would have to be altered. Also, in compound numbers the order of 20 and 10 would have to be inverted. For example, in square script 17 is שבע עשרה (with 10 after the unit), and 27 is עשרים ושבע (with 20 before the unit). If written as words, therefore, how could 17 and 24 (עשרים וארבע) be confused, or 14 and 27?

---

21. See my previous comments (§5.3.1) on 1 Kgs 15:16, which says, "There was war between Asa and King Baasha of Israel all their days." This verse may not have been in the original text.

22. Vaticanus has the variant of Asa's death in his 40th year.

23. For an overview, see J. P. Siegel, "The Evolution of Two Hebrew Scripts," *Biblical Archaeology Review* 5/3 (1979): 28–33.

24. Y. Aharoni, "The Use of Hieratic Numerals in Hebrew Ostraca and the Shekel Weights," *BASOR* 184 (1966): 13–19; W. H. Shea, "Israelite Chronology and the Samaria Ostraca," *Zeitschrift des Deutschen Palästina-Vereins* 101 (1985): 14–19.

The change from 6 to 3 in words is possible, but it involves—again using the square script—שלש (3) being confused with שש (6). My analysis indicates, however, that 6 is the correct number for Abijam's regnal years, so the change to 3 incurs the addition of a letter, suggesting an intentional rather than an accidental change. An intentional change is hard to explain, raising further doubt that the earlier number 6 was written as a word.

The likelihood that 10 could have been confused with 30 in the example concerning Baasha's war with Asa when written as words is unlikely, as 15 is חמש ועשרה and 35 is שלשים וחמש. Not only are 10 and 30 spelled differently, but 10 and 30 are inverted. Various scholars propose textual corruption between 15th and 35th and between 16th and 36th, where numbers have been indicated by Hebrew letters. In this case, in the paleo-Hebrew 10 (*yod*) has been mistaken for 30 (*lamed*), a feasible case of confusion between letters graphically alike.[25] Other scholars propose that the change in the numbers, crediting Baasha with more years actually reigned, was prompted by a theological motive.[26] Accidental change is less speculative.

Numerals in the Samaria ostraca are written as words in a paleo-Hebrew script[27] in one group of ostraca, having either "in the 9th year" or "in the 10th year" without identifying what or to whom the years refer. But a different group of ostraca use Egyptian hieratic numerals or signs for "in year 15" and one debated case of "in year 17."[28] The year dates in both groups of ostraca are interpreted by scholars as referring to a year in the reign of an Israelite king, even though no king is named.[29] The first group of ostraca appear to be dockets for the distribution of oil and wine;[30] the second group may be dockets for military conscripts.[31] The hieratic symbols for 5 to 50 are reproduced in table 7.2.[32]

Ostraca discovered at Tell Arad written in paleo-Hebrew contain numbers written in either Hebrew or hieratic script, and at least one ostracon from Arad exhibits Hebrew writing and hieratic symbols in combination.[33] Of particular interest to our inquiry is how the numbers 15 and 35

---

25. C. F. Keil, *The Books of the Chronicles* (trans. A. Harper; Biblical Commentary on the Old Testament 7; repr. Grand Rapids: Eerdmans, n.d.), 366–67; E. L. Curtis and A. A. Madsen, *A Critical and Exegetical Commentary on the Books of the Chronicles* (International Critical Commentary; Edinburgh: Clark, 1910), 387; S. J. De Vries, "Chronology of the OT," in *Interpreter's Dictionary of the Bible* (ed. G. A. Buttrick; New York: Abingdon, 1962), 1.591; V. Pavlovský and E. Vogt, "Die Jahre der Könige von Juda und Israel," *Biblica* 45 (1964): 329–30; G. L. Archer, *Encyclopaedia of Bible Difficulties* (Grand Rapids: Zondervan, 1982), 225–26; R. Dillard, *2 Chronicles* (Word Biblical Commentary 15; Waco: Word, 1987), 124. The 38th year appears in codexes Vaticanus and Alexandrinus at 2 Chr 16:1 instead of 36th, showing a possible confusion between 6 and 8.

26. Curtis and Madsen, *Chronicles*, 387–88; W. Rudolph, "Der Aufbau der Asa-Geschichte (2 Chr. xiv–xvi)," *VT* 2 (1952): 367–68; R. Dillard, "The Reign of Asa (2 Chronicles 14–16): An Example of the Chronicler's Theological Method," *Journal of the Evangelical Theological Society* 23 (1980): 211–14; W. T. Pitard, *Ancient Damascus* (Winona Lake, Ind.: Eisenbrauns, 1987), 113–14.

27. For an overview, see I. T. Kaufman, "The Samaria Ostraca: An Early Witness to Hebrew Writing," *Biblical Archaeologist* 45 (1982): 229–39.

28. Y. Aharoni, *The Land of the Bible* (London: Burns & Oates, 1967), 315–21; W. H. Shea, "The Date and Significance of the Samaria Ostraca," *Israel Exploration Journal* 27 (1977): 17–18; idem, "Israelite Chronology," 14.

29. E.g., Aharoni, *Land of the Bible*, 323–24; Shea, "Date and Significance," 16–27; cf. A. F. Rainey, "Toward a Precise Date for the Samaria Ostraca," *BASOR* 272 (1988): 69–74.

30. Shea, "Israelite Chronology," 16–17; A. F. Rainey, "The Samaria Ostraca in the Light of Fresh Evidence," *Palestine Exploration Quarterly* 99 (1967): 32–35.

31. Shea, "Israelite Chronology," 18.

32. Aharoni, "Use of Hieratic Numerals," 19.

33. S. Yeivin, "A Hieratic Ostracon from Tel Arad," *Israel Exploration Journal* 16 (1966): 153–59; idem, "An Ostracon from Tel Arad Exhibiting a Combination of Two Scripts," *Journal of Egyptian Archaeology* 55 (1969): 98–102; cf. Y. Aharoni,

Table 7.2. Egyptian Hieratic Symbols in the Samaria Ostraca

5	10	20	30	40	50
⌐	∧	⋋	⋌	(⌴)	⊀

(and 16 and 36) and 17 and 24 were written in hieratic. The hieratic symbol for 24 (designating a day of the month) is found on an ostracon from Arad represented by the sign for 20 plus 4 vertical strokes.[34] The number 15 comprises hieratic 5 and 10, as shown on the Samaria ostraca. The number 17 may appear on one Samaria ostracon (#63) comprised of what appear to be three adjacent symbols, the second (5) being uncertain.[35] If 17 is meant, it is represented by the symbols for 10 and 5 followed by two vertical strokes. With little resemblance between 17 and 24 in the hieratic notational system, the hieratic script would not explain the supposed confusion.

Allrik's analysis of the numbers of returned exiles found in Ezra 2 and Neh 7 suggests that the differences between numbers that ought to be the same in both lists are best accounted for (with the exception of careless omissions) by a numerical system using vertical lines for units and horizontal hooks for tens. Allrik points out that this system is well known from ancient Aramaic documents, which he regards has having "certain affinities to the hieroglyphic numeral notation and also to the cuneiform."[36] Earlier, S. R. Driver supposed that the Hebrews used a notational system similar to that of their neighbors: Phoenician, Palmyrene, Nabatean, and Old Aramaic,[37] a view consonant with Allrik's proposal. Even if Allrik's argument is valid for the lists in Ezra and Nehemiah, it does not necessarily follow that numbers used in the regnal formulas of Kings were written in the same manner. Instances where the numbers 4 and 7 or 10 and 20 have been inverted, or 6 mistaken for 3 do not occur in the Ezra-Nehemiah lists.

There are many proponents of the view that numbers were written using letters and values of the Hebrew consonants. As early as 1874, John W. Haley cited thirteen scholars who had come to this conclusion.[38] And in 1910 E. Kautzsch commented,

> In default of special arithmetical figures, the consonants were used also as numerical signs. . . . The earliest traces of this usage are, however, first found on the Maccabean coins. . . . These numerical letters were afterwards commonly employed, e.g. for marking the numbers of chapters and verses in the editions of the Bible. The units are denoted by ט-א, the tens by צ-י, 100–400 by ת-ק, the numbers from 500–900 by ת (= 400), with the addition of the remaining hundreds, e.g. תק 500.[39]

"Hebrew Ostraca from Tel Arad," *Israel Exploration Journal* 16 (1966): 1–3, in which an abbreviation and down strokes are used to designate *baths* of wine.

34. Aharoni, "Use of Hieratic Numerals," 14–16; I. T. Kaufman, "New Evidence for Hieratic Numerals on Hebrew Weights," *BASOR* 188 (1967): 39.

35. Shea, "Israelite Chronology," 16; G. I. Davies, *Ancient Hebrew Inscriptions: Corpus and Concordance* (Cambridge: Cambridge University Press, 1991), 51.

36. H. L. Allrik, "The Lists of Zerubbabel (Nehemiah 7 and Ezra 2) and the Hebrew Numeral Notation," *BASOR* 136 (1954): 23. See §6.1.2 #3 for Kidner's comment on the same lists.

37. S. R. Driver, *Notes on the Hebrew Text and the Topography of the Books of Samuel* (Oxford: Clarendon, 1960), 97 n. 2; cf. J. Naveh, "More Hebrew Inscriptions from Meṣad Ḥashavyahu," *Israel Exploration Journal* 12 (1962): 29 n. 4; Archer, *Encyclopaedia of Bible Difficulties*, 206–7.

38. J. W. Haley, *Alleged Discrepancies of the Bible* (repr. Grand Rapids: Baker, 1977), 19–24; see also 380–83.

39. E. Kautzsch, *Gesenius' Hebrew Grammar* (2nd ed.; trans. A. E. Cowley; Oxford: Clarendon, 1910), §5k.

The phenomenon of graphically similar letters being confused in either the paleo-Hebrew or Aramaic script is undeniable.[40] While no extant copy of an early Bible manuscript shows numbers written as letters of the Hebrew alphabet, its use in later times is thought to hark back to a much earlier and well-known practice. C. F. Keil notes that the employment of the alphabet as numeral signs among the Greeks coincides with the Hebrew alphabet, presupposing Hebrew usage of consonants as numbers.[41] When the confusion of letters is applied to numbers, the number takes on another value. Corruption in the years given for Abijam's reign, 6 to 3, could have been caused by graphic similarity in the letters *gimel* and *waw* in the paleo-Hebrew or Aramaic script (see table 7.3).

While the square Hebrew letters for 10 (י) and 20 (כ) do not resemble each other, in the paleo-Hebrew script *kaph* (20) was written in both medial and final forms.[42] The final form was the earlier form, having a straight down stroke that developed into a curved shape through the tendency to form ligatures.[43] In the early 4th century *kaph* had a narrow ticked head,[44] which may have led to its confusion with *yod* (10), written with a long down stroke, not unlike *waw* ו (6) with which it was often mistaken.[45] In addition, *dalet* (4) could be confused with *zayin* (7).[46] Since *zayin* was often confused with *waw*,[47] it follows that *dalet* and *zayin* had shapes similar to *waw*. Individual handwriting styles add further ambiguity.

Of the current proposals concerning confusion of numbers, numbers written as letters of the Hebrew alphabet thus seems the most plausible. The data given in the OG/L and MT/KR for the EDK have all been accounted for in my analyses above. I have not introduced any data not already indicated by the texts.[48] My analyses do not employ coregencies (or interregnums), antedating or postdating systems, switches in dating systems, years beginning with Nisan in Israel and with Tishri in Judah, or variant recordings kept in Israel and Judah for the kings' reigns. The resolution to DK chronology comes from a critical analysis of the data in the Hebrew and Greek texts, not in assumed dating systems like those proposed by Thiele and other scholars. The proposal that numbers were written as letters in an early Hebrew script leading to the confusion between graphically similar letters is a topic that needs further investigation by experts in that field.

7.4. Assessment of the Early Divided Kingdom Chronology by Thiele and Other Scholars

Before proceeding to LDK chronology, I will review how the preceding chronology has been understood by scholars who show some awareness of the Greek data.

---

40. See §6.1.2 nn. 1 and 3 (p. 94) for bibliography.

41. Keil, *Books of the Chronicles*, 44–45.

42. E. Tov, *Textual Criticism of the Hebrew Bible* (2nd ed.; Minneapolis: Fortress, 2001), 210, 254–55.

43. F. M. Cross Jr., "The Development of the Jewish Scripts," in *The Bible and the Ancient Near East: Essays in Honor of William Foxwell Albright* (ed. G. E. Wright; New York: Doubleday, 1961), 180.

44. Ibid., 182.

45. P. K. McCarter, *Textual Criticism: Recovering the Text of the Hebrew Bible* (Philadelphia: Fortress, 1986), 47; Tov, *Textual Criticism of the Hebrew Bible*, 244–46.

46. See table 7.3 for comparison of early and late forms; cf. Cross, "Jewish Scripts," 181–82; Tov, *Textual Criticism of the Hebrew Bible*, 409–10.

47. McCarter, *Textual Criticism*, 47.

48. As explained, Baasha's 17 years is not extant in any text but is called for by Elah's accession in Asa's 20th year (1 Kgs 16:6 OG/L), followed by Zimri's accession in Asa's 22nd year (16:15 be$_2$). Similarly, Asa's 38 years are demanded by the synchronism for Jehoshaphat's accession in Omri's 11th year (16:28a OG/L) and Ahab's accession in Jehoshaphat's 2nd year (16:29 OG/L).

Table 7.3. Hebrew Alphabets
(source: M. Lidzbarski in *Gesenius' Hebrew Grammar* [ed. E. Kautzsch; trans. A. E. Cowley; 2nd ed.; Oxford: Clarendon, 1920], facing p. xvi)

TABLE OF ALPHABETS

7.4.1. Abijam and Asa

How have scholars treated the 6 years attributed to Abijam's reign in OG/L and the 3 years in the MT? Thiele explains that the 6 years of Abijam's reign in "LXX and Luc[ianic]" was an attempt by the Greek texts to "make possible the same total of years for Judah in this period [the EDK] as for Israel" (*MNHK*[1] 184).[49] He notes that in the MT Judah has 95 years and Israel has 98. Further on, Thiele claims that Asa's accession in Jeroboam I's 24th year in the Greek texts was necessary because of "the increase in the length of Abijam's reign from three years to six, and the reckoning of these reigns according to the inconsequent accession-year system. Under the Greek arrangement only this new synchronism will fit" (*MNHK*[1] 187). In neither of these contexts does Thiele consider the possibility that the reign for Abijam in the MT has been reduced from 6 to 3 years or that the MT altered Asa's synchronism to Jeroboam I's 20th year. The second and third editions of *MNHK* do not mention that the Greek texts give Abijam 6 years, not even in the tabulation of Greek variants at the end of his book. Thiele takes these from Burney, who notes that Abijam reigned 6 years in both LXX and L (*MNHK*[2] 198; *MNHK*[3] 209).[50] In Thiele's latter works he has ignored this vital datum completely.

Shenkel notes that Abijam's 6-year reign fully accords with Asa's accession in Jeroboam I's 24th year and that MT gives Abijam 3 years, with Asa's accession in Jeroboam I's 20th year. But apart from noting that c_2 adopted the MT numbers (*CRD* 34–35), Shenkel has little else to say about the variant data, even though he urges the use of Greek data in reconstructing the chronology (*CRD* 4–5). He also misses the significance of the OG/L data for the reconstruction of the EDK chronology. Shenkel writes, "Beginning with the reign of Elah until the establishment of the new dynasty under Omri the details of the history of the northern kingdom are confused. This confusion is reflected in the Greek texts, which are defective in their chronological data" (*CRD* 35). My analysis shows that the confusion began with the shortening of Abijam's reign from 6 years to 3 years, not with the establishment of the reign of Omri and supposed defects in the Greek texts.

Other scholars, too, even if they acknowledge the OG/L and MT variants for the reigns of Abijam, Jeroboam I, and Asa, do not notice their significance for the subsequent MT chronology.[51]

7.4.2. The Omride Period to the End of the Early Divided Kingdom

Scholars have concentrated their attention on the problems of the Omride period, not realizing that the difficulties stem from the initial reduction of Abijam's reign from 6 to 3 years and from the change of Baasha's regnal years from 17 to 24.[52]

---

49. J. M. Miller seems to agree with Thiele; see "Another Look at the Chronology of the Early Divided Monarchy," *JBL* 86 (1967): 281.

50. C. F. Burney, *Notes on the Hebrew Text of the Books of Kings* (Oxford: Clarendon, 1903), xlii.

51. See comments by Hughes, *Secrets of the Times*, 38, 77, 88, 123, 189–90, 275–76; Galil, *CKIJ* 16 n. 13, 135–36.

52. See the extensive literature, including C. F. Keil, *The Books of the Kings* (trans. J. Martin; Biblical Commentary on the Old Testament 6; repr. Grand Rapids: Eerdmans, n.d.), 224–25; J. Skinner, *I and II Kings* (Century Bible; Edinburgh: Jack, 1904), 217–20; Burney, *Hebrew Text of the Books of Kings*, 203–4; W. F. Albright, "The Chronology of the Divided Monarchy of Israel," *BASOR* 100 (1945): 20–21; J. A. Montgomery, *A Critical and Exegetical Commentary on the Books of Kings* (ed. H. S. Gehman; International Critical Commentary; Edinburgh: Clark, 1951), 283–84; Miller, "Another Look," 281–87, esp. 283; J. Gray, *1 and 2 Kings* (Old Testament Library; London: SCM, 1970), 64; K. T. Andersen, "Die Chronologie der Könige von Israel und Juda," *Studia Theologica* 23 (1969): 81; D. W. Gooding, review of *CRD* in *Journal of Theological Studies* 21 (1970): 123–25; E. R. Thiele, "Coregencies and Overlapping Reigns among the Hebrew Kings," *JBL* 93 (1974): 175–81; S. J. De Vries, "Chronology, OT," in *Interpreter's Dictionary of the Bible: Supplementary Volume* (ed. K. Crim; Nashville: Abingdon, 1976), 163; idem, *1 Kings*, 200–202; J. M. Miller, "So Tibni Died (1 Kings xvi 22)," *VT* 18

Thiele, whose explanation for the data of the Omride period was summarized in §6.3.4.1, ignores the data of the be$_2$ manuscripts locating the accessions of Zimri and Omri in Asa's 22nd year (1 Kgs 16:15–18). He proposes a 4-year coregency between Tibni and Omri to fill the years from Asa's 27th year (when he assumes that Omri acceded to the throne; 16:15 MT) to Asa's 31st year (16:23). Thiele proposes Asa's 31st year as the Greek datum commencing Omri's sole reign. He claims that the 12 years for Omri's reign in the Hebrew chronology extended from Asa's 27th to 38th years, but the Greek chronology was forced to extend Omri's reign to Ahab's 2nd year to give Omri 12 years. Thiele claims that the MT sequence for the reigns of the kings following Omri is original, proved by the inconsistency of the Greek's two accounts for the reign of Jehoshaphat (16:28; 22:41–51). He assumes the account at 16:28 was secondarily placed and resulted in variant data (*MNHK*³ 88–92).[53] Thiele does not recognize that Vaticanus consists of two independent texts, each having Jehoshaphat's narrative positioned according to their own sequence of kings' reigns.

Thiele does not realize that the 31st year is an aberrant synchronism from a pre-MT, accompanied by the 41 years given to Asa's reign at 15:10. The 4 years supposedly between Asa's 27th and 31st years is a misconception because the 27th and 31st both refer to Omri's 1st year in Samaria in different texts (see their virtual alignment in calendar year 51 in table 7.1). No explanation of the chronology can be based on the assumption that there were 4 years between the 27th and 31st years of Asa. It is evident that Tibni never reigned. Thiele's hypothesis, and others like it, rely on a false premise.

Like Thiele, Shenkel also does not perceive that Asa's 27th and 31st years refer to the same year in different texts. Shenkel proposes that Zimri's death was followed by 4 years of internecine strife between troops of Omri and Tibni, culminating in Tibni's death. These years were "assigned to Tibni, although he is not listed officially among the kings of Israel" (*CRD* 40). Shenkel seeks support for Tibni's reign by appealing to the words *Omri began to reign after* (μετά) *Tibni*. The words *after Tibni* appear in the extension of 16:22 OG/L, and Shenkel proposes that they mean after Tibni *reigned*. The more appropriate reading, however, is after Tibni *died*, since he had just been slain. No regnal formulas or regnal years are attributed to Tibni.

Even though Shenkel assigns the 4 years of internecine strife to Tibni, he also proposes that "in the Hebrew chronology the four years after the death of Zimri are reckoned as part of the total of regnal years for Omri." He admits, "It should be observed that this procedure of reckoning the years before a king's official accession as part of his regnal years is completely anomalous, having no parallel elsewhere in Kings" (*CRD* 40).[54] According to Shenkel, the Hebrew chronology gives Omri only 7 years of sole reign (*CRD* 41), and the Greek chronology "regards the

---

(1968): 392–94; idem, *The Old Testament and the Historian* (London: SPCK, 1976), 3; Green, "Regnal Formulas," 170–71; G. H. Jones, *1 and 2 Kings* (New Century Bible Commentary; Grand Rapids: Eerdmans, 1984), 22–23, 294–97; E. W. Faulstich, *History, Harmony, and the Hebrew Kings* (Spencer, Iowa: Chronology Books, 1986), 53; Miller and Hayes, *HAIJ* 229, 264–65; J. H. Hayes and P. K. Hooker, *A New Chronology for the Kings of Israel and Judah and Its Implications for Biblical History and Literature* (Atlanta: John Knox, 1988), 27–28; Hughes, *Secrets of the Times*, 83–84; L. McFall, "A Translation Guide to the Chronological Data in Kings and Chronicles," *Bibliotheca Sacra* 148 (1991): 16; Galil, *CKIJ* 21–23, 28–29; M. Cogan, *1 Kings: A New Translation with Introduction and Commentary* (Anchor Bible 10; New York: Doubleday, 2000), 415–17.

53. Cf. Thiele, "Coregencies and Overlapping Reigns," 175–82.

54. Gooding (review of *CRD*, 123) points out what he considers to be a perfect analogy, viz., the 40 years of David's reign includes Ishbosheth's reign before David was officially made king over Israel (1 Kgs 2:11). Note, however, that David was officially king over Judah at this time (2 Sam 5:3–5), and the sum of his years is taken from the time he began his reign at Hebron.

twelve years of Omri's reign to have begun with his official accession as sole ruler of Israel in the thirty-first year of Asa" (*CRD* 40).

Shenkel regards Asa's 31st year as the Greek datum even though he knows that L minuscules be$_2$ place Zimri's (and therefore Omri's) accession in Asa's 22nd year at 16:15 (*CRD* 36). Since Shenkel writes elsewhere that "proto-Lucian agrees with the Old Greek wherever the latter is extant" (*CRD* 10), we expect Shenkel to use Asa's 22nd year as the Greek datum for Omri's accession. Shenkel also points out that the verb מלך used for the duration of reign at 16:23 ("Omri reigned over Israel 12 years; he reigned 6 years at Tirzah") is translated with the historical present, when elsewhere it is translated by the aorist (*CRD* 51). These considerations should have cautioned Shenkel against attributing Asa's 31st year to the Greek texts.

Nevertheless, Shenkel asserts that "the period of four years, more or less, that constitutes the discrepancy between the two chronologies . . . entails an alteration in all the synchronisms that follow. . . . The variation of four years in the chronology also entails a divergence in the order of the text itself" (*CRD* 40–41). The fallacy of these comments was noted above. The addition of 3 years to Asa's original 38 years to give him 41 years in a pre-MT caused the initial divergency. When 41 years were added to a text having the original 6 years for Abijam's reign, Asa's reign was forced to extend 3 years beyond Ahab's accession in Asa's 38th year, to Ahab's 4th year. This caused the change in synchronisms in the MT and the alteration to its sequence of reigns.

Shenkel takes his hypothesis a step further when he argues that divergence in the MT and OG chronologies in the reign of Omri was effected in the MT in order to identify Jehoshaphat as the good king of Judah in the Moabite campaign of 2 Kings 3 (*CRD* 107, 111). A pious redactor "wished to justify Elisha's intervention on behalf of the king of Judah by identifying the latter with the religiously acceptable Jehoshaphat" (*CRD* 111; see also 105). This produced an alteration in the chronology so that Jehoshaphat and Joram could be contemporaries. A compensating adjustment had to be made, which Shenkel sees as the reason for Omri's sole reign beginning in Asa's 27th year in the Hebrew texts, but the 31st in the Greek. After this adjustment was made, Joram's accession "was synchronized with the eighteenth year of Jehoshaphat, making the encounter of the two kings, Jehoshaphat and Joram, possible from a chronological viewpoint" (*CRD* 107). Shenkel also proposes that the naming of Jehoshaphat in the Moabite campaign was influenced by the parallel account of the battle at Ramoth-gilead in 1 Kings 22 (*CRD* 106–7).

In fact, the MT arrangement of reigns does not synchronize Joram's accession with Jehoshaphat's 18th year, but rather with the 22nd, though it is the 18th that is given (2 Kings 3:1). The MT does overlap Joram's reign with Jehoshaphat's, but this is due to the chronological rearrangement of the MT data and can scarcely be attributed to "a piety motive" of a redactor.

Gooding's review of Shenkel's book seeks to evaluate the chronological data of the Hebrew and Greek texts:

> The MT's chronology, as expounded by Thiele and Gray, is at least a consistent system; the Greek chronology, in favour of which Shenkel would discard the MT's scheme, is unfortunately self-contradictory, incomplete and incompletable. The trouble stems from the Greek's insistence that Omri's twelve regnal years began after the death of his rival Tibni (μετὰ Θαμνει I Kings xvi. 22) in the 31st year of Asa, whereas the MT counts the years from the 27th of Asa.[55]

The Greek, of course, does not insist that Omri's 12 years begin in Asa's 31st year. This is an aberrant pre-MT datum and has nothing whatever to do with the Greek chronology. Therefore "the trouble" does not originate with the Greek text at 16:23, and the Greek chronology is not

---

55. Review of *CRD*, 123; see also 118–19.

"self-contradictory, incomplete and incompletable." The OG/L data is much more consistent than the MT data and, furthermore, completable!

Using the nonaccession-year dating system for Baasha's reign (which reduces Baasha's reign from 24 years to 23) Gooding fills in Baasha's 24 years between Asa's 3rd and 26th years. This gave Elah a 1-year reign (reduced from 2 by antedating), thus enabling Zimri's 7-day reign and Omri's accession to synchronize with Asa's 27th year. Gooding hypothesizes that Omri's 12 years were "partly disputed by Tibni" until Omri began his sole reign in Asa's 31st year.[56] Gooding sees the MT as a consistent system, not recognizing that the OG/L system giving Baasha 17 years, Elah 2, and Omri 18 (from Asa's 22nd year) is a far more consistent system because it does not need to reduce Baasha's 24 years to 23 or Elah's 2 years to 1 year.

Gooding then compares the MT's "consistent system" with the "B-text" (he does not differentiate between the OG and KR of Codex Vaticanus) and notes that Zimri is credited with 7 years not 7 days. Gooding theorizes that if the 7 years are reckoned from the 27th, even on nonaccession-year reckoning, Zimri's rule would run to Asa's 33rd year, 2 years after the commencement of Omri's sole reign. The B-text "therefore does some drastic surgery."[57] Gooding notes that the B-text gives 24 years for Baasha's reign as in MT, "but then . . . inserts into I Kings xvi. 6 a synchronism which, of course, is not in the MT." He means the accession of Elah in Asa's 20th year. In other words, because the B-text credits Zimri with 7 years preceding Asa's 31st year, using postdating Gooding proposes that Omri and Tibni dispute leadership from the 29th to the 31st, and the prior 7 years are occupied by Zimri who begins to reign in Asa's 23rd year. Elah was given a new accession synchronism, the 20th instead of the 26th.[58] Gooding assumes that the B-text inserted the synchronism of Elah's accession into 16:6. In §5.3.4, my detailed analysis of 16:6–8 MT/OG/L concluded that the OG/L synchronism (16:6) for Elah's accession in Asa's 20th year was more likely to be original than the MT synchronism for the 26th at 16:8.

Moreover, the foregoing analysis saw that the 24 years assigned to Baasha conflicted with the be_2 synchronism for Zimri's and Omri's accessions in Asa's 22nd year and that in the MT the extra 7 years of Baasha's reign (his 18th–24th years) replaced the 6 years of Omri's reign at Tirzah (the 22nd to 27th years of Asa). Baasha's 24 years is the discrepant datum, not Elah's accession in Asa's 20th year at 16:6. Furthermore, the discrepant 24 years caused the alteration in MT of Elah's accession from Asa's 20th to 26th year. It is this MT synchronism for the 26th that is discrepant, not the OG/L. Gooding writes, "How the B-text intends the next years to be filled in is left uncertain, for in xvi. 8 it omits altogether Elah's synchronism, and likewise in xvi.15 it omits Zimri's synchronism."[59] In response, I note that the B-text did not omit the synchronism for Elah because it has already given its synchronism in 16:6. Prior to 16:7's intruding between 16:6 and 16:8, the end of 16:6 (with the synchronism) and the beginning of 16:8 comprised one verse consisting of Elah's opening regnal formula. In MT, 16:7 was placed before the opening formula so that the entire opening formula appears in 16:8. The B-text and MT have one place for one synchronism, and therefore it is inappropriate to ask, as Gooding does, how the B-text intended to fill in 16:8. The B-text does not have Zimri's accession at 16:15, probably having deleted "the 22nd year of Asa" when Baasha's additional years extended from Asa's 18th to 24th year. It is likely to have been deleted from OG on account of the conflict in its text when Baasha's 24 years

---

56. Ibid., 124.
57. Ibid.
58. Galil (*CKIJ* 136 n. 28) questions Gooding's assumption that the 7 years credited to Zimri were responsible for the changes in Vaticanus and influenced changes in L.
59. Review of *CRD*, 124.

were inserted incorrectly. The discussion about 7 years in the B-text is utterly hypothetical, as the correct length for Zimri's reign is 7 days. Whether 7 years was a scribal lapse or an attempt by a later redactor to fill in the years between Zimri's accession (deleted) and Omri's presumed accession in Asa's 31st year is a moot point.

Gooding next compares L with the MT and B-text and notes that L has 24 years for Baasha, but unlike the B-text does not give Zimri 7 years to be filled in from Asa's 23rd to 31st year. Instead, it has 7 days for Zimri as in MT. He notes that L attempts "the very lame 'while Asa was king of Judah,'"[60] not realizing that this is a repetition of the synchronism given in 16:6, but in 16:8 L has left out the year of Asa's reign. To have introduced Asa's 26th year at 16:8 to bring it into conformity with the MT would have brought a conflict into the L texts, with Asa's 20th year at 16:6. Gooding states that L supplies a synchronism at 16:15, which is not found in the B-text, for Asa's 22nd year, "which is simply 20 [years for] Asa plus the two years of Elah,"[61] inferring that it too is discrepant. The be$_2$ synchronism indicates that Omri reigned 18 years altogether, a number apparently corroborated by the Moabite Stone, thus confirming the accession of Omri, and therefore Zimri's 7 days previously, in Asa's 22nd year. The Moabite Stone invalidates Omri's initial reign from Tirzah in the 27th year of Asa as assumed by scholars from the MT data. This indicates the secondary nature of the MT; and Gooding dismisses one of the most important synchronisms representing an original Hebrew datum that has all but disappeared except in be$_2$.

Gooding does not realize that Omri reigned 18 years from Asa's 22nd year and thinks that the L text leaves the "excessively long period from the 22nd to the 31st of Asa to be filled in with the dispute between Omri and Tibni."[62] He continues, "The B-text and the Lucianic, then, have a sorry mess of a chronology precisely at the crucial point that has determined their peculiar order of text. The Lucianic chronology is an unintelligent hotch-potch of the MT and the B-text."[63] As noted earlier, it is not the reign of Omri that determined the difference in the Greek and Hebrew order of the texts, but the extension to the reign of Asa when Abijam was already correctly credited with 6 years. Nor is there the long period from Asa's 22nd to 31st year filled in with the dispute between Omri and Tibni. Asa's 22nd to 27th years are Omri's years at Tirzah, and the 31st is a secondary datum replacing the 27th at 16:23. The L text is not an "unintelligent hotch-potch of the MT and the B-text." It actually reflects the original more closely than the OG and MT.

The next area of Shenkel's thesis addressed by Gooding is the relative merits of the OG/L and MT sequence of kings' reigns. I noted in §5.4 that one outcome of the extension of Asa's reign from 38 years to 41 is that Jehoshaphat's narrative at 1 Kgs 16:28a–h OG/L, coming before Ahab's at 16:29–21:40 is now placed after Ahab's in 22:41–51 MT/KR. Gooding reasons that Jehoshaphat's reign could not be original in the Greek position because all it included was a summary of Jehoshaphat's reign, with the content of the summary placed later in Ahab's reign. It would have included the alliance of Ahab and Jehoshaphat at the battle of Ramoth-gilead in Jehoshaphat's narrative, whereas it is now in 1 Kings 22. Then the summary appears again at 22:41–51, the same summary as at 16:28a–h OG/L.[64] Gooding sees this as an inconsistency in the B-text:[65] "There remains, therefore, a difficulty in thinking that the placing of the Jehoshaphat

---

60. Ibid., 125.
61. Ibid.
62. Ibid.
63. Ibid. Cf. Gooding's similar comments in "A Recent Popularisation of Professor F. M. Cross' Theories on the Text of the Old Testament," *Tyndale Bulletin* 26 (1975): 127–28.
64. Review of *CRD*, 125–26; cf. 119, 121.
65. Ibid., 119.

summary at xvi. 28ᵃ⁻ʰ represents the free-composition of the original Hebrew."[66] It is, however, not inconsistent that the B-text has two accounts of Jehoshaphat's reign, because OG and KR are two independent texts, the KR following the MT chronology and sequence of reigns.

In 1965 Gooding was influenced in his thinking by certain passages in the Greek texts that have a different order in the MT:

> That the Old Greek has a markedly different order from the MT is obvious almost at first sight, and most people would perhaps agree with Montgomery's dictum: "But all presumption is against Greek rearrangements in general." Yet in a number of places ... the leading consideration has been a desire to put things in a strictly logical order of temporal sequence, to denote which I propose, for convenience of frequent reference, to use the term "timetable." The reasoning behind this "timetable" has, however, been at best pedantic and not seldom perverse and mistaken; it is demonstrably the work of a literalistically minded reviser.[67]

Gooding takes this perception a step further in 1975:

> But a thorough-going interest in a timetable that is prepared to re-order the contents of the book is not far removed from an interest in chronology. The Greek's special chronology likewise involves a special ordering of some of the contents of Kings. Shenkel and Cross think that the chronology represents the original Hebrew. But if the timetabling does not, is it likely that the chronology does?[68]

If logic is responsible for secondary and pedantic timetabling as Gooding proposes, the "logical" 22:41–51 MT/KR is secondary, and the "illogical" 16:28a–h OG/L is primary. But Gooding argues that the Greek, illogical for having the Jehoshaphat summary before that which it summarizes, is secondary! It is not the logicality or illogicality that positions the narratives, but the order of the kings' accessions in the respective texts dictated by the variant chronologies.

I noted in §5.4 that when two kings are involved in one event, the incident is recounted under the narrative of the main participant. The battle at Ramoth-gilead involving the alliance of Jehoshaphat and Ahab against the Syrians (1 Kings 22) was initiated by Ahab, took place in Israel, and was the cause of Ahab's death. The battle account properly belongs to Ahab's reign and is thus found in 1 Kings 22 at the end of Ahab's narrative and not in Jehoshaphat's at 16:28a–h OG/L.

The criticism directed at Shenkel's work by Gooding leads De Vries to write:

> D. W. Gooding showed that 1 Kgs 16:28+, drawing Jehoshaphat's reign forward, is a doctrinaire adaptation of 22:41–51. The obvious explanation for Gᴸ's revision is that it is a misguided attempt to make sense out of apparently conflicting evidence for Omri's reign in 16:23. The MT meant the synchronism with Asa's thirty-first year to mark Omri's victory over Tibni, and the length of Omri's reign to begin with his seizure of power from Zimri. It is only by following the MT and applying all the methods of the Hebrew scribes, not by adopting Gᴸ, that this fits into the overall chronology of the various kings.[69]

---

66. Ibid., 126.

67. "D. W. Gooding, "Pedantic Timetabling in 3rd Book of Reigns," *VT* 15 (1965): 154; quotation cited from Montgomery, *Books of Kings*, 319. See also Gooding, "Ahab according to the Septuagint," *Zeitschrift für die alttestamentliche Wissenschaft* 76 (1964): 269–80; idem, "An Impossible Shrine," *VT* 15 (1965): 405–20; idem, "Temple Specifications: A Dispute in Logical Arrangement between the MT and the LXX," *VT* 17 (1967): 143–72; idem, "Text-Sequence and Translation-Revision in 3 Reigns ix 10–x 33," *VT* 19 (1969): 448–63.

68. "Recent Popularisation," 131.

69. De Vries, *1 Kings*, 182; see also lix; cf. also comments by De Vries in "Chronology, OT," 163, on the relative merits of the Hebrew and Greek texts as espoused by Thiele and Shenkel.

I have responded to most of these criticisms of L above. De Vries asserts that the chronology fits together "only by following the MT and applying all the methods of the Hebrew scribes" (a likely reference to Thiele's dating systems). This is completely discounted by my reconstruction of the chronology from an analysis of all the textual data without applying Thiele's principles.

Gooding also criticizes Shenkel's work for the piety motive that Shenkel attributed to an MT redactor in naming Jehoshaphat as the "good king of Judah" in the Moabite campaign of 2 Kings 3, indicating the secondary nature of the MT. Gooding compares the piety motive with the order of the temple and palace plans of 1 Kings 6–7: "The MT has: Temple, Temple, Palace, Temple; the B-text and the Lucianics have: Temple, Temple, Temple, Palace."[70] The Greek texts are more pious and, therefore, secondary,[71] so the naming of Jehoshaphat should be Greek and secondary, but Shenkel asserts it is Hebrew and secondary. Gooding notes that if there is no piety motive in naming Jehoshaphat as the king of Judah in the MT, then "the MT may after all be original, and the Lucianics' reading, Ahaziah[-J] instead of Jehoshaphat, a secondary adaptation to the Lucianics' secondary chronology."[72]

According to my analysis, piety was not the motive for the insertion of Jehoshaphat's name in 2 Kings 3; this was rather the result of the change in the sequence of the king's narratives. Neither view—Gooding's argument that piety is Greek and secondary, or Shenkel's argument that the naming of Jehoshaphat shows the MT to be pious and secondary—applies. Gooding is correct in claiming that the naming of Ahaziah-J in the L texts is secondary as it is completely at variance with its own data, which make Jehoram the king of Judah in the Moabite campaign (discussed in §5.4). It may not, however, be argued that the MT is original merely because L has secondarily named Ahaziah-J as the king of Judah in 2 Kings 3. The MT's naming of Jehoshaphat is also secondary!

Scholars have not sufficiently understood the significance of differences in the Greek and Hebrew data for Abijam, Jeroboam I, and Asa and the resultant changes that are shown in the MT for the chronology that stemmed from the Omride period to the end of the EDK. The chronology presented in the earlier part of this chapter shows that the OG/L data have more of the original chronology than the MT. They produce a coherent chronology when divested of their extraneous data; the latter coming, as it seems, from a pre-MT, the proto-MT, or the MT itself.

---

70. Review of *CRD*, 127.

71. See A. G. Auld, *Kings without Privilege: David and Moses in the Story of the Bible's Kings* (Edinburgh: Clark, 1994), 24–25, who notes J. Trebolle Barrera's citation of the common view that the Greek sequence in 1 Kings 6–7 "reflects a secondary improvement of the original," but that Trebolle Barrera says it can be reversed on an analysis of the text and on grounds that the Greek has a more logical sequence with less textual contortion; *Salomán y Jeroboán: Historia de la recensión y redacción de I Reyes 2–12; 14* (Bibliotheca Salamanticensis. Dissertationes 3; Salamanca: Universidad Pontificia/ Jerusalem: Instituto Español Bíblico y Arqueológico, 1980); excerpted in English in "Redaction, Recension, and Midrash in the Books of Kings," *Bulletin of the International Organization for Septuagint and Cognate Studies* 15 (1982): 24–28.

72. Review of *CRD*, 127.

8

Relative Chronology of the Late Divided Kingdom

8.1. Explanation of Table 8.1

In the LDK material in 2 Kings, the MT/KR and L (excluding c_2 and L's extension at 2 Kgs 10:36+) exhibit the same chronological data except for the reign of Pekahiah (2 Kgs 15:23). MT/KR assign Pekahiah 2 years, L 10 years, and c_2 12 years. The LDK is not, however, without its chronological problems. The main problems (see §3.2.3) are Azariah's accession in Jeroboam II's 27th year (15:1) followed by the accession synchronisms for Zechariah, Shallum, and Menahem in Azariah's 38th/39th years and the length of Pekahiah's and Pekah's reigns. The alternative c_2 data, which give a consistent chronology, albeit with a downward trend due to its year-for-year approach (see §4.2), suggest how some of the problems may be resolved.

Table 8.1 represents my reconstruction of LDK chronology based on the following textual analysis. Although consisting of only one set of data, table 8.1 is constructed in the same manner as table 7.1 (see §7.1 for further explanation).

8.2. Explanation of Late Divided Kingdom Chronology

8.2.1. Athaliah and Joash-J (Judah); Jehu and Jehoahaz (Israel)

Athaliah's regnal years are not explicitly stated, but she was succeeded by Ahaziah-J's rightful heir, the 7-year-old Joash-J, whose accession is synchronized with Jehu's 7th year (2 Kgs 12:1–2 MT). This indicates that Athaliah ruled somewhat more than 6 full years. Jehu reigned 28 years (10:36) and was succeeded by Jehoahaz in Joash-J's 23rd year (13:1). The regnal years and synchronisms concur.

8.2.2. Joash-J, Amaziah, Azariah (Judah); Jehoahaz, Joash-I, Jeroboam II (Israel)

Jehoahaz reigned 17 years (2 Kgs 13:1). The accession of his successor, Joash-I, should synchronize with Joash-J's 39th year. This is supported by the accession of Amaziah in Joash-I's 2nd year (14:1) after Joash-J had reigned 40 years (12:1). Instead, Joash-I's synchronism at 13:10 is Joash-J's 37th year. But Joash-I's accession in Joash-J's 39th year agrees with the associated data.[1] I noted in §3.2.3 that the 37th year may be a textual error for the 39th, or it could derive from a defective L manuscript that located Jehu's accession in Athaliah's 2nd year (10:36), causing a change in the following two synchronisms.

---

1. The 39th appears in late Greek manuscripts Nefgjmnpqstuw–z.

Table 8.1. Late Divided Kingdom Chronology
Reconstructed from MT/KR, L, and c_2 Data

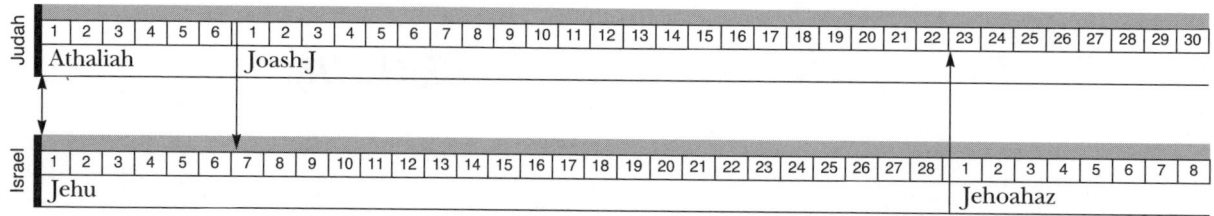

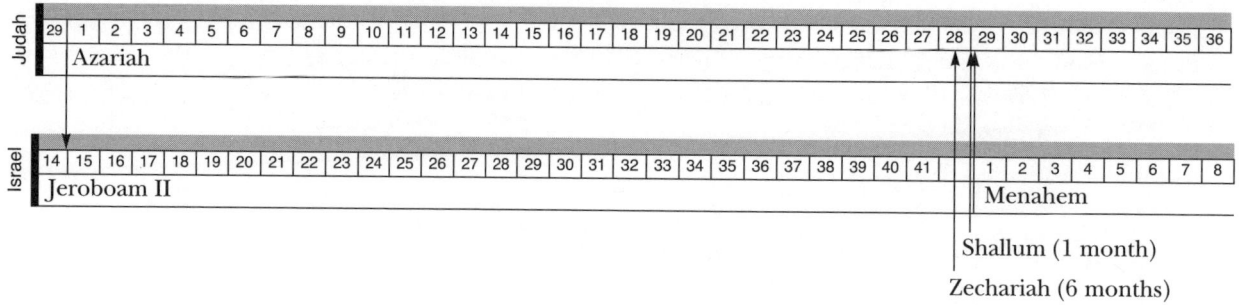

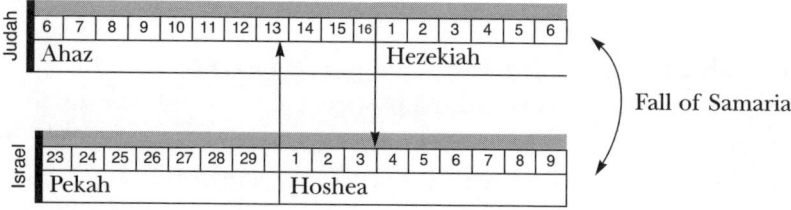

Table 8.1. Late Divided Kingdom Chronology Reconstructed from MT/KR, L, and c_2 Data (cont.)

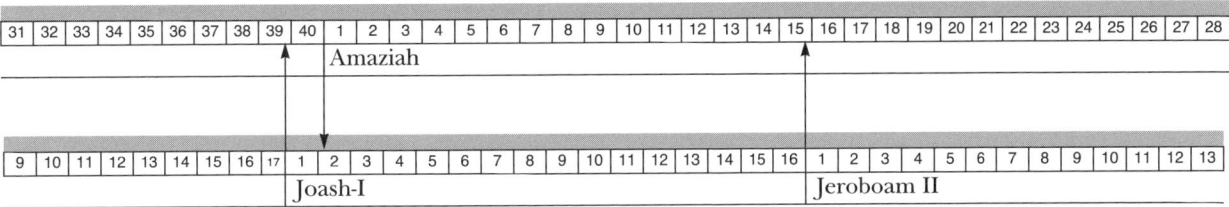

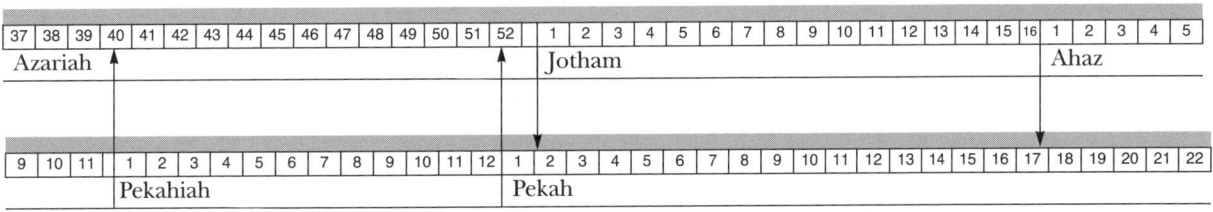

Joash-I reigned 16 years (13:10). His successor, Jeroboam II, began to reign in Amaziah's 15th year (14:23). Amaziah reigned 29 years (14:2). 2 Kings 14:17 states that Amaziah lived 15 years after Joash-I died. In §5.3.9 I noted that Joash-I's closing formula is not in its original position at 13:12–13 or its duplicate at 14:15–16. L, however, has Joash-I's closing formula in the appropriate position at the end of 13:25 before Amaziah's opening formula at 14:1. The disturbance of text at 14:15–16 may mean that 14:17 is a late textual addition. Furthermore, 14:17 is unique in stating the number of years that a king lived after the death of his contemporary of the other kingdom. Josephus indicates that the war between Amaziah and Joash-I occurred in Amaziah's 14th year (*Antiquities* 9.203), information not in the extant biblical text. The 15 years Amaziah lived after Joash-I died is correct when reckoned from his 15th rather than his 16th year.

With Jeroboam II's accession located in Amaziah's 15th year (14:23) and Amaziah spanning a 29-year reign (14:2), the synchronism for his successor, Azariah, would be expected in Jeroboam II's 14th or 15th year. The MT places Azariah's accession in Jeroboam II's 27th year (15:1), plainly in conflict with the previous synchronism. Azariah's accession 15 years after the death of Joash-I makes the 27th impossible. Josephus has the variant 14th year (*Antiquities* 9.216), which is consistent with the previous data. If the 14th is correct, whence came the 27th? Perhaps it is another

Table 8.2. Calendar Years 196–229 according to MT/KR

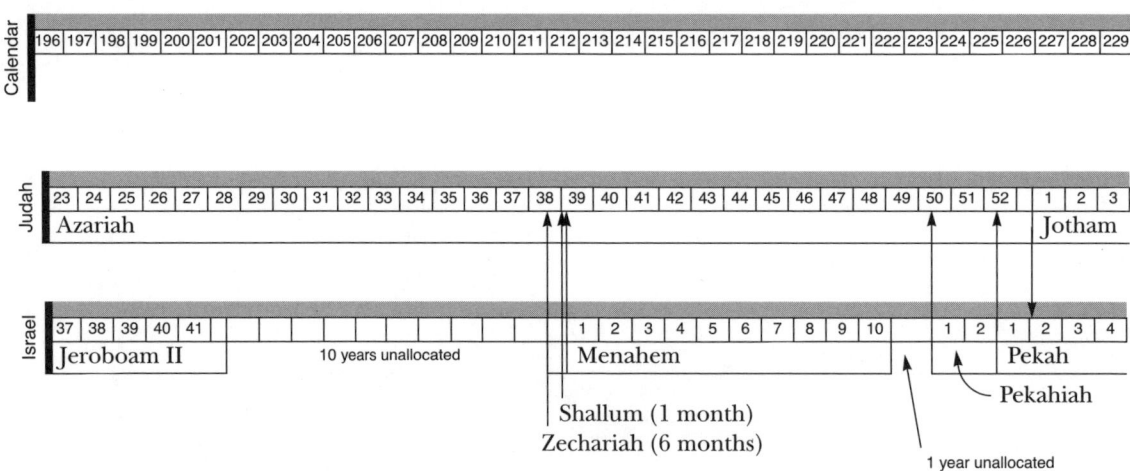

indication of confusion between 24 and 17, as we saw with Baasha's reign in the EDK (given as 24 years at 1 Kgs 15:33 but apparently originally 17 years, as required by the synchronism for Elah's accession in Asa's 20th year in 16:6 OG/L) and Ahaziah-I's accession (synchronized with the 17th in 22:52 MT but the 24th in L). With new confusion arising between 27 and 14 at 2 Kgs 15:1, these examples show that 10 and 20 can be confused as well as 7 and 4 (see §7.3.6). Josephus's alternative of Azariah's accession in Jeroboam II's 14th year appears to reflect the original number. c_2 aligns Azariah's accession with Jeroboam II's 15th year, having previously aligned Jeroboam II's accession with Amaziah's 16th year, instead of the correct 15th (see table 4.4 and §4.2). This shows the effect of the year-for-year alignment. If this 1-year downward trend is corrected, the c_2 synchronism agrees with Azariah's accession in Jeroboam II's 14th year.

Jeroboam II reigned 41 years (14:23), so the expected accession synchronism for his successor, Zechariah, would be Azariah's 27th or 28th year depending on the length of Jeroboam II's final year. Zechariah's accession, however, is synchronized with Azariah's 38th year (15:8), which leaves 10 years between Jeroboam II's death and his son's accession. An interregnum is so far unprecedented in the chronology of Judah and Israel and raises doubts over the authenticity of Jeroboam II's 41 years or the accession of Zechariah in Azariah's 38th year.

8.2.3. Azariah (Judah); Jeroboam II, Zechariah, Shallum, Menahem, and Pekahiah (Israel)

Zechariah's accession is the first of the problematic synchronisms in 2 Kings 15. Of the seven regnal formulas in this chapter, four of them use pattern B2, where the usual rhetorical question in the referral notice is turned into a statement: Zechariah (15:11), Shallum (15:15), Pekahiah (15:26), and Pekah (15:31). Pattern 2 of opening formulas (acceding king's name first) occurs in 15:13 MT for Shallum's reign, while KR and L exhibit an irregular Pattern 2. As discussed in chapter 5, changes in the predominant pattern of regnal formulas raise doubts about the authenticity of the associated regnal data. It is obvious that the construction of the chronology in the MT/KR has significant gaps, implying discrepancy.

Table 8.3. Calendar Years 196–229 according to L

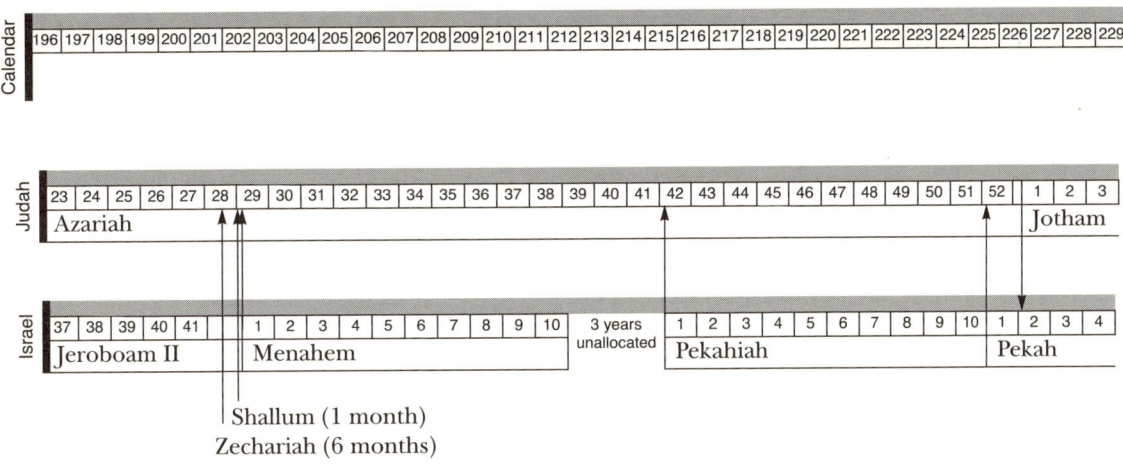

In MT/KR (table 8.2), Zechariah's accession is synchronized with Azariah's 38th year. Zechariah reigns 6 months before being killed by Shallum (15:8–10). Shallum's accession is synchronized with Azariah's 39th year, and Shallum is killed after 1 month by Menahem (15:13–14), whose accession is also synchronized with Azariah's 39th year. Menahem reigns 10 years (15:17), and Pekahiah succeeds him in Azariah's 50th year and reigns 2 years (15:23). Zechariah's reign begins 10 years after Jeroboam II's death in Azariah's 28th year, leaving 10 unallocated years in the chronology. In addition, Menahem's reign begins in Azariah's 39th year and lasts 10 years, leaving 1 year unaccounted for between the end of Menahem's reign in Azariah's 49th year before Pekahiah's accession in Azariah's 50th year. Pekahiah's 2 years in MT/KR concur with the accession of Pekah in Azariah's 52nd year.

The L texts (table 8.3) assign the same accession synchronisms as MT/KR to the reigns of Zechariah, Shallum, and Menahem and also assign Pekahiah's accession to Azariah's 50th year. But unlike MT/KR, the L texts assign to Pekahiah 10 years not 2 years. If Pekah's accession remains in Azariah's 52nd year as stated in all texts (15:27), Pekahiah's 10 years cannot begin in Azariah's 50th year; this datum needs to be adjusted to Azariah's 42nd year. But this accession synchronism for Pekahiah does not appear in L. Furthermore, Menahem's accession is synchronized with Azariah's 39th year as in MT/KR, but if Pekahiah's accession is in Azariah's 42nd year, there would be an overlap in the reigns of Menahem and Pekahiah from the 42nd to 49th years of Azariah, which is unattested. It also leaves unresolved the gap of 10 years from the end of Jeroboam II's reign in Azariah's 28th year and the accession of Zechariah in the 38th, followed by Shallum's and Menahem's accessions in the 39th.

Alternatively, if Pekahiah's accession in Azariah's 42nd year was preceded 10 years earlier by Menahem's accession in Azariah's 32nd year, with Shallum's 1 month in the same year and Zechariah's 6 months earlier in the 31st, this accounts for 10 of the unallocated years but leaves unaccounted 3 years from the end of Jeroboam II's reign in Azariah's 28th year and the accession of Zechariah in the 31st. Another proposal is to commence Zechariah's reign in Azariah's 28th year and Shallum's and Menahem's in the 29th. Menahem's 10 years would then end in Azariah's 39th

Table 8.4. Calendar Years 196–229 according to c_2

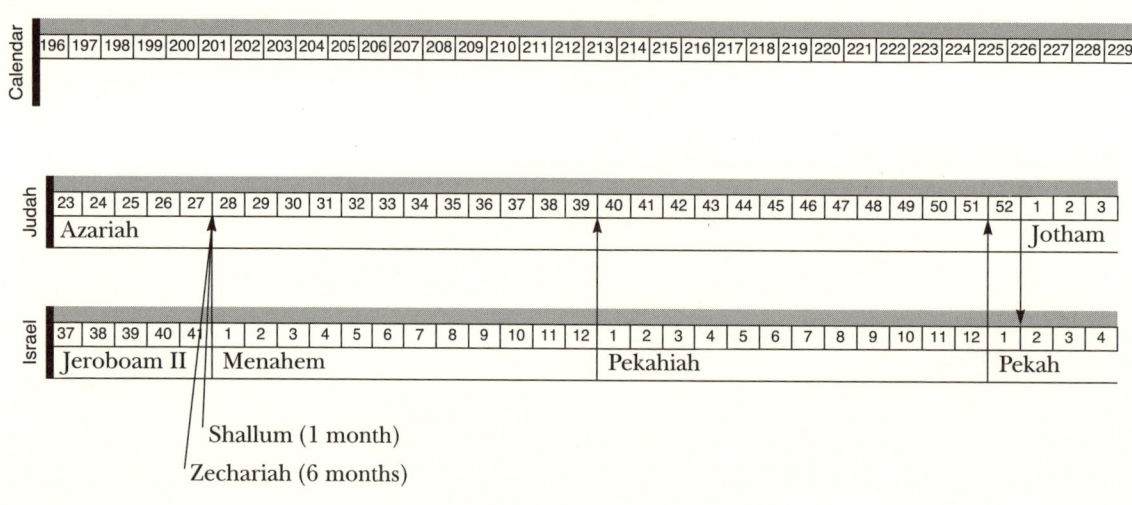

year, indicating a gap of 3 years before Pekahiah's reign begins in the 42nd. Alternatively again, Pekahiah's 10 years could begin in the 39th, leaving a 3-year gap between the 49th and Pekah's accession in Azariah's 52nd year.

The L variant of 10 years for Pekahiah's reign obviously affects the reigns of his predecessors, Zechariah, Shallum, and Menahem. It eliminates some of the years of the gap between the reigns of Jeroboam II and Zechariah unaccounted for in MT/KR, but 3 years are still outstanding, and a gap like this implies discrepancy.

The c_2 (table 8.4; see also table 4.1 and §4.2) chronology reflects the year-for-year alignment of regnal years in Israel and Judah. No allowance is made for final years being part years; each final year is reckoned as a full year.

c_2 has variants for the reigns of Zechariah, Shallum, Menahem, and Pekahiah. Following the 41-year reign of Jeroboam II, the accession of Zechariah is synchronized with Azariah's 28th year. The accessions of Shallum and Menahem are also synchronized with Azariah's 28th year. Zechariah is assigned 6 months and Shallum 1 month as in MT/KR and L. Menahem, however, is assigned 12 years, not L's 10 or MT's 2. Pekahiah's accession is synchronized with Azariah's 40th year, not the 50th, and after 12 years is succeeded by Pekah in Azariah's 52nd year (2 Kgs 15:27). This arrangement has no gap in the years between Menahem's accession in Azariah's 28th year and Pekah's accession in Azariah's 52nd year.

If Pekahiah reigned 12 years and not 2, his accession occurred in either Azariah's 39th or 40th year, depending on the length of his final year. If 10 years have been inadvertently deleted from his length of reign in MT and his accession later altered to accommodate the change, his present accession attribution in Azariah's 50th year suggests that the original may have been the 40th as given in c_2.

Menahem's accession, now given for Azariah's 39th year in MT/KR/L, if subject to the same 10-year downdating, would originally have been in Azariah's 29th year. c_2, with its variant of Azariah's 28th year, is probably illustrating its year-for-year approach. It aligns Jeroboam II's 41st year with Azariah's 27th year, whereas the synchronisms for Zechariah and Shallum show that

Jeroboam II must have reigned partway into Azariah's 28th year, assuming that Zechariah reigned only 6 months from the 28th and that Shallum began his reign in the 29th. If c_2 began Menahem's reign 1 year earlier than the actual, then its 12-year reign for Menahem is probably 1 year too many. This concurs with the MT/KR, which indicate the requirement for Menahem to reign 11 years from the 39th to the 50th years of Azariah (if updated as proposed, these years correspond to the 29th to the 40th years of Azariah).

This analysis of the variants in MT/KR, L, and c_2 for the reigns of Zechariah to Pekahiah proposes the following as the most likely reconstruction of the original (see table 8.1). Zechariah's accession is synchronized with Azariah's 28th year. After 6 months, Shallum's accession is synchronized with Azariah's 29th year, and, after a month, Menahem also begins to reign in Azariah's 29th year. Menahem's reign is 11 years. Pekahiah's accession is synchronized with Azariah's 40th year, and he reigns for 12 years. Pekah succeeded Pekahiah in Azariah's 52nd year. At this point all texts concur.

If inadvertent, the deletion of 10 years in the MT/KR from the 12 assigned to Pekahiah's reign (leaving 2 years) and the deletion of 2 years in the L manuscripts (leaving 10 years) suggests that part of the original number was not transmitted accurately. If the numbers were written in words, a word may have been left out. If written in Hebrew consonants, 10 (*yod*) may not have been copied into the MT/KR texts (presumably from a proto-MT), and in the L texts 10 may have been copied, but not 2 (*beth*). A 10-year reign instead of 11 for Menahem also suggests a transmission fault. The same argument is applicable if symbols were used for numbers. The error may be due to the illegible condition of the *Vorlage*(*n*) (moldy, moth-eaten, cracked, etc.), or the lapse of a scribe. On the other hand, if the changes were deliberate, the reasons are now known only to those who made them.

My observation that the text of the four regnal formulas for Zechariah, Shallum, Pekahiah, and Pekah (yet to be discussed) has suffered accords with my prior proposal that reworked formulas may coincide with altered data.

8.2.4. Jotham, Ahaz, and Hezekiah (Judah); Pekah and Hoshea (Israel)

Pekah's accession is synchronized with Azariah's 52nd year in all texts (including c_2). The 52nd is Azariah's last year, and Jotham's accession is synchronized with Pekah's 2nd year (15:32). Jotham reigned 16 years (15:33), and the accession of his successor, Ahaz, is synchronized with Pekah's 17th year (16:1). c_2 synchronized Ahaz's accession with Pekah's 18th year, showing its downward alignment of kings in its year-for-year approach (see table 4.1 and §4.2).

Ahaz too reigned 16 years (16:2), and the accession of his successor, Hezekiah, is synchronized with Hoshea's 3rd year (18:1). This indicates that Hoshea's expected synchronism would be Ahaz's 13th or 14th year, depending on the length of Ahaz's final year, the length of Pekah's final year, and at what time in Hoshea's 3rd year Hezekiah began to reign. Hoshea's accession, however, at 17:1 has Ahaz's 12th year. But the 12th is not possible if Ahaz's accession is correctly given for Pekah's 17th year, because if Hoshea's accession was in Ahaz's 12th year, Hezekiah's accession could not have been earlier than Hoshea's 5th year. Ahaz's accession to the throne of Judah in Pekah's 17th year followed 16 years later by Hezekiah's accession in Hoshea's 3rd year seems to indicate that Pekah reigned 29–30 years, that is, from Azariah's 52nd year to Ahaz's 13th or 14th year. But according to 15:27 Pekah reigned only 20 years, which would place Hoshea's accession in Ahaz's 4th year—an unattested synchronism. In §3.2.3 it was proposed that Hoshea's accession was secondarily placed in Jotham's 20th year at 15:30 after Pekah's reign had inadvertently been reduced to 20 years.[2] (The synchronism is not given in L texts and is misplaced in a closing formula.) Jotham, of course, did not reign 20 years, only 16, but if he had, Hoshea's accession would have been in Jotham's 20th year. As it is, Pekah's 20th year corresponds to Ahaz's 3rd/4th year.

It seems that only 20 instead of 29 was copied into the text, presumably a pre-MT or proto-MT (and subsequently brought into the MT/KR and L texts). The presence of 20 suggests that 29 rather than 30 was the original figure for Pekah's reign. This returns us to the conclusion that Hoshea's accession must have occurred in Ahaz's 13th or 14th year if Hezekiah's accession is to synchronize with Hoshea's 3rd year (18:1). (See table 8.1.)

That Hoshea's accession could not have been in Ahaz's 12th year is further confirmed by the synchronization of Hoshea's and Hezekiah's regnal years with the siege and fall of Samaria in 2 Kgs 18:9–10, which asserts that the siege began in Hezekiah's 4th year = Hoshea's 7th year and lasted 3 years, ending in Hezekiah's 6th year and Hoshea's 9th year. These synchronisms confirm Hezekiah's 1st year in either Hoshea's 3rd or 4th year. The 3rd year is given at 18:1, though c_2 gives the 4th year, probably reflecting the downward trend of its alignment. The 3rd year is likely to be correct. Three years earlier, Hoshea's accession must have occurred in Ahaz's 13th or 14th year, not the 12th. Why then does the 12th year appear at 17:1? Perhaps the original text had the 14th year, and during transmission the graphic similarity of the letters *beth* and *dalet* caused 14th to be mistaken for 12th. In the Hebrew square script the letters are יד (14) and יב (12), and the similarity is even more evident in earlier Hebrew scripts (see table 7.3). On the other hand, if the *Vorlage* was damaged or illegible the 12th may have been a secondary calculation, whether the original was 13th or 14th.[3] In the final synchronization, Hezekiah's accession begins at the end of Hoshea's 3rd year and Hoshea's accession falls in Ahaz's 13th year, correlated with the Assyrian chronology (see table 8.6).

The siege of Samaria began in Hezekiah's 4th year, which was Hoshea's 7th year. "At the end of 3 years" the city fell in Hezekiah's 6th year and Hoshea's 9th year (18:9–10). My chronology thus concurs with the biblical data. The DK lasted 263 years, contrasting with Thiele's chronology, which allows only 208 years (931/930–723/722) (*MNHK*[3] 79, 122, 137, 217). The fall of Samaria brings us to the end of the DK.

8.2.5. Summary of Late Divided Kingdom Chronology

The LDK chronology has been affected by transmission errors and attempts to correct apparent errors, which led to further corruption. To recapitulate the foregoing discussion, I note the following textual discrepancies and the proposed reconciliations based on their associated textual data:

1. Joash-I's accession in Jehoahaz's 37th year (2 Kgs 13:10) should be the 39th.
2. Azariah's accession in Jeroboam II's 27th year (2 Kgs 15:1) should be the 14th.
3. Menahem's 10-year reign (2 Kgs 15:17) should be 11 years.
4. Pekahiah's reign, now allotted 2 years in MT/KR and 10 years in L (2 Kgs 15:23), should be 12 years.

---

2. See T. R. Hobbs, *2 Kings* (Word Biblical Commentary 13; Waco: Word, 1985), 204–5, for comments on the difficulty of the chronology.

3. The late Greek manuscripts hivz assign Pekah 28 years, which may be dependent on the synchronism at 17:1 that Hoshea began to reign in Ahaz's 12th year or possibly vice versa.

5. The foregoing deletion in Pekahiah's reign caused an alteration in the accession synchronisms for Zechariah, Shallum, Menahem, and Pekahiah, locating them all 10 years later than they should be (2 Kgs 15:8, 13, 17, 23).
6. Pekah's reign of 20 years (2 Kgs 15:27) should be 29 years.
7. The deletion of 9 years from Pekah's reign caused an incorrect synchronism at 2 Kgs 15:30 MT/KR of Hoshea's accession in Jotham's 20th year.
8. Hoshea's accession in Ahaz's 12th year (2 Kgs 17:1) should be the 13th.

When secondary alterations and additions are eliminated and the text restored as indicated above, the years of the kings of Israel and Judah — their reign lengths and accession synchronisms — exhibit a coherent chronology. The resolution of problems has been sought through textual analysis, with no need to resort to unattested dating systems, hypothetical coregencies, the distortion of regnal formulas, or the manipulation of associated narratives.

8.3. Establishing a Starting Date: The Fall of Samaria

It still remains for my chronology to be dated to the Julian calendar and to locate it and explore its corroboration in the context of ancient Near Eastern history. The Hebrew and Assyrian histories converge in the years surrounding the fall of Samaria, providing an opportunity to date the Hebrew kings to the Julian calendar. If a reliable date for the fall of Samaria can be established, the dates for the Hebrew kings can be worked backward to the beginning of the DK. Comparison can then be made between the dates of the Hebrew kings given in this chronology and those based on the AEC as proposed by Thiele and others.

8.3.1. The Earliest Established Date

To date the fall of Samaria, a synchronism must be found between a Hebrew king and a king or event dated to a specific year of the Julian calendar. The earliest established date applicable to Hebrew chronology is the battle of Megiddo, when Josiah was killed by Pharaoh Neco of Egypt (2 Kgs 23:28-30; 2 Chr 35:20-24) sometime between Siwan (May/June) and Tammuz (June/July)[4] in 609 B.C.E.[5]

Reckoning backward from mid-609 to the fall of Samaria in Hezekiah's 6th year requires 31 years for Josiah (2 Kgs 22:1), 2 for Amon (21:19), 55 for Manasseh (21:1), and 23 for the remainder of Hezekiah's reign (18:2), totaling 111 years. This produces the date mid-720 for the fall of Samaria. The date is approximate since the length of each king's final year is not known. Allowing a year on either side of 720 tentatively dates the fall of Samaria to 721-719 B.C.E.

8.3.2. Sennacherib's Campaign to Jerusalem

According to the validated data of 2 Kgs 18:10, Samaria fell in Hezekiah's 6th year, and according to 18:13 Sennacherib's army came against Jerusalem in Hezekiah's 14th year, 8 years later. Most scholars understand 18:13 to refer to Sennacherib's third campaign in his 4th regnal

---

4. S. H. Horn, "The Babylonian Chronicle and the Ancient Calendar of the Kingdom of Judah," *Andrews University Seminary Studies* 5 (1967): 18; A. Malamat, "The Last Kings of Judah and the Fall of Jerusalem," *Israel Exploration Journal* 18 (1968): 139.

5. See D. J. Wiseman, *Chronicles of Chaldean Kings (626-556 B.C.) in the British Museum* (London: British Museum, 1956), 19, 45, 63; D. N. Freedman, "The Babylonian Chronicle," *Biblical Archaeologist* 19 (1956): 51-55; Horn, "Babylonian Chronicle," 16-20; G. Galil, "The Babylonian Calendar and the Chronology of the Last Kings of Judah," *Biblica* 72 (1991): 376.

year in 701 B.C.E.[6] But if this was Hezekiah's 14th year, his 6th year would have been in 709. Alternatively, if Hezekiah's 6th year fell in 721–719, his 14th year fell in 713–711, not 701—a discrepancy of 10–12 years.

Sennacherib's coming to Jerusalem in 713–711 is problematic because these years fall in the reign of Sargon II (722–705), not Sennacherib (705–680). Sargon's commander-in-chief was involved in a campaign against Ashdod (Isa 20:1) in 712 when the AEC notes that Sargon was "in the land," that is, Assyria. But this Ashdod campaign cannot be identified with the Jerusalem campaign of Sennacherib described in 2 Kgs 18:13–19:36 and Isa 36:1–37:37.[7]

Although Sennacherib's campaign to Judah cannot be placed in 713–711, Hezekiah's 14th year can be located in these years, as deduced from 2 Kgs 20:1–11 and Isa 38:1–8. These parallel passages recount Hezekiah's illness and the extension of his life by 15 years. Since Hezekiah reigned 29 years (2 Kgs 18:2), his illness would have occurred in his 14th year. When the Babylonian king, Merodach-baladan, heard that Hezekiah had been ill he sent an envoy to Jerusalem (2 Kgs 20:12–19; Isa 39:1–8). Merodach-baladan reigned from 721 to 709,[8] so Hezekiah's 14th year could have occurred in 713–711, but not in 701. Merodach-baladan's dates invalidate Thiele's claim that "full confidence can be placed in 701 as the fourteenth year of Hezekiah" (*MNHK*[3] 174; see also 175, 120, 124–25).[9] If one year during 713–711 coincides with Hezekiah's 14th year, 701 will coincide with his 24th, 25th, or 26th year.

Various scholars acknowledge that the dating of Sennacherib's campaign to Hezekiah's 14th year in 2 Kgs 18:13 is inconsistent with other textual data and offer suggestions to account for the occurrence.[10] Among these is the suggestion that 14th is a textual corruption of 24th (see §6.3.4.9 n. 76, p. 117). If 701 is Hezekiah's 24th year, the fall of Samaria in Hezekiah's 6th year should be dated to 719, not 721 or 720.[11]

---

6. For the evidence see *ARAB* 2: §§231–82; J. Hughes, *Secrets of the Times: Myth and History in Biblical Chronology* (Journal for the Study of the Old Testament Supplement 66; Sheffield: JSOT Press, 1990), 210 n. 101.

7. For comments about the Ashdod campaign, see Y. Aharoni, *The Land of the Bible* (London: Burns & Oates, 1967), 334–35; G. L. Mattingly, "An Archaeological Analysis of Sargon's 712 Campaign against Ashdod," *Near East Archaeological Society Bulletin* 17 (1981): 47–64.

8. Hughes (*Secrets of the Times*, 183 n. 54) notes, "The total lunar eclipse which is recorded as having occurred on the night of Thoth 29/30 in the first year of Merodachbaladan is astronomically datable to March 19 721 B.C." Merodach-baladan also reigned for 9 months in 704–703 (M. Cogan and H. Tadmor, *II Kings: A New Translation with Introduction and Commentary* [Anchor Bible 11; Garden City, N.Y.: Doubleday, 1988], 259, 260–61) succeeded by Bel-ibni (*ABC* 77).

9. Thiele explains this anomaly by claiming that Merodach-baladan was a king in exile in 701 (*MNHK*[3] 176). Hobbs has a similar explanation (*2 Kings*, 289). Others who date Hezekiah's 14th year to 701 include G. H. Jones, *1 and 2 Kings* (New Century Bible Commentary; Grand Rapids: Eerdmans, 1984), 564; and L. McFall, "Did Thiele Overlook Hezekiah's Coregency?" *Bibliotheca Sacra* 143 (1989): 404; idem, "A Translation Guide to the Chronological Data in Kings and Chronicles," *Bibliotheca Sacra* 148 (1991): 36.

10. Cogan and Tadmor (*II Kings*, 228) propose that the 14th year was originally placed with the prophetic tradition about Hezekiah's illness and recovery and that "the present position of the date in v. 13a is secondary." J. H. Hayes and P. K. Hooker suggest that a number of events have been correlated, "beginning with the fourteenth year of Hezekiah and his illness. It appears that 2 Kings 18:13 and following, and thus the fourteenth-year reference, were not part of the first edition of the Deuteronomistic History"; *A New Chronology for the Kings of Israel and Judah and Its Implications for Biblical History and Literature* (Atlanta: John Knox, 1988), 74–75. Galil (*CKIJ* 102–3) suggests that the 14th year is based on a calculation of the redactor who assumed that Hezekiah's sickness and Sennacherib's campaign occurred in the same year.

11. Sennacherib's siege of Jerusalem in Hezekiah's 24th year produces a conflict in that Sennacherib's campaign to Judah (2 Kgs 18:13; Isa 36:1) comes before the account of Hezekiah's sickness in his 14th year (2 Kgs 20:1–11; Isa 38:1–8). Cogan and Tadmor (*II Kings*, 262–63) propose that the transposition of the texts occurred at a later stage of the

The mention of Tirhakah of Ethiopia advancing toward the Assyrian army in Judah (2 Kgs 19:9; Isa 37:9) is used by some scholars to argue that Sennacherib undertook two campaigns to Jerusalem on the assumption that Tirhakah was too young to lead a campaign in 701.[12] The two-campaign hypothesis has no support from Assyrian sources and is now generally abandoned on evidence that Tirhakah was 20 years old in 701 and could have commanded his brother Shebitku's army.[13] Thus Sennacherib's campaign may be dated to 701 and the fall of Samaria to 719.

8.3.3. Tiglath-pileser III and Hoshea's Accession

The attempt to find Assyrian and biblical corroboration for 719 as the fall of Samaria begins with the reign of Tiglath-pileser III and the accession of Hoshea (2 Kgs 15:30; 17:1). The fall of Samaria occurred in Hoshea's 9th year (18:10), which, if in 719, locates Hoshea's 1st year in 727 after he killed Pekah. Pekah had allied himself with Rezin of Damascus in laying siege to Jerusalem during the reign of Ahaz (16:5–9). Ahaz then sent messengers with treasures from the temple to Tiglath-pileser requesting military assistance against Rezin and Pekah. Tiglath-pileser marched against Damascus, killed Rezin,[14] and sent captives to Kir (16:9).[15] Hoshea "made a conspiracy against Pekah and struck him down and slew him" (15:30). The conspiracy may refer to Hoshea's collaboration with Tiglath-pileser, who claims to have appointed Hoshea as king of Israel, as two records from his reign state:

> [. . .] I carried off [to] Assyria. Peqah, their king [I/they killed] and I installed Hoshea [as king] over them. 10 talents of gold, x talents of silver, [with] their [property] I received from them and [to Assyria I car]ried them.[16]

---

development of the Books of Kings in order to give the Assyrian campaign precedence over Hezekiah's illness. Perhaps the change from 24th to 14th in an early text prompted a later redactor to interchange the order of these events?

12. E.g., J. Bright, *A History of Israel* (London: SCM, 1960), 282–87; S. H. Horn, "Did Sennacherib Campaign Once or Twice against Hezekiah?" *Andrews University Seminary Studies* 4 (1966): 1–28; B. S. Childs, *Isaiah and the Assyrian Crisis* (Studies in Biblical Theology 2/3; London: SCM, 1967), 14–17 and n. 8; W. H. Shea, "Sennacherib's Second Palestinian Campaign," *JBL* 104 (1985): 401–18; cf. W. H. Barnes, *Studies in the Chronology of the Divided Monarchy of Israel* (Harvard Semitic Monographs 48; Atlanta: Scholars Press, 1991), 73–130.

13. K. A. Kitchen, *The Third Intermediate Period in Egypt (1100–650 B.C.)* (2nd ed.; Warminster: Aris & Phillips, 1986), 157–61; idem, review of *Studies in the Chronology of the Divided Monarchy of Israel* by W. H. Barnes in *Evangelical Quarterly* 65 (1993): 250–51; H. H. Rowley, *Studies in Old Testament History and Prophecy* (London: Nelson, 1963), 98–132; A. R. Millard, "Sennacherib's Attack on Hezekiah," *Tyndale Bulletin* 36 (1985): 63–64; F. J. Yurco, "The Shabaka-Shebitku Coregency and the Supposed Second Campaign of Sennacherib against Judah: A Critical Assessment," *JBL* 110 (1991): 35–45.

14. Two fragmentary inscriptions relating to Tiglath-pileser, designated by H. Tadmor as Annals 18 and 24 (*The Inscriptions of Tiglath-pileser III King of Assyria* [Jerusalem: Israel Academy of Sciences and Humanities, 1994], 82–83), state that Mitinti of Ashkelon revolted against Tiglath-pileser and witnessed Rezin's defeat. See also J. K. Kuan, *Neo-Assyrian Historical Inscriptions and Syria-Palestine* (Jian Dao Dissertation Series 1; Hong Kong: Alliance Bible Seminary, 1995), 168.

15. See wider context in Isa 7:1–9, which infers that Rezin and Pekah died because they attacked Jerusalem. The deportation of the Syrians to Kir is also referred to in Amos 1:3–5.

16. Summary Inscription 4, rev. lines 17–19 = Tadmor, *Inscriptions of Tiglath-pileser III*, 141. This inscription was previously known as III R 10,2 (= H. C. Rawlinson, *The Cuneiform Inscriptions of Western Asia* [London: British Museum, 1875], 3: pl. 10 no. 2); see also *ARAB* 1: §816; *ANET* 284; S. A. Irvine, *Isaiah, Ahaz, and the Syro-Ephraimitic Crisis* (Society of Biblical Literature Dissertation Series 123; Atlanta: Scholars Press, 1990), 62–65; Kuan, *Neo-Assyrian Historical Inscriptions*, 176–82, 190–91. For previous publications of the annals, see Tadmor, *Inscriptions of Tiglath-pileser III*, 283–86. For previous comments on the annals of Tiglath-pileser III, see idem, "Introductory Remarks to a New Edition of the Annals of Tiglath-pileser III," *Proceedings of the Israel Academy of Sciences and Humanity* 2/9 (1967): 168–87.

[The land of Bīt-Ḫumria (Israel)] to its fu[ll extent I captured . . . together with] their belongings [I carried off] to Assyria.] [. . . Hoshea] over them as king [I placed.] [. . .] before me to the city of Sarrabani [. . .].[17]

The correlation of biblical and Assyrian records indicates that Pekah's death and Hoshea's accession occurred when Tiglath-pileser was in Syria (Damascus) or Israel.[18] According to my chronology Hoshea's 1st year was 727. Since Tiglath-pileser reigned from 745 to 727, Hoshea could have been appointed in 727 if Tiglath-pileser was in Damascus or Israel that year.

The AEC notation for 727 has only "to [ ]; [Shalman]eser (V) [sat on the throne]."[19] Tiglath-pileser campaigned in 727 but the location is destroyed on extant lists. For the previous year, 728, Smith (followed by Kuan and Irvine) reads "the city of Di[. . .]."[20] Millard translates "to Hi[. . .]."[21] And Tadmor renders "the City of [. . . was conquered]."[22] Cogan and Tadmor say of the broken sign that Smith reads as *di* and Olmstead interprets as "Damascus"[23] that "the name of the place referred to cannot presently be known."[24] The original designation in the AEC for the year 728 is thus unclear. The chronological reconstruction, if not the textual, points to Tiglath-pileser's presence in Damascus in 727, intriguing the question whether the AEC had "to Damascus" for 728 and 727.

If Tiglath-pileser was present in Damascus in 727, it was an event separate from his earlier campaign in 733/732 when the AEC notes he went "to Damascus." Scholars usually assume that the campaign of 733/732 is referred to in 2 Kgs 15:29 when Tiglath-pileser captured towns of northern Israel and carried captives off to Assyria. They also refer these years to the campaign of 16:5–9 when Tiglath-pileser marched against Damascus in response to Ahaz's appeal for help, the same year they understand Hoshea killed Pekah (15:30).[25] Nevertheless, Tadmor cites a passage that reads:

[The land of Bīt-Ḫumria (Israel),] all [of whose] cities I had [devastated] in my former campaigns, [. . .] its livestock I had despoiled and had spared Samaria alone — (now) [they overthrew Peqa]h, their king.[26]

---

17. Summary Inscription 9, rev. lines 9–11 = Tadmor, *Inscriptions of Tiglath-pileser III*, 189; published by D. J. Wiseman, "A Fragmentary Inscription of Tiglath-pileser III from Nimrud," *Iraq* 18 (1956): 121, 124–26. The inscription comes from two fragments previously known as ND 4301 and ND 4305; Kuan, *Neo-Assyrian Historical Inscriptions*, 182–86, 190–91. Hoshea's tribute was apparently sent on to Tiglath-pileser in Sarrabani, a city in southern Babylonia. See R. Borger and H. Tadmor, "Zwei Beiträge zur alttestamentlichen Wissenschaft aufgrund der Inschriften Tiglatpilesers III," *Zeitschrift für die alttestamentliche Wissenschaft* 94 (1982): 244–49.

18. Tadmor, *Inscriptions of Tiglath-pileser III*, 189, 277–78; N. Naʾaman, "Historical and Chronological Notes on the Kingdoms of Israel and Judah in the Eighth Century B.C.," *VT* 36 (1986): 71–72.

19. G. Smith, "On a New Fragment of the Assyrian Canon Belonging to the Reigns of Tiglath-pileser and Shalmaneser," *Transactions of the Society of Biblical Archaeology* 2 (1873): 322, 331; A. R. Millard, *The Eponyms of the Assyrian Empire, 910–612 B.C.* (State Archives of Assyria Studies 2; Helsinki: Neo-Assyrian Text Corpus Project, 1994), 45, 59; similarly Kuan, *Neo-Assyrian Historical Inscriptions*, 137–38. Tadmor (*Inscriptions of Tiglath-pileser III*, 236) reconstructs it as "Against the city of [. . .]."

20. Smith, "On a New Fragment," 322, 331; Kuan, *Neo-Assyrian*, 137–38 and n. 6; Irvine, *Isaiah, Ahaz*, 25 n. 6.

21. Millard, *Eponyms of the Assyrian Empire*, 45, 59, followed by K. L. Younger, "The Fall of Samaria in Light of Recent Research," *Catholic Biblical Quarterly* 61 (1999): 463–64.

22. Tadmor, *Inscriptions of Tiglath-pileser III*, 236. Tadmor notes that Luckenbill (*ARAB* 2: §1198) mistakenly attributes the sign *di* to the following year, 727. Luckenbill is followed by Thiele, *MNHK*³ 224.

23. A. T. Olmstead, "The Assyrian Chronicle," *Journal of the American Oriental Society* 34 (1915): 357.

24. Cogan and Tadmor, *II Kings*, 198–99 n. 4.

25. E.g., K. L. Younger, "The Deportations of the Israelites," *JBL* 117 (1998): 201–11.

26. Summary Inscription 13, lines 17–18 = Tadmor, *Inscriptions of Tiglath-pileser III*, 203, 281. This inscription was previously known as Layard 66; A. H. Layard, *Inscriptions in the Cuneiform Character from Assyrian Monuments* (London:

Tadmor comments, "This is, then, a general statement to the effect that Tiglath-pileser mounted not one, but several campaigns against Israel prior to Peqah's fall."[27]

Another passage states:

> That (king of Damascus), in order to save his life, fled alone, and entered the gate of his city [like] a mongoose. His chief ministers I impaled alive and had his country behold them. For 45 days my camp I set up around his city, and I cooped him up like a bird in a cage. His gardens, [. . .] orchards without number I cut down; I did not leave a single one.[28]

According to Tadmor, "the hyperbole is employed as a face-saving device to cover for a failure to take the enemy's capital and punish the rebellious king. In the case of Rezin, this was accomplished the following year (732)."[29] Since Tadmor does not place Tiglath-pileser in Damascus in 727, he naturally refers Rezin's "punishment" (death) to the 2nd year of the first campaign in 732.[30] Tiglath-pileser claimed campaigns in Israel before Pekah was overthrown, and Pekah's death is not mentioned in Annal 23. This suggests that Tiglath-pileser killed Rezin on a later campaign to Damascus (16:9), and during this campaign Hoshea conspired to kill Pekah (15:30), probably in collaboration with Tiglath-pileser who received tribute from Hoshea. Hoshea slew Pekah, and Tiglath-pileser installed Hoshea as king of Israel. Tiglath-pileser died later that same year (727) and was succeeded by Shalmaneser V.

The above analysis suggests that Tiglath-pileser III had a campaign "to Damascus" in 727, the year of Hoshea's accession. Hoshea's 7th–9th years, the 3 years of the siege (18:10), may be dated to 721–719, and this indicates 719 as the date of the fall of Samaria.[31]

8.3.4. Who Was King of Assyria When Samaria Fell?

Second Kings 17:3–6 asserts that Shalmaneser came against Hoshea, who became his vassal and paid him tribute. In an unspecified year Hoshea sent messengers to "King So of Egypt"[32] and stopped paying tribute to the Assyrian king "as he had done year by year." For this offense the king of Assyria "shut him up and bound him in prison." Then comes a curious statement: "Then

---

Harrison, 1851); P. Rost, *Die Keilschriftexte Tiglat-pilesers III* (Leipzig: Pfeiffer, 1893), lines 227–28; see Irvine, *Isaiah, Ahaz*, 37–40; Kuan, *Neo-Assyrian Historical Inscriptions*, 173–75.

27. Tadmor, *Inscriptions of Tiglath-pileser III*, 281.

28. Annal 23, lines 8–12 = Tadmor, *Inscriptions of Tiglath-pileser III*, 78–79. The inscription was formerly known as Layard 72b+73a; Rost, *Die Keilschriftexte Tiglat-pilesers III*, lines 200–204; see Irvine, *Isaiah, Ahaz*, 28–29; Kuan, *Neo-Assyrian Historical Inscriptions*, 171–73.

29. Tadmor, *Inscriptions of Tiglath-pileser III*, 79.

30. Cf. B. Becking, *The Fall of Samaria: An Historical and Archaeological Study* (Studies in the History of the Ancient Near East 2; Leiden; Brill, 1992), 14.

31. Hezekiah's 29th and last year fell in 696. Manasseh reigned for 55 years (696–641); Amon for 2 years (641–639); and Josiah 31 years (639–609).

32. For the identification of "So," consult S. Yeivin, "Who Was Sōʾ the King of Egypt?" *VT* 2 (1952): 164–68; Cogan and Tadmor, *II Kings*, 196; H. Goedicke, "The End of 'So, King of Egypt,'" *BASOR* 171 (1963): 64–66; W. F. Albright, "The Elimination of King 'So,'" *BASOR* 171 (1963): 66; Kitchen, *Third Intermediate Period in Egypt*, 372–76; Barnes, *Chronology of the Divided Monarchy*, 131–35; D. L. Christensen, "The Identity of 'King So' in Egypt (2 Kings xvii 4)," *VT* 39 (1989): 140–53; J. Day, "The Problem of 'So, King of Egypt' in 2 Kings xvii 4," *VT* 42 (1992): 289–301; P. T. Crocker, "Recent Discussion on the Identity of King 'So' of Egypt," *Buried History* 29 (1993): 68–73; N. Naʾaman, "The Historical Background to the Conquest of Samaria (720 B.C.)," *Biblica* 71 (1990): 216–17; Becking, *Fall of Samaria*, 47 n. 2 for bibliography; A. R. Green, "The Identity of King So of Egypt—An Alternative Interpretation," *Journal of Near Eastern Studies* 52 (1993): 99–108.

the king of Assyria invaded all the land and came to Samaria, and for 3 years he besieged it. In Hoshea's 9th year, he captured Samaria, and he carried the Israelites away to Assyria." What were the circumstances surrounding the imprisonment of Hoshea and the siege and capture of Samaria? Were these parts of a single event or two separated events?

The AEC for the last two years of Tiglath-pileser's reign (728–727), the 5 years of Shalmaneser's reign (727–722), and the first 5 years of Sargon's reign (722–718) is shown in table 8.5.[33]

Table 8.5. The Assyrian Eponym Canon during the Fall of Samaria

728	Dur-Ashur	of Tushhan	to Hi[...]; the king took the hands of Bel
727	Bel-Harran-belu-usur	of Guzana	to [ ]; [Shalman]eser (V) [sat on the throne]
726	Marduk-belu-usur	[of Ame]di	i[n]
725	Mahde	of Nineveh	to [ ]
724	Ashur-ishmanni	[of Kili]zi	to [ ]
		[ ] years	
723	Shalmaneser (V)	king [of Assyria]	t[o]
722	Ninurta-ilaya	[	]
721	Nabu-taris	[	t]i
720	Ashur-nirka-da''in	[	]
		[ ] years	
719	Sargon [II]	king of [Assyria]	[ent]ered
718	Zeru-ibi	governor of Rasappa	[to Ta]bal

The horizontal rule between the years 728 and 727 indicates that Tiglath-pileser died in 727 and Shalmaneser came to the throne, with his 1st regnal year being 726. The rule between the years 723 and 722[34] indicates that Shalmaneser died in 722 and Sargon II became king, with his 1st regnal year being 721 (Assyrians used postdating).[35] Shalmaneser V was king of Assyria for the period 727–722, which also corresponds to the 1st–6th years of Hoshea's reign. In his accession year, Shalmaneser may have continued Tiglath-pileser's campaign of 728/727 when Tiglath-pileser went "to Damascus," killed Rezin, and appointed Hoshea as king of Israel. In Shalmaneser's 1st regnal year, 726, he was "i[n the land]."[36] If Shalmaneser did not go "against Hoshea" until his

---

33. Taken from Millard, *Eponyms of the Assyrian Empire*, 59–60. A horizontal rule is shown in two eponym lists (Millard's designation: A3 and A7; p. 46) after 720 and before Sargon's eponym in 719, but this does not indicate Sargon's 1st year.

34. Millard, *Eponyms of the Assyrian Empire*, 46, 59.

35. H. Tadmor, "The Campaigns of Sargon II of Assur: A Chronological-Historical Study," *Journal of Cuneiform Studies* 12 (1958): 27; A. K. Grayson, "Assyria: Ashur-dan II to Ashur-Nirari V (934–745 B.C.)," in *Cambridge Ancient History*, vol. 3/1: *The Prehistory of the Balkans; and the Middle East and the Aegean World, Tenth to Eighth Centuries B.C.* (ed. J. Boardman et al.; Cambridge: Cambridge University Press, 1982), 245.

36. See Millard, *Eponyms of the Assyrian Empire*, 59; Cogan and Tadmor, *II Kings*, 198 n. 4; J. H. Hayes and J. K. Kuan, "The Final Years of Samaria (730–720 B.C.)," *Biblica* 72 (1991): 160; Younger, "Fall of Samaria," 467.

2nd regnal year in 725 it leaves less time for Hoshea to have paid tribute "year by year," since Shalmaneser reigned only 3 more full regnal years.

After several years of paying tribute Hoshea appealed to "King So of Egypt" for help and stopped paying tribute to Shalmaneser, who then imprisoned Hoshea for his treachery (2 Kgs 17:4). Shalmaneser died in 722, so Hoshea must have been "shut up and bound" no later than 722 and possibly in 723, which is Shalmaneser's eponym year (see below). The reign of Shalmaneser V and the accession of Sargon are referred to in Babylonian Chronicle 1.27–31:

On the twenty-fifth day of the month Tebet Shalmaneser (V)
ascended the throne in Assyria ⟨and Akkad⟩. He ravaged Samaria.

The fifth year: Shalmaneser (V) died in the month Tebet.
For five years Shalmaneser (V) ruled Akkad and Assyria.
On the twelfth day of the month Tebet Sargon II ascended the throne in Assyria.[37]

The only event in Assyrian records relating to the reign of Shalmaneser is the ravaging of Samaria.[38] The exact meaning of the Assyrian verb *ḫepû* is uncertain. Na'aman concludes that in the context of the Babylonian Chronicle it means "'to plunder' or 'to ravage,' and that other verbs were selected to designate the breaking of walls after a siege."[39] This concurs with the proposal that the ravaging of Samaria by Shalmaneser was distinct from the capture of the city by Sargon at the end of the siege.

It seems, therefore, that Shalmaneser died before Samaria was put to siege and that the king of Assyria who invaded the land and besieged Samaria was Sargon II. Sargon's first 3 regnal years were 721–719, which correspond to the siege during Hoshea's 7th–9th years. This recognition of Sargon II as the king of Assyria during the years of the siege identifies him as the unnamed king of Assyria in 2 Kgs 17:5–6 and distinguishes him from Shalmaneser of Assyria in 17:3–4.

Sargon II's yearly activities are reported in the Khorsabad Annals.[40] Line 10 contains the words *i-na rē*[ ], which Tadmor reconstructs as *i-na rē*[*š šarrū-ti-ia*][41] (with or without additional text) and translates it, "In the begin[ning of my reign]."[42] Line 11 continues: "[When I took (my) seat on the royal throne and was crowned with a lordly crown." The text then continues in parallel with the Nimrud Prism.[43] Cogan and Tadmor restore the two inscriptions as follows:

With the strength of my gods, I fought with and defeated the Samarians, who had come
to an agreement with a hostile king not to be my vassals and not to pay tribute, and who

---

37. Transliteration and translation in *ABC* 73. Tebet is the 10th month of the Hebrew and Babylonian year, corresponding approximately to mid-December through mid-January.

38. See Hayes and Kuan, "Final Years of Samaria," 158–59.

39. Na'aman, "Historical Background to the Conquest," 211; cf. Becking, *Fall of Samaria*, 24–25; Younger, "Fall of Samaria," 465–67.

40. Tadmor, "Campaigns of Sargon II," 94–97. Eight Assyrian inscriptions record Sargon's claim to have conquered Samaria; see Becking, *Fall of Samaria*, 21, 25–45; Younger, "Deportations," 215–19; idem, "Fall of Samaria," 461, 468–70 and n. 31.

41. Tadmor, "Campaigns of Sargon II," 31 n. 82; cf. 33, 35 n. 108.

42. Ibid., "Campaigns," 34.

43. The Nimrud Prism lines 28–37 parallel the Khorsabad Annals lines 11b–16a; Tadmor, "Campaigns of Sargon II," 34.

opened hostilities (against me). I took captive 27,290 of its inhabitants. . . . The city of Samaria I rebuilt and repopulated more than before.[44]

This inscription thus indicates that early in his reign Sargon II confronted the Samarians and a hostile king who had rebelled. Stephanie Dalley translates Cogan and Tadmor's "hostile king" as "the king, my predecessor,"[45] but Hayes and Kuan say Dalley's restoration is impossible.[46] In the context of 2 Kgs 17:3 the hostile king likely refers to either Hoshea or King "So" of Egypt (provided the latter refers to a person and not a place).

The suppression of rebellion in Samaria during Shalmaneser's reign by the exaction of tribute, the "ravaging" of Samaria, and the imprisonment of Hoshea was followed by Sargon's besieging the city. Samaria was taken at the end of 3 years in Hoshea's 9th year (18:10). Thus the siege began early in Hoshea's 7th year. According to my reconstruction (table 8.6), Hoshea's 7th year in 721 begins at approximately the same time as Sargon's 1st regnal year. Tadmor notes that Sargon II suppressed a domestic crisis after his accession, discounting any expedition of Sargon to Samaria in his accession and 1st regnal years.[47] Cogan and Tadmor assert, "Despite Sargon's claim in the final edition of the Khorsabad annals, it was in his 2nd year, 720, and not during his accession and 1st year, that he set out to reconquer the West."[48] This not only contradicts Sargon's own account in the Khorsabad Annals, but conflicts with my chronological analysis. Contrary to Cogan and Tadmor, it seems that Sargon did have time to deal with the crisis in 722 before invading Israel and besieging Samaria in 721.

The Khorsabad Annals go on to speak of Sargon's battle at Der and defeat of Merodach-baladan (*ARAB* 2: §4), attributed to Sargon's 2nd regnal year in Babylonian Chronicle lines 33–37 (*ABC* 73–74).[49] This corresponds to the year 720, showing that the earlier events concerning Samaria belong to Sargon's accession and 1st years, 722/721. The Khorsabad Annals for Sargon's 2nd year (numbering intact) speak of the "quelling of the rebellion in Syria, reconquest of Samaria; fall of Gaza and Raphiah (lines 23–58),"[50] indicating Sargon's presence in Samaria in 720. Many scholars view 720 as the year of Sargon's reconquest of Samaria after its fall to Shalmaneser in 722 (see below).

For Sargon's 3rd year, 719, the Nineveh Prism is not preserved and the Khorsabad Annals report that Sargon went "against some cities in the land of the Manneans and on the border of Urartu (lines 58–68)."[51] The AEC entry has only a reconstructed "[ent]ered."[52] Sargon's eponym year, 719, may, however, have special significance. I noted above that Shalmaneser V's eponym year is his last full year, 723, probably the year he imprisoned Hoshea in Samaria. His

---

44. Cogan and Tadmor, *II Kings*, 200; see also 336. Cf. S. Dalley, "Foreign Chariotry and Cavalry in the Armies of Tiglath-pileser III and Sargon II," *Iraq* 47 (1985): 36; Na'aman, "Historical Background to the Conquest," 209–10; Hayes and Kuan, "Final Years," 170–75; Becking, *Fall of Samaria*, 28–31. Cf. Sargon's Display Inscription, lines 23–25. Line 23 reads, "I besieged and conquered Samerina"; Becking, *Fall of Samaria*, 26; cf. 27–33; Younger, "Fall of Samaria," 469–70.

45. Dalley, "Foreign Chariotry and Cavalry," 36; supported by Na'aman, "Historical Background to the Conquest," 209; cf. Younger, "Fall of Samaria," 470–71.

46. Hayes and Kuan, "Final Years," 171–72.

47. Tadmor, "Campaigns of Sargon II," 30–31, 37–38; cf. Dalley, "Foreign Chariotry and Cavalry," 33; Becking, *Fall of Samaria*, 36–38; Hayes and Kuan, "Final Years," 170–71.

48. Cogan and Tadmor, *II Kings*, 200.

49. Discussed by Barnes, *Chronology of the Divided Monarchy*, 116–18 n. 128; 121–22 n. 139.

50. Tadmor, "Campaigns of Sargon II," 94.

51. Ibid.

52. Millard, *Eponyms of the Assyrian Empire*, 60. Tadmor ("Campaigns of Sargon II," 94) reconstructs the notation to read, "[God x has en]tered his Temple."

Table 8.6. Years 746–717 Synchronized with Assyrian and Hebrew Chronology

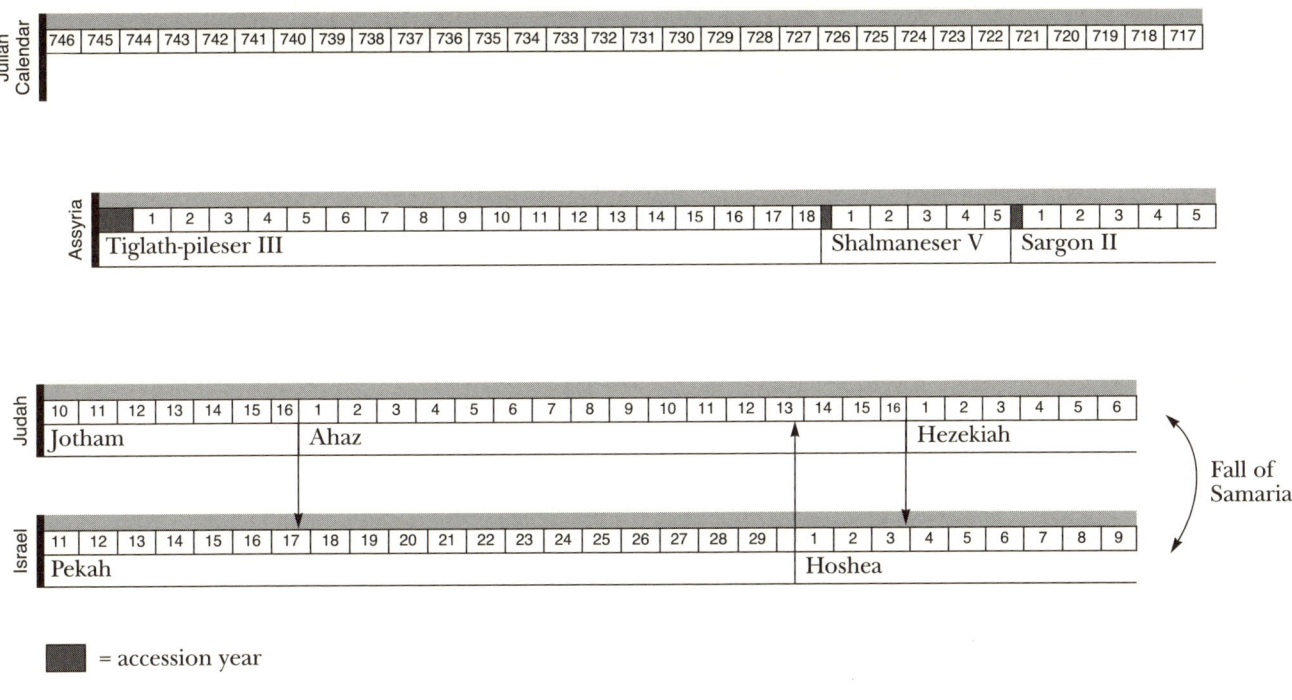

= accession year

eponym possibly marks the year he "ravaged Samaria," the only event of his reign singled out by the Babylonian Chronicle. By analogy, Sennacherib's eponym year is 687, probably referring to his conquest of Babylon,[53] his most notable victory. Sargon II's eponym year in 719 thus marks the most important happening in his reign—the fall of Samaria (see §6.2.1 for comments on the practice of assigning eponyms). The siege lasted 3 years (2 Kgs 17:5; 18:10), the first 3 years of Sargon's reign, from 721 to 719.

The Hebrew and Assyrian calendar year begins about $2\frac{1}{2}$ months after the Julian year. Sargon's 1st regnal year begins in Nisan 721 and coincides with Hezekiah's 4th year and Hoshea's 7th year (2 Kgs 18:9). The fall of Samaria may have occurred in the early months of a new Julian calendar year before the Hebrew calendar had changed to the new year, thus giving two dates to the fall of Samaria: 719 Hebrew reckoning, 718 Julian reckoning. (For the correlation of Hebrew and Assyrian chronology dated to Julian years for the reigns of Tiglath-pileser III to Sargon II see

---

53. Sargon II died in Abu (July/August) 705 (Tadmor, "Campaigns of Sargon II," 97). The Canon of Ptolemy omits after Sargon's reign the 1-month reign of Marduk-zakir-shumi and the 9-month reign of Merodach-baladan (Cogan and Tadmor, *II Kings*, 260). The "kingless period" of 2 years that followed (ibid., 261 and n. 3), dated in the canon as 704–703, should be 703–702 (L. Depuydt, "'More Valuable than All Gold': Ptolemy's Royal Canon and Babylonian Chronology," *Journal of Cuneiform Studies* 47 [1995]: 108). The Canon of Ptolemy then gives to Bel-ibni 3 years, Ashur-nadin-shumi 6 years, Nergal-ushezib 1 year, and Mushezib-Marduk 4 years. Sennacherib captured Babylon in his eighth campaign on Kislev 1 (November/December) and deported Mushezib-Marduk to Assyria (L. D. Levine, "Sennacherib's Southern Front: 704–689 B.C.," *Journal of Cuneiform Studies* 34 [1982]: 48). Fourteen years from 702 is 688, indicating that Sennacherib ousted Mushezib-Marduk in 688 not 689 as is usually given (e.g., Levine, p. 52). According to Levine the campaign lasted at least 23 months and possibly longer, so Sennacherib's eponym entry in 687 appears to commemorate the capture of Babylon in his eighth campaign.

table 8.6.) I conclude, therefore, that Shalmaneser V is correctly referred to as the king of Assyria in 2 Kgs 17:3–4, but the unnamed "king of Assyria" in 17:5–6 refers to Sargon II. 2 Kings 17:3–4 has no textual parallel, but the 3-year siege of Samaria and the deportation of its people in 17:5–6 is expanded in 18:9–11 with the addition of synchronisms.[54]

The naming of Shalmaneser in 2 Kgs 18:9, when Sargon II is otherwise indicated, may have occurred because the kings of Assyria were often not named in the biblical record. The king of Assyria is mentioned by title alone in 17:4 (thrice), 5, 6, 24, 26, 27; 18:7, 11, 14 (twice), 16, 17, 19, 23, 28, 30, 31, 33 (see my comments on the anonymous king of Judah in 2 Kings 3 in §5.4). It is possible that the king of Assyria at 18:9 was originally similarly indicated only by title, and at a later stage Shalmaneser's name was appropriated from 17:3 into 18:9 on the assumption that 17:5–6 also referred to Shalmaneser.

8.3.5. Date of Samaria's Fall

My analysis indicates that Tiglath-pileser "marched against Damascus" (2 Kgs 16:9) in 727 in response to Ahaz's plea for help against Rezin and Pekah, who were besieging Jerusalem. Tiglath-pileser killed Rezin, and Hoshea killed Pekah and was appointed king of Israel by Tiglath-pileser. Thus Hoshea's 1st year can be dated to 727 and his 9th year to 719. Tiglath-pileser died in 727, and Shalmaneser V ascended the Assyrian throne. Shalmaneser "came against" Hoshea, probably in his accession year, and Hoshea became his vassal. After several years Hoshea stopped paying tribute and called on the help of an Egyptian king. Shalmaneser apparently returned to Samaria and imprisoned Hoshea, probably the year he "ravaged Samaria," Shalmaneser's eponym year, 723. Shalmaneser died in 722 and was succeeded by Sargon II. Sargon dealt with a domestic crisis before invading Israel, which had continued the rebellion begun under Shalmaneser. Sargon put Samaria under siege in 721, and 720 was the 2nd year of the siege. At the end of the 3rd year Samaria fell in 719 or 718. The fall of Samaria equates with Hoshea's 9th year, Hezekiah's 6th year (18:10), and Sargon's 3rd year.

Chronology that places Hoshea's accession in 727 leaves the biblical synchronisms at 18:1 and 18:9–10 undisturbed. Hezekiah becomes king in Hoshea's 3rd year (18:1); the siege of Samaria begins in Hezekiah's 4th year and Hoshea's 7th year; and the fall of Samaria occurs in Hezekiah's 7th year and Hoshea's 9th year (18:9–10). The fall of Samaria is placed in 719/718, Sargon's 3rd regnal year.[55]

On the other hand, placing Hoshea's accession in 732/731, the 2nd year of Tiglath-pileser's earlier campaign, puts Hoshea's 9th year in 724/723, the year before Shalmaneser V died in 722. Although this seems to concur with Shalmaneser's being responsible for the siege of Samaria, it runs into difficulties with the reign of Hezekiah. Hezekiah's 1st year, synchronized with Hoshea's 3rd year (18:1) in 730/729, puts Hezekiah's 14th year in 717/716 in the reign of Sargon, whereas 18:13 synchronizes Hezekiah's 14th year with Sennacherib's expedition to Jerusalem, generally acknowledged as his third campaign of 701. Even assuming that 14th is a corruption of 24th at 18:13, on the above dates Hezekiah's 24th year falls in 707/706, and his 29th year is 702/701.

---

54. Some scholars see two traditions or archival sources referred to here, while others deny this concept. See W. F. Albright, "The Original Account of the Fall of Samaria in II Kings," *BASOR* 174 (1964): 67; Na'aman, "Historical Background to the Conquest," 212–13; Becking, *Fall of Samaria*, 49–52 and bibliography nn. 8–9; Galil, *CKIJ* 96–97; Younger, "Fall of Samaria," 477–79.

55. See M. C. Tetley, "The Date of Samaria's Fall as a Reason for Rejecting the Hypothesis of Two Conquests," *Catholic Biblical Quarterly* 64 (2002): 59–77.

Various scholars conclude that the synchronisms of 18:1 and 18:9–10 are inauthentic (*MNHK*³ 136–37, 168–71, 174–75). They are attributed to a scribe or redactor ignorant of the actual situation (*MNHK*³ 201).[56] Dating the fall of Samaria to Shalmaneser's last year in 723/722 does not explain Sargon's claim to have conquered Samaria.[57] Some deny Sargon's claim,[58] and at least one scholar rejects Samaria as the city referred to in Sargon's annals.[59] Yet others believe that after Shalmaneser conquered Samaria in 722, Sargon reconquered Samaria in 720, in his 2nd regnal year.[60] This diminishes Sargon's claim to have fought the Samarians at the beginning of his reign. The years between 724/723 (assumed to be Hoshea's last year) and 720 are generally understood as a time when Samaria's throne was unoccupied[61] or occupied by an unidentified king.[62] Some view this person as the "hostile king" who agreed with the Samarians to withhold tribute.[63] Various scholars understand 2 Kgs 17:3–6 and 18:9–11 to refer to Shalmaneser V.[64] Na'aman says that 17:3–4 refers to Shalmaneser V, and 17:5–6 and 18:9–11 refer to Sargon II;[65] while Cogan and Tadmor assume that Shalmaneser is referred to in 17:3–6a and was responsible for the capture of Samaria, but 17:6b refers to Sargon who exiled the people.[66] This supposes that the one verse refers to two consecutive kings without a break. I conclude that 17:3–4 refers to Shalmaneser V and 17:5–6 to Sargon II, with a definite break in the continuity of the narrative between 17:4 and 17:5. It is evident that proposals that date Hoshea's accession to 732/731 cannot reconcile his 7th–9th years in 726/725–724/723 with Samaria's siege and the claims of Sargon II that he besieged and conquered Samaria.

My effort to correlate the biblical and Assyrian records with the reconstructed chronology noted two areas of inconsistency: (1) the attribution of the siege of Samaria to Shalmaneser at 2 Kgs 18:9 (and by inference at 17:5–6), when other factors show it to be Sargon II; and (2) the attribution of Sennacherib's campaign to Hezekiah's 14th year (18:13), when it should be the 24th year. The first can be explained as a secondary editorial addition at 18:9 involving the addition of the name *Shalmaneser*, and the second as textual corruption probably involving only one letter, *yod*, graphically confused with *kaph*, in an early Hebrew script (see §7.3.6). These same problems beset the alternative proposals referred to above—that 18:9–10 is inauthentic; that the siege of Samaria lasted only 2 years not 3; that Sargon's claim of conquering Samaria at the start of his reign is false; or that Samaria had no king when it was captured or that another unidentified (and

---

56. A. Laato, "New Viewpoints on the Chronology of the Kings of Judah and Israel," *Zeitschrift für die alttestamentliche Wissenschaft* 98 (1986): 218; Cogan and Tadmor, *II Kings*, 216; cf. 195; Na'aman, "Historical Background to the Conquest," 220–25; cf. 211 §F; Galil, *CKIJ* 93–94.

57. Younger reviews four theories: "Fall of Samaria," 461–62, 479–82.

58. *MNHK*³ 164–68; citing A. T. Olmstead, "The Fall of Samaria," *American Journal of Semitic Languages and Literatures* 21 (1904–5), 179–82; cf. similar comments by Gray, *1 and 2 Kings*, 60–62.

59. Becking, *Fall of Samaria*, 39–45.

60. Tadmor, "Campaigns of Sargon II," 36–38 (see comments by Becking, *Fall of Samaria*, 34–45); Cogan and Tadmor, *II Kings*, 197, 199–200; Hughes, *Secrets of the Times*, 208 and n. 97; Galil, *CKIJ* 91; contra Na'aman, "Historical Background to the Conquest," 223–25; Younger, "Fall of Samaria," 471–73, 482.

61. Tadmor, "Campaigns of Sargon II," 37; Cogan and Tadmor, *II Kings*, 195, 199, 216; cf. Na'aman, "Historical Background to the Conquest," 218, 220; cf. 224–25; Galil, *CKIJ* 91.

62. Tadmor, "Campaigns of Sargon II," 37; Hayes and Kuan, "Final Years," 176–77.

63. Suggestions include Yaubi'di of Hamath, Shalmaneser V, and a native Israelite king. Cf. Dalley, "Foreign Chariotry and Cavalry," 36; Na'aman, "Historical Background to the Conquest," 209–10; Hayes and Kuan, "Final Years," 172–75; Becking, *Fall of Samaria*, 30.

64. Hughes, *Secrets of the Times*, 205–7; Hayes and Kuan, "Final Years," 169, 180.

65. Na'aman, "Historical Background to the Conquest," 206, 217–20.

66. Cogan and Tadmor, *II Kings*, 197; cf. 199–200.

unattested) king reigned in Israel between Shalmaneser V and Sargon II. When compared with these proposals, my chronology shows greater plausibility.

I conclude that Hoshea's accession took place in 727, his imprisonment by Shalmaneser V in 723, and the siege of Samaria in 721–719/718 ending in Sargon's 3rd regnal year. Establishing this date for the fall of Samaria provides the starting date by which to date the preceding kings' reigns.

Table 7.1 commences at year 1 with the accessions of Rehoboam and Jeroboam I, and table 8.1 ends with the fall of Samaria in year 263, indicating that the DK spanned 263 years. Projecting back 263 years from the end of the DK in 719/718 locates its commencement in 981 in the Julian calendar. This is 50 years earlier than the date 931/930 given by Thiele based on synchronisms with the AEC (*MNHK*[3] 79).

9

Absolute Chronology of the Divided Kingdom

To conclude this study of Hebrew chronology, it is necessary to correlate relative DK chronology to the Julian calendar to provide absolute chronology. This involves reconciling the regnal years of the Assyrian kings given in the AEC with the jointly reconstructed chronologies of Israel and Judah. This reconciliation also forces a new appraisal of contemporary Egyptian chronology and provides a list of significant dates for ancient Near Eastern history.

9.1. The Priority of the Hebrew Record

It is evident in the Hebrew chronology of 1–2 Kings that the regnal formulas of the Hebrew kings were composed with the overt intention of demonstrating the years of each king's reign by anchoring each king's accession to a regnal year of the contemporary king of the other kingdom. Opening and closing regnal formulas associating each king with his predecessor and successor reinforces regnal continuity over the 263-year period. Evidence that some of the synchronisms and regnal years have been altered over centuries of transmission does not vitiate the original intention of the writer(s)/editor(s) of the regnal formulas to preserve a factual record of the kings' reigns derived from the annals of Israel and Judah. The use of such a system by the compilers of 1–2 Kings infers that they had adequate data for the task and that they intended to provide a complete and coherent account. It may be that the compilers were aware of the propensity for numbers to become corrupt in copying and transmission and devised the synchronization system in an effort to prevent errors entering the text.

Although not wholly successful in preserving all the original data, the Hebrew system of safeguarding the regnal years with an interlocking continuum provides a framework whereby text-critical analysis can be employed to reveal or extrapolate the authentic regnal data. This medium contrasts with the Assyrian system, which relies upon a single composite linear arrangement of eponyms representing consecutive years. The omission of an eponym causes a corresponding and possibly irretrievable deletion to a king's regnal years. The Assyrian system is not a synchronistic system, nor does it employ regnal formulas that link one king's accession to his predecessor or successor. The AEC comprises one list of overlapping fragments of dubious provenance, with no assurance that they derive from a *Vorlage(n)* that contained all the eponyms intact. The omission of regnal years in the Assyrian chronology may be detected only against a framework of contemporary kings.

9.2. Explanation of the Julian-Year Tables

Since reconstructed Hebrew chronology conflicts with the years afforded to the AEC, it is necessary to correlate the reigns of the kings of Israel and Judah with those of Assyrian kings according to the Julian calendar. Because Assyrian kings prior to Shalmaneser III have no known synchronisms with the DK kings and because their years in the AEC have not been validated, kings prior to Shalmaneser III do not appear on the tables in this chapter. Julian dates for Assyrian kings commence with Shalmaneser III's 1st regnal year in 902 (his eponym is his 2nd regnal year; see §9.3.1).

Tables 9.1–8 assist with the discussion, while table 9.9 presents a continuous chronology for the entire DK (for further explanation of table 9.9, see §9.4.1). Where extant, the years of the Assyrian kings are represented by eponyms.[1] Table 9.10 tabulates DK reigns and table 9.11 provides dates of significant ANE events.

9.3. Synchronization of Hebrew, Assyrian, Tyrian, and Egyptian Chronologies

As noted in §8.3.5, the date 981 for the commencement of the DK in my reconstructed Hebrew chronology is 50 years earlier than Thiele's date based on the AEC. Is it possible to reconcile this date with the AEC?

In the following discussion I will suggest that the Assyrian kings' reigns, now deficient in the AEC, might be reconciled with the reconstructed Hebrew chronology before 763. New dates will be proposed for three Assyrian kings: Shalmaneser III (902–867), Shamshi-Adad V (866–832), and Adad-nirari III (831–782). Pul, the Assyrian king contemporary with Menahem, will be identified as Shalmaneser IV, not Tiglath-pileser III. And Shoshenq I's accession will be revised from 945 to 997.

9.3.1. Shalmaneser III of Assyria; Ahab and *Iaúa* "Son of Omri"

The earliest known synchronism between Assyrian and Israelite kings occurs in the reign of Shalmaneser III. In the eponymate of Dayan-Ashur, Shalmaneser's 6th regnal year, Shalmaneser is reported to have fought *A-ḫa-ab-bu* KUR *Sir-'i-la-a-a*, presumed to be Ahab, in the battle of Qarqar.[2] In the chronologies of Thiele and others, the battle of Qarqar is dated to 853 in dependence on the AEC. Shalmaneser's 18th year, when he received tribute from *Iaúa* "son of Omri," is then synchronized with Jehu's 1st year in 841.[3] From these unsubstantiated dates, Thiele dates the division of the kingdom to 931/930.

In §7.2.7 I concluded that *Iaúa* "son of Omri" who paid tribute to Shalmaneser III in the latter's 18th year can no longer be identified as Jehu, but rather as Joram, grandson of Omri. This places Shalmaneser's 18th year during the 12 years of Joram's reign, which, by my reconstruction spanned the years 895–883 (table 9.1). According to Assyrian records, in Shalmaneser's 18th year

---

1. The eponyms are taken from A. Millard, *The Eponyms of the Assyrian Empire 910–612 B.C.* (State Archives of Assyria Studies 2; Helsinki: Neo-Assyrian Text Corpus Project, 1994), 56–60, but the Julian dates have been changed to concur with the Hebrew chronology.

2. Collated from Bull Inscription (*ARAB* 1: §§646–47; *ANET* 279), Black Obelisk (*ARAB* 1: §563; *ANET* 279), and Monolith Inscription (*ARAB* 1: §§610–11; *ANET* 278–79; *HAIJ* 258–59; J. K. Kuan, *Neo-Assyrian Historical Inscriptions and Syria-Palestine* [Jian Dao Dissertation Series 1; Hong Kong: Alliance Bible Seminary, 1995], 27–31).

3. Thiele, *MNHK*³ 50, 72–78, 104, 121–22, 162; idem, "An Additional Chronological Note on 'Yaw, Son of 'Omri,'" *BASOR* 222 (1976): 19.

Table 9.1. Correlation of Reigns of Joram and Shalmaneser III

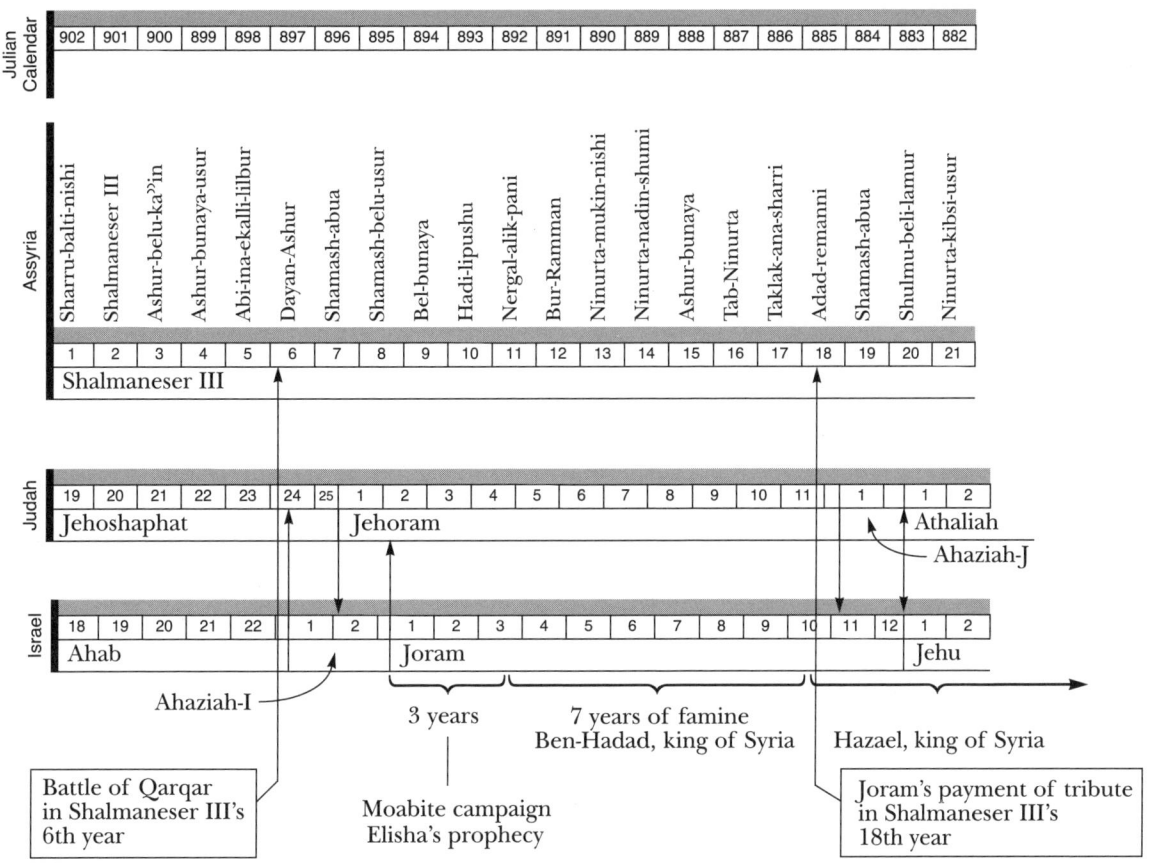

he fought and pursued Hazael to Damascus—indicating that *Adad-idri* was no longer king of Syria—and subsequently received tribute from Joram.[4] An undated inscription relates the defeat of *Adad-idri* of Damascus together with 12 kings whose armies were cast into the Orontes by Shalmaneser's troops. *Adad-idri* disappeared and Hazael "the son of a nobody" seized the throne. Hazael and his army engaged the Assyrians in battle, were defeated, and were pursued to Damascus. This record also appears to refer to Shalmaneser's 18th year.[5] *Adad-idri* is understood here to be the Ben-Hadad of 2 Kgs 8:7-15 who was murdered by Hazael.[6] Determining which year during his reign that Joram paid tribute to Shalmaneser after the accession of Hazael enables us to identify Shalmaneser's 18th year.

---

4. See *ARAB* 1: §672; *ANET* 280; M. Cogan and H. Tadmor, *II Kings: A New Translation with Introduction and Commentary* (Anchor Bible 11; Garden City, N.Y.: Doubleday, 1988), 334-35; Kuan, *Neo-Assyrian Historical Inscriptions*, 51-63; K. L. Younger, *Ancient Conquest Accounts: A Study in Ancient Near Eastern and Biblical History Writing* (Journal for the Study of the Old Testament Supplement 98; Sheffield: JSOT, 1990), 105-10.

5. Text on a basalt statue, known as *KAH* 1, 30. See *ARAB* 1: §§679-81; *ANET* 280; W. T. Pitard, *Ancient Damascus* (Winona Lake, Ind.: Eisenbrauns, 1987), 132-38; Cogan and Tadmor, *II Kings*, 334; Kuan, *Neo-Assyrian Historical Inscriptions*, 53-54.

6. G. H. Jones, *1 and 2 Kings* (New Century Bible Commentary; Grand Rapids: Eerdmans, 1984), 442-43.

Table 9.2. Correlating Adad-nirari III with Joash-I on Current AEC Reckoning of Shamshi-Adad V's Reign

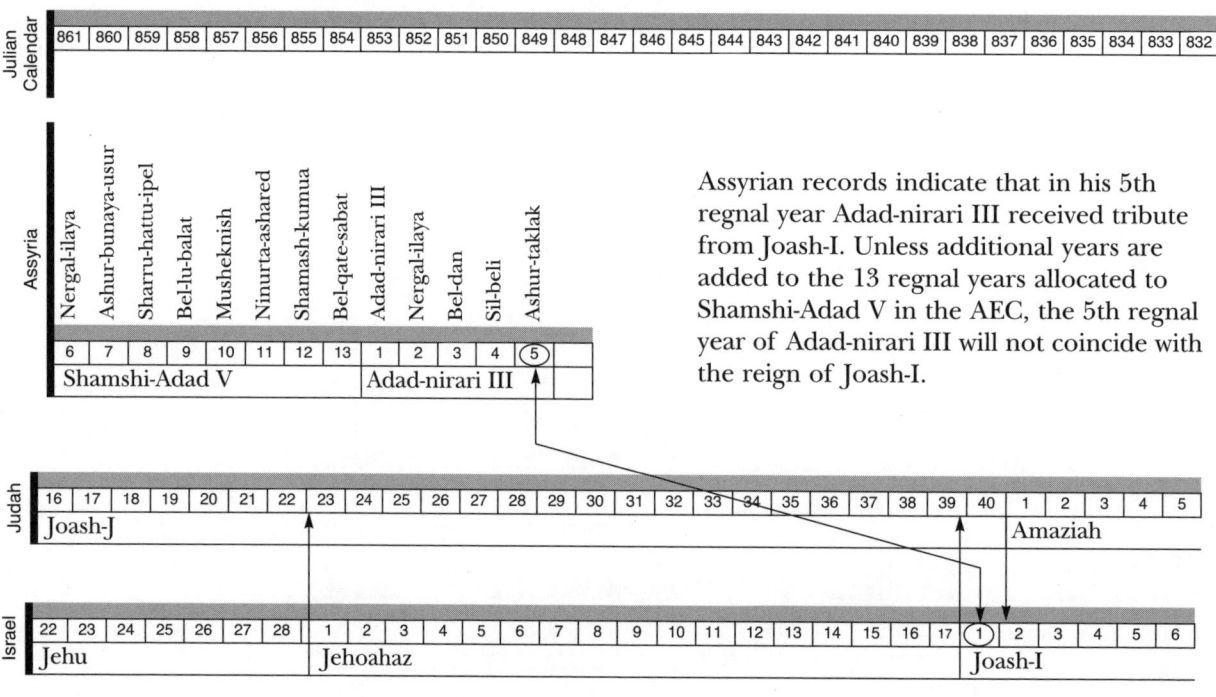

Joram's early years involved the Moabite campaign (2 Kings 3; see §7.2.4), Elisha's prophecy of a son born to a Shunammite woman (4:11–16) and its fulfillment after a year (4:17), and the child's subsequent death and revival by Elisha (4:18–37). These events may have involved 2–3 years and were followed by 7 years of famine in Israel, during which Ben-Hadad of Damascus besieged Samaria (6:24–8:6). After these events Elisha prophesied in Damascus that Hazael would murder Ben-Hadad and seize the throne (8:7–15). At least 10 years must have elapsed in Joram's reign for these events to occur.[7] In Joram's 11th or 12th year Hazael fought Joram and Ahaziah-J at Ramoth-gilead (8:28–29), and Ahaziah-J and Joram were killed by Jehu in Joram's 12th year (8:25–9:29). Therefore, Joram's 10th or 11th year was the only year he could have paid tribute to Shalmaneser after Hazael became king of Damascus. One of these must coincide with Shalmaneser's 18th year. A corroborating and decisive factor is that Shalmaneser's 6th year fell during Ahab's reign. Ahab's last year dates to 897, so Shalmaneser's 6th year falls no later than 897 and makes Shalmaneser's 18th year fall no later than Joram's 10th year (table 9.1). Shalmaneser's 6th year is confirmed for 897 and Shalmaneser's 18th year for 885, Joram's 10th year. This date concurs with Ben-Hadad's murder, Hazael's accession to the throne of Damascus soon after the

---

7. A. R. Green concurs; "Regnal Formulas in the Hebrew and Greek Texts of the Books of Kings," *Journal of Near Eastern Studies* 42 (1983): 177.

Table 9.3. Revised Correlation of Adad-nirari III and Joash-I

siege ended in Samaria, and Hazael's subsequent battle at Ramoth-gilead with Ahaziah-J and Joram before the latter were killed by Jehu in 883.

The AEC attributes 36 eponyms to Shalmaneser's reign, indicating he reigned 36 years, from 902 to 867, assuming that my analysis and the 36 years are correct. Between Thiele's chronology—which places Shalmaneser's 18th year in 841 in dependence on the AEC—and my chronology placing it in 885 is a discrepancy of 44 years.

9.3.2. Adad-nirari III of Assyria and Joash-I

Taken together, the Assyrian inscriptions seem to indicate that Joash-I paid tribute to Adad-nirari III in Arpad in the latter's 5th year (see §6.2.2.2). Thiele does not mention Adad-nirari's 5th year, which in his chronology did not fall in Joash-I's reign. Instead, Thiele assigns Joash-I's tribute to the 14th eponym of Adad-nirari's reign, when, the AEC notes, Adad-nirari III went "to Manṣuate" in 796, Joash-I having begun his reign in 798 (according to Thiele, *MNHK*[3] 112–13).

As seen in table 6.4, a synchronism between Joash-I and Adad-nirari's 5th year is possible only if the 13 years allocated in the AEC to Shamshi-Adad V (successor to Shalmaneser III) are extended. At least 8 years (or more, depending on which year during Joash-I's reign he paid tribute to Adad-nirari) are required for the reign of Shamshi-Adad V if Adad-nirari's 5th year is to coincide with Joash-I's 1st year. With Shalmaneser's 18th year and Joram's 10th year now reconstructed as 885, some 11 to 26 additional years are required (table 9.2).

As noted in §6.2.2.2, Babylonian King List A and Babylonian Chronicle 24 infer that Shamshi-Adad V ruled over Babylonia in a kingless period following the removal of Baba-aha-iddina. The number of kingless years can be read as 12 or 22. Shamshi-Adad went "to Babylon" in the 12th year of his reign, the eponymate of Shamash-kumua, and it seems probable that the kingless years began at this time. Only one further eponym, Bel-qate-sabat, remains for the reign of Shamshi-Adad.

An addition of either 12 or 22 years to the reign of Shamshi-Adad allows Adad-nirari's 5th year to fall in Joash-I's reign. Adding 12 years causes Adad-nirari's 5th year to coincide with Joash-I's 2nd year in 837, and adding 22 years to coincide with Joash-I's 11th/12th year in 827. The decision to allot 22 years, not 12, is determined by the consideration that in only one other area in the AEC—the reign of Adad-nirari III—could years have been lost (see §9.3.3, §9.3.4). It seems preferable to attribute to Adad-nirari a further 22 years rather than 32 years, making a 50-year reign, not 60. Therefore, I allocate to Shamshi-Adad V a further 22 years for the kingless period in Babylonia, commencing with his assumption of sovereignty in the eponymate of Shamash-kumua. The remaining eponym Bel-qate-sabat is not now Shamshi-Adad's 13th eponym as in the AEC, but his 35th, when the AEC notes that the king was "in the land" (see table 9.3). Shamshi-Adad can be attributed 35 regnal years from 866 to 832 (table 9.9).

The inserted 22 years span the years 854–833 and are concurrent in Judah with the 23rd to 40th regnal years of Joash-J followed by the first 4 regnal years of Amaziah and in Israel with the 17 regnal years of Jehoahaz followed by the first 6 regnal years of Joash-I. Adad-nirari's 5th year falls in 827 coincident with Joash-I's 11th/12th year, making feasible Joash-I's payment of tribute to Adad-nirari III as indicated by the Assyrian records.

9.3.3. Hebrew Chronology and the Kings of Tyre

Also spanning the years between Shalmaneser III and Adad-nirari III is a list of Tyrian kings beginning with Hiram, a contemporary of David and Solomon (2 Sam 5:11; 1 Kgs 9:10–14), and ending with Balezeros, Mattenos, and Pygmalion.[8] The Marble Slab inscription of Shalmaneser's 18th year names Ba'li-manzer as the king of Tyre who, with *Iaúa* (Joram), paid tribute to Shalmaneser III. Ba'li-manzer is commonly recognized as Balezeros, noted on the Tyrian king list preceding Mattenos.

According to Josephus (*Against Apion* 1.125, quoting Menander),[9] Pygmalion murdered the husband of his older sister, Dido,[10] in Pygmalion's 7th regnal year. Being 11 at his accession, Pygmalion then would have been 18 years old.[11] Dido fled to Libya where she founded the city of Carthage, an event usually dated to 825 B.C.E. or 814 B.C.E.[12]

---

8. For relevant information on this subject, see W. F. Albright, "The New Assyro-Tyrian Synchronism and the Chronology of Tyre," *Annuaire de l'Institut de Philologie et d'Historie Orientales et Slaves* 13 [Mélanges Isidore Levy] (1953): 1–9; J. Liver, "The Chronology of Tyre at the Beginning of the First Millennium B.C.," *Israel Exploration Journal* 3 (1953): 113–20; F. M. Cross, "An Interpretation of the Nora Stone," *BASOR* 208 (1972): 17 n. 11; H. J. Katzenstein, *The History of Tyre* (Jerusalem: Schocken Institute for Jewish Research, 1973), 116–20, 129–30, 167–69, 175; A. R. Green, "David's Relations with Hiram: Biblical and Josephan Evidence for Tyrian Chronology," in *The Word of the Lord Shall Go Forth* (ed. C. L. Meyers and M. O'Connor; Winona Lake, Ind.: Eisenbrauns, 1983), 373–97, esp. 382–88; W. H. Barnes, *Studies in the Chronology of the Divided Monarchy of Israel* (Harvard Semitic Monographs 48; Atlanta: Scholars Press, 1991), 29–55; Kuan, *Neo-Assyrian Historical Inscriptions*, 55, 61–62.

9. Katzenstein, *History of Tyre*, 78–79.

10. For the political intrigue, see Katzenstein, *History of Tyre*, 188–89.

11. Pygmalion lived 58 (variant 56) years, reigned 47, so was 18 in his 7th regnal year; see Katzenstein, *History of Tyre*, 167.

12. Katzenstein, *History of Tyre*, 120; Green, "David's Relations with Hiram," 379, 393 nn. 15–16.

An unnamed king of Tyre, noted on the Tell al-Rimah inscription, paid tribute to Adad-nirari III at the same time as Joash-I (see §6.2.2.2 n. 32, p. 99). My chronology places Joash-I's payment in 827 (§9.3.2). The founding of Carthage in 825 points to Pygmalion as the Tyrian king mentioned on the stela; a date of 814 for the founding of Carthage postpones Pygmalion's 1st year to 820, 2 years after Joash-I died. The question to be determined is whether the reigns of the three Tyrian kings spanning the period from Shalmaneser III's 18th year to the founding of Carthage in 825 or 814 concur with the regnal years of the Hebrew kings for the same period.

Extant Tyrian king lists are poorly preserved, and variants for the kings' regnal years and ages are given in various texts.[13] The length of Balezeros's reign is variously given as 6, 7, 8, or 18 years; Mattenos's reign as 9, 25, or 29 years; and Pygmalion's as 40, 47, or 7 years.[14]

Table 9.4 explores three scenarios for reconciling the three Tyrian kings' reigns with the reconstructed Hebrew chronology in which Shalmaneser's 18th year coincides with Joram's 10th year in 885 and Adad-nirari's 5th year coincides with Joash-I's 11th/12th year in 827. Pygmalion's 7th year aligns with 825 in the first and second options. The shortest time indicated by the variants for the reigns of Balezeros (6), Mattenos (9), and Pygmalion (7) is illustrated in option 1, with the reigns constructed backward from 825 so that Pygmalion's 1st year is 831, Mattenos's in 840, and Balezeros's in 846. This scenario demonstrates a shortfall in the Tyrian kings' reigns of some 40 years. The second option represents the longest chronology indicated by the variants (Balezeros 18 years, Mattenos 29 years, and Pygmalion 47 years), again proceeding backward from Pygmalion's 7th year in 825 so that Mattenos's 1st year is 860 and Balezeros's is 878. This scenario demonstrates that even with the longest variants the Tyrian chronology falls short of 885 by 7 years. It is also dubious because it has Mattenos becoming king at age 3.[15]

A third scenario is possible. The text relating that Dido fled from Pygmalion in his 7th year may have been incorrectly transmitted and should read Pygmalion's 47th year (his final year). If Pygmalion's 47th year was 825, his 1st year would be 871. If Mattenos reigned 9 years, his 1st year would have been 880. Five years previously, Balezeros—whether he reigned 6, 7, 8, or 18 years— would have been king of Tyre in Shalmaneser's 18th year when he and Joram paid Shalmaneser tribute. If, alternatively, Pygmalion's reign ended in 814 and began in 860, Mattenos's 1st year would be 869,[16] and another 16 years would be required if Balezeros's 1st year is to coincide with 885 (the variant 18 years makes this possible, but not the variants 6, 7, or 8). If Balezeros reigned 18 years, his 3rd year would then coincide with 885.

The scenario of Pygmalion ordering the death of his sister's husband in his 47th (and final) regnal year when he was a mature 58 years in either 825 or 814 seems more plausible than his doing so as a youth of 18. Emending Pygmalion's 7th year to 47th year assumes the omission of one word or symbol in a text that was translated from Phoenician into Greek and copied many times in the eight centuries between Pygmalion and Josephus.[17] The multiple variants already noted for these three Tyrian kings makes a transmission error from the 47th to the 7th not implausible.

---

13. Green, "David's Relations with Hiram," 383.

14. Barnes, *Chronology of the Divided Monarchy*, 43, 44 nn. l, m, and o.

15. If Mattenos reigned 29 years and lived only 32 years as recorded, he would have become king at age 3; but if he reigned 9 years, he became king at 23, which seems more likely.

16. This assumes a 9-year reign for Mattenos. A variant of 25 years for Mattenos's reign commences his reign in 885. Balezeros might have paid tribute before his death that same year. A 29-year reign for Mattenos commences his reign in 889 and makes it impossible for Balezeros to give tribute in 885.

17. Katzenstein, *History of Tyre*, 79, 117; Green, "David's Relations with Hiram," 388.

Table 9.4. Tyrian Data and Reconstructed Late Divided Kingdom Chronology

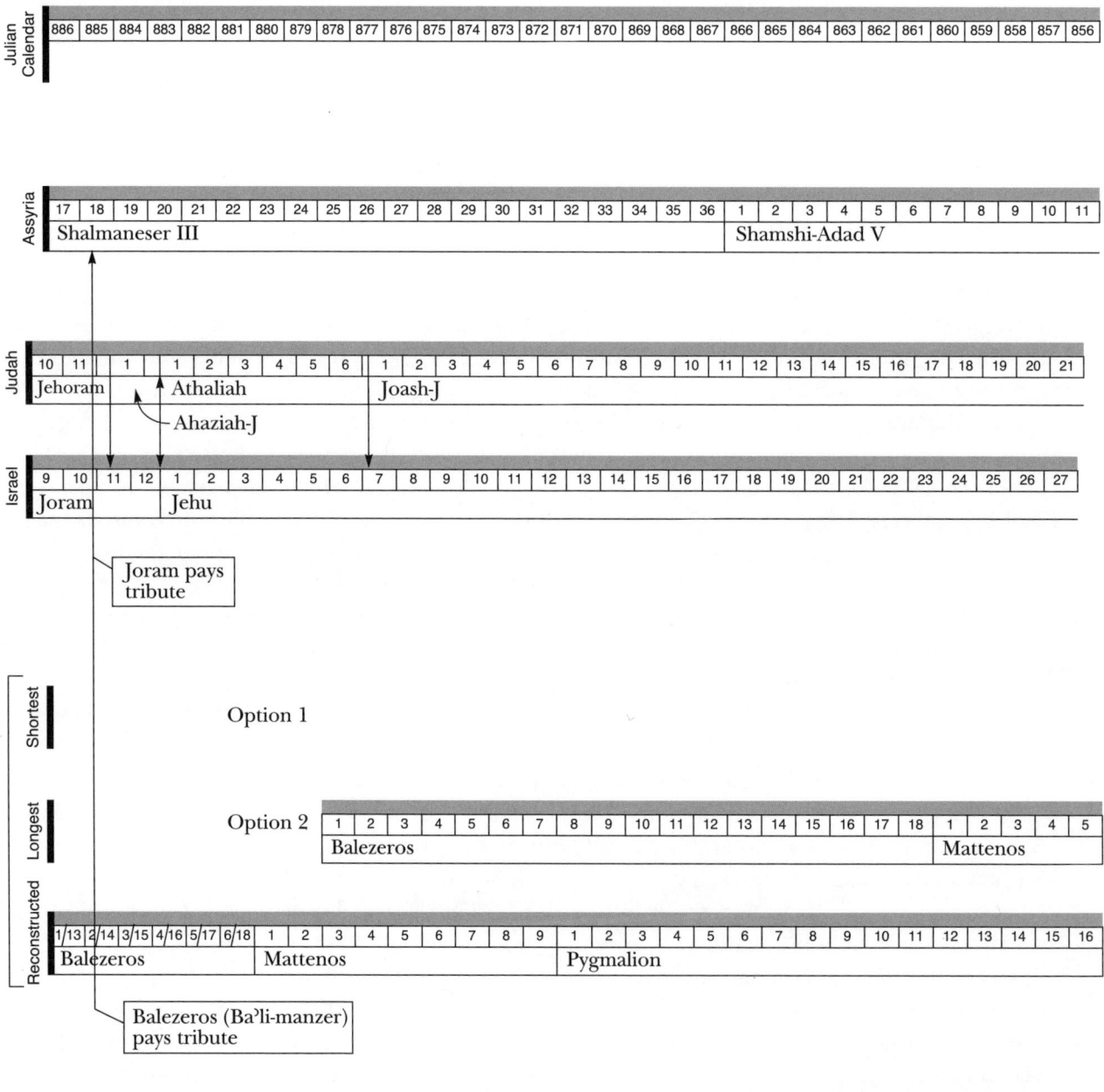

It is thus possible to reconcile the Tyrian and Hebrew chronologies for the period from Shalmaneser III's 18th year in 885 to the founding of Carthage in Pygmalion's 47th year during the reign of Adad-nirari III in either 825 or 814. This period includes the addition of 22 years to the reign of Shamshi-Adad V in the AEC as discussed previously. The entire Tyrian chronology from Hiram to Pygmalion requires reexamination in light of the reconstructed Hebrew chronology.

Table 9.4. Tyrian Data and Reconstructed Late Divided Kingdom Chronology (cont.)

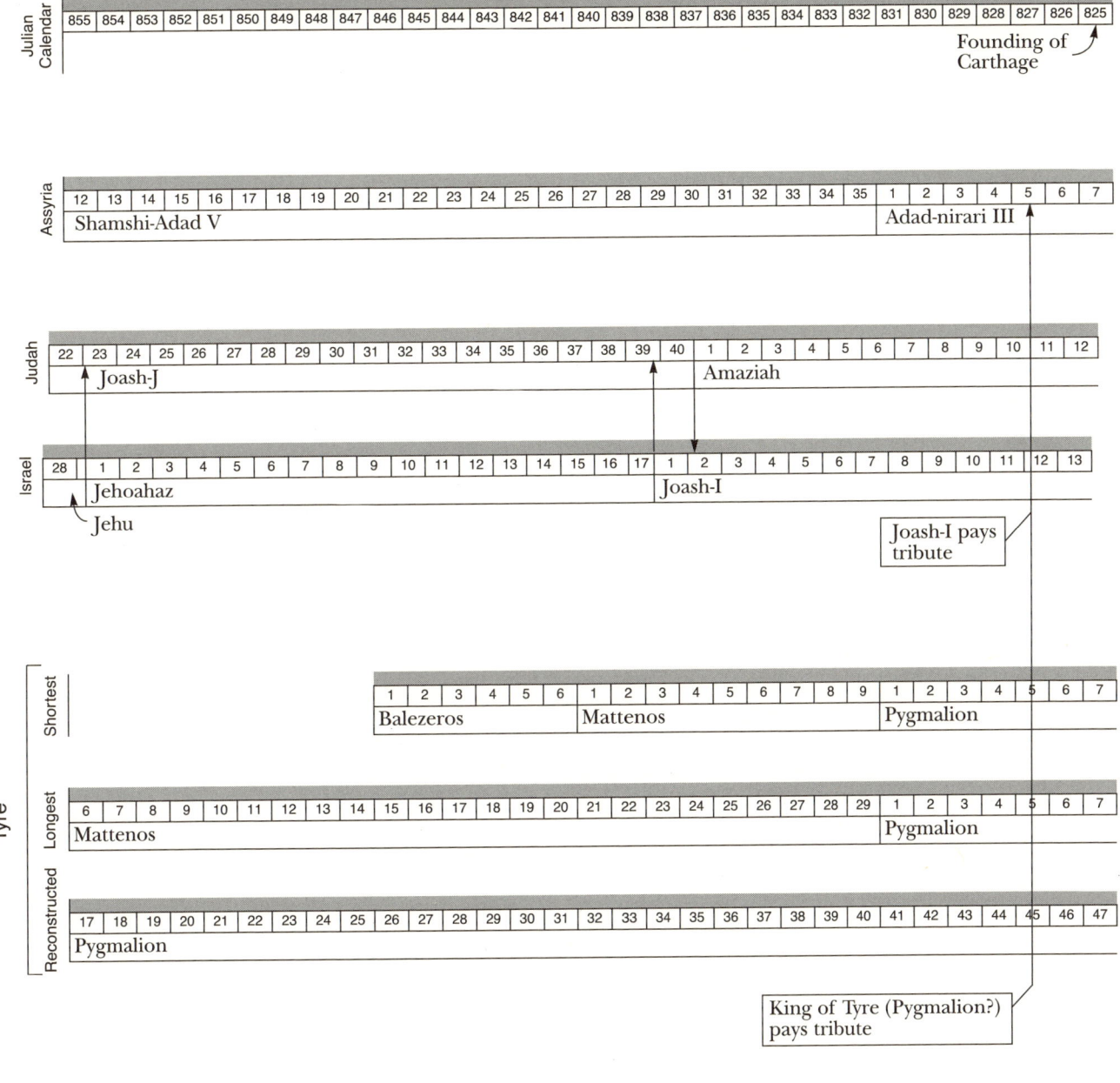

9.3.4. Adad-nirari III of Assyria and a Discontinuity in the Eponyms of His Reign

Of the 44 years missing in the AEC, 22 remain to be accounted for. In §6.2.2.1, I discussed the possibility of a break in the eponyms of Adad-nirari III's reign, seemingly the only break among the remaining eponyms before the confirmed dating of the eclipse in 763. The combined lists of C^a6, C^b2, C^c, Sultantepe Tablet 150, and Sultantepe Tablet 18 show a break between Nabu-

Table 9.5. Assyrian Eponym Canon 810–781

	Cᵃ6, Cᵇ2, Cᶜ, Sultantepe 150, Sultantepe 18	Cᵃ3
810	Adad-mushammer	Adad-mushammer
809	Sil-Ishtar	Sil-Ishtar
808	Nabu-sharru-usur	[eponym missing]
	[21 eponyms missing]	[21 eponyms missing]
786	[eponym missing]	Balatu
785	Adad-uballit	Adad-uballit
784	Marduk-sharru-usur	Marduk-sharru-usur
783	Ninurta-nasir	Ninurta-nasir
782	Iluma-leʾi	Iluma-leʾi
781	Shalmaneser IV	Shalmaneser IV

sharru-usur and Adad-uballit representing 22 eponyms, while Cᵃ3 shows a similar break between Sil-Ishtar and Balatu (table 9.5). Both lists thus have 22 missing eponyms, but the gap in the right column of table 9.5 starts and ends 1 year earlier than the left column. While 22 eponyms are missing in both columns, 21 eponyms are missing between Nabu-sharru-usur (left column) and Balatu (right column).[18]

The previous synchronization of Adad-nirari's 5th year with Joash-I's 11th/12th year in 827 and the dating of Shalmaneser IV's 1st year in 781 according to the AEC, presumed to be correct, indicates that 21 additional years must be included in the AEC between the eponyms of Nabu-sharru-usur and Balatu in order for Assyrian chronology to align with Hebrew chronology (table 9.6). The 21 years, 807 to 787, are concurrent with the 2nd to 22nd years of Azariah and the 16th to 36th years of Jeroboam II.

A much discussed Assyrian inscription about Hamath[19] may shed light on these 21 years: "19 districts of Hamath together with the cities of their environs, which are on the seacoast of the west, which in rebellion were seized for Azriyau, I annexed to Assyria."[20] Most commentators locate this event in the reign of Tiglath-pileser and identify *Azriyau* with an unidentified ruler of

---

18. The dates are according to my reconstructed chronology; the date 810 for Adad-mushammer's eponym corresponds to 788 in the AEC, or 789 if Balatu is assigned a year.

19. *ANET* 283; *ARAB* 1: §770; H. Tadmor, *The Inscriptions of Tiglath-pileser III King of Assyria* (Jerusalem: Israel Academy of Sciences and Humanities, 1994), 62–63; 273–76. For discussion, see H. M. Haydn, "Azariah of Judah and Tiglath-pileser III," *JBL* 28 (1909): 182–99; H. Tadmor, "Azriyau of Yaudi," *Scripta Hierosolymitana* 8 (1961): 232–71; M. Haran, "The Rise and Decline of the Empire of Jeroboam ben Joash," *VT* 17 (1967): 290–97; N. Naʾaman, "Sennacherib's 'Letter to God' on His Campaign to Judah," *BASOR* 214 (1974): 25–39; Thiele, *MNHK*³ 139–62; Jones, *1 and 2 Kings*, 518–19; J. Hughes, *Secrets of the Times: Myth and History in Biblical Chronology* (Journal for the Study of the Old Testament Supplement 66; Sheffield: JSOT Press, 1990), 195–96 n. 64; Kuan, *Neo-Assyrian Historical Inscriptions*, 149–50 and n. 57.

20. Tadmor's Annal 19, lines 9–11 restored from Annal 26 (*Inscriptions of Tiglath-pileser III*, 62–63). The inscription was previously referred to as Layard 65.

Table 9.6. Revised Correlation of Adad-nirari III's Later Reign with Hebrew Chronology

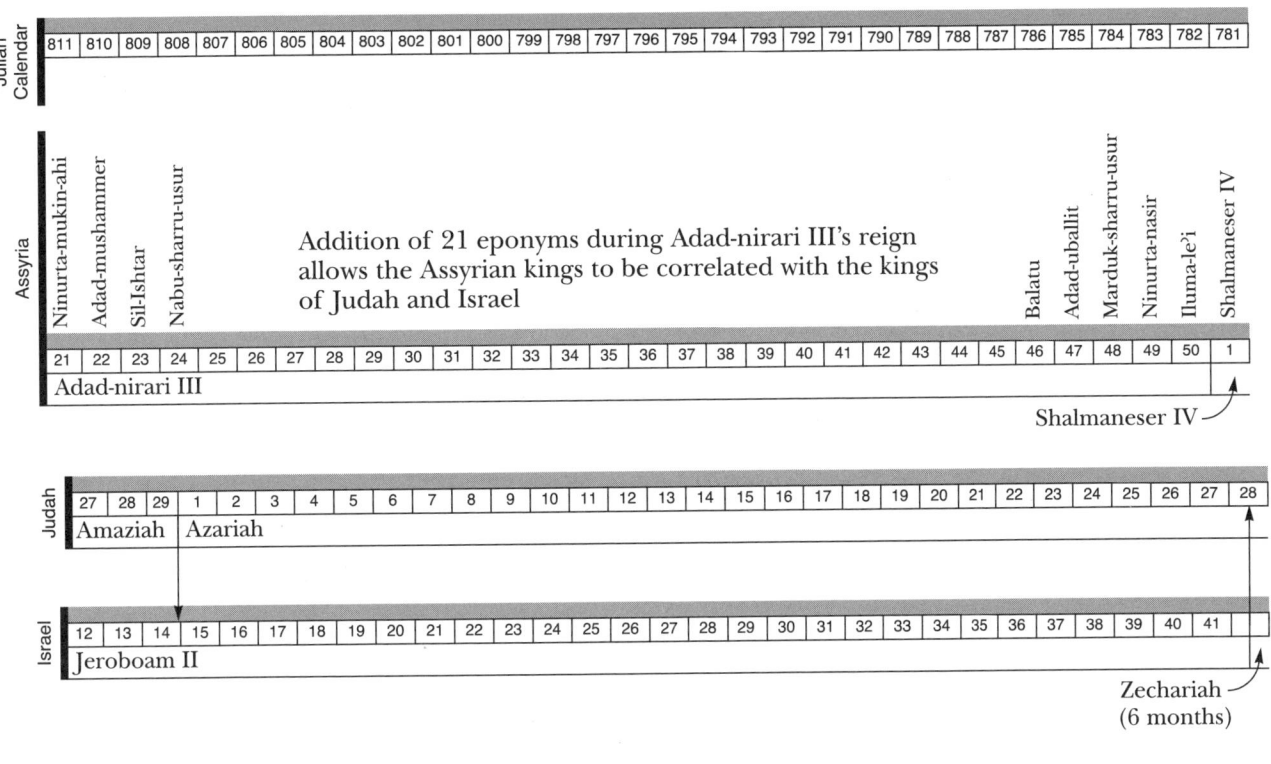

Ja'udi in northwest Syria or a ruler of Hamath.[21] Cogan and Tadmor point out that the name is Israelite.[22] If an Israelite, *Azriyau* could be Azariah, Jeroboam II's contemporary for 27 years, from 808 to 782, when the Assyrian king was Adad-nirari III (table 9.6).

The Assyrian inscription may be considered in the light of 2 Kgs 14:25: "[Jeroboam II] restored the border of Israel from the entrance of Hamath as far as the Sea of the Arabah"; and 14:28: "How [Jeroboam II] fought, and how he recovered for Israel Damascus and Hamath, which had belonged to Judah."[23] Both the Assyrian and biblical texts refer to Hamath and its territories, which seem to have been a "political football" in the campaigns of Assyria and Israel/Judah.

---

21. J. A. Montgomery, *A Critical and Exegetical Commentary on the Books of Kings* (ed. H. S. Gehman; International Critical Commentary; Edinburgh: Clark, 1951), 446–47; W. H. Shea, "Menahem and Tiglath-pileser III," *Journal of Near Eastern Studies* 37 (1978): 46–47; S. Herrmann, *A History of Israel in Old Testament Times* (Philadelphia: Fortress, 1981), 246; T. R. Hobbs, *2 Kings* (Word Biblical Commentary 13; Waco: Word, 1985), 194; Hughes, *Secrets of the Times*, 195–96 n. 64, 198 n. 73; Tadmor, *Inscriptions of Tiglath-pileser III*, 273–74; Kuan, *Neo-Assyrian Historical Inscriptions*, 149–50 n. 57.

22. Cogan and Tadmor, *II Kings*, 165–66; cf. 162.

23. See comments by Montgomery, *Kings*, 444; Haran, "Rise and Decline," 296–97; Hobbs, *2 Kings*, 183–84; Jones, *1 and 2 Kings*, 516–17; Pitard, *Ancient Damascus*, 176; Cogan and Tadmor, *II Kings*, 161–62; N. Na'aman, "Azariah of Judah and Jeroboam of Israel," *VT* 43 (1993): 230–32; Kuan, *Neo-Assyrian Historical Inscriptions*, 123–24.

Hamath, Damascus and associated territories were Assyrian possessions in the early years of Adad-nirari's reign, known from the Tell al-Rimah Stela and other inscriptions (§6.2.2.2). Jeroboam II recovered Damascus and Hamath for Israel, which had "belonged to Judah." The inscription speaks of Assyria regaining this territory, which had "been seized for Azriyau," possibly a reference to the exploits of contemporaries Azariah and Jeroboam II.

Of the 27 years when Jeroboam II, Azariah, and Adad-nirari were contemporaries, 21 of them coincide with the eponyms presumed missing from the AEC (807–787). Since a western campaign is not mentioned in the extant portion of eponyms for this latter period of Adad-nirari's reign, it is possible that this event occurred in one (or more) of the years now missing from the AEC. Also missing from the eponyms of Adad-nirari's reign is Shamshi-ilu, Adad-nirari's commander-in-chief, and any mention of a western campaign in which they established the border between Hamath and Arpad.[24] Nor is there mention of the battle they fought with Artashumki of Arpad and eight kings, and the setting up in this same year of a boundary stone between Kummuh and Gurgum.[25] Since Shamshi-ilu is second eponym in the subsequent reigns of Shalmaneser IV (780) and Ashur-nirari V (752), the omission of his eponym from Adad-nirari's reign is inexplicable. The recurrence of eponyms of the king and his officials after 30 years would place Adad-nirari's and Shamshi-ilu's eponyms between those of Nabu-sharru-usur and Balatu—where it is presumed eponyms are missing.

Robert Whiting observes that more eponyms exist than years: "Since all Neo-Assyrian eponyms down to 649 are known from the canon, any eponym from a Neo-Assyrian text that is not in the canon is post-canonical. However, 648 to 612 requires 37 eponyms while the number of attested PC eponyms is ≈ 50."[26] I contest his assertion that "all Neo-Assyrian eponyms down to 649 are known" and wonder if some of the excess eponyms might belong to the years recovered in my proposal.

At year 786 (eponym Balatu), the AEC coincides with Hebrew chronology and remains reconciled to the end of the DK. Adad-nirari III may be assigned 50 years, from 831 to 782. The reigns of Shalmaneser III, Shamshi-Adad V, and Adad-nirari III should be reexamined in the light of the new dates assigned to these kings.

9.3.5. Pul of Assyria and Menahem

The revised dates for the Hebrew kings have implications for the identity of Pul, the king of Assyria, to whom Menahem paid tribute (2 Kgs 15:19). Most chronologists, including Thiele (*MNHK*³ 125, 139–41), identify Pul as Tiglath-pileser III on the basis of 1 Chr 5:26 (which uses an alternative spelling for Tiglath-pileser's name): "The God of Israel stirred up the spirit of Pul king of Assyria and/even the spirit of Tilgath-pilneser." *Waw* here is understood as "even" or "that is," thus identifying Pul as Tiglath-pileser.[27] Furthermore, Babylonian Chronicle 1, lines 22–24, records Tiglath-pileser's last 2 years in Babylon (*ABC* 72). Babylonian King List A, column 4, refers these 2 years to Pul (*ANET* 272), thus identifying Pul as Tiglath-pileser III.[28] In addition, several

---

24. Noted on the Antakya stele; Veysel Donbaz, "Two Neo-Assyrian Stelae in the Antakya and Kahramanmaraş Museums," *Annual Review of the Royal Inscriptions of Mesopotamia Project* 8 (1990): 7.

25. Noted on the Pazarcik Stela; Donbaz, "Two Neo-Assyrian Stelae," 9.

26. R. Whiting, "The Post-Canonical and Extra-Canonical Eponyms," in Millard, *Eponyms of the Assyrian Empire*, 72.

27. D. J. Wiseman, "Some Historical Problems in the Book of Daniel," in *Notes on Some Problems in the Book of Daniel* (London: Tyndale, 1965), 12; D. W. Baker, "Further Examples of the *Waw Explicativum*," *VT* 30 (1980): 129–36.

28. The Canon of Ptolemy combines the reigns of Ukinzer and Pulu (where he is called Πῶρος) for a total of 5 years. For comments on the name Pul, see J. A. Brinkman, *A Political History of Post-Kassite Babylonia, 1158–722 B.C.* (Analecta Orientalia 43; Rome: Pontifical Biblical Institute Press, 1968), 61–62.

Table 9.7. Menahem and Tiglath-pileser III

Julian Calendar	771	770	769	768	767	766	765	764	763	762	761	760	759	758	757	756	755	754	753	752	751	750	749	748	747	746	745	744	743	742
Assyria (eponym)	Ashur-dan III	Shamshi-ilu	Bel-ilaya	Aplaya	Qurdi-Ashur	Mushallim-Ninurta	Ninurta-mukin-nishi	Sidqi-ilu	Bur-Saggile	Tab-belu	Nabu-mukin-ahi	La-qipu	Pan-Asur-lamur	Ana-beli-taklak	Ninurta-iddin	Bel-shadua	Iqisu	Ninurta-shezibanni	Ashur-nirari V	Shamshi-ilu	Marduk-shallimanni	Bel-dan	Shamash-kenu-dugul	Adad-belu-ka''in	Sin-shallimanni	Nergal-nasir	Nabu-belu-usur	Bel-dan	Tiglath-pileser III	Nabu-da''inanni
Regnal	1	2	3	4	5	6	7	8	9	10	11	12	13	14	15	16	17	18	1	2	3	4	5	6	7	8	9	1	2	3

Ashur-dan III / Ashur-nirari V / Tiglath-pileser III (accedes to the throne on 13 Ayar 745)

Judah	38	39	40	41	42	43	44	45	46	47	48	49	50	51	52	1	2	3	4	5	6	7	8	9	10	11	12	13	14

Azariah / Jotham

Israel	10	11	1	2	3	4	5	6	7	8	9	10	11	12	1	2	3	4	5	6	7	8	9	10	11	12	13	14	15

Menahem / Pekahiah / Pekah

■ = accession year

solar eclipse 15/16 June 763

---

tribute lists seem to ascribe the payment of tribute by *Me-ni-ḫi-im-me* URU *Sa-me-ri-na-a+a*, understood to be Menahem, to Tiglath-pileser III.[29]

In the reconstructed Hebrew chronology 24 years exist between the death of Menahem in 769 and Tiglath-pileser's accession in 745 (table 9.7), and so Menahem was not alive in the reign of Tiglath-pileser. Neither Assyrian inscriptions nor biblical text indicate any personal contact between Menahem and Tiglath-pileser. On the other hand, Pekah and Hoshea are mentioned both in Assyrian inscriptions (discussed in §8.3.3) and in 2 Kgs 15:29–16:18 as Tiglath-pileser's contemporaries. Furthermore, based on Thiele's dates for Menahem, scholars have been unable

---

29. Annal 13, with Annals 3 and 27 covering lines 10–11 of Annal 13. See Tadmor, *Inscriptions of Tiglath-pileser III*, 68–69, 89. Kuan, *Neo-Assyrian Historical Inscriptions*, 153–57. For the Iran Stela, see L. D. Levine, *Two Neo-Assyrian Stelae from Iran* (Occasional Paper 23; Toronto: Royal Ontario Museum, 1972), 5–24; idem, "Menahem and Tiglath-pileser: A New Synchronism," *BASOR* 206 (1972): 40–42; Tadmor, *Inscriptions of Tiglath-pileser III*, 92, 106–9; Kuan, *Neo-Assyrian Historical Inscriptions*, 146–57. For Summary Inscription 7 (Nimrud Tablet K 3751), which does not mention Menahem in its list of other tributaries but includes Jehoahaz of Judah, see *ARAB* 1: §801; Hughes, *Secrets of the Times*, 202–3 and nn. 83, 84; S. A. Irvine, *Isaiah, Ahaz, and the Syro-Ephraimitic Crisis* (Society of Biblical Literature Dissertation Series 123; Atlanta: Scholars Press, 1990), 40–44; Tadmor, *Inscriptions of Tiglath-pileser III*, 170–71; Kuan, *Neo-Assyrian Historical Inscriptions*, 161–64.

to agree on the year of Tiglath-pileser's reign that the tribute lists refer to; suggested dates are 743, 740, 738, or 737.[30]

My reconstructed chronology places Menahem's reign in the years 780–769 and locates him as a contemporary of Shalmaneser IV of Assyria in 781–772. The AEC notes that Shalmaneser went "to Damascus" in his 9th (penultimate) year in 773, which coincides with Menahem's 8th regnal year (see table 9.9).

The Pazarcik Stela records an expedition led by Shalmaneser IV's commander-in-chief, Shamshi-ilu, to Damascus to exact tribute from Hadiyani, the Aramean king.[31] It is probable that during this same campaign Shalmaneser IV "came against Israel" and received payment from Menahem (2 Kgs 15:19). The reconstructed chronology makes concurrent the reigns of Menahem and Shalmaneser IV, and the AEC supplies the year 773 as the most likely year that Menahem paid tribute to Shalmaneser IV. Scholarly indecision about when Menahem might have paid tribute to Tiglath-pileser is resolved if we understand that the recipient of Menahem's tribute was Shalmaneser IV when he went "to Damascus" in 773.

Assyrian and Babylonian records and 1 Chr 5:26 indicate that Tiglath-pileser III was known as Pul (or Pulu). Synchronized chronology, however, identifies the Pul who was a contemporary of Menahem (2 Kgs 15:19) as Shalmaneser IV. Thus, two Assyrian kings were known as Pul: Shalmaneser IV and Tiglath-pileser III. Pul of 2 Kgs 15:19 should not be identified as Pul of 1 Chr 5:26. Assyrian records that purportedly identify Menahem as a contemporary of Tiglath-pileser III must be reconsidered in the light of Menahem's being contemporary with Shalmaneser IV.

9.3.6. Shishak of Egypt and Rehoboam

One other synchronism appearing near the beginning of the DK—this one concerning an Egyptian king—deserves mention because it too relies on the AEC. A campaign by Pharaoh Shishak (also spelled Shoshenq I), the first ruler of Egypt's 22nd Dynasty, to Jerusalem occurred in Rehoboam's 5th year (1 Kgs 14:25–26; 2 Chr 12:1–12). In my chronology this is dated to 977.

Kitchen writes, "the founder of the next line, Shoshenq I, can be closely dated by a synchronism with the Hebrew monarchy, whose dates in turn are closely fixed with reference to Assyrian chronology."[32] Kitchen then outlines the dating systems used by Thiele, approves them as valid methods for dating the kings of Israel and Judah, including Thiele's coregency hypothesis,[33] and places Shoshenq I's expedition to Judah in Shoshenq's 20th regnal year. Using Thiele's date of 853 for Ahab's last year, based on it being Shalmaneser III's 6th year in the AEC, Kitchen accepts that Rehoboam's 5th year fell in 925 and adopts this date as the 20th year for Shoshenq I.[34]

---

30. For discussion see Thiele, *MNHK*³ 139–62; V. Pavlovský and E. Vogt, "Die Jahre der Könige von Juda und Israel," *Biblica* 45 (1964): 334–36; Levine, *Two Neo-Assyrian Stelae from Iran*, 13–15, 18–19; idem, "Menahem and Tiglath-pileser," 40–42; M. Cogan, "Tyre and Tiglath-pileser III," *Journal of Cuneiform Studies* 25 (1973): 96–99; M. Weippert, "Menahem von Israel und seine Zeitgenossen in einer Steleninschrift des assyrischen Königs Tiglathpileser III. aus dem Iran," *Zeitschrift des Deutschen Palästina-Vereins* 89 (1973): 26–53; Shea, "Menahem and Tiglath-pileser III," 43–49; Hobbs, *2 Kings*, 198, 201; Cogan and Tadmor, *II Kings*, 5, 172; Tadmor, *Inscriptions of Tiglath-pileser III*, 274–77; Hughes, *Secrets of the Times*, 198–201; Kuan, *Neo-Assyrian Historical Inscriptions*, 127, 150–52, 187–88, 192.

31. Donbaz, "Two Neo-Assyrian Stelae," 9–10; Kuan, *Neo-Assyrian Historical Inscriptions*, 115–16.

32. K. A. Kitchen, *The Third Intermediate Period in Egypt (1100–650 B.C.)* (2nd ed; Warminster: Aris & Phillips, 1986), 72.

33. Ibid., 74–75; idem, review of *Studies in the Chronology of the Divided Monarchy of Israel* by W. H. Barnes in *Evangelical Quarterly* 65 (1993): 249.

34. Kitchen, *Third Intermediate Period in Egypt*, 74–76; idem, "Egypt, History of," in *Anchor Bible Dictionary* (ed. D. N. Freedman et al.; New York: Doubleday, 1992), 2:327; idem, "How We Know When Solomon Ruled," *Biblical Archaeology Review* 27/5 (2001): 34–35.

Table 9.8. Egypt's 22nd Dynasty according to Kitchen

945–924	Shoshenq I	21y
924–889	Osorkon I	35y
ca. 890	Shoshenq II	(x years as coregent)
889–874	Takelot I	15y
874–850	Osorkon II	24y
ca. 870–860	Harsiese	(ca. 10 years as coregent)
850–825	Takelot II	25y
825–785	Shoshenq III	40y
785–773	Shoshenq IV	12y[a]
773–767	Pimay	6y
767–730	Shoshenq V	37y
730–715	Osorkon IV	15y

a. Previously, Kitchen assigned 52 years to Shoshenq III alone, i.e., not including Shoshenq IV; *Third Intermediate Period in Egypt*, 102–5, 588.

Kitchen's dates for the upper limit of the 22nd Dynasty are restricted by the dates provided by Thiele's chronology for Ahab in 853 and Jehu in 841. "Earlier this latter king [Shoshenq I] cannot be, because of the synchronism with the 5th year of Rehoboam of Judah in 925 B.C. . . . heading a line of rulers tied firmly (via Ahab and Jehu of Israel) to a fixed Assyrian chronology."[35] Though Kitchen stresses that the 130 years or so of the 22nd Dynasty cannot be stretched or contracted appreciably due to genealogical considerations of priestly families in Thebes and Memphis,[36] this argument depends on reckoning the length of a generation by the prior assumption of the length of the 22nd Dynasty.[37] The discrepancy between the reconstructed Hebrew chronology that places Rehoboam's 5th year in 977 and Kitchen's and Thiele's chronology in 925 is 52 years.

Based on its system of interlocking reigns and synchronisms for Israel and Judah, Hebrew chronology accounts for all years in this period. On the other hand, the regnal years of the 22nd Dynasty kings are not definitely known.[38] Kitchen gives the kings of Dynasty 22 their highest known regnal years, which produces a minimum chronology (table 9.8).[39]

Shoshenq I's reign of 21 years, said to be "indisputable" by Kitchen,[40] is in fact disputed by Wente, who assigns 34 years to Shoshenq I. Nor do they agree on the regnal years of Osorkon I and Osorkon II.[41] Furthermore, Kitchen writes, "Pimay's monuments are few, hence he will be

---

35. K. A. Kitchen, "The Historical Chronology of Ancient Egypt, A Current Assessment," *Acta Archaeologica* 67 (1996): 3.
36. Ibid.
37. M. L. Bierbrier, *The Late New Kingdom in Egypt (c. 1300–664 B.C.)* (Warminster: Aris and Phillips, 1975), 99–100.
38. See Kitchen's discussion in *Third Intermediate Period in Egypt*, 100–122.
39. Kitchen, "Historical Chronology of Ancient Egypt," 12.
40. Kitchen, *Third Intermediate Period in Egypt*, 450; cf. idem, review of *Chronology of the Divided Monarchy* by Barnes, 250.
41. E. F. Wente, review of *Third Intermediate Period in Egypt* by K. A. Kitchen in *Journal of Near Eastern Studies* 35 (1976): 276–78; cf. A. R. Green, "Solomon and Siamun: A Synchronism between Early Dynastic Israel and the Twenty-First Dynasty of Egypt," *JBL* 97 (1978): 356–59; Barnes, *Chronology of the Divided Monarchy*, 58–60.

Table 9.9. Reconstructed Divided Kingdom Chronology for Julian Years 981–718

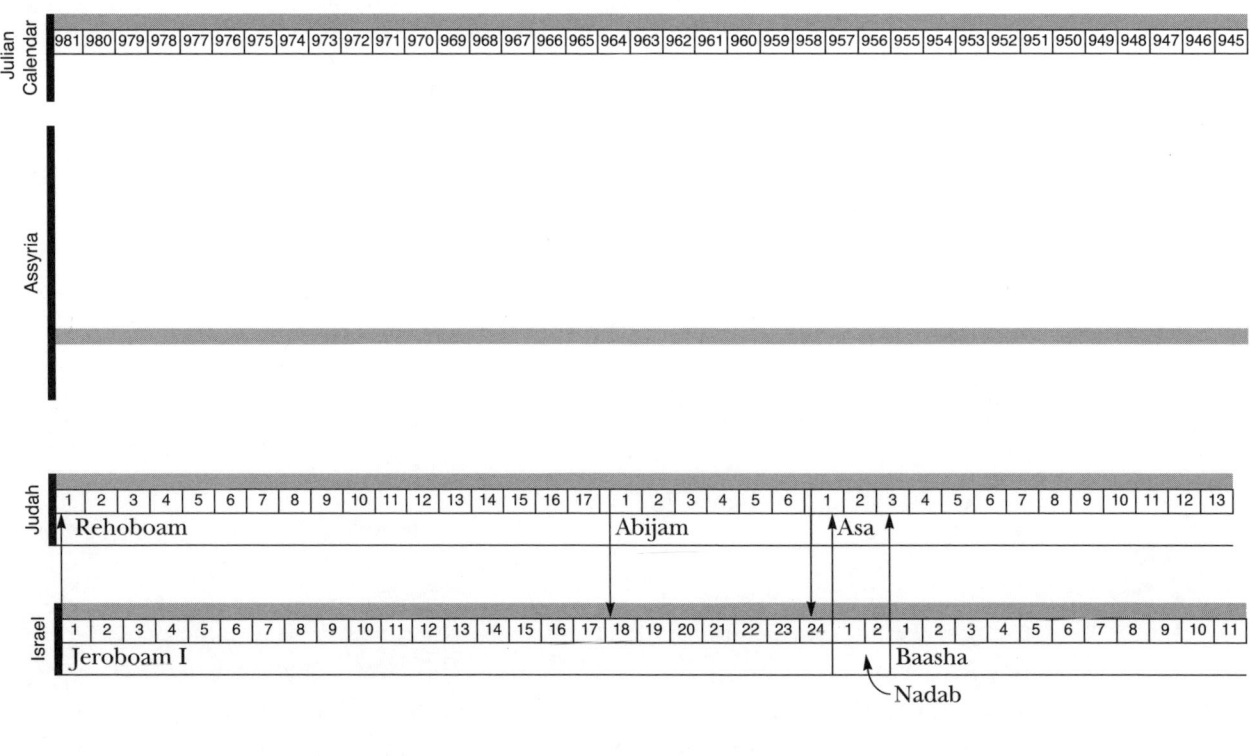

allowed just 6 full years here."[42] If Pimay reigned more than 6 years the accession of Shoshenq I occurred before 945, making untenable the synchronism between Shoshenq I and Rehoboam in 925. Other kings, too, may have had longer reigns than presently reckoned. Previous discussion indicates that no reliance can be placed on Thiele's chronology and the dates afforded to the AEC earlier than 763, and therefore Kitchen's date for Shoshenq I's accession cannot be sustained.

The reigns of the 22nd Dynasty kings should be reinvestigated by Egyptologists in light of the reconstructed Hebrew chronology. Shoshenq I's accession in 997 — not 945 — has obvious implications for the dating of the preceding Egyptian dynasties as well.

9.4. A New Julian Chronology for the Divided Kingdom

9.4.1. Explanation of Table 9.9

Reconstructed DK chronology is set out in table 9.9 and correlated to Julian years. The kings of Assyria are represented from 902 (Shalmaneser III's 1st year) to 712 (Sargon II's 10th year). Prior to the accession of Tiglath-pileser III in 745, regnal years are aligned with Julian years be-

---

42. Kitchen, *Third Intermediate Period in Egypt*, 103.

Table 9.9. Reconstructed Divided Kingdom Chronology for Julian Years 981–718 (cont.)

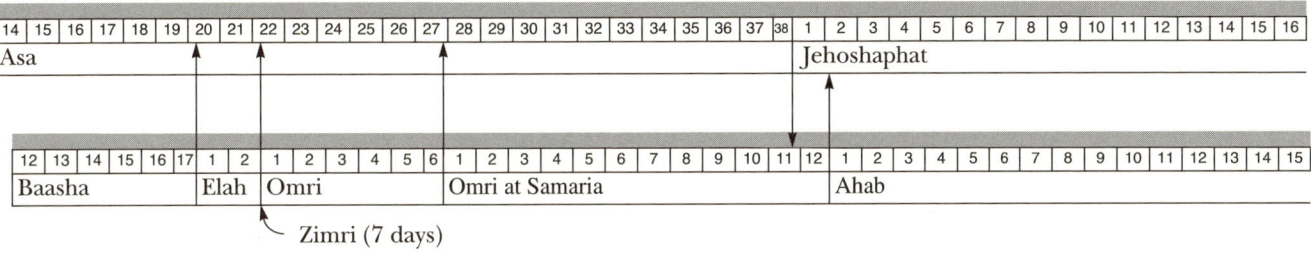

cause the lengths of Assyrian kings' accession years (the partial year that a king reigned after his predecessor died and before the new year began) are not known. The accession of Tiglath-pileser III is recorded in the AEC as occurring on Ayar 13 (around the end of April/early May), with his 1st regnal year beginning on the following new year on Nisanu 1 (= mid-March to mid-April). Beginning, then, with the 1st regnal year of Tiglath-pileser in 744, the years of the Assyrian kings are aligned with the Assyrian new year.

Ashur-nirari V has a partial 9th year beginning in January 745, followed by Tiglath-pileser's accession year ending in mid-March (Nisanu) 744. Ashur-nirari's 9th year lasted only a few weeks but appears longer on the table because the beginnings of his regnal years have been aligned with January not Nisanu.

The accession years of Shalmaneser V and Sargon II are not indicated on table 9.9 to avoid confusion in portraying accession years within eponyms. The accession years for these kings may be seen on table 8.6. The dates provided for the eponyms of Tiglath-pileser III, Shalmaneser V, and Sargon II indicate the years they came to the throne, though their 1st regnal years do not begin until the following new year.

I propose that 22 years have been lost from the AEC in the reign of Shamshi-Adad V and 21 years in the reign of Adad-nirari III. The inclusion of these years reconciles Assyrian chronology with the dual interlocking chronological system of Israel and Judah.

Table 9.9. Reconstructed Divided Kingdom Chronology for Julian Years 981–718 (cont.)

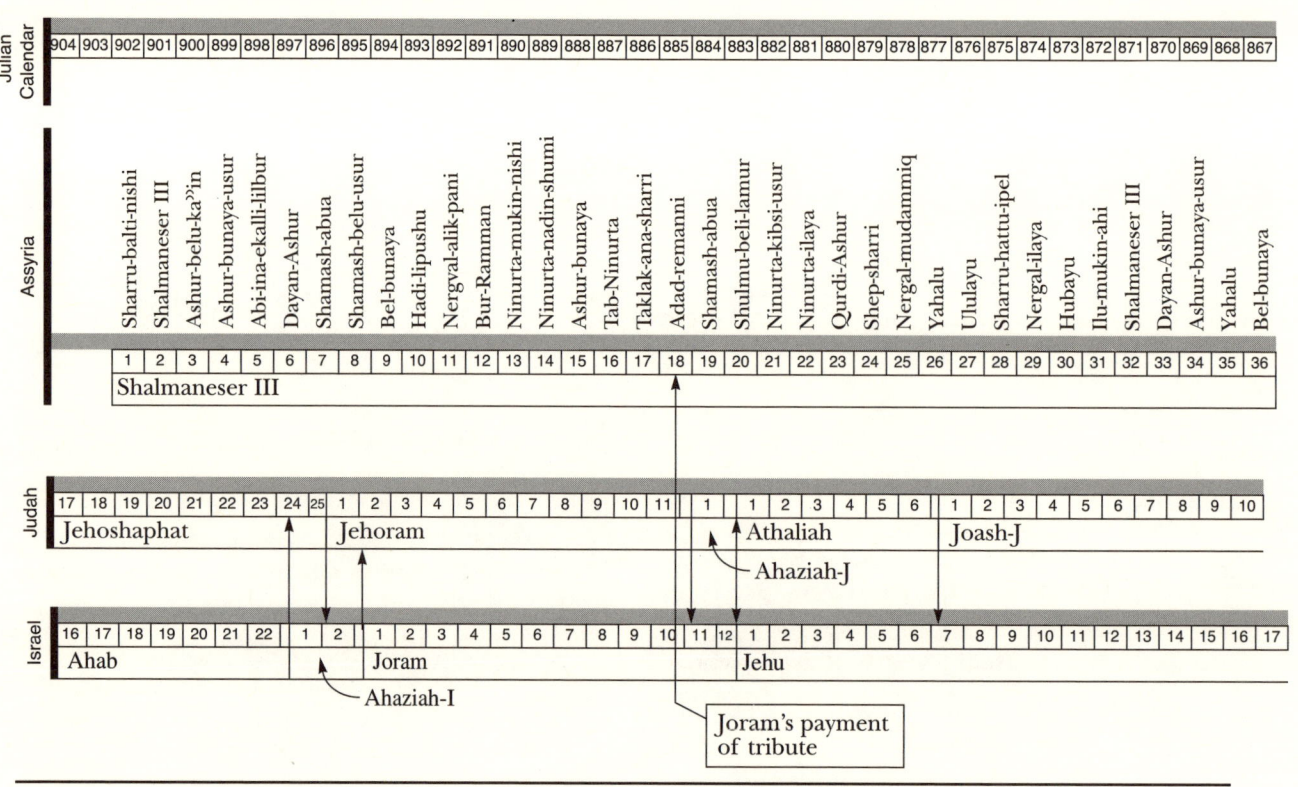

Table 9.10. Reigns for the Divided Kingdom

Kings of Judah			Kings of Israel		
981–964	Rehoboam	17 years	981–957	Jeroboam I	24 years
964–958	Abijam	6 years	957–956	Nadab	2 years
958–921	Asa	38 years	956–939	Baasha	17 years
921–896	Jehoshaphat	25 years	939–937	Elah	2 years
896–884	Jehoram	11 years	937–	Zimri	7 days
884–883	Ahaziah	1 year	937–919	Omri	18 years
883–877	Athaliah	6 years	919–897	Ahab	22 years
877–837	Joash	40 years	897–895	Ahaziah	2 years
837–808	Amaziah	29 years	895–883	Joram	12 years
808–756	Azariah/Uzziah	52 years	883–855	Jehu	28 years
756–740	Jotham	16 years	855–838	Jehoahaz	17 years
740–724	Ahaz	16 years	838–822	Joash	16 years

Table 9.9. Reconstructed Divided Kingdom Chronology for Julian Years 981–718 (cont.)

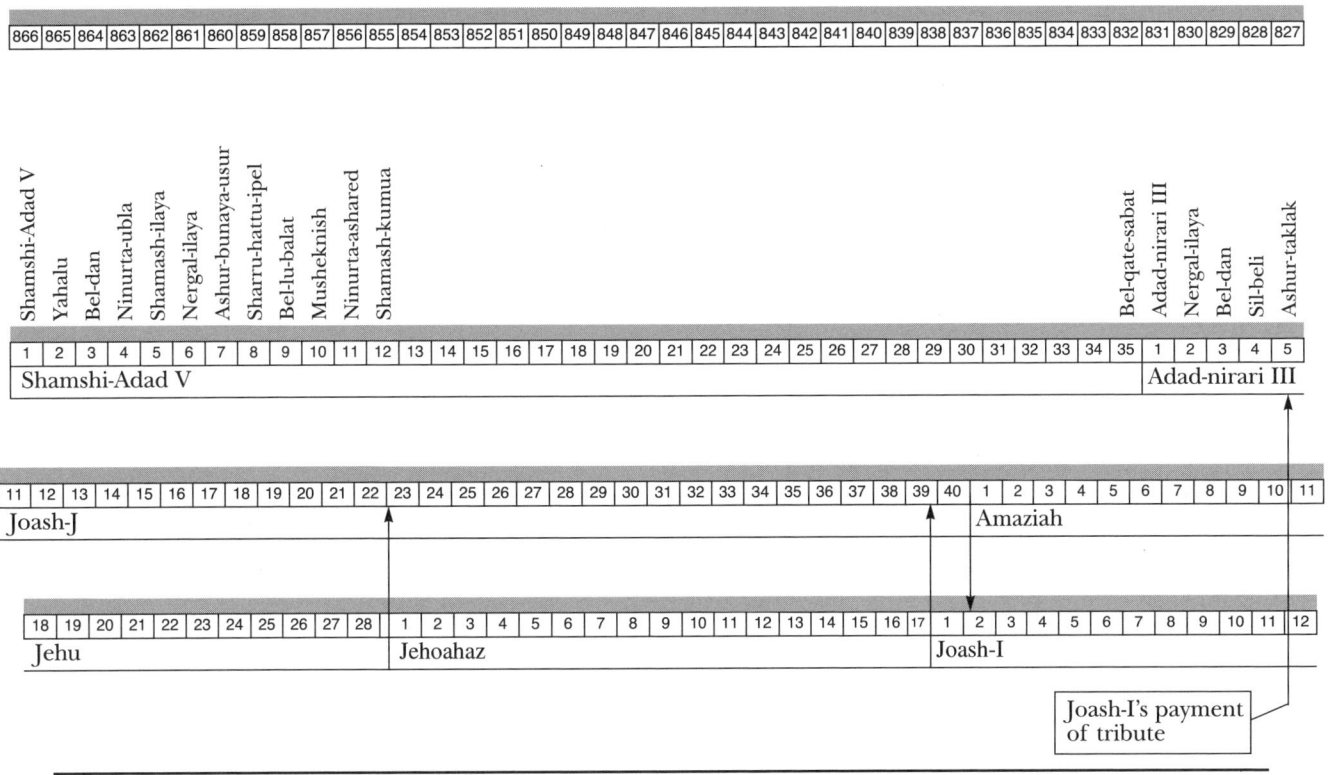

Table 9.10. Reigns for the Divided Kingdom (cont.)

Kings of Judah			Kings of Israel		
724–719/718	Hezekiah (to his 6th year at the fall of Samaria)		822–781	Jeroboam II	41 years
			781–780	Zechariah	6 months
			780–	Shallum	1 month
			780–769	Menahem	11 years
			769–757	Pekahiah	12 years
			757–727	Pekah	29 years
			727–719/718	Hoshea	9 years

9.4.2. Significant Dates in Ancient Near Eastern History

The following dates based on the above synchronizations of Hebrew and Assyrian records are proposed as fixed dates from which other dates pertinent to ancient Near Eastern history may be reckoned.

Table 9.9. Reconstructed Divided Kingdom Chronology for Julian Years 981–718 (cont.)

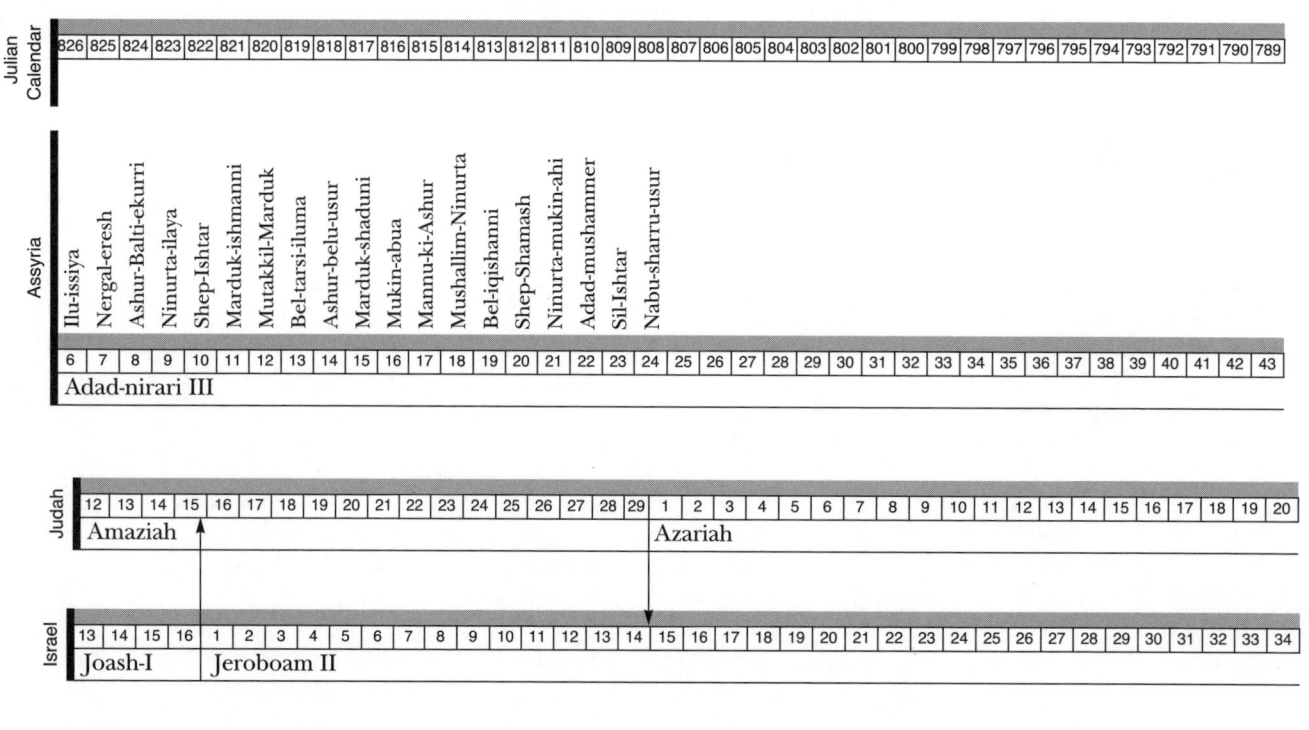

Table 9.11. Significant Dates in Ancient Near Eastern History

Julian Year B.C.E.	Event
981	Beginning of the DK and the accessions of Rehoboam and Jeroboam I
977	Rehoboam's 5th year; Shishak (Shoshenq I) of Egypt campaigns against Judah
897	Ahab's last year and Shalmaneser III's 6th year; battle of Qarqar
885	Shalmaneser III's 18th year and Joram's 10th year; *Iaúa* (Joram) pays tribute to Shalmaneser III
827	Adad-nirari III's 5th year; Joash-I pays tribute to Adad-nirari III
773	Shalmaneser IV's 9th year; Menahem pays tribute to Shalmaneser IV
719/718	Fall of Samaria in Hezekiah's 6th year, Hoshea's 9th year, and Sargon II's 3rd year

Table 9.9. Reconstructed Divided Kingdom Chronology for Julian Years 981–718 (cont.)

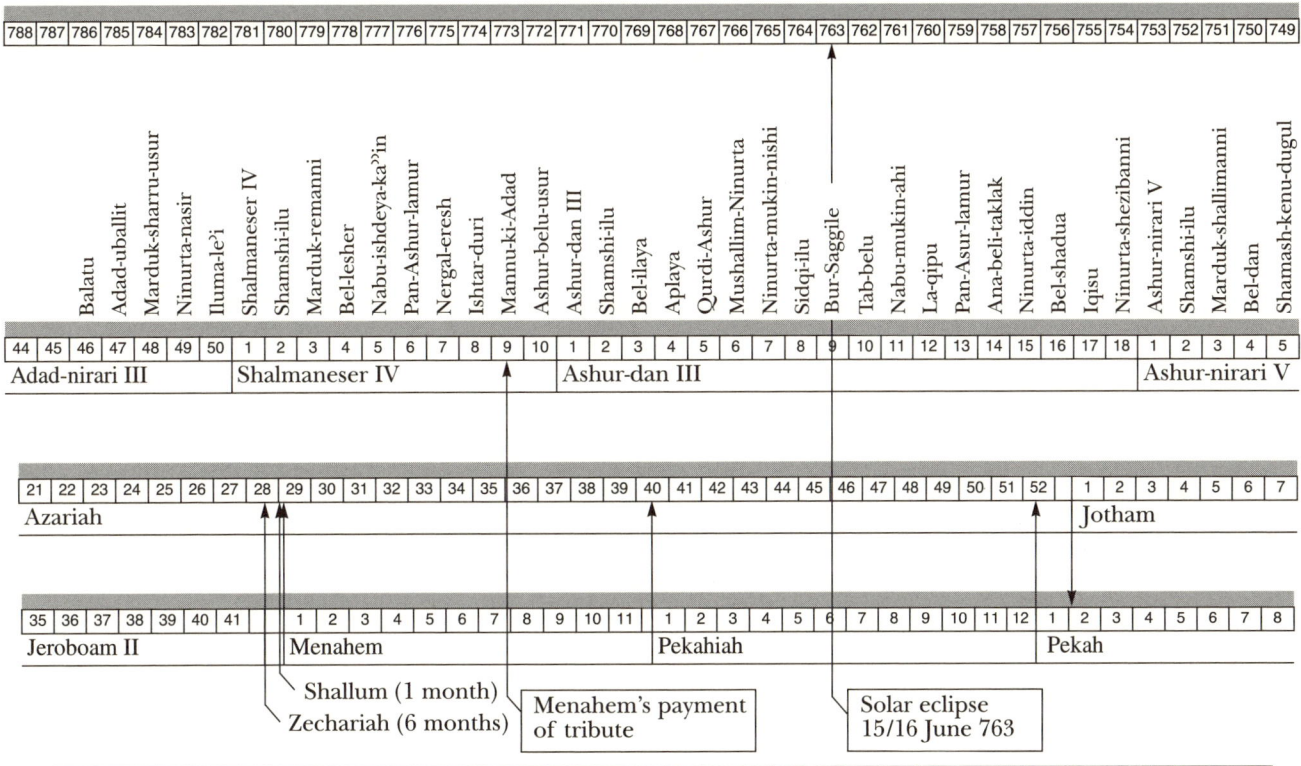

9.5. Resolution to the Problems of Divided Kingdom Chronology

In the preceding pages a solution has been proposed to resolve the 2,000-year-old chronological problems in the Books of 1–2 Kings. The dates provided have the benefit of confirmation by a dual record of consecutive reigns in Judah and Israel, linked by a unique feature—a deliberate system of synchronization. This chronology has three distinguishing features.

1. It is based on the earliest extant Greek and Hebrew texts, evaluating the variant data within each text-type rather than relying primarily on the MT.
2. It is constructed on a dating system consistent with the literary form of the regnal formulas used by the compiler(s) of 1–2 Kings.
3. It places greater reliance on the synchronized dual-dating system found in the Books of Kings rather than on a hypothetical collation of the single lineage of Assyrian kings found in the present reconstruction of the AEC and does not resort to manipulation via antedating, postdating, coregencies, etc.

The first feature takes into account Shenkel's 1968 book. Shenkel's thesis, based on the recensional development of the Greek texts of Kings, urges that any chronology of Kings must take into account the Greek data (*CRD* 5, 22). This present book proposes the chronology that Shenkel's

Table 9.9. Reconstructed Divided Kingdom Chronology for Julian Years 981–718 (cont.)

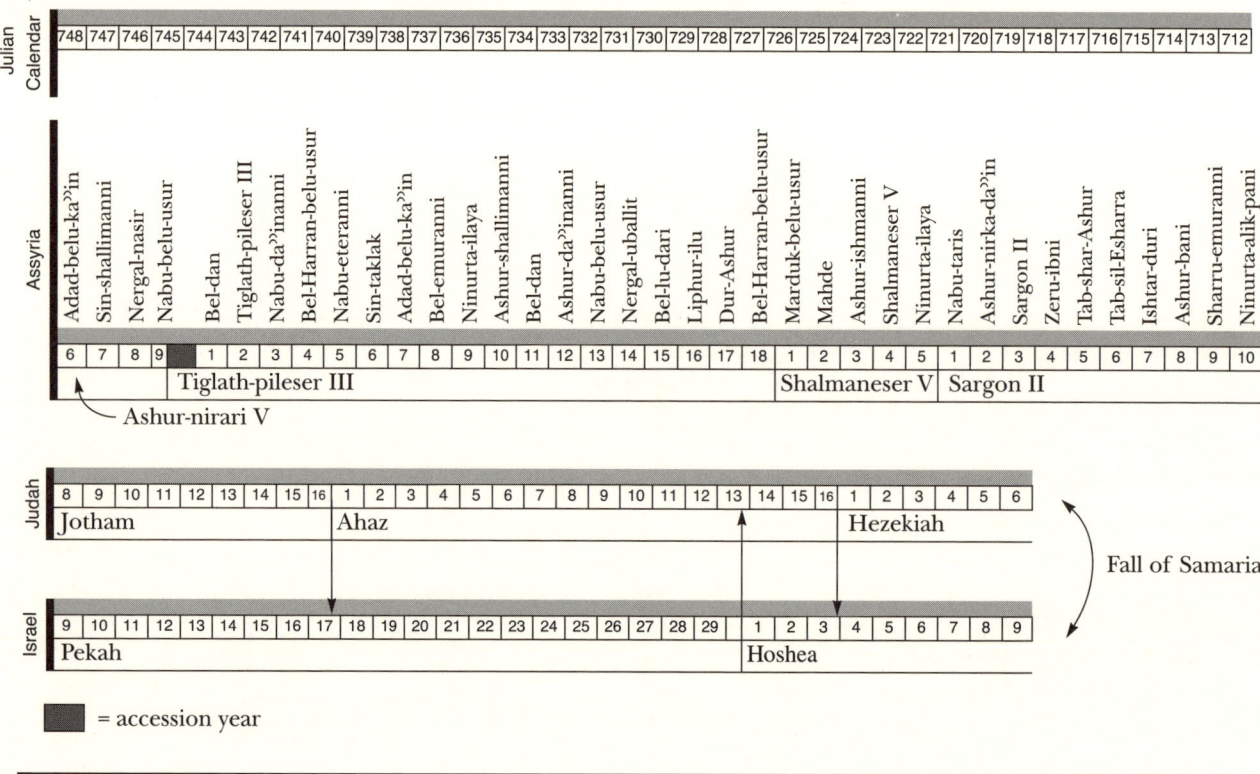

work lacked and validates the OG/L texts with their data as important witnesses to the earliest Hebrew text and chronology.

The priority of the Greek texts of the Books of Kings and the chronological framework now provided have important implications for applied Old Testament scholarship, especially in textual translation and the explanation of the DK in its historical context. The updating of the DK chronology by 50 years to 981 from the currently accepted date of 931/930 gives new dates for the Hebrew kings. These dates not only give a new perspective to the histories of Israel and Judah but also supply a new absolute chronology (replacing the AEC) with which all other connected chronologies should synchronize.

In the course of my discussion I critiqued Edwin Thiele's chronological hypothesis propounded in *The Mysterious Numbers of the Hebrew Kings*. His dates for Israel and Judah have been quoted extensively in the last half century. My analysis, however, concludes that Thiele's chronology relies on faulty methodology and the dubious premise that the AEC as currently represented is a credible tabulation of the Assyrian kings' regencies. Similar chronologies, likewise, cannot be recommended.

My reconstruction of DK chronology is offered in hope of challenging and changing present perceptions of the chronology and history of the ancient Near East.

Indexes

Index of Authors

Aharoni, Y.   133-135, 154
Albright, W. F.   4-5, 7, 9, 16, 29, 102, 126, 138, 157, 162, 170
Allen, L. C.   94
Allrik, H. L.   135
Andersen, K. T.   5, 7-8, 138
Archer, G. L.   94, 117, 134-135
Auld, A. G.   15, 144

Baker, D. W.   176
Barnes, W. H.   5-9, 14, 65, 109, 155, 157, 160, 170-171, 178-179
Barr, J.   6
Barthélemy, D.   18-22, 24
Becking, B.   157, 159-160, 162-163
Begrich, J.   7, 9
Bennett, W. H.   126
Bickerman, E. J.   106
Bierbrier, M. L.   179
Bin-Nun, S. R.   14, 65, 72
Borger, R.   156
Bright, J.   155
Brinkman, J. A.   97-98, 102-103, 176
Brock, S. P.   21, 25
Burney, C. F.   27, 29, 60, 90, 138

Campbell, A. F.   14, 65
Childs, B. S.   4, 9, 155
Christensen, D. L.   157
Clines, D. J. A.   105
Cody, A.   99-100
Cogan, M.   5, 7, 83, 101-102, 115, 130, 139, 154, 156-161, 163, 167, 175, 178
Cook, H. J.   116
Crocker, P. T.   157
Cross, F. M.   9, 14-18, 22, 26, 29, 136, 143, 170
Curtis, E. L.   134

Dalley, S.   160, 163
Davies, G. I.   135
Day, J.   157
De Vries, S. J.   9, 14, 19, 75, 113, 127, 134, 138, 143-144
Deboys, D. G.   22
Depuydt, L.   3, 95, 161
Dillard, R. B.   9, 134
Donbaz, V.   100, 176, 178
Driver, G. R.   94

Driver, S. R.   79-80, 94, 135

Faulstich, E. W.   95, 139
Fernández Marcos, N.   22
Finegan, J.   3
Freedman, D. N.   153

Galil, G.   4-9, 60-63, 67, 83, 101, 107, 109, 113, 115-116, 138-139, 141, 153-154, 162-163
Galling, K.   126
Garbini, G.   126
Gelb, I. J.   97
Gibson, J. C. L.   126
Goedicke, H.   157
Gooding, D. W.   9, 78, 82-83, 85-86, 107, 138-144
Gray, J.   3, 6, 19, 94, 113, 138, 163
Grayson, A. K.   102-103, 158
Green, A. R.   9, 83-84, 107, 126, 139, 157, 168, 170-171, 179
Greenberg, M.   15
Grindel, J. A.   19
Gurney, O. R.   97-98

Haley, J. W.   94, 135
Halpern, B.   15, 65, 67, 130
Haran, M.   14, 64, 174-175
Haydn, H. M.   174
Hayes, J. H.   5-8, 99-102, 139, 154, 158-160, 163
Herrmann, S.   126, 175
Hobbs, T. R.   1, 4, 9, 45, 152, 154, 175, 178
Hooker, P. K.   5-7, 139, 154
Horn, S. H.   15, 126, 153, 155
Hughes, J.   4-8, 60, 101, 109, 113, 116, 130, 138-139, 154, 163, 174-175, 177-178

Irvine, S. A.   155-157, 177

Jellicoe, S.   19, 21, 23
Jepsen, A.   7, 99
Jones, G. H.   4-6, 9, 14, 29, 45, 83, 105, 117, 139, 154, 167, 174-175
Josephus   11, 17, 22, 30, 34, 37-39, 44, 46-48, 51-52, 54-55, 57, 59, 63, 83, 87, 112-113, 147-148, 170-171

Kahle, P. E.   25
Katz, P.   18
Katzenstein, H. J.   102, 170-171

Kaufman, I. T.   134-135
Kautzsch, E.   94, 135, 137
Keil, C. F.   94, 134, 136, 138
Kidner, D.   94, 135
Kitchen, K. A.   7, 95, 155, 157, 178-180
Klein, R. W.   9, 25, 83
Kuan, J. K.   95-96, 99-102, 155-160, 163, 166-167, 170, 174-175, 177-178

Laato, A.   163
Layard, A. H.   156-157, 174
Lemaire, A.   15, 126
Levine, L. D.   161, 177-178
Lipiński, E.   101, 126
Liver, J.   126, 170
Long, B. O.   65
Longman, T.   9
Luckenbill, D.   156

Madsen, A. A.   134
Malamat, A.   99, 153
Mattingly, G. L.   154
McCarter, P. K.   23, 94, 103, 130, 136
McFall, L.   4-8, 139, 154
McKenzie, S. L.   15, 67, 85, 87
Meer, P. van der   96
Metzger, B. M.   21-23, 25
Mez, A.   22
Millard, A. R.   3, 9, 95-98, 100-102, 155-156, 158, 160, 166, 176
Miller, J. M.   6-10, 67, 99-102, 107-108, 126, 138-139
Mitchell, T. C.   7, 95
Montgomery, J. A.   78, 117, 138, 143, 175
Muraoka, T.   20

Na'aman, N.   156-157, 159-160, 162-163, 174-175
Naveh, J.   135
Nelson, R. D.   14, 65
Noth, M.   14

O'Brien, M. A.   14, 65
O'Connell, K. G.   18-19, 24
Olmstead, A. T.   156, 163

Page, S.   99
Pavlovský, V.   5, 8, 134, 178
Payne, J. B.   28
Pietersma, A.   22
Pitard, W. T.   101, 134, 167, 175
Poebel, A.   97, 102-103
Ptolemy, C.   3

Rainey, A. F.   134
Rawlinson, H. C.   102, 155
Reade, J.   8
Ronan, C. A.   3
Rost, P.   157
Rowley, H. H.   117, 155

Rudolph, W.   134

Schedl, C.   5, 8
Scheil, V.   100
Schneider, T.   130
Schramm, W.   100
Shea, W. H.   97, 99-100, 133-135, 155, 175, 178
Shenkel, J. D.   6, 8-10, 14-15, 18-19, 22-26, 29, 52, 54, 56, 60-61, 76, 78, 80-86, 90, 104, 107-109, 126-127, 138-140, 142-144, 185
Siegel, J. P.   133
Skehan, P. W.   24
Skinner, J.   79, 138
Smith, G.   95, 117, 156
Smith, M.   19
Soggin, J. A.   99
Stade, B.   83
Stanley, C. D.   22
Strand, K. A.   4
Stuart, D.   116
Swete, H. B.   25

Tadmor, H.   5, 7-8, 83, 99-102, 113, 115, 130, 154-161, 163, 167, 174-175, 177-178
Talmon, S.   16
Tetley, M. C.   162
Thackeray, H. St. J.   19-20, 22, 27-28
Thiele, E. R.   4-9, 11, 27-29, 33-34, 48-53, 60-61, 87, 89-90, 95, 98, 101-102, 104-118, 130, 136, 138-140, 143-144, 152-154, 156, 164, 166, 169, 174, 176-180, 186
Tov, E.   15-16, 18-20, 22, 24-26, 28, 94, 136
Trebolle Barrera, J.   9, 15-16, 18-20, 22, 24-26, 87, 144

Ulrich, E. C.   17, 22-23, 54, 64
Ungnad, A.   95, 97-98

Vanderhooft, D. S.   15, 65, 67
Vogt, E.   5, 8, 134, 178

Weippert, M.   130, 178
Wenham, J. W.   28
Wente, E. F.   179
Wevers, J. W.   25
Whiting, R.   176
Wifall, W. R.   60
Williams, P. J.   9
Williamson, H. G. M.   106
Wiseman, D. J.   4, 153, 156, 176

Yeivin, S.   134, 157
Young, E. J.   117
Younger, K. L.   102, 156, 158-160, 162-163, 167
Yurco, F. J.   155

Zawadzki, S.   96
Zöckler, O.   94

Index of Scripture

2 Samuel
- 1:1–9:13   19
- 1:1–11:1   19
- 5:3–5   139
- 5:4–5   92
- 5:11   170
- 10:1–1 Kgs 2:11   19
- 11:2–1 Kgs 2:11   19, 22

1 Kings
- 1:1–48   7
- 2:11   20, 22, 139
- 2:12–21:43   19
- 6–7   144
- 6:1   92, 105
- 6:37   92, 105
- 6:38   92, 105
- 9:10–14   170
- 11:41   14
- 12   92
- 12:2–3   119
- 12:20   119
- 12:24   119
- 14:19–20   67
- 14:20   5, 31, 34–35, 39, 49, 54, 66–67, 69, 72, 121
- 14:21   31, 35, 88, 92, 119
- 14:25–26   178
- 14:25–27   95
- 14:30   72–73
- 15:1   50, 56, 70, 75, 92, 119
- 15:1–2   35, 65, 88
- 15:1–21:43   21
- 15:2   31, 54, 130, 133
- 15:6   72–73
- 15:7   72–73
- 15:7–8   66
- 15:8   32, 34–35, 67, 76
- 15:8–9   34–35
- 15:9   31–32, 34, 49–50, 56, 67, 70, 75–76, 93, 120, 130
- 15:9–10   35, 88
- 15:10   31, 49, 57, 80, 108, 125–126, 131–132, 139
- 15:16   72–73, 133

1 Kings (cont.)
- 15:23   14, 73, 108
- 15:23–24   133
- 15:24   76
- 15:25   31, 35, 49–50, 56, 65, 69–72, 75–76, 88, 120–121, 132
- 15:27–30   65
- 15:28   56, 67–69, 72, 120
- 15:28–31   67
- 15:29–30   68, 73, 75
- 15:31   14, 72
- 15:32   68, 72–73
- 15:33   31, 35, 49–50, 56, 68, 70, 75, 88, 120, 125, 128, 131–133, 148
- 16:6   35, 56, 67, 70, 73, 75, 88, 123, 132, 136, 141–142, 148
- 16:6–8   73–75, 123, 141
- 16:7   73–75, 123, 141
- 16:8   31, 35, 39, 57, 70, 73–75, 88, 123, 132, 141–142
- 16:10   35, 67–68, 87, 123
- 16:10–14   67
- 16:11–13   68, 73, 75
- 16:14   68, 76
- 16:15   23, 31, 35, 37, 39, 67, 70, 76, 88, 107, 123–124, 132, 136, 139–142
- 16:15–16   87
- 16:15–18   107, 139
- 16:15–24   108
- 16:16   35
- 16:17–20   67
- 16:20   75
- 16:21–22   75
- 16:22   108, 139–140
- 16:23   31, 36–37, 39, 41, 57, 70, 75, 87–88, 107, 124, 126–127, 131–132, 139–140, 142–143
- 16:27–28   66, 76
- 16:28   21, 29, 31, 36, 40–41, 57, 65, 67, 69–70, 75–76, 80, 83, 85–89, 126–127, 131, 136, 139, 142–143
- 16:28–29   93
- 16:29   31, 36, 40, 57, 70–71, 76, 80, 86–89, 107–108, 125–127, 131, 136
- 16:29–21:40   142

1 Kings (cont.)
  16:29–22:40 85, 126, 131
  16:31–22:38 65
  20 20
  20:43 20
  21 20
  21:43 20, 80
  22 2, 20, 85, 140, 142–143
  22:1 20
  22:1–38 67
  22:1–40 8, 85
  22:1–2 Kgs 25:30 19
  22:35–37 67
  22:37 67
  22:40 67, 76
  22:41 29, 40, 69–70, 76, 80, 86, 88, 108, 127
  22:41–42 21, 36
  22:41–51 21, 41, 75, 85–86, 90, 126, 131, 139, 142–143
  22:42 31, 57, 65, 127, 129
  22:46 76
  22:47–50 41, 76
  22:48 83
  22:51 76, 85
  22:52 3, 21, 31, 36, 57, 70–71, 76, 80–81, 86, 88, 108, 110, 127–128, 132–133, 148

2 Kings
  1 84–85, 90
  1:1 83, 127
  1:16 69
  1:17 21, 23–24, 32, 36, 43, 53, 70–71, 76, 78–81, 84, 86, 90, 94, 109–110, 128, 132
  1:17–18 69, 76–77, 128
  1:18 21, 24, 32, 36, 42–43, 53–54, 57, 62, 70–72, 78, 80–82, 84–88, 90, 94, 110, 121, 127–129, 132
  2 78, 80, 82, 84–85, 131
  3 9, 29, 82–83, 85, 131, 140, 144, 162, 168
  3:1 3, 21, 24, 31, 36, 43, 53–54, 57, 62, 70–71, 78–82, 85, 88, 94, 109–110, 127–129, 131–132, 140
  3:1–3 82, 84
  3:2 82
  3:4–5 127
  3:4–8:15 65
  3:5–6 83
  3:6 83
  3:7 83
  3:8 83
  3:9 83
  3:10 83
  3:11 83
  3:11–20 84

2 Kings (cont.)
  3:12 83
  3:13 83
  3:14 83
  4:11–16 168
  4:17 168
  4:18–37 168
  6:24–8:6 168
  8:7–15 167–168
  8:15 78, 82, 84
  8:16 24, 33, 43, 57, 70, 78, 84–86, 93, 109–110, 127, 129, 131–132
  8:16–17 36, 86, 88
  8:16–24 81–82, 84–85, 131
  8:17 31, 42, 54, 65, 86, 129, 132
  8:19–22 80
  8:20–22 83
  8:22 84
  8:23–24 66, 76
  8:24 84
  8:25 32, 37, 41–42, 44, 53, 57, 70, 85–86, 129, 131
  8:25–26 37, 83, 88
  8:25–9:29 168
  8:26 31
  8:28–29 168
  9:9 25
  9:23–24 69
  9:24–28 21, 44
  9:24–29 83
  9:27–28 66, 85
  9:28 25, 66, 85
  9:29 32, 37, 41, 44, 53, 57, 70, 85–86, 88, 129, 131
  9:30 85
  10:17 130
  10:24 25
  10:25 25
  10:34–35 76
  10:35 67
  10:36 31, 34, 38, 44–45, 70, 84–86, 88, 101, 145
  11:1 25
  11:1–12:1 66
  11:4 31
  11:21 78
  12:1 65, 78, 86, 145
  12:1–2 38, 57, 70, 89, 145
  12:2 31, 78
  12:20–22 78
  12:21–22 66
  13:1 31, 38, 57, 70, 89, 101, 145
  13:8–9 78
  13:9 67

2 Kings (cont.)
  13:10   31, 38, 46, 57, 70, 89, 145, 147, 152
  13:10-11   78
  13:12-13   76, 78-79, 147
  13:13   78
  13:14   78
  13:25   78, 147
  14:1   13, 57, 70, 78, 145, 147
  14:1-2   38, 89
  14:1-14   78
  14:2   31, 51, 147
  14:8-14   51, 113
  14:13-14   113
  14:15-16   76, 78-79, 147
  14:16   67, 78
  14:17   38, 112-113, 147
  14:18-22   78-79
  14:19   79
  14:19-20   66
  14:19-22   67
  14:21   51, 113
  14:22   66, 79
  14:23   31, 38, 57, 62, 71, 89, 112-113, 147-148
  14:25   175
  14:28   79, 175
  14:28-29   79
  14:29   67
  15   63, 68-69, 148
  15:1   51, 62, 71, 112, 133, 145, 147-148, 152
  15:1-2   38, 46, 89
  15:2   31, 112
  15:5   7, 113
  15:6   69
  15:6-7   66
  15:8   31, 38, 46, 48, 62, 71, 89, 112-113, 148, 153
  15:8-10   149
  15:10-11   79
  15:10-12   68
  15:11   69, 148
  15:12   68-69, 79
  15:13   31, 38, 48, 62, 71-72, 79, 89, 121, 148, 153
  15:13-14   149
  15:15   69, 79, 148
  15:16   69, 79
  15:17   31, 39, 48, 58, 62, 71-72, 79, 89, 149, 152-153
  15:17-23   8
  15:19   4, 7, 176, 178
  15:21   69
  15:22   67
  15:23   31, 39, 47, 58, 71, 89, 145, 149, 152-153
  15:25   65, 106, 115

2 Kings (cont.)
  15:26   69, 148
  15:27   31, 39, 47-48, 58, 71, 85, 89, 113, 116, 149-151, 153
  15:29   8, 63, 156
  15:29-16:18   177
  15:30   39, 48, 59, 68, 85, 114-116, 151, 153, 155-157
  15:30-31   79
  15:31   69, 85, 148
  15:32   39, 71, 114, 151
  15:32-33   39, 89, 114
  15:33   31, 48, 114, 116, 151
  15:36   69
  15:36-38   79
  15:37   79, 116
  16:1   59, 71, 114, 116, 151
  16:1-2   39, 65, 89
  16:1-18   8
  16:1-20   85
  16:2   31, 151
  16:5-7   85, 116
  16:5-9   155-156
  16:9   155, 157, 162
  16:19-20   66, 76
  16:28   76
  17   115
  17:1   31, 39, 48, 68, 71, 79, 89, 114-116, 151-153, 155
  17:1-6   85
  17:3   160, 162
  17:3-4   159, 162-163
  17:3-6   157, 163
  17:4   159, 162-163
  17:5   161-163
  17:5-6   159, 162-163
  17:6   162-163
  17:24   162
  17:26   162
  17:27   162
  18   115
  18:1   47-48, 71, 89, 114, 151-152, 162-163
  18:1-2   39
  18:2   153-154
  18:7   162
  18:9   161-163
  18:9-10   39, 47, 59, 85, 115, 152, 162-163
  18:9-11   162-163
  18:10   30-32, 114, 153, 155, 157, 160-162
  18:11   162
  18:13   117, 133, 153-154, 162-163
  18:13-19:36   154
  18:14   162
  18:16   162

2 Kings (cont.)
   18:17   162
   18:19   162
   18:23   162
   18:28   162
   18:30   162
   18:31   162
   18:33   162
   19:9   155
   20:1–11   154
   20:12–19   154
   21:1   153
   21:19   153
   22:1   153
   22:3   105
   23:23   105
   23:28–30   153
   23:29–30   67
   23:33   25
   23:35   25
   24:6   67
   24:18   92
   25:2–7   92

1 Chronicles
   5:26   8, 176, 178

2 Chronicles
   12:1–12   178
   12:2–4   95
   12:9–10   95
   13   12
   13:23–14:7   133
   14–16   134
   14:8–14   133
   15:10–11   133
   15:19   73
   15:19–16:1   132–133
   16:1   73, 134
   16:8   133
   16:12   108
   16:12–13   73, 133
   21:8–10   83

2 Chronicles (cont.)
   21:12–15   84
   25:21–24   51, 113
   26   13
   26:1–3   51
   35:20–24   153
   36:6   67

Ezra
   2   135
   2:2–35   94

Nehemiah
   1:1   105–106
   2:1   105–106
   7   135
   7:7–38   94

Isaiah
   7:1–9   155
   20:1   154
   36:1   154
   36:1–37:37   154
   37:9   155
   38:1–8   154
   39:1–8   154

Jeremiah
   22:18–19   67
   36:22   106
   36:30–31   67
   39:2   92
   52:6   92

Ezekiel
   19:8–9   67

Hosea
   5:5   116

Amos
   1:3–5   155

New Testament

Romans
   11:3–4   22

Index of Royal Names

Pages on which royal names occur in time-lines are displayed in this index in bold type.

Abijah *see* Abijam
Abijam   12-13, 28-35, 37, **40**, 49-50, 54-56, **58**, 60-61, 65-67, 70, 72-73, 76, 92-93, 119-120, 122-125, 127-128, 130-131, 134, 136, 138, 140, 142, 144, **180**, 182
Adad-idri (of Damascus)   167
Adad-nirari III   7, 11, 97-103, 166, **168**-176, 181, **183-185**
Ahab   2-3, 7-8, 12-13, 20-21, 28-29, 31, 33, 36-37, 40-43, 55, 57-61, 65-67, 69-71, 76-77, 80, 82-83, 85-87, 89, 93, 107-108, 114, 117, 119, **121-122**, 125-128, 130-132, 136, 139-140, 142-143, 166-168, 178-179, **181-182**, 184
Ahaz   8, 12-13, 31, 39, **46**-48, 55, 58-60, 63, 65-66, 68, 71, 76, 79, 85, 114-116, **146-147**, 151-153, 155-156, **161-162**, 182, **186**
Ahaziah-I   3, 7, 12-13, 21, 23-24, 28, 31-33, 36, 41-43, 55, 57-**58**, 60, 67, 69-71, 76-78, 80-81, 83, 86, 108-110, 117, **122**, 126-132, 148, **167**, 182
Ahaziah-J   2, 9, 12-13, 21, 28, 31-32, 34, 37, 41-42, 44-45, 53, 55, 57-**58**, 66, 70, 76, 78, 83-86, 110, **122**, 128-129, 131, 144-145, **167**-169, **172**, 182
Amaziah   12-13, 31, 38, **43**-46, 50-51, 55, 57-**59**, 62, 66-67, 70-71, 78-79, **101**, 111-113, 145, 147-148, **168**-170, **173**, **175**, 182-**184**
Amon   153, 157
Artashumki (of Arpad)   100, 176
Artaxerxes   105-106
Asa   12-13, 21, 23, 31-37, 39-41, 43-44, 49-50, 55-60, 65-76, 80, 87, 93, 107-110, 120-134, 136, 138-144, 148, **180**-182
Ashur-dan III   3, 95-96, **177**, **185**
Ashur-nadin-shumi   161
Ashur-nirari V   176-**177**, 181, **185-186**
Athaliah   2, 12-13, 21, 31, 33-34, 38, **42**, 44-45, 55, 57-**58**, 66, 70, 78, 84, 86, **100**, **122**, 145-**146**, **167**, **172**, 182
Azariah   8, 12-13, 31, 38-39, **44**-48, 51-52, 55, 57-**59**, 61-63, 66, 69, 71-72, 79, 107, 112-114, 145-152, 174-**177**, 182, **184-185**

Ba'li-manzer (of Tyre)   170
Baasha   12-13, 31, 33, 35, 37, 39-**41**, 44, 49-50, 55-56, **58**-60, 67-68, 70, 72-75, 120-121, 123-125, 127-128, 130-134, 136, 138, 141-142, 148, **180-182**

Baba-aha-iddina   102-103, 170
Balezeros (of Tyre)   170-**173**
  see also Ba'li-manzer
Bel-ibni   161
Ben-Hadad (of Damascus)   167-168

David   1, 7, 20, 66, 92, 139, 170

Elah   12-13, 31, 33, 35, 37, 39-**41**, 55-56, **59**-60, 66-68, 70, 73-76, **121**, 123-125, 132, 136, 138, 141-142, 148, **181**-182

Hadiyani (Aramean)   178
Harsiese (pharaoh)   179
Hazael (of Damascus)   167-169
Hezekiah   12-13, 30-31, 39, **46**-48, 55, **58**-59, 71, 85, 114-118, **146**, 151-155, 157, 161-163, 183-184, **186**
Hiram (of Tyre)   170, 172
Hoshea   12-13, 30-31, 39, **46**-48, 55, **58**-59, 62-63, 68, 71, 79, 85-86, 114-116, **146**, 151-153, 155-164, 177, 183-184, **186**

Jehoahaz   8, 12-13, 31, 38, **43**, 45-46, 50, 55, 57, **59**, 67, 70, 78, **100-101**, 145-**146**, 152, **168**-170, **173**, 182-**183**
Jehoahaz of Judah   177
Jehoash   *see* Joash-I, Joash-J
Jehoiakim   67
Jehoram   9, 12-13, 21, 23-24, 28-33, 36-37, 41-45, 50-51, 53-55, 57-58, 60-62, 65-66, 70-71, 75-78, 80-86, 90, 92, 94, 108-111, **122**, 127-132, 144, **167**, **172**, 182
Jehoshaphat   9, 12-13, 21, 24, 28-29, 31, 33, 36, 40-44, 49, 53, 55, 57-61, 65, 67, 69-72, 75-78, 80-87, 89-90, 93-94, 107-111, 119, **121-122**, 125-132, 136, 139-140, 142-144, **167**, **181**-182
Jehu   2-3, 7, 12-13, 21, 31, 33-34, 38, **42**-46, 55, 57-**59**, 61-62, 67-70, 73, 75-76, 79, 84-86, **100**-101, 103, 114, 117, **122**-123, 129-130, **145-146**, 166-169, **172-173**, 179, 182-**183**
Jeroboam I   5, 12-13, 30-35, 37, 39-**40**, 49-50, 54-56, **58**, 60-62, 65-67, 69-70, 72-73, 76, 92, 119-125, 130-131, 138, 144, 164, **180**, 182, 184
Jeroboam II   12-13, 31, 38, **44**-48, 51-52, 55, 57-**59**, 61-63, 67, 71, 78-79, 93, 111-113, 145-152, 174-176, 183-**185**

193

Joahaz *see* Jehoahaz
Joash-I 12–13, 31, 38, **43**–46, 50–51, 55, 57–**59**, 67, 70, 76, 78–79, 97, 99–103, 111–113, 145, 147, 152, **168**–171, **173**–174, 182–184
Joash-J 12–13, 31, 38, **42–43**, 45–46, 50, 55, 57–**59**, 65–66, 70, 78, **100–101**, 145–**146**, **168**–170, **172–173**, 182–**183**
Joram 2–3, 7, 9, 12–13, 21, 23–24, 28–29, 31–34, 36–37, 41–45, 53–55, 57–**58**, 60–62, 65, 69–71, 76–87, 90, 92–94, 103, 108–110, 117, **122**, 126–132, 140, 166–**172**, 182, 184
Josiah 67, 105, 153, 157
Jotham 7, 12–13, 31, 39, **45**–48, 55, 58–59, 63, 68–69, 71, 79, 113–117, **147**–153, **161**, **177**, 182, **185–186**

Manasseh 117, 153, 157
Marduk-balatsu-iqbi 102–103
Marduk-zakir-shumi 161
Mari' (of Damascus) 100, 102
Mattenos (of Tyre) 170–**173**
Menahem 4, 7–8, 12–13, 31, 39, **45**–48, 55, 57–59, 61–63, 67, 69, 71–72, 79, 113–114, 116, 145–**146**, 148–153, 166, 176–178, 183–**185**
Merodach-baladan 154, 160–161
Mitinti (of Ashkelon) 155
Mushezib-Marduk 161

Nabonassar 95
    see also Nabu-nasir
Nabu-nasir 3
Nadab 12–13, 31, 33–35, 37, 39–**40**, 44, 49–50, 55–56, **58**, 60–61, 65, 67–73, 75–76, 120–123, 130–132, **180**, 182
Neco (pharaoh) 67, 153
Nergal-ushezib 161
Ninurta-apl?-[x] 103

Omri 8–9, 12–13, 21, 29, 31, 33–37, 39–42, 44, 52, 55, 57, **59**–61, 66–67, 69–70, 75–76, 80, 87, 89, 93, 103, 107–108, **121**, 123–132, 136, 138–144, 166, **181**–182
Osorkon I (pharaoh) 179
Osorkon II (pharaoh) 179
Osorkon IV (pharaoh) 179

Pekah 8, 12–13, 31, 39, **45**–48, 55, 58–59, 61–63, 68–69, 71, 79, 85, 106, 113–117, 145–153, 155–157, **161**–162, 177, 183, **185–186**
Pekahiah 2, 8, 12–13, 21, 31–32, 34, 39, **45**–48, 55, 58–**59**, 61–63, 65, 68–69, 71, 106, 113–115, 145, **147**–153, **177**, 183, **185**

Pimay (pharaoh) 179–180
Pul 4, 7–8, 166, 176, 178
    see also Tiglath-pileser III
Pygmalion (of Tyre) 170–**173**

Rehoboam 12–13, 28, 30–31, 33–35, **40**, 49, 55–56, **58**, 72–73, 92, 95, 119–**120**, 164, 178–180, 182, 184
Rezin (of Damascus) 79, 85, 155, 157–158, 162

Sargon II 33, 96, 103, 130, 154, 158–164, 180–181, 184, **186**
Saul 1
Sennacherib 96, 103, 115, 117, 153–155, 161–163
Shallum 12–13, 31, 38, **45**, 48, 55, 57–**59**, 61–63, 68–69, 71–72, 79, 145–**146**, 148–151, 153, 183, **185**
Shalmaneser III 33, 96, **100**–102, 117, 129–130, 166–**172**, 176, 178, 180, **182**, 184
Shalmaneser IV 96, 166, 174–176, 178, 184–**185**
Shalmaneser V 3, 96, 103, 156–164, 181, **186**
Shamshi-Adad V 11, 102–103, 166, **168**–170, 172, 176, 181
Shebitku (of Ethiopia) 155
Shishak 95, 178, 184
Shoshenq I (pharaoh) 95, 166, 178–180, 184
    see also Shishak
Shoshenq II (pharaoh) 179
Shoshenq III (pharaoh) 179
Shoshenq IV (pharaoh) 179
Shoshenq V (pharaoh) 179
So (pharaoh) 157, 159–160
Solomon 1, 6–7, 30, 34, 92, 105, 170

Takelot I (pharaoh) 179
Takelot II (pharaoh) 179
Tiglath-pileser III 4, 7–8, 62–63, 96, 103, 114, 116, 130, 155–158, 161–162, 166, 174, 176–178, 180–181, **186**
    see also Pul
Tirhakah (of Ethiopia) 155

Uzziah *see* Azariah

Zechariah 12–13, 31, 38, **45**–48, 55, 57–**59**, 61–63, 68–69, 71, 79, 112–113, 145–**146**, 148–151, 153, **175**, 183, **185**
Zedekiah 92
Zimri 12–13, 23, 31, 33, 35, 37, 39–**41**, 55, 57, **59**–60, 67–68, 70, 73, 75–76, 107–108, **121**, 123–124, 132, 136, 139–143, **181**–182